National Space Law in the Republic of Korea

A Comprehensive Analysis of the Present Landscape and Proposals for the Future Legal Framework

By

Youngshin Ahn

BRILL | NIJHOFF

LEIDEN | BOSTON

Library of Congress Cataloging-in-Publication Data

Names: Ahn, Youngshin, author.
Title: National space law and policy in the Republic of Korea : a comprehensive analysis of the present landscape and proposals for the future legal framework / by Youngshin Ahn.
Description: Boston : Brill/Nijhoff, 2024. | Series: Studies in space law, 1871-7659 ; volume 23 | Includes bibliographical references and index. | Summary: "Embark on a journey into South Korea's remarkable rise as a space power. Discover how this technological giant has secured its place among a select group of seven nations capable of launching one-ton satellites using domestically engineered rockets. Delve into South Korea's intricate space legislation, dissecting four pivotal laws and regulations through a global lens"– Provided by publisher.
Identifiers: LCCN 2023058134 (print) | LCCN 2023058135 (ebook) | ISBN 9789004694736 (hardback) | ISBN 9789004694743 (ebook)
Subjects: LCSH: Space law–Korea (South) | Space law.
Classification: LCC KPA3469 .A94 2024 (print) | LCC KPA3469 (ebook) | DDC 341.4/7095195–dc23/eng/20240117
LC record available at https://lccn.loc.gov/2023058134
LC ebook record available at https://lccn.loc.gov/2023058135

Typeface for the Latin, Greek, and Cyrillic scripts: "Brill". See and download: brill.com/brill-typeface.

ISSN 1871-7659
ISBN 978-90-04-69473-6 (hardback)
ISBN 978-90-04-69474-3 (e-book)
DOI 10.1163/9789004694743

This book is printed on acid-free paper and produced in a sustainable manner.

Our planet is a lonely speck in the great enveloping cosmic dark. In our obscurity, in all this vastness, there is no hint that help will come from elsewhere to save us from ourselves.

CARL SAGAN, *Pale Blue Dot: A Vision of the Human Future in Space,* 1994

There is never a day without space.

United States Space Command, Commander's Strategic Vision, January 2021

Contents

Preface

The Republic of Korea, commonly known as South Korea, is recognized as one of the seven nations worldwide capable of launching a satellite weighing over one ton into orbit using a domestically developed launch vehicle from its own territory. Moreover, South Korea has pledged its commitment to the Artemis Accords and placed its lunar orbiter carrying the US ShadowCam around the Moon to conduct research that will be leveraged for the Artemis Program.

Given South Korea's ambitious goals in the space sector, this book aims to provide a comprehensive evaluation of the current state of Korean space legislation and offer recommendations for improvement. The research primarily focuses on South Korea's four domestic space laws and their corresponding regulations, which are analyzed from an international space law perspective and compared with the laws of selected countries.

The analysis reveals that the Korean space legislation encompasses almost every aspect of outer space exploration and utilization under international space law. However, the legal framework is a collection of processes centered on South Korea's early viable space activities, which makes it unsuitable for regulating emerging space activities in the present climate of the space industry. Consequently, South Korea lacks an overarching, all-inclusive legislation that would entirely regulate current and future national space activities.

This book is the first of its kind in the Korean academic community, and it illuminates the extent of South Korea's compliance with its international obligations and how its domestic regulations apply in the context of real-world application to national space activities. Finally, this book proposes possible revisions to the current Korean space legislation and provides practical recommendations for policymakers and stakeholders to create a better legal framework for South Korea.

Acknowledgements

This book represents a revised publication of my doctoral dissertation, originally composed to fulfill the requirements of my *Juridicae Scientiae Doctor* (JSD) Program in Space Law at the University of Nebraska-Lincoln College of Law. My time in Lincoln, Nebraska, marked a distinct phase in my life, characterized by engagements in various activities and participation in lectures and conferences. The onset of the COVID-19 pandemic, while undeniably challenging, provided an environment conducive for me to focus on my dissertation. Nevertheless, it is imperative to recognize that the completion of this work was not a solitary endeavor but, rather, a collective effort, for which I remain indebted to numerous individuals.

First and foremost, I extend my immense gratitude to Professor Frans von der Dunk and Professor Matthew Schaefer at the University of Nebraska-Lincoln College of Law, alongside Professor Mark Sundahl, the Director of the Global Space Law Center at Cleveland State University. Professor Frans von der Dunk served as my dedicated advisor during my time in the JSD Program in Space law, assisting me with multiple draft versions of chapters and the completed dissertation. Professors Schaefer and Sundahl played pivotal roles as members of the Defense Committee for my dissertation, and I owe them much for their guidance on this project and my future pursuits. This work would not have been as comprehensively researched without their invaluable support.

Next, I wish to express my heartfelt gratitude to Ms. Lauren Bydalek, the Associate Director of the Space, Cyber, and Telecommunications Law Program, and Ms. Vicki Lill, the Registrar of the Nebraska College of Law. Their crucial roles in guiding me through my journey in the JSD Program, from admission to graduation, were instrumental.

Furthermore, I would like to acknowledge the invaluable support of my friends in the United States, Europe, and the Republic of Korea. Their steadfast support significantly contributed to maintaining my mental and physical well-being while I pursued my studies abroad.

Finally, I must express my deepest gratitude to my family, whose unwavering support has been the cornerstone of my endeavor throughout the years devoted to writing and developing this project. This book is dedicated to them, and I am profoundly grateful for their enduring love and support.

Youngshin Ahn, JSD
Attorney at Law
Seoul, Republic of Korea, October 2023

Figures and Tables

Figures

Tables

Abbreviations and Acronyms

ADD	Agency for Defense Development
ASI	Agenzia Spaziale Italiana, or Italian Space Agency
BLT	Ballistic Lunar Transfer
BR IFIC	Radiocommunication Bureau International Frequency Information Circular
CFR	Code of Federal Regulations
CNES	Centre National d'Études Spatiales, or National Center for Space Studies
CNSA	China National Space Administration
COPUOS	Committee on the Peaceful Uses of Outer Space
CSA	Canadian Space Agency
DECCA	Hyperbolic Curve Radionavigation
DLR	Deutsche Zentrum für Luft- und Raumfahrt, or German Aerospace Center
DMB	Digital Multimedia Broadcasting
DTNPL	Delay-Tolerant Networking Experiment
EDT	Eastern Daylight Time
EIAST	Emirates Institution for Advanced Science and Technology
ESA	European Space Agency
ETRI	Electronic Telecommunication Research Institute
FAA	Federal Aviation Administration
FAI	Fédération Aéronautique Internationale, or World Air Sports Federation
FCC	Federal Communications Commission
GATT	General Agreement on Tariffs and Trade
GEO	Geosynchronous Equatorial Orbit
GIO	Geosynchronous Inclined Orbit
GMDSS	Global Maritime Distress and Safety System
GMT	Greenwich Mean Time
GNSS	Global Navigation Satellite System
GPS	Global Positioning System
IADC	Inter-Agency Space Debris Coordination Committee
ICAO	International Civil Aviation Organization
ICBM	Intercontinental Ballistic Missile
ICT	Information and Communications Technology

IMO	International Maritime Organization
IMSO/INMARSAT	International Mobile Satellite Organization
ISAS	Institute of Space and Astronautical Science
ISES	International Space Environment Service
ISO	International Organization for Standardization
ISS	International Space Station
ITSO/INTELSAT	International Telecommunications Satellite Organization
ITU	International Telecommunication Union
JAXA	Japan Aerospace Exploration Agency
KAAIB	Korea Aviation Accident Investigation Board
KAI	Korea Aerospace Industries
KAIS	Korea Advanced Institute of Science
KAIST	Korea Advanced Institute of Science and Technology
KARI	Korea Aerospace Research Institute
KARIST	Korea Aerospace Research Institute International Space Training
KASA	Korea AeroSpace Administration
KASI	Korea Astronomy and Space Science Institute
KASP	Korea Association for Space Technology Promotion
KASS	Korea Augmentation Satellite System
KCA	Korea Communications Agency
KCC	Korea Communications Commission
KGRS	KPLO Gamma Ray Spectrometer
KIMM	Korea Institute of Machinery and Materials
KITSAT	Korea Institute of Technology Satellite
KLEP	Korea Lunar Exploration Program
KMAG	KPLO Magnetometer
KOMPSAT	Korea Multi-Purpose Satellite
KPLO	Korea Pathfinder Lunar Orbiter
KPS	Korea Positioning System
KSLS	Korea Space Launch System
KSLV	Korea Space Launch Vehicle
KSR	Korea Sounding Rocket
KT	Korea Telecommunication Corporation
LSA	Luxembourg Space Agency
LUTI	Lunar Terrain Imager
MBRSC	Mohammed Bin Rashid Space Centre
MOU	Memorandum of Understanding
NACA	National Advisory Committee for Aeronautics

NAL	National Aerospace Laboratory of Japan
NASA	National Aeronautics and Space Administration
NASA Act	National Aeronautics and Space Act
NASDA	National Space Development Agency of Japan
NEO	Near Earth Object
NEXT Sat	Next Generation Satellite
NOAA	National Oceanic and Atmospheric Administration
NSSAO	National Space Situational Awareness Organization
PolCam	Wide-Angle Polarimetric Camera
PTO	Public Telecommunications Operator
RAPA	Radio Promotion Association
ROSCOSMOS	State Space Corporation of the Russian Federation
RRA	Radio Research Agency
SaTRec	Satellite Technology Research Center
SI	Satrec Initiative
SIIS	Satrec Initiative Imaging Service
SLBM	Advanced Submarine Launched Ballistic Missile
SPREC	Space Policy Research Center
SSAU	State Space Agency of Ukraine
SSO	Sun-synchronous orbit
STEPI	Science and Technology Policy Institute
STIT	Science, Technology, Information and Telecommunications
STSAT	Science and Technology Satellite
UAE	United Arab Emirates
UAESA	United Arab Emirates Space Agency
UEL	Unmanned Exploration Laboratory
UKSA	United Kingdom Space Agency
UN	United Nations
UN Charter	Charter of the United Nations
UNCOPUOS	United Nations Committee on the Peaceful Uses of Outer Space
UNGA	United Nations General Assembly
UNOOSA	United Nations Office for Outer Space Affairs
USC	United States Code
USGS	United States Geological Survey
WTO	World Trade Organization

Introduction

Within the serene canvas of the night sky, ancient Koreans shared a profound belief – an enduring tale of a rabbit that had journeyed from Earth to the Moon, diligently pounding rice cakes in a colossal stone mortar.[1] Remarkably, this whimsical narrative finds its reflection in the lunar terrain, an intricate mosaic of craters discernible from our terrestrial vantage point (Figure 1). For nearly two millennia, this oral folklore has persevered,[2] a testament to the abiding inquisitiveness of the Korean people concerning the mysteries that lie beyond our planet's boundaries.[3]

While the Republic of Korea, by historical happenstance, found itself a latecomer to the realm of national space programs, it has traversed remarkable distances in a relatively brief span.

Since launching its inaugural national space program in 1996,[4] the Korean government has systematically cultivated the nation's space capabilities. The culmination of these endeavors was the unveiling of "The Fourth Five-Year Basic Plan for the Promotion of Space Development" in December 2022.[5] This visionary document outlines a transformative mission – a paradigm where private enterprise spearheads space development, fostering the incremental growth of Korea's burgeoning commercial space industry.

This paradigm shift mirrors the global trend propelling private enterprise to the forefront of the space sector. The advent of cost-effective and innovative technologies has ushered in a new era, characterized by a surge of private entities entering the space domain, commonly referred to as "NewSpace."[6]

---

1 The rabbit is called *Oktoki* (옥토끼) in Korean, which literally means a rabbit living on the Moon. Coincidentally, this book is being revised in the Year of the Rabbit, which corresponds to 2023 in the Korean zodiac.

2 Jitae Jang, "방아 찧는 토끼 (A rabbit pounding rice cakes [English title added])," Busanilbo, October 31, 2012, https://news.naver.com/main/read.nhn?oid=082&aid=0000362799.

3 As a side note, in South Korea, there is an astronomical observatory constructed in the 7th century, called *Cheomseongdae* (첨성대), which means 'star-gazing tower' in Korean. *Cheomseongdae* is the oldest surviving astronomical observatory in Asia, and possibly even the world (David Kelley and Eugene Milone, "Exploring Ancient Skies: A Survey of Ancient and Cultural Astronomy," 79; Helaine Selin, "Encyclopaedia of the History of Science, Technology, and Medicine in Non-Western Cultures," 503).

4 제1차 우주개발중장기기본계획 (The First Medium to Long-Term Basic Plan for the Space Development [English title added]).

5 English title added, "제4차 우주개발진흥기본계획" in Korean.

6 The term "NewSpace" can be found in the following articles and websites: Hamid Kazemi, S. Hadi Mahmoudi and Ali Akbar Golroo, "The Need to Regulate New Space Activities on Exploration of Space Resources and Off-Earth Mining," in Proceedings of the International

 | DOI:10.1163/9789004694743_002

FIGURE 1 Shape of the rabbit and mortar imagined by ancient Koreans

This transformation, far from being a transient phenomenon, epitomizes a global movement, an inventive industrial environment ignited by the recent commercialization of space activities. However, the transition to "NewSpace" not only presents entrepreneurial opportunities but also poses intricate legal challenges, both at the international and national levels.

Acknowledging this transformative shift, this book aspires to undertake a comprehensive evaluation of current Korean space legislation. Its primary objective is to scrutinize the existing legal framework and provide insightful recommendations for enhancement. The ultimate goal is to establish a more robust legal regime in alignment with the anticipated evolution of the space domain. The uniqueness of this endeavor lies in its pioneering role within the

Institute of Space Law 2017 (2018), 227–228; Xiaodan Wu, "NewSpace in China in Needs of New Laws," in Proceedings of the International Institute of Space Law 2017 (2018), 501; Airbus, "New Space: Europe should shape the future of space," accessed November 14, 2019, https://www.airbus.com/public-affairs/brussels/our-topics/space/new-space.html; Gary Martin, "NewSpace: The Emerging Commercial Space Industry," accessed November 14, 2019, https://ntrs.nasa.gov/archive/nasa/casi.ntrs.nasa.gov/20160001188.pdf.

Korean academic community and its commitment to shaping the national and, eventually, international space landscape.

The rationale for enacting national space legislation derives primarily from Articles VI, VII, and VIII of the Outer Space Treaty,[7] notably in the context of regulating private space endeavors. As per the tenets of international space law, States are responsible for their national space activities, irrespective of whether these ventures are State-driven or undertaken by private entities.[8] The incorporation of these private entities within the framework of international space law, through the conduit of national legal systems, ensures conformity with international obligations.

South Korea is a party to the four United Nations (UN) space treaties – the Outer Space Treaty, the Rescue Agreement,[9] the Liability Convention,[10] and the Registration Convention.[11] Furthermore, it stands as a member of the International Telecommunication Union (ITU) and the World Trade Organization (WTO). Therefore, as part of its comprehensive mandate, this study endeavors to assess the extent to which Korea has assimilated the imperatives of *corpus juris spatialis internationalis* into its legal architecture. This critical inquiry discerns the alignment of Korea's legal infrastructure with prevailing international benchmarks.

As a satellite producer, space service provider, and a nation launching space vehicles, it is crucial for South Korea to reflect on its past achievements and embark on a path of forward-thinking space policy. This journey begins with an

---

7 Treaty on Principles Governing the Activities of States in the Exploration and Use of Outer Space, including the Moon and Other Celestial Bodies (hereinafter the "Outer Space Treaty), London/Moscow/Washington, done January 27, 1967, entered into force October 10, 1967; 610 UNTS 205; TIAS 6347; 18 UST 2410; UKTS 1968 No. 10; Cmnd. 3198; ATS 1967 No. 24; 6 ILM 386 (1967).

8 Article VI of the Outer Space Treaty.

9 Agreement on the Rescue of Astronauts, the Return of Astronauts and the Return of Objects Launched into Outer Space (hereinafter the "Rescue Agreement"), London/Moscow/Washington, done April 22, 1968, entered into force December 3, 1968; 672 UNTS 119; TIAS 6599; 19 UST 7570; UKTS 1969 No. 56; Cmnd. 3786; ATS 1986 No. 8; 7 ILM 151 (1968).

10 Convention on International Liability for Damage Caused by Space Objects (hereinafter the "Liability Convention"), London/Moscow/Washington DC, done March 29, 1972, entered into force September 1, 1972; 961 UNTS 187; TIAS 7762; 24 UST 2389; UKTS 1974 No. 16; Cmnd. 5068; ATS 1975 No. 5; 10 ILM 965 (1971).

11 Convention on Registration of Objects Launched into Outer Space (hereinafter the "Registration Convention"), New York, done January 14, 1975, entered into force September 15, 1976; 1023 UNTS 15; TIAS 8480; 28 UST 695; UKTS 1978 No. 70; Cmnd. 6256; ATS 1986 No. 5; 14 ILM 43 (1975).

exhaustive review of its current national space legislation. In general, research in the field of national space law holds significant value in two distinct aspects:

First, with the increasing commercialization and privatization of space activities, a comprehensive analysis of a specific State's national space law provides insights into how it addresses domestic space-related matters. Professor Dr. Frans von der Dunk has observed that "the establishment of national space legislation is usually considered the most comprehensive and preferable method of ensuring the direct application of international space law as relevant to the private sector."[12] In this regard, Korean space law is no exception, faithfully adhering to this principle.

Second, the relentless progress in space science and technology demands a nuanced legal framework. As international collaboration between government agencies and private enterprises burgeons, the practical implementation of national and international space law assumes heightened significance. In this context, research findings on Korean space law serve as a valuable asset in addressing the emerging challenges of our times.

To fulfill its research objectives, this book employs descriptive, comparative, and analytical methodologies. Each approach is seamlessly integrated with the others, ensuring a holistic and discerning examination. The initial phase adopts a descriptive stance, offering a historical perspective to illuminate Korea's past and contemporary space endeavors. Archival materials sourced from Korean public and private institutions serve as the bedrock of this investigation. The second phase delves into the application of comparative and analytical techniques, meticulously dissecting Korean space legislation, with particular emphasis on scrutinizing the legal semantics underpinning each clause. Finally, when proposing recommendations for Korea's future legal framework, the study harmoniously combines all three approaches to yield a comprehensive and well-informed conclusion.

The primary ambition of this book extends beyond a mere introduction to Korean national space legislation. Rather, it unveils a comprehensive and profound exploration thereof. Comprising six chapters, each section advances a distinct purpose, collectively contributing to the overarching objective of unearthing the intricacies enshrined in Korean space laws. This intricate tapestry weaves a nuanced and multifaceted comprehension of the legal framework governing Korea's space endeavors, including its policies, regulations, and enforcement mechanisms.

12 Frans von der Dunk, "Scoping National Space Law: The True Meaning of 'National Activities in Outer Space' of Article VI of the Outer Space Treaty," in *Proceedings of the International Institute of Space Law 2019*, 227–237.

Chapters 1 and 2 serve as the foundation, providing essential contextual knowledge for subsequent chapters. Chapter 1 meticulously scrutinizes Korea's participation in international space law and its affiliations with international organizations dedicated to space activities. It examines the influence of these treaties and organizations on Korea's domestic legal framework and delves into the symbiotic relationships forged between Korea and other nations in the dynamic sphere of space exploration. Chapter 2 provides an in-depth overview of Korea's national space activities, encompassing a panorama of space-related committees, public institutions, private enterprises, and ongoing space programs. These elements intricately interlace with Korea's space policy and national space legislation.

Chapters 3 through 6 embody the crux of our analysis, with each chapter dedicated to one of the core space laws and their complementary regulations. Within these chapters, the provisions of each law are dissected from the vantage point of *corpus juris spatialis internationalis*, juxtaposed against analogous laws in select countries where relevant. The laws are assessed in chronological order, shedding light on the evolving trajectory of Korean space laws. This evaluation reveals South Korea's fidelity to its international commitments and the practical application of its domestic regulations in the arena of national space activities.

The book concludes by distilling insights from the preceding chapters, providing potential amendments to Korea's existing space legislation, and proposing a novel paradigm necessitating a unique legal framework. It proffers valuable insights for future research and delineates a path forward for Korea's space development, thereby furnishing actionable recommendations for policymakers and stakeholders.

CHAPTER 1

Korea's Participation in International Space Law

1 A Party to the UN Space Treaties

The United Nations (UN) announced five major space treaties in the late 1960s and 1970s. Like most of the other space-faring nations, South Korea is a party to the four UN space treaties: the Outer Space Treaty, the Rescue Agreement, the Liability Convention, and the Registration Convention. However, South Korea is neither a signatory nor a party to the Moon Agreement.[1]

Pursuant to Article 6(1) of South Korea's Constitution,[2] a duly concluded and promulgated treaty has a legal status equal to national law, which is generally superior to a presidential decree and inferior to the Constitution. Since the four aforementioned space treaties entered into force for South Korea through constitutional due process, they have the same legal effect as Korean national law. By signing these treaties and relevant instruments almost immediately after their conclusion, South Korea actively participated in the international space law regime, long before launching its first national space program in 1996.[3]

1.1 *The Outer Space Treaty*

On January 27, 1967, South Korea signed the Outer Space Treaty and ratified it on October 13 of the same year, assigning the Treaty No. 262 under the domestic treaty numbering system. The Outer Space Treaty entered into force for Korea on the date of ratification. Five days after the ratification, the Ministry of the Interior and Safety promulgated the Outer Space Treaty in the Korean official gazette upon request from the International Legal Affairs Division of the Ministry of Justice.[4]

---

1 Agreement Governing the Activities of States on the Moon and Other Celestial Bodies (hereinafter the "Moon Agreement), New York, done December 18, 1979, entered into force July 11, 1984; 1363 UNTS 3; ATS 1986 No. 14; 18 ILM 1434 (1979).

2 Constitution of the Republic of Korea, Constitution No. 10 as wholly amended on October 29, 1987, entered into force on February 25, 1988.

3 For more information, *see* Youngshin Ahn, "Recent Developments in the Republic of Korea's Space Policy: An Overview of Space Activities and National Laws," Air & Space Law 44, no. 2 (2019), 169–184.

4 Ministry of Foreign Affairs, "Multilateral Treaty Book No. 2," accessed January 1, 2020, http://www.mofa.go.kr/www/wpge/m_3835/contents.do.

 | DOI:10.1163/9789004694743_003

1.1.1 The Advent of the Outer Space Treaty

In 1958, the United Nations General Assembly (UNGA) adopted Resolution 1348 (XIII) on the Questions of the Peaceful Use of Outer Space. This Resolution served as a starting point for the conclusion of the Outer Space Treaty. In the Resolution, the UNGA recognized the importance of international cooperation in space affairs and established an *ad hoc* Committee on the Peaceful Uses of Outer Space (COPUOS).[5] In the following year, the UNGA furthered these endeavors by establishing a permanent COPUOS under Resolution 1472 (XIV).[6] Notably, both Resolutions presciently referred to the study of legal problems in space exploration as one of COPUOS's founding purposes, even before substantive legal issues had yet to arise.

In line with these endeavors, the Legal Subcommittee of COPUOS was formed in 1961 and entrusted with the task of addressing legal issues intensively. Through its sessions, the Legal Subcommittee was faced with the need to elaborate a set of basic principles to serve as the foundation for detailed rules in the exploration and use of outer space.[7]

The results of their undertakings are reflected in the unanimous adoption of the "Declaration of Legal Principles Governing the Activities of States in the Exploration and Use of Outer Space" (Resolution 1962)[8] by the UNGA in 1963.[9] The nine principles outlined in the Resolution 1962 were later incorporated into the first-ever space treaty, the Outer Space Treaty.[10] The difference between the Resolution 1962 and the Outer Space Treaty in terms of legal effect is that the former is not legally binding,[11] whereas the latter has binding force

5 UNGA Res. 1348 (XIII), December 13, 1958, UN Doc. A/RES/1348 (XIII). For more information, see Chapter 1 § 3.1 *UNCOPUOS*.

6 UNGA Res. 1472 (XIV) A, December 12, 1959, UN Doc. A/RES/1472 (XIV).

7 Manfred Lachs, The Law of Outer Space: An Experience in Contemporary Law-Making (1972), 30.

8 Hereinafter the "Resolution 1962," UNGA Res. 1962 (XVIII), December 13, 1963, UN Doc. A/RES/1962 (XVIII).

9 *Supra* Chapter 1, n. 7, Manfred Lachs.

10 The nine principles are as follows: Principle 1 on benefit of all mankind, Principle 2 on freedom of exploration and use, Principle 3 on non-appropriation, Principle 4 on compliance with international law, Principle 5 on state responsibility for national activities, Principle 6 on cooperation and mutual assistance, Principle 7 on national registration and jurisdiction, Principle 8 on launching state and liability, and Principle 9 on astronauts as envoys of mankind.

11 Nonetheless, through State practice and attendant *opinio juris*, it could be recognized as customary international law and thus would be binding upon States. *See*, Frans von der Dunk, "International Space Law," in Frans von der Dunk (ed.), Handbook of Space Law (2014), 31.

among member States. As such, the rules of the Outer Space Treaty ought to be interpreted as legally authoritative norms that fundamentally govern all space activities.[12] The Outer Space Treaty is widely credited as the "Magna Carta" of contemporary space law and is considered the cornerstone of the international legal framework governing space activities, from which other subsequent space treaties originated.

1.1.2 International Responsibility for "National Activities"

Among other core principles set forth in the Outer Space Treaty, Article VI attracts special attention as it foresightedly anticipated the involvement of private entities, even though at the time of its drafting, most space activities were primarily being conducted by governmental agencies. The first sentence of Article VI stipulates that States bear "international responsibility for national activities in outer space" whether these activities are carried on by governmental agencies or non-governmental entities.[13]

A question of cardinal importance arises as to which category of private space activities can be deemed as "national activities" under the regime of the Outer Space Treaty. In addressing this question, academia has propounded three distinct approaches:

The first theory construes "national activities" as activities conducted by a State's nationals, based on the concept of 'nationals' appearing in Article IX of the Outer Space Treaty.[14]

---

12 Ram Jakhu, "Legal Issues Relating to the Global Public Interest in Outer Space," Journal of Space Law 32, no. 1 (Summer 2006), 34.

13 The full language of Article VI of the Outer Space Treaty is as follows: "States Parties to the Treaty shall bear international responsibility for national activities in outer space, including the Moon and other celestial bodies, whether such activities are carried on by governmental agencies or by non-governmental entities, and for assuring that national activities are carried out in conformity with the provisions set forth in the present Treaty. The activities of non-governmental entities in outer space, including the Moon and other celestial bodies, shall require authorization and continuing supervision by the appropriate State Party to the Treaty. When activities are carried on in outer space, including the Moon and other celestial bodies, by an international organization, responsibility for compliance with this Treaty shall be borne both by the international organization and by the States Parties to the Treaty participating in such organization."

14 The paragraph where 'nationals' appears in Article IX of the Outer Space Treaty is as follows: "If a State Party to the Treaty has reason to believe that an activity or experiment planned by it or its *nationals* in outer space, including the Moon and other celestial bodies, would cause potentially harmful interference with activities of other States Parties in the peaceful exploration and use of outer space, including the Moon and other celestial bodies, it shall undertake appropriate international consultations before proceeding with any such activity or experiment." [Italics added]. Dr. Bin Cheng argued that

The second approach connects the activities to qualifications for the 'launching State,' as specified in both Article VII of the Outer Space Treaty and Article I(c) of the Liability Convention.[15]

The third approach interprets the activities as those over which a State has jurisdiction under the general concept of public international law, where the State in question can exercise its legal authority to regulate or control the activities.[16]

Given defining what constitutes "national activities" is ultimately related to the issue of determining which State is responsible for private space activities, it appears reasonable to conclude that space activities falling under a State's legal power or control – under effective jurisdiction – should be subject to the State's responsibility, regardless of whether such activities are conducted by governmental agencies or by non-governmental entities.[17]

---

relying on 'nationals' has two drawbacks. First, a State may "assume responsibility over persons and activities that are beyond its effective jurisdiction." Second, it "leaves out space activities by non-nationals within a State's territory, or on board, or from on board, ships or aircraft of its nationality." *See*, Bin Cheng, "Article VI of the 1967 Space Treaty Revisited: 'International Responsibility,' 'National Activities' and 'The Appropriate State'" in Journal of Space Law Vol. 26 (1998), 22.

15 The full language of Article VII of the Outer Space Treaty is as follows: "Each State Party to the Treaty that launches or procures the launching of an object into outer space, including the Moon and other celestial bodies, and each State Party from whose territory or facility an object is launched, is internationally liable for damage to another State Party to the Treaty or to its natural or juridical persons by such object or its component parts on the Earth, in air space or in outer space, including the Moon and other celestial bodies. In addition, Article I(c) of the Liability Convention provides that the term "*launching State*" means: (i) A State which launches or procures the launching of a space object; (ii) A State from whose territory or facility a space object is launched." [Italics added]. *See*, Valérie Kayser, "Commercial Exploitation of Space: Developing Domestic Regulation," Annals of Air and Space Law 17 (1992), 188–189; Stephen Gorove, "Liability in Space Law: An Overview," Annals of Air and Space Law 8 (1983), 377; Hanneke L. van Traa-Engelman, "Problems of State Responsibility in International Space Law" in Proceedings of the 26th Colloquium on the Law of Outer Space (1983), 140–141.

16 *Supra* Chapter 1, n. 14, Bin Cheng at 23–26. *See also,* Ricky J. Lee, "Liability Arising from Article VI of the Outer Space Treaty: States, Domestic Law, and Private Operators," in Proceedings of the 48th Colloquium on the Law of Outer Space (2005), 219; Bin Cheng, Studies in International Space Law (1997), 626–627.

17 For more discussion, *see supra* Chapter 1, n. 14, Bin Cheng at 24; Michael Gerhard, "Article VI," in Stephan Hobe, Bernhard Schmidt-Tedd and Kai-Uwe Schrogl (eds.), Cologne Commentary on Space Law, Vol. 1 (2013), 112–114; Henri A. Wassenbergh, "The Law Governing International Private Commercial Activities of Space Transportation," Journal of Space Law 21, no. 2 (1993), 109. *See also,* Frans von der Dunk, Advanced Introduction to Space Law (2020), 121–125; "Private Enterprise and Public Interest in the European 'Spacescape': towards harmonized national space legislation for private space activities

Another instrument addressing "national activities" is the Recommendations on National Legislation relevant to the Peaceful Exploration and Use of Outer Space, adopted by the UN General Assembly in 2013.[18] This document presents a set of eight elements that States should consider when enacting regulatory frameworks for their space activities. These elements include: (1) the scope of space activities targeted by its national space law; (2) the ascertainment of national jurisdiction over space activities; (3) authorization by a competent national authority; (4) conditions for authorization; (5) procedures for continuing supervision of authorized space activities; (6) establishment of a national registry of space objects; (7) insurance requirements and indemnification procedures for damage claims; and (8) the transfer of ownership or control of a space object in orbit.

Of these eight elements, the first and second are particularly relevant to defining "national activities." Specifically, the first element enumerates examples of space activities that may be addressed in national space legislation. These include launching and returning space objects, operating launch or reentry sites, controlling space objects in orbit, designing and manufacturing spacecraft, applying space science and technology, and conducting exploration and research.

The second element pertains to ascertaining national jurisdiction over space activities. It emphasizes a State's obligation to authorize and supervise space activities that are conducted from its territory (territorial/quasi-territorial jurisdiction) or by its nationals (personal jurisdiction). These two elements, in conjunction with the aforementioned theories, aid in better understanding the implications of "national activities" under Article VI of the Outer Space Treaty.

Nonetheless, since the Outer Space Treaty does not provide an explicit definition of "national activities," and there is no international consensus thereon, member States still have the discretion to legislate for their space activities based on their apprehension. Therefore, it is worth examining the extent to which South Korea's national space law covers such activities, which may invoke international responsibility in a certain situation.

---

in Europe" (1998), 19, 297; "Fundamental Provisions for National Space Laws" (2006), Space, Cyber, and Telecommunications Law Program Faculty Publications 11, 93–94; "The Origins of Authorization: Article VI of the Outer Space Treaty and International Space Law" (2011) in Space, Cyber, and Telecommunications Law Program Faculty Publication 69, 5–6.

18 UNGA Res. 68/74 of December 11, 2013; UN Doc. A/RES/68/74.

1.1.3 Authorization and Continuing Supervision by the "Appropriate State"

The second sentence of Article VI of the Outer Space Treaty further provides that the activities of non-governmental entities in outer space require authorization and continuing supervision by the "appropriate State" to the Treaty.[19] Unlike Principle 5 of the Resolution 1962,[20] which uses the term "State concerned,"[21] this sentence refers to the term "appropriate State."

There are divergent opinions as to which State should be qualified as an "appropriate State." Some scholars argue that the "appropriate State" should essentially be the 'launching State' in accordance with Article VII of the Outer Space Treaty, as the launching State is internationally liable for space damage.[22] Others contend that the "appropriate State" is the State of registry, which exercises jurisdiction and control over the space object.[23] Still, others maintain that the identification of the "appropriate State" should be understood in relation to the first sentence of Article VI of the Outer Space Treaty, in which the State responsible for national activities is the appropriate State to accordingly authorize and continually supervise such activities.[24]

It appears that the above approaches are not mutually exclusive, and each approach can be valid from case to case depending on the situation.[25] The "appropriate State" should be determined by identifying the particular activities and States concerned in the light of "national activities" at issue. From this perspective, it would be meaningful to examine State practice relating to mechanisms for authorizing and supervising private space activities.

---

19 *Supra* Chapter 1, n. 13, the second sentence of Article VI of the Outer Space Treaty.

20 *Supra* Chapter 1, n. 8, UNGA Res. 1962 (XVIII); *supra* Chapter 1 §1.1.1.

21 The second sentence of Principle 5 of Resolution 1962 is as follows: The activities of non-governmental entities in outer space shall require authorization and continuing supervision by the *State concerned.* [Italics added].

22 *Supra* Chapter 1, n. 15, Hanneke L. van Traa-Engelman; *Supra* Chapter 1, n. 15 Stephen, S Gorove. *Cf.* Istvan Herczeg, "Problems of Interpretation of the Space Treaty of 27 January 1967" in Proceedings of the 10th Colloquium on the Law of Outer Space (1967), 107–108.

23 *Supra* Chapter 1, n. 16, Ricky J. Lee; Michel Bourely, "Rules of International Law Governing the Commercialization of Space Activities" in Proceedings of the 29th Colloquium on the Law of Outer Space (1986), 159–160.

24 *Supra* Chapter 1, n. 17, Michael Gerhard at 111–112; Armel Kerrest, "Remarks on the Responsibility and Liability for Damage Caused by Private Activity in Outer Space" in Proceedings of the 42nd Colloquium on the Law of Outer Space (1997), 139; *Cf. Supra* Chapter 1, n. 14, Bin Cheng at 14; Tanja Masson-Zwaan and Mahulena Hofmann, Introduction to Space Law (2019), 43.

25 Karl-Heinz Böckstiegel, "The Term 'Appropriate State' in International Space Law," in Proceedings of the 37th Colloquium on the Law of Outer Space (1994), 79.

With regard to such mechanisms, however, there is no explicit provision in the Outer Space Treaty that obliges States Parties to enact specific national laws. The Outer Space Treaty merely prescribes that the private space activities require authorization and continuing supervision.[26] Therefore, how to fulfill the obligation is left up to each State Party. Some States have implemented the obligation through their national space legislation, while others have adopted different approaches, such as holding governmental shares in the relevant private entities or including authorization conditions in other administrative procedures.[27] The contents of authorization and supervision are also at the discretion of States, provided that they comply with the provisions of the Outer Space Treaty.[28]

1.2 *The Rescue Agreement*

The UN General Assembly adopted the Rescue Agreement on December 19, 1967, which was opened for signature on April 22, 1968, and entered into force on December 3 of the same year.

South Korea signed the Rescue Agreement on May 9, 1968, in Washington, and ratified it on April 4, 1969, which entered into force for Korea on the same day.[29] The Ministry of the Interior and Safety promulgated it as Treaty No. 296 in the Korean official gazette on April 15, 1969.[30]

1.2.1 The Structure of the Rescue Agreement

Shortly after the Outer Space Treaty's completion, the United States and the Soviet Union – the two space powers most concerned at that time – as well as some other COPUOS' members sought further protection for their astronauts and space objects.[31] The Rescue Agreement is a product of these efforts, which elaborates two provisions of the Outer Space Treaty: Article V regarding the rescue of astronauts[32] and Article VIII regarding the return of space

26 *Supra* Chapter 1, n. 17, Michael Gerhard at 117; *Supra* Chapter 1, n. 15, Valérie Kayser at 190.

27 *Supra* Chapter 1, n. 17, Michael Gerhard at 119.

28 The first sentence of Article VI of the Outer Space Treaty.

29 United Nations Treaty Collection, accessed on December 18, 2019, https://treaties.un.org/Pages/showDetails.aspx?objid=080000028012504f.

30 Ministry of Foreign Affairs of the Republic of Korea, accessed on December 18, 2019, https://www.mofa.go.kr/www/wpge/m_3835/contents.do.

31 Frans von der Dunk, "A Sleeping Beauty Awakens: The 1968 Rescue Agreement after Forty Years," Journal of Space Law 34, no. 2 (2008), 417–418.

32 Article V of the Outer Space Treaty stipulates that "States Parties to the Treaty shall regard astronauts as envoys of mankind in outer space and shall render to them all possible assistance in the event of accident, distress, or emergency landing on the territory of another State Party or on the high seas. When astronauts make such a landing, they shall

objects.[33] The preamble of the Rescue Agreement explicitly refers to the Outer Space Treaty, which calls for "the rendering of all possible assistance to astronauts in the event of accident, distress or emergency landing, the prompt and safe return of astronauts, and the return of objects launched into outer space[.]"[34]

In line with the letter and the spirit of the Outer Space Treaty, the Rescue Agreement focuses on two main subject matters: (i) "the personnel of a spacecraft" in Articles 1 through 4 and (ii) "a space object or its component parts" in Article 5.

Regarding the first subject matter, it appears evident that the Rescue Agreement places a high priority on ensuring the safety of space personnel. Article 2, in this context, requires States to "immediately take all possible steps" to rescue and assist the personnel of a spacecraft in distress that has landed in their territory.

As for the second subject matter, the Rescue Agreement establishes a duty to return space objects. Article 5 stipulates that the nation where space objects have been discovered is required to take "practical" steps to recover those

---

be safely and promptly returned to the State of registry of their space vehicle. In carrying on activities in outer space and on celestial bodies, the astronauts of one State Party shall render all possible assistance to the astronauts of other States Parties. States Parties to the Treaty shall immediately inform the other States Parties to the Treaty or the Secretary-General of the United Nations of any phenomena they discover in outer space, including the moon and other celestial bodies, which could constitute a danger to the life or health of astronauts."

33 Article VIII of the Outer Space Treaty provides that "[a] State Party to the Treaty on whose registry an object launched into outer space is carried shall retain jurisdiction and control over such object, and over any personnel thereof, while in outer space or on a celestial body. Ownership of objects launched into outer space, including objects landed or constructed on a celestial body, and of their component parts, is not affected by their presence in outer space or on a celestial body or by their return to the Earth. Such objects or component parts found beyond the limits of the State Party to the Treaty on whose registry they are carried shall be returned to that State Party, which shall, upon request, furnish identifying data prior to their return."

34 The full language of the preamble is as follows: "The Contracting Parties, *Noting* the great importance of the Treaty on Principles Governing the Activities of States in the Exploration and Use of Outer Space, including the Moon and Other Celestial Bodies, which calls for the rendering of all possible assistance to astronauts in the event of accident, distress or emergency landing, the prompt and safe return of astronauts, and the return of objects launched into outer space, *Desiring* to develop and give further concrete expression to these duties, *Wishing* to promote international co-operation in the peaceful exploration and use of outer space, *Prompted* by sentiments of humanity, *Have agreed* on the following."

objects upon the request of the "launching authority."[35] Given the wording in Article 5, the duty to retrieve the space object is less stringent than the duty to return the personnel of a spacecraft with "all possible" steps taken.

1.2.2 The Term "Personnel of a Spacecraft"

The Rescue Agreement does not define the term "personnel of a spacecraft" used in Articles 1 to 4. As such, the primary question is whether this term has the same meaning as "astronauts" in Article V of the Outer Space Treaty, from which the Rescue Agreement was derived.[36]

In their drafts of the Soviet Union and the United States as historical background, both "astronauts" and "personnel [or "crew" in the Soviet Union's draft] of a spacecraft" were referred to without a clear preference or explanation.[37] This implies that at the time of the Rescue Agreement's conclusion, the two space powers did not intend to differentiate one from another. It is also notable that the Rescue Agreement employs both terms, with "astronauts" appearing in the title and the preamble[38] and "personnel of a spacecraft" appearing in the subsequent operative provisions.

Given the historical context and the language of the Rescue Agreement *per se*, it appears that the two terms do not have different meanings for the purpose of the rescue and return of such personnel.[39]

---

35 Paragraph 2 of Article 5 of the Rescue Agreement. According to Article 6 of the Rescue Agreement, the term "launching authority" refers to the State or intergovernmental organization responsible for launching.

36 *Supra* Chapter 1 §2.1; *supra* Chapter 1, n. 33; *supra* Chapter 1, n. 35.

37 For more information, Irmgard Marboe, Julia Neumann, and Kai-Uwe Schrogl, "Preamble ARRA," in Stephan Hobe, Bernhard Schmidt-Tedd and Kai-Uwe Schrogl (eds.), *Cologne Commentary on Space* Law, Vol. II (2013), 33–35; UN Doc. A/AC.105/C.2/L.2, International Agreement on the Rescue of Astronauts and Spaceships making Emergency Landings, USSR Proposal, June 6, 1962; UN Doc. A/AC.105/C.2/L.2/Rev.l, Agreement on the rescue of astronauts and spaceships in the event of accident or emergency landing, USSR Revised Draft, March 9, 1964; UN Doc. A/AC.105/ C.2/L.2/Rev.2, Agreement on the rescue of astronauts and spaceships in the event of accident or emergency landing, USSR Revised Draft, October 26, 1964; UN Doc. A/AC.105/C.2/L.9, International Agreement on Assistance to and Return of Astronauts and Objects Launched into Outer Space, United States Proposal, March 9, 1964; UN Doc. WG. I/33, USA: Proposal, in UN Doc. A/AC. 105/29, Report of the Legal Sub-Committee on the Work of its Fourth Session (20 September – 1 October 1965), Annex I, Proposals and Amendments Relating to Assistance to and Return of Astronauts and Space Vehicles, October 1, 1965 at 2.

38 *Supra* Chapter 1, n. 34.

39 For further discussion of these terms especially in relation to commercial space flights, *see* Mark J. Sundahl, "The Duty to Rescue Space Tourists and Return Private Spacecraft," Journal of Space Law 35, no. 1 (Spring 2009), 163–200; Mark J. Sundahl, "Rescuing Space Tourists: A Humanitarian Duty and Business Need," in Proceedings of the Fiftieth

1.2.3 The Term "Launching Authority"

The usage of "launching authority" in the Rescue Agreement is unique in comparison to other UN space treaties that came out later, such as the Liability Convention and the Registration Convention, which refer to the "launching State." This difference in terminology was the result of the negotiating history between the two major space powers at the time of the agreement's drafting.

The United States proposed that international organizations should have the same rights and obligations as States in the event that the organizations dispatch astronauts or launch space objects.[40] In contrast, the Soviet Union objected to an explicit reference to international organizations but ultimately did not insist on their exclusion.[41] As a compromise, the term "launching authority" was selected and defined in Article 6 of the Rescue Agreement as follows:

> For the purposes of this Agreement, the term "launching authority" shall refer to *the State responsible for launching*, or, *where an international intergovernmental organization is responsible for launching, that organization*, provided that that organization declares its acceptance of the rights and obligations provided for in this Agreement and a majority of the States members of that organization are Contracting Parties to this Agreement and to the Treaty on Principles Governing the Activities of States in the Exploration and Use of Outer Space, including the Moon and Other Celestial Bodies. [Italics added]

In summary, the term "launching authority" includes both the launching States and international intergovernmental organizations that have declared acceptance of the rights and obligations under the Rescue Agreement and whose

Colloquium on the Law of Outer Space (2008), 204–214; Francis Lyall, "Who is an astronaut? The inadequacy of current international law," Acta Astronautica 66 (2010), 1613–1617.

40 The United States had made reference to "the State or international organization responsible for launching" and later to "the State of registry or international organization responsible for launching." *Supra* Chapter 1, n. 37, Irmgard Marboe, Julia Neumann, and Kai-Uwe Schrogl, at 71.

41 Irmgard Marboe, "Agreement on the Rescue and Return of Astronauts and Objects Launched into Outer Space," the Oxford Research Encyclopedias, 7, available at https://oxfordre.com/planetaryscience/view/10.1093/acrefore/9780190647926.001.0001/acrefore-9780190647926-e-65.

majority of member States are contracting parties to the Rescue Agreement and the Outer Space Treaty.[42]

1.3 *The Liability Convention*

South Korea signed the Liability Convention on March 29, 1972, and later ratified it on January 14, 1980, under Treaty No. 702.[43] Prior to the ratification, the Ministry of Foreign Affairs obtained consent from the National Assembly on December 3, 1979,[44] in accordance with Article 60(1) of the South Korean Constitution. This provision grants the National Assembly the authority to give consent to the ratification of certain types of treaties, including those related to mutual assistance, national security, financial obligations, or legislative actions.[45]

The minutes of the 103rd National Assembly plenary session describe how their discussion for ratification proceeded to consensus.[46] In the Foreign Affairs Subcommittee of the National Assembly, some members expressed skepticism about the necessity and benefits of joining the Liability Convention. On the other hand, others emphasized that, as a party to the Outer Space Treaty, South Korea should prepare for potential damage caused by space objects and the resulting compensation claims.[47] Among the four UN space treaties that South Korea has joined, the Liability Convention was the only one that required prior consent from the National Assembly in terms of the ratification procedure. The minutes and relevant documents from the time of deliberation do not

---

42 Regarding the terms used in South Korea's national space legislation, *see infra* Chapter 5 §4.5.

43 National Archives of the Republic of Korea, accessed on December 18, 2019, http://theme.archives.go.kr/viewer/common/archWebViewer.do?bsid=200300839869&dsid=000000000019&gubun=search#1.

44 National Assembly of Republic of Korea, *Bill Information*, accessed on January 15, 2020, http://likms.assembly.go.kr/bill/billDetail.do?billId=008797&ageFrom=20&ageTo=20.

45 Regarding treaties subject to the National Assembly's prior consent, the full language of Article 60(1) of the Constitution of the Republic of Korea is as follows: "The National Assembly shall have the right to consent to the conclusion and ratification of treaties pertaining to *mutual assistance or mutual security*; treaties concerning important *international organizations;* treaties of *friendship, trade and navigation*; treaties pertaining to any *restriction in sovereignty*; *peace* treaties; treaties which will burden the State or people with an important *financial obligation*; or treaties related to *legislative matters*." [Italics added].

46 "The minutes of the 103rd National Assembly plenary session," No. 10, December 3, 1979, 10–11.

47 The bill of ratification of the Liability Convention, "The minutes of the Foreign Affairs Subcommittee of the 103rd National Assembly," 23–25. Available at http://likms.assembly.go.kr/bill/billDetail.do?billId=008797&ageFrom=20&ageTo=20.

clearly state the reason for this particular consent. However, the minutes of the plenary session and subcommittee reveal some members expressing concerns about whether a separate budgetary measure was required due to the financial implications of the Liability Convention. Therefore, it appears that the members considered the nation's financial obligation during their deliberations. Since Article 60(1) of the Constitution includes treaties that may impose a financial burden on the nation or its nationals among the treaties subject to prior consent, it can be inferred that the Liability Convention was ratified with prior consent, taking into consideration the potential financial burden.

1.3.1 The Background of the Liability Convention

The Liability Convention was finalized nearly five years after the effectuation of the Outer Space Treaty. Article VII of the Outer Space Treaty stipulates that States are liable for damage caused by space objects launched or procured by them or launched from their territory or facility.

The Liability Convention builds upon this essential principle of the Outer Space Treaty and expands upon the categories of liability and the compensation procedure in greater detail. The preamble of the Liability Convention explicitly references the Outer Space Treaty, and specifically Paragraph 5 of the preamble emphasizes the significance of providing effective international rules concerning liability for space damage and ensuring the prompt and equitable compensation for victims of such damage. The Liability Convention is designed with a victim-oriented approach, aiming to balance the imperative of space development and the protection of innocent victims.[48] This approach benefits all State Parties to the Liability Convention, as space objects can cause damage in any State, regardless of whether it has space capabilities or not.[49]

1.3.2 The Definition of the "Launching State" in the Liability Convention

The fundamental principle of the Liability Convention is that it attributes international liability for damage to the "launching State." Article I provides the definitions for key terms such as "damage," "launching State," and "space object" before further elaborating on the liability regime. This is in marked contrast to the Outer Space Treaty, which does not contain any definitions, and the Rescue Agreement, which only defines the meaning of "launching authority."

48 Joseph A. Burke, "Convention on International Liability for Damage Caused by Space Objects: Definition and Determination of Damages After the Cosmos 954 Incident," Fordham International Law Journal Vol.8 (1984), 257.

49 The United Nations, Proceedings of the United Nations/International Institute of Air and Space Law Workshop on Capacity Building in Space Law (2004), 33, 546.

According to Paragraph (c) of Article I, the "launching State" means:
(i) A State which launches or procures the launching of a space object;
(ii) A State from whose territory or facility a space object is launched.
While it is true that this definition helps to understand the concept of the "launching State," there is still room for further interpretation, particularly regarding instances where private entities conduct space activities without any active involvement of their States. For example, if a private entity procured the launching of a space object from a private facility outside the territory of a State, would any State be classified as the "launching State" under Article I(c)(i) of the Liability Convention?

The Liability Convention remains unclear on that question. If Article I(c)(i) of the Liability Convention is understood to include the activities of non-governmental entities like the concept of Article VI of the Outer Space Treaty, the State concerned can fall under this criterion, and thus is internationally liable for space damage. In contrast, if the text is interpreted most narrowly, there may be no "launching State" under the criterion of Article I(c)(i) in this particular case.[50] States' approaches can be varying, and it appears up to States' discretion to what extent they cover private space activities through their authorization regimes.[51] In practice, qualifying a State as a "launching State" can be determined based on a specific situation and a State's interest, along with the parameters contained in the definition of the "launching State."

1.3.3 The Recovery of Damages under the Liability Convention

The term "damage" is defined in Article I(a) of the Liability Convention as "loss of life, personal injury or other impairment of health; or loss of or damage to property of States or of persons, natural or juridical, or property of international intergovernmental organizations." Articles II and III of the Convention flow from the foregoing definition of "damage" to which the wording 'caused by a space object' is added.[52] From the text of those provisions, it is obvious

50 For more discussion about the term "launching State," *see supra* Chapter 1, n. 11, Frans von der Dunk, "International Space Law," Handbook of Space Law, 83–84. *See* also, Carl Q. Christol, The Modern International Law of Outer Space (1982), 115; Karl-Heinz Böckstiegel, "The Term 'Appropriate State' in International Space Law" in Proceedings of the 37th Colloquium on the Law of Outer Space (1994), 80–82; Frans von der Dunk, "The Origins of Authorization: Article VI of the Outer Space Treaty and International Space Law," in Frans von der Dunk (ed.), National Space Legislation in Europe (2011), 21–24.

51 For further discussion on South Korea's approach, *see infra* Chapter 6.

52 The full text of Article II is as follows: "A launching State shall be absolutely liable to pay compensation for *damage caused by its space object* on the surface of the Earth or to aircraft in flight" and Article III "In the event of *damage being caused* elsewhere than on the surface of the Earth to a space object of one launching State or to persons or property on

that direct damage caused by physical contact with a space object falls under this definition.

Nonetheless, the critical question remains as to whether indirect or consequential damage can be covered under the Liability Convention. There is no unanimous point of view among commentators on this issue.[53] Stephen Gorove argues that the limitation 'caused by' a space object could relate only to direct physical damage or impact.[54] In contrast, Carl Q. Christol suggests that the expression 'caused by' should "allow for recovery of damages both for a direct hit and for the indirect or consequential aspects of an accident involving a space object."[55] He adds, "if a valid causal relationship could be established between the malfunctioning of a space object [...] and an injury to persons or to property, recovery would be allowed for such indirect damage."[56]

With the uncertainty over the scope of damage under the Liability Convention, States can have differing viewpoints regarding the extent of coverage when establishing their respective liability regimes.[57] In this regard, Article XII of the Convention helps to provide some understanding of compensable damage, although it does not explicitly address the scope of damage. The text "[t]he compensation [...] shall be determined in accordance with *international law* and *principles of equity and justice*"[58] suggests that a broader interpretation of damage can be acceptable within these parameters. This approach aligns with the growing need to protect innocent victims, especially in light of the increasing emergence of new technologies in outer space.

---

board such a space object *by a space object* of another launching State, the latter shall be liable only if the damage is due to its fault or the fault of persons for whom it is responsible." [Italics added].

53 Lesley Jane Smith & A. Kerrest de Rozavel, "The 1972 Convention on International Liability for Damage Caused by Space Objects," in Stephan Hobe, Bernhard Schmidt-Tedd and Kai-Uwe Schrogl (eds.), *Cologne Commentary on Space Law*, Vol. II (2013), 111–113.

54 Stephen Gorove, "Cosmos 954: Issues of Law and Policy," Vol. 6 Journal of Space Law (1978), 141.

55 Carl Q. Christol, "International Liability for Damage Caused by Space Objects," Vol. 74 American Journal of International Law (1980), 362. *Cf.* Jerzy Rajaki, "Convention on International Liability for Damage caused by Space Objects – An Important Step in the Development of the International Space Law," Proceedings on the Law of Outer Space 17 (1974), 246, 257.

56 *Ibid.* Carl Q. Christol at 370. *Cf.*, Stephan Hobe, Space Law (2019), 81–82.

57 For the viewpoint of South Korea, *see infra* Chapter 6 §3.

58 Italics added.

1.3.4 Absolute Liability and Fault Liability

The Liability Convention sets out a distinction between absolute liability and fault liability. Article II of the Convention specifies absolute liability for "damage caused by its space object on the surface of the Earth or to aircraft in flight," while Article III applies a fault-liability regime to "the event of damage being caused elsewhere than on the surface of the Earth to a space object of one launching State or to persons or property on board such a space object by a space object of another launching State."

Exoneration from absolute liability can be granted to the extent that "gross negligence" or "an act or omission" on the claimant State or its natural or juridical persons has resulted in the damage.[59] This exemption does not apply to cases of fault liability.

Compensation for damage is awarded to restore the victims "to the condition which would have existed if the damage had not occurred."[60] In this regard, reparations under the Liability Convention are unlimited.

A claim for compensation is required to be presented "not later than one year following the date of the occurrence of the damage or the identification of the launching State which is liable."[61] However, claims lodged with national courts under national law are not affected by this one-year time limit. Thus, States have flexibility to establish their own timeframes in their domestic legal regimes.[62]

1.3.5 Article XXVI: Regulatory Review of the Liability Convention

The Liability Convention has a specific clause regarding systematic reexamination after a certain time of its effective date. The first sentence of Article XXVI stipulates that States shall include the question of its review in the provisional agenda of the UN General Assembly, ten years after the Convention's entry into force, in order to assess whether the Convention requires revision based on past application. The second sentence further provides that a conference of the States Parties shall be convened to review the Convention at any time five years after the Convention's entry into force, if requested by one-third of and supported by the majority of the States Parties.

Accordingly, pursuant to the first sentence of Article XXVI, the Liability Convention was indeed reviewed by the UN General Assembly in 1982, ten

59 Paragraph 1 of Article VI of the Liability Convention.

60 Article XII of the Liability Convention.

61 Article X of the Liability Convention.

62 For more about the time limits of South Korea, *see infra* Chapter 6 §3.5.

years after it had entered into force.[63] The Convention is the first UN space treaty that contains an explicit provision on its possible revision, which later became a model for almost identical provisions of the other two UN space treaties – Article X of the Registration Convention and Article 18 of the Moon Agreement.

Following the regulatory review concept set forth in the Liability Convention, States can also establish a similar assessment system within their national space legislation to periodically reexamine the validity of certain provisions. This system enables a State to assess whether any particular provision of its national space law is still effective over time.[64]

1.4 *The Registration Convention*

South Korea acceded to the Registration Convention on October 15, 1981, which came into effect for Korea on the same day.[65] The Convention was promulgated in the Korean official gazette on October 19, 1981, with Treaty No. 761 granted under the domestic treaty numbering system.[66]

1.4.1 The Background of the Registration Convention

The framework for the registration of space objects originated from Resolution 1721 B (XVI) adopted by the UN General Assembly in 1961,[67] which called upon States to provide information regarding their launching on a voluntary basis and also requested the Secretary-General to maintain a public registry of such information.

Two other references to registration are found in the Outer Space Treaty. Article V of the Outer Space Treaty stipulates the State's obligation to return astronauts in distress to the "State of registry of their space vehicles." The Outer

63 UNGA Res. 37/91, Question of the review of the Convention on International Liability for Damage Caused by Space Objects, December 10, 1982.

64 For further discussion about South Korea's approach, *see infra* Chapter 6 §3.6.

65 According to the UN archives, Korea's accession date of the Registration Convention was on October 14, whereas in the Korean national archives it was on October 15. This is because of the time difference between the two. The UN archives, available at https://treaties.un.org/Pages/showDetails.aspx?objid=08000002800361b4&clang=_en.

66 Ministry of Foreign Affairs of the Republic of Korea, *Multilateral Treaties*, accessed on January 15, 2020, https://www.mofa.go.kr/www/wpge/m_3835/contents.do.

67 UNGA Res. 1721 B (XVI), December 20, 1961, UN Doc. A/RES/1721 (XVI). Paragraph 1 of Resolution "[c]alls upon States launching objects into orbit or beyond to furnish information promptly to the Committee on the Peaceful Uses of Outer Space, through the Secretary-General, for the registration of launchings;" and Paragraph 2 "[r]equests the Secretary-General to maintain a public registry of the information furnished in accordance with paragraph 1 above."

Space Treaty further provides in Article VIII that "[a] State Party to the Treaty on whose registry an object launched into outer space is carried shall retain jurisdiction and control over such object, and over any personnel thereof, while in outer space or on a celestial body."

The Registration Convention elaborated upon the aforementioned principles with a desire to establish provisions for national registration and to maintain a mandatory UN register.[68] The Convention's primary purpose is to create "a legal link between the object launched into outer space and the launching State on whose registry this object is carried,"[69] ensuring jurisdiction and control over the object.

1.4.2 The National Registry

The Registration Convention requires a launching State to establish a national registry of space objects, register those objects in the registry, and furnish the UN Secretary-General with relevant information about the objects.[70] By complying with these obligations, each State can secure accurate information about the activities conducted by non-governmental entities, in particular.[71]

The Convention does not necessarily imply that States shall enact domestic legislation to fulfill these obligations. Therefore, States have the freedom to determine how they will comply with the obligations.[72] Besides, Paragraph 3 of Article II allows the "State of registry"[73] to determine the contents and conditions for maintaining the registry. Consequently, each State has discretion in managing its national registry, while information transmitted to the United Nations still requires complying with Paragraph 1 of Article IV of the Registration Convention.[74]

68 Paragraphs 5 and 6 of the Preamble of the Registration Convention.

69 Vladimir Kopal, "The 1975 Convention on Registration of Objects Launched into Outer Space in View of the Growth of Commercial Space Activities," in Benko, Marietta/Kroll, Walter (eds.), Air and Space Law in the 21st Century (2001), 375.

70 Paragraph 1 of Article II of the Registration Convention.

71 Michel Bourely, "Is it Necessary to Renegotiate the Convention on Registration," in Proceedings on the Law of Outer Space 31 (1988), 229.

72 Julian Hermida, "Legal Basis for a National Space Legislation," McGill University (2003), 80; *Cf., supra* Chapter 1, n. 15, Valérie Kayser, 190.

73 The term "State of registry" is defined in Article I(c) as "a launching State on whose registry a space object is carried in accordance with Article II."

74 *Infra*, Chapter 1 §1.4.3.

1.4.3 The UN Register

The Registration Convention further stipulates that the UN Secretary-General shall maintain an international register in which the information of space objects shall be recorded.[75] Paragraph 1 of Article IV enumerates a list of the mandatory information to be furnished to the UN Secretary-General: (a) Name of launching State or States; (b) An appropriate designator of the space object or its registration number; (c) Date and territory or location of launch; (d) Basic orbital parameters;[76] and (e) General function of the space object.

The Convention, however, does not specify the exact timeframe for providing the required information to the United Nations. Instead, it merely states that each State shall furnish the information "as soon as practicable,"[77] which leaves a legal loophole that may result in non-registration.[78] Given that timely national registration is a prerequisite for fulfilling the international obligation,[79] one solution could be for States to set a specific timeframe for their domestic procedures to encourage opportune registration. This approach would enable the national registration system to clarify the somewhat ambiguous wording of "as soon as practicable."[80]

2 A Party to Other Space-Related Treaties

2.1 *The ITU Constitution and Convention*

2.1.1 South Korea's Membership of the ITU

The International Telecommunication Union (ITU)[81] is a specialized agency for information and communication technologies under the United Nations. The ITU was originally founded in 1865 as the International 'Telegraph' Union to promote international cooperation of telegraphy networks. As communication

75 Paragraph 1 of Article III of the Registration Convention.

76 They include: (i) Nodal period; (ii) Inclination; (iii) Apogee; and (iv) Perigee.

77 Paragraph 1 of Article IV of the Registration Convention.

78 For further discussion on non-registration, *see* Frans von der Dunk, "Registration Convention: Background and Historical Context," Proceedings on the Law of Outer Space 46 (2003), 450–453; Setsuko Aoki, "In Search of the Current Legal Status of the Registration of Space objects," Proceedings of the International Institute of Space Law 53 (2010), 252–255.

79 Bernhard Schmidt-Tedd, Nataliia Malysheva and Olga Stelmakh, "The 1975 Convention on Registration of Objects Launched into Outer Space," in Stephan Hobe, Bernhard Schmidt-Tedd and Kai-Uwe Schrogl (eds.), *Cologne Commentary on Space Law*, Vol. II (2013), 301.

80 Regarding South Korea's approach, *see infra* Chapter 5 §4.3.

81 Hereinafter referred to as the "ITU."

technologies gradually developed, the International 'Telegraph' Union was renamed the International Telecommunication Union in 1932, which has continued to this day.[82] The ITU's primary role is to coordinate the global use of the radio spectrum, allocate satellite orbits, and assist in developing worldwide technical standards. Its main decision-making body is the Plenipotentiary Conference, where the ITU Member States meet every four years. The ITU membership includes 193 Member States as well as some 900 companies, universities, and international and regional organizations as of 2019.[83]

Korea participated in the ITU interim and regional conferences for the first time in 1948,[84] although it had no diplomatic sovereignty while under US military control. With this valuable participation experience, the nation submitted an application for ITU membership in November 1949. However, its entry into the ITU was disapproved due to insufficient support, falling short of the requisite two-thirds majority. Despite the previous rejection, Korea remained undeterred and resubmitted its application in May 1950, obtaining the necessary approval of forty-seven out of sixty-one Member States, surpassing the required two-thirds majority. This time, however, the outbreak of the Korean War in June 1950 caused a delay in the membership joining process. After all the twists and turns, South Korea ultimately attained ITU membership status on January 30, 1952, and made its debut at the Plenipotentiary Conference in Buenos Aires, Argentina, on October 3, 1952.

South Korea has been an active participant in ITU conferences and relevant meetings, and has hosted several major ITU conferences since 1988, including the 2014 Plenipotentiary Conference in Busan.[85] As of 2019, there are sixteen sector members and seven academic members of the ITU in South Korea.[86] As the first country in the world to bring 5G – the fifth generation of mobile

---

82 *See* further, Frans von der Dunk, "Legal Aspects of Satellite Communications," in Frans von der Dunk (Ed) *Handbook of Space Law* (2015), 460–461; Francis Lyall and Paul B. Larsen, *Space law: A Treatise* (2009), 200–206.

83 ITU, "About ITU," last accessed on October 27, 2020, https://www.itu.int/en/about/Pages/default.aspx.

84 "우리나라와 ITU 전권회의 (South Korea and the ITU Plenipotentiary Conference [English title added])," October 19, 2014, available at https://www.etnews.com/20141017000139; Korea ITU Committee, "History," accessed on July 20, 2020, https://www.koreaitu.or.kr/introduce_ITU/menu4/intro_history.do?menu_gubun=mid&menu_no=0&menu_no2=3&menu_no3=&params=.

85 Korea ITU Committee, "Annual Report of Korea ITU Committee 2017," at 5.

86 ITU, "List of member States," accessed on January 27, 2020, https://www.itu.int/online/mm/scripts/gensel8.

technologies – into reality in 2019, South Korea is endeavoring to develop international standards for high-performance 5G networks.[87]

2.1.2 The ITU Regime

The ITU Constitution[88] and Convention,[89] together with the Administrative Regulations,[90] form an international legal framework governing the use of radio frequencies.[91]

South Korea ratified the ITU Constitution and Convention on August 5, 1994, shortly after these instruments had entered into force in July 1994.[92] Both were promulgated in the official gazette on August 22 of the same year under Treaty No. 1237 and 1238, respectively, based on South Korea's treaty numbering system.[93] These ITU instruments are binding upon its Member States.[94]

2.1.2.1 *International Frequency Management*

The ITU's main objectives are to harmonize international telecommunications practices and minimize harmful interference between radio stations of different countries. Achieving these goals depends on the adequate implementation of principles and requirements enshrined in the ITU Constitution and Convention as well as the Administrative Regulations.

87 ITU Media Center, "5G – Fifth generation of mobile technologies," accessed on January 27, 2020, https://www.itu.int/en/mediacentre/backgrounders/Pages/5G-fifth-generation-of-mobile-technologies.aspx.

88 Constitution of the International Telecommunication Union (hereinafter "ITU Constitution"), Geneva, done 22 December 1992, entered into force 1 July 1994; 1825 UNTS 1; UKTS 1996 No. 24; Cm. 2539; ATS 1994 No. 28; Final Acts of the Additional Plenipotentiary Conference, Geneva, 1992 (1993), at 1.

89 Convention of the International Telecommunication Union (hereinafter "ITU Convention"), Geneva, done 22 December 1992, entered into force 1 July 1994; 1825 UNTS 1; UKTS 1996 No. 24; Cm. 2539; ATS 1994 No. 28; Final Acts of the Additional Plenipotentiary Conference, Geneva, 1992 (1993), at 71.

90 They include "Radio Regulations" and "International Telecommunication Regulations," which contain provisions of a technical nature governing international telecommunications. For more detail, *see* https://www.itu.int/en/history/Pages/RegulationsCollection.aspx.

91 Article 4 of the ITU Constitution.

92 In addition to these treaties, South Korea ratified on the same day the "Optional Protocol on the Compulsory Settlement of Disputes relating to the Constitution of the International Telecommunication Union to the Convention of the International Telecommunication Union and to the Administrative Regulations" as Treaty No. 1239.

93 The Ministry of Foreign Affairs of the Republic of Korea, Multilateral Treaties, accessed on January 15, 2020, https://www.mofa.go.kr/www/wpge/m_3835/contents.do.

94 Article 6 of the ITU Constitution.

The ITU Constitution emphasizes that the ITU's activities focus on 1) extending constructive international cooperation among all its Member States for the improvement and rational use of telecommunications and 2) promoting the development of technical facilities and their efficient operation.[95] To that end, the ITU plays a key role in allocating bands of the radio-frequency spectrum, allotting radio frequencies, and registering radio-frequency assignments.[96]

2.1.2.2 *Principles and Regulatory Requirements*

Specific rules and procedures pertaining to the use of radio frequencies and satellite orbits are elaborated in the Radio Regulations, which complement the ITU Constitution and Convention.[97]

The main principles in the ITU process are stipulated in Article 44(2) of the ITU Constitution and reiterated in the Preamble of the Radio Regulations as follows:

> In using frequency bands for radio services, Member States shall bear in mind that radio frequencies and any associated orbits, including the geostationary-satellite orbit, are limited natural resources and that they must be used rationally, efficiently and economically, in conformity with the provisions of the Radio Regulations, so that countries or groups of countries may have equitable access to those orbits and frequencies, taking into account the special needs of the developing countries.

Other principles that the Member States abide by are to 1) avoid harmful interference to other radio services,[98] 2) prioritize distress calls and messages and immediately take necessary actions,[99] and 3) properly maintain and safeguard telecommunication channels and installations within their jurisdiction and control.[100] In addition to these obligations, the Member States reserve the rights to cut off any private telecommunications appearing dangerous to national security or public order[101] and to suspend their international telecommunication service with immediate notification.[102]

95 Article 1(1) of the ITU Constitution.
96 Article 1(2) of the ITU Constitution.
97 Article 4(3) of the ITU Constitution.
98 Article 45 of the ITU Constitution.
99 Article 46 of the ITU Constitution.
100 Article 38 of the ITU Constitution.
101 Article 34(2) of the ITU Constitution.
102 Article 35 of the ITU Constitution.

The mechanisms to implement these principles are i) a *priori* allocation for equitable access to orbits and frequency bands for future use and ii) the coordination procedures to achieve efficient and interference-free operation of international satellite services.[103]

2.1.2.3 *An Overview of Frequency Arrangement and Coordination*

Article 5 of the Radio Regulations provides for frequency allocations, which contains the Table of Frequency Allocations[104] that divided the world into three regions and allocated frequency bands to services for ITU purposes.[105]

The next course is the allotment of a radio frequency or radio frequency channel, which is defined as an "[e]ntry of a designated frequency channel in an agreed plan, adopted by a competent conference, for use by one or more administrations for a terrestrial or space radiocommunication service in one or more identified countries or geographical areas and under specified conditions."[106]

The allotment process mingles with or leads to the next step of assignment by each ITU Member State for specific operators under its national regulations. When the Member States assign frequencies to stations that may cause harmful interference to the services rendered by another country's stations, such assignments are to be made in accordance with the Table of Frequency Allocations and other provisions of the Radio Regulations.[107]

Additionally, the administrations of Member States are prohibited from assigning radio frequencies to stations in a manner that contradicts the established Table of Frequency Allocations or other provisions of the Radio Regulations.[108] Nonetheless, this prohibition does not apply if the station is assigned a frequency under the express condition that it will not cause any harmful interference to any station operating in accordance with the ITU regime and will not claim protection from such interference.[109]

---

103 *See* further, Yvon Henri *et al.*, "Regulation of telecommunications by satellites," in Ram Jakhu and Paul Stephen Dempsey (Eds), Routledge Handbook of Space Law, 121.

104 Section IV of Article 5 of the Radio Regulations.

105 No. 5.2 of the Radio Regulations.

106 No. 1.17 of the Radio Regulations.

107 No. 4.2 of the Radio Regulations. Its full text is as follows: "Member States undertake that in assigning frequencies to stations which are capable of causing harmful interference to the services rendered by the stations of another country, such assignments are to be made in accordance with the Table of Frequency Allocations and other provisions of these Regulations."

108 The first half of No. 4.4 of the Radio Regulations.

109 The second half of No. 4.4 of the Radio Regulations. This allows for some flexibility in frequency assignments. The full text of No. 4.4 of the Radio Regulations is as

The coordination procedures following frequency assignments are stipulated in Articles 9 and 11 of the Radio Regulations. These procedures include notifying the ITU Radiocommunication Bureau and recording the frequency assignment in the Master International Frequency Register.

The coordination of international frequency usage is a formal process by which administrations of Member States can request frequency allotments/assignments, or negotiate agreements related to affected services.

The notification of a frequency assignment to the ITU Radiocommunication Bureau is a final step leading up to the recording of the frequency assignment in the Master International Frequency Register.

The significance of the recording of those assignments is stated in No. 8.1 of the Radio Regulation that "[t]he international rights and obligations of administrations in respect of their own and other administrations frequency assignments shall be derived from the recording of those assignments in the Master International Frequency Register or from their conformity, where appropriate, with a plan."

As such, the ITU Member States obtain international recognition of the right to use the registered frequencies without harmful interference.[110] In this regard, it is essential for the Member States to adopt appropriate national legislation and to discharge the obligations established in the ITU regulatory regime.[111]

2.2 *The INTELSAT / ITSO Agreement*

2.2.1 A Brief History of INTELSAT's Privatization

The International Telecommunications Satellite Organization (INTELSAT)[112] was an intergovernmental organization that enshrined the principle in UNGA Resolution 1721 (XVI), stating that "communications by means of satellites should be available to the nations of the world as soon as practicable on a

follows: "Administrations of the Member States shall not assign to a station any frequency in derogation of either the Table of Frequency Allocations in this Chapter or the other provisions of these Regulations, except on the express condition that such a station, when using such a frequency assignment, shall not cause harmful interference to, and shall not claim protection from harmful interference caused by, a station operating in accordance with the provisions of the Constitution, the Convention and these Regulations."

110 For more information about the whole ITU procedures, *see supra* Chapter 1, n. 82, Frans von der Dunk, 474–475, 482–484; *supra* Chapter 1, n. 103, Yvon Henri *et al.*, 123–129.

111 Further discussion on South Korea's approach to the ITU regime will be addressed in Chapter 4.

112 Hereinafter referred to as "INTELSAT."

global and non-discriminatory basis."[113] Until the dawn of the twenty-first century, INTELSAT, established in 1973, operated a global fleet of international communications satellites that provided the connectivity of the world's telecommunications networks and infrastructures.[114] INTELSAT aimed to achieve a single global telecommunications satellite system for expanded telecommunications services to all areas of the world.[115]

In 2001, INTELSAT was restructured into two separate entities, a private corporation – Intelsat S.A. – and a residual intergovernmental organization under a new acronym – the International Telecommunications Satellite Organization (ITSO),[116] completing its five-year privatization process in 2005.[117] Although ITSO no longer operates satellites, its key function remains to ensure that every country on Earth receives international communications services without discrimination.[118]

2.2.2 South Korea's Membership: from INTELSAT to ITSO

2.2.2.1 *A Party to the INTELSAT Agreement*

South Korea ratified the INTELSAT Agreement[119] on December 12, 1972, under the Korean National Assembly's prior consent on November 28, 1972, and promulgated it under Treaty No. 456 on January 18, 1973.[120] The INTELSAT

113 The Preamble of UNGA Resolution 1721 (XVI) D, December 20, 1961, UN Doc. A/RES/1721 (XVI).

114 Kenneth Katkin, "The Global Broadband Satellite Infrastructure Initiative," University of Louisville Law Review 48, no. 4 (2010), 977.

115 Paragraph 4 of the Preamble of the Agreement Relating to the International Telecommunications Satellite Organization (hereinafter the "INTELSAT Agreement"), Washington, done 20 August 1971, entered into force 12 February 1973; 1220 UNTS 21; TIAS 7532; 23 UST 3813; UKTS 1973 No. 80; Cmnd. 4799; ATS 1973 No. 6; 10 ILM 909 (1971).

116 Hereinafter referred to as "ITSO" for the residual International Telecommunications Satellite Organization after privatization.

117 *See* further, Francis Lyall, "On the Privatization of INTELSAT," Journal of Space Law 28, no. 2 (2000), 101–120; Kenneth Katkin, "Communication Breakdown: The Future of Global Connectivity after the Privatization of INTELSAT," Vanderbilt Journal of Transnational Law 38, no. 5 (2005), 1323–1402; Sylvia Ospina, "International Satellite Organizations: Their Evolution from ISOS to GSCS and the Further Privatization/Commercialization of Space Activities," Proceedings of the International Institute of Space Law 53 (2010), 337–348; ITSO "About us," available at https://itso.int/about-us/.

118 Article III of the amended INTELSAT Agreement, done in Washington on November 17, 2000, entered into force on November 30, 2004 (hereinafter the "ITSO Agreement" for the amended version); *supra* Chapter 1, n. 114, Kenneth Katkin, 978.

119 *Supra* Chapter 1, n. 115.

120 The Ministry of Foreign Affairs of the Republic of Korea, Multilateral Treaties, *Multilateral Treaties*, accessed on January 15, 2020, http://www.mofa.go.kr/www/wpge/m_3835/contents.do.

Agreement provided important technical and economic safeguards against harm to INTELSAT.[121] These safeguards were specified in Article XIV: Where the INTELSAT members intended to establish separate space segment facilities, they were required to consult with the Assembly of Parties to ensure that their facilities are technically compatible with those of INTELSAT and to "avoid significant economic harm" to the global INTELSAT system.

Until being restructured in 2001, INTELSAT was a hybrid of (i) States Parties for which the INTELSAT Agreement entered into force and (ii) Public Telecommunications Operators (PTOs) designated by State Parties as signatories for which the INTELSAT Operating Agreement[122] entered into force.[123] The PTOs were the actual users of the INTELSAT satellite infrastructure through their ground stations.[124] The PTO of South Korea in those days was the Korea Telecommunication Public Corporation (KT) established in 1981 by the Korea Telecommunication Public Corporation Act.[125]

2.2.2.2 *Alterations Following the Restructuring of INTELSAT*

In the course of facilitating the privatization, the INTELSAT Agreement was amended rather than terminated. Thus, INTELSAT States Parties remained members of ITSO upon privatization.[126] Accordingly, as an original INTELSAT State Party, South Korea ratified the ITSO Agreement[127] on January 10, 2003.[128]

In line with this transition, the only PTO of South Korea, KT, was privatized entirely in May 2002, changing its name into KT Corporation. As a result, KT Corporation could no longer maintain a monopoly in the satellite communications business and started competing with emerging private companies while adapting to a new market environment.

Meanwhile, as the competition system was introduced into the telecommunications market in South Korea, the "*Public* Telecommunications Business

---

121 Bert W. Rein & Carl R. Frank, "The Legal Commitment of the United States to the INTELSAT System," 14 N.C. J. Int'l L. & Com. Reg. sp219 (1989), 233.

122 The Operating Agreement Relating to the International Telecommunications Satellite Organization (hereinafter the "INTELSAT Operating Agreement"), Washington, done 20 August 1971, entered into force 12 February 1973; 1220 UNTS 149; TIAS 7532; 23 UST 4091; UKTS1973 No. 80; Cmnd. 4799; ATS 1973 No. 6; 10 ILM 946 (1971).

123 Articles I(f) and (g) of the INTELSAT Agreement. *See*, Frans von der Dunk, "International Organizations in Space Law" in Handbook of space law, 286.

124 *Ibid.*

125 Entered into force on March 14, 1981, Act No. 3385. The Act was completely repealed in 2001.

126 *Supra* Chapter 1, n. 114, Kenneth Katkin, 977.

127 *Supra* Chapter 1, n. 118.

128 Promulgated as Treaty No. 1694 on November 15, 2004.

Act"[129] that dealt with telecommunications service providers designated by the government was entirely amended under a new title of "Telecommunications Business Act."[130] The new Act aimed to stimulate fair competition among telecommunications operators by encouraging private corporations to infiltrate the satellite telecommunications market that had traditionally been reserved for the INTELSAT regime. This Act covers various aspects of the telecommunications businesses, including technical standards of telecommunications equipment and obligations of registration or report of their businesses. Article 1 of the Act provides that its purpose is to contribute to the public welfare by facilitating the sound development of telecommunications businesses and ensuring users' convenience through proper and efficient management thereof. The Act has since been amended several times in response to global telecommunications market changes relating to negotiations with the WTO.[131]

2.2.2.3 *The ITSO Principles and Obligations*

The last paragraph of the Preamble of the ITSO Agreement[132] highlights "a need for an intergovernmental supervisory organization, to which any State member of the United Nations or the International Telecommunication Union may become a Party, to ensure that the Company[133] fulfills the Core Principles on a continuing basis" The ITSO Agreement further stipulates in Article III(a) that "the main purpose of ITSO is to ensure [...] that the Company provides, on a commercial basis, international public telecommunications services, in order to ensure the performance of the Core Principles." The Core Principles are (i) maintaining global connectivity and global coverage, (ii) serving its lifeline connectivity customers, and (iii) providing non-discriminatory access to the Company's system.[134] Thus, ITSO's mission is fundamentally to monitor the performance of Intelsat's public service obligations and to safeguard the Parties' orbital locations and associated frequency assignments.[135]

---

129 Enacted on December 30, 1983, Act No. 3686, entered into force on September 1, 1984. [Italics added].

130 Entirely amended on August 10, 1991, Act No. 4394, entered into force December 11, 1991.

131 For further discussion on the amendments to the new Telecommunications Business Act, *see* Chapter 1 §2.4.

132 *Supra* Chapter 1, n. 118.

133 "Company" is defined in Article I(d) of the ITSO Agreement as follows: "the private entity or entities established under the law of one or more States to which the international telecommunications satellite organization's space system is transferred and includes their successors-in-interest."

134 Article III(b) of the ITSO Agreement.

135 ITSO, "Milestones," accessed on November 10, 2020, available at https://itso.int/about-us/milestones/.

South Korea has been actively participating in ITSO's activities of monitoring Intelsat's performance as one of the representatives of the ITSO Advisory Committee since 2008.[136] The Advisory Committee comprises twenty-three of the one hundred forty-nine States Parties to the ITSO Agreement, which provides consultative advice and feedback to the Director-General of ITSO on any matters requested.[137]

2.3 *The INMARSAT / IMSO Convention*

2.3.1 INMARSAT Prior to Privatization

The International Mobile Satellite Organization (INMARSAT)[138] was established by the INMARSAT Convention in 1976[139] under the auspices of the International Maritime Organization[140] to oversee maritime satellite communications for safety purposes modeled after INTELSAT. INMARSAT's organizational structure was analogous to that of INTELSAT, which featured a hybrid of Member States under the INMARSAT Convention and their PTOs as signatories of the INMARSAT Operating Agreement.[141]

South Korea acceded to the original INMARSAT Convention on August 21, 1985, which entered into force for Korea on September 16 of the same year, assigned domestic Treaty No. 868. In a similar manner to INTELSAT, the designated signatory or the PTO of South Korea for the original INMARSAT Convention was KT.

Meanwhile, the initial purpose of INMARSAT was extended to include aeronautical and land mobile communications services through Amendments to the INMARSAT Convention.[142] Accordingly, to stay up-to-date with this trend

136 The Korea Communications Commission, press release on October 26, 2010, p. 2, available at https://www.korea.kr/news/pressReleaseView.do?newsId=155695908.

137 ITSO, accessed on November 11, 2020, available at https://itso.int/about-us/more/.

138 Hereinafter referred to as "INMARSAT."

139 Convention on the International Maritime Satellite Organization (hereinafter the "INMARSAT Convention"), done at London on September 3, 1976, came into force on July 16, 1979; 1143 UNTS 105; TIAS 9605;31 UST 1; UKTS 1979 No. 94; Cmnd. 6822; ATS 1979 No. 10; 15 ILM 1052 (1976).

140 International Maritime Organization, "IMO Convention on the International Maritime Satellite Organization," https://www.imo.org/en/About/Conventions/Pages/Convention-on-the-International-Maritime-Satellite-Organization.aspx.

141 The Operating Agreement on the International Maritime Satellite Organization (hereinafter the "INMARSAT Operating Agreement"), London, done 3 September 1976, entered into force 16 July 1979; 1143 UNTS 213; TIAS 9605; 31 UST 1; UKTS 1979 No. 94; Cmnd. 6822; ATS 1979 No. 10; 15 ILM 233, 1075 (1976). *Supra* Chapter 1, n.123, Frans von der Dunk, International Organizations in Space Law, in Handbook of space law, 291–292.

142 Amendments to the Convention on the International Maritime Satellite Organization, done on January 19, 1989, came into force on June 26, 1997.

in satellite communications, the Korean government ratified the Amendments to the INMARSAT Convention on February 2, 1996. To reflect the amended purpose, the title of the Convention was changed to the "Convention on the International Mobile Satellite Organization (Inmarsat)"

2.3.2 The IMSO Regime

After operating more than two decades, the Inmarsat Assembly adopted Amendments to the Inmarsat Convention in 1998.[143] The Amendments aimed to privatize the Organization while retaining its intergovernmental oversight role. The Korean government ratified the Amendments on December 20, 1999, assigning domestic Treaty No. 1708 with the prior consent of the National Assembly.[144]

Following these Amendments, INMARSAT was reorganized into two entities: The current International Mobile Satellite Organization (under a new acronym IMSO), which operates as a residual intergovernmental body, and Inmarsat Ltd. as a public limited company, which serves as the commercial arm of Inmarsat.

The PTO of South Korea – KT – was accordingly transformed into one of Inmarsat's investors. Upon KT's privatization with a new name of KT Corporation, its affiliate – KT Sat – has been operating an Inmarsat station in South Korea, furnishing satellite communications services worldwide.[145] The satellite communication industry in South Korea has changed in line with the global transformation that affects the domestic telecommunication market.

The restructured residual intergovernmental organization, IMSO, focuses on overseeing the provision of public services, particularly the Global Maritime Distress and Safety System (GMDSS), established under the legal framework of the International Maritime Organization (IMO).[146] In performing this role, IMSO acts as an ally of IMO to ensure that Inmarsat Ltd. properly implements services worldwide in a non-discriminatory manner.[147] Additionally, Article

143 Amendments to the Convention on the International Mobile Satellite Organization, done on April 24, 1998, came into force on July 31, 2001.

144 The National Assembly completed its consent process on December 2, 1999.

145 KT Sat, "Facilities," accessed on April 1, 2020, https://www.ktsat.net/kr/content/view.do?cttNm=facilities&cttNo=011.

146 Article 3(1) of the IMSO Convention.

147 *See* further, Francis Lyall, "Protection of the Public Interest in the Light of the Commercialization and Privatization of the Providers of International Satellite Telecommunications," Proceedings on the Law of Outer Space 47 (2004), 441–451; Jerzy W. Vonau, "Restructured Inmarsat and Public Service Obligations," Annals of Air and Space Law 26 (2001), 367–372.

6(1) of the IMSO Convention emphasizes that States Parties are required to take appropriate measures to enable service providers to furnish GMDSS services in accordance with national laws.

2.4 *The GATT, GATS and WTO Regimes*

2.4.1 The WTO and Satellite Communications

The World Trade Organization (WTO)[148] is an international organization that aims to promote trade liberalization by establishing trade rules among nations. The WTO replaced its precursor, General Agreement on Tariffs and Trade (GATT) established in 1947,[149] and officially commenced in 1995 under the Agreement Establishing the World Trade Organization (the WTO Agreement) concluded in 1994.[150] The establishment of the WTO was in line with the growing trend in the 1990s for commercialization and privatization in various businesses. This trend was also evident in the restructuring and privatization of INTELSAT and INMARSAT as previously discussed, which resulted in a procompetitive satellite communications market.

2.4.2 South Korea's Membership and Participation

South Korea has been a WTO member since its formal commencement on January 1, 1995, as well as a party to the GATT since April 14, 1967.[151] As a WTO member, South Korea is also a party to the GATS[152] that extends the open trading system to service sectors. The Korean government further signed the

148 The World Trade Organization (hereinafter the "WTO"). For more information about the WTO's history and function, *see* Frans von der Dunk, "International Trade Aspects of Space Services," in Frans von der Dunk (ed) *Handbook of Space Law* (2015), 814–873; Ram Jakhu, "Emerging Legal Issues of Satellite Telecommunications and Broadcasting," Proceedings on the Law of Outer Space 43 (2000), 428–439; S. G. Sreejith, "When Sputnik orbits Geneva: Legal Reflections on WTO Governance in Respect of Commercial Space Activities," Proceedings on the Law of Outer Space 47 (2004), 403–413.

149 The General Agreement on Tariffs and Trade (hereinafter the "GATT"), Geneva, done on October 30, 1947, entered into force on January 1, 1948; 55 UNTS 194; TIAS 1700; ATS 1948 No. 23.

150 The WTO was founded by the Agreement Establishing the World Trade Organization (hereinafter the "WTO Agreement"), Marrakesh, done 15 April 1994, entered into force 1 January 1995; 1867 UNTS 154; UKTS 1996 No. 57; ATS 1995 No. 8; 33 ILM 1125, 1144 (1994).

151 The World Trade Organization, WTO Memberships, Republic of Korea, https://www.wto.org/english/thewto_e/countries_e/korea_republic_e.htm.

152 The General Agreement on Trade in Services (hereinafter the "GATS"), Marrakesh, done 15 April 1994, entered into force 1 January 1995; 1869 UNTS 183; UKTS 1996 No. 58; Cm. 3276; ATS 1995 No. 8.

Fourth Protocol to the GATS[153] on November 27, 1997.[154] The Protocol aims to liberalize the international telecommunications market.

South Korea's participation in these regimes has affected its domestic telecommunications policy. In accordance with the Schedule of Specific Commitments on Basic Telecommunications,[155] South Korea's national telecommunications law – Telecommunications Business Act – was amended in 1997.[156] The government stated that the amendment was to loosen the restrictions on the aggregate voting shares owned by foreign entities and promote vigorous competition between domestic and international telecommunications operators, following the WTO negotiation on basic telecommunications.[157] In the Schedule of Specific Commitments of South Korea, the nation does not single out or make any particular reference to satellite communications. Therefore, the regime of basic telecommunications is essentially applied to all telecommunications sectors.

Furthermore, another amendment to the Telecommunications Business Act was made to facilitate a more accessible market to global operators. Although there is a maximum forty-nine percent limit of foreign equities to the telecommunications business as per the Schedule of Specific Commitments,[158] Article 8(3)(ii) of the Telecommunications Business Act as amended in 2013[159] stipulates that a case where 'the foreign entity is unlikely to harm public interest'[160] and 'the largest shareholder thereof is the foreign government or foreigner of the other party to bi/multi-lateral free trade agreements with South Korea' is *not* considered to be foreign. In other words, if the two aforementioned

153 The Fourth Protocol to the General Agreement on Trade and Services (hereinafter the "Fourth Protocol to the GATS"), Geneva, done 15 April 1997, entered into force 5 February 1998; WTO Doc. S/L/20 of 30 April 1996 (96–1750); 2061 UNTS 209; ATS 1998 No. 9; 33 ILM 1167 (1994); 36 ILM 354 (1997).

154 Promulgated on April 6, 1998 as Notification No. 337.

155 WTO, the Schedule of Specific Commitments: Republic of Korea, accessed on April 1, 2020, http://i-tip.wto.org/services/ComparativeReports.aspx.

156 Partially amended on August 28, 1997, Act No. 5385, entered into force January 1, 1998. *See, supra* Chapter 1 §2.2.2.2.

157 The first paragraph of "전기통신사업법 개정이유 (The Reason for the Amendment to the Telecommunications Business Act [English title added])" released in 1997, available at http://www.law.go.kr/lsInfoP.do?lsiSeq=6303&ancYd=19970828&ancNo=05385&efYd=19980101&nwJoYnInfo=N&efGubun=Y&chrClsCd=010202&ancYnChk=0.

158 *Supra* Chapter 1, n. 155, WTO, the Schedule of Specific Commitments, Republic of Korea.

159 Partially amended on August 13, 2013, Act No. 12035. The amendments are to implement the provisions of the free trade agreements with the US and the EU.

160 The Minister of Science and ICT has the authority to confirm if the foreign entity is unlikely to harm public interest.

requirements are met, there is no restriction on stock ownership of the particular foreign entity. In this manner, South Korea mitigates constraints imposed on the telecommunications market in line with the WTO's fundamental principles of trade liberalization.

2.5 *The Partial Test Ban Treaty and the Comprehensive Nuclear Test Ban Treaty*

2.5.1 An Overview of the Two Treaties

The Treaty Banning Nuclear Weapon Tests in the Atmosphere, in Outer Space and Under Water (the Partial Test Ban Treaty)[161] is an arms control agreement that aims to restrict nuclear weapons testing and limit nuclear proliferation.[162] The Partial Test Ban Treaty is the first international treaty on arms limitations in outer space, which entered into force in 1963, preceding Article IV of the Outer Space Treaty that addresses arms control and military activities in outer space.[163]

The Partial Test Ban Treaty is comprised of five articles with its main principle enshrined in Article I. The other provisions mainly prescribe signature, ratification, and amendment procedures. According to Article I(1)(a) of the Partial Test Ban Treaty, any nuclear tests and explosions are prohibited in the atmosphere, outer space, or underwater. Article I(2) further stipulates that each Party to the Treaty undertakes to refrain from causing, encouraging, or participating in nuclear tests and explosions. However, the Treaty permits underground testing, so long as radioactive debris is not released outside the testing State's territorial limits.[164]

Beyond the Partial Test Ban Treaty, the Comprehensive Nuclear Test Ban Treaty was adopted by the United Nations General Assembly on September 10, 1996.[165] As its name implies, the Comprehensive Nuclear Test Ban Treaty

---

161 Treaty Banning Nuclear Weapon Tests in the Atmosphere, in Outer Space and Under Water (hereinafter the "Partial Test Ban Treaty"), done at Moscow on August 5, 1963, came into force October 10, 1963.

162 Atomic Heritage Foundation, "Limited or Partial Test Ban Treaty (LTBT/PTBT)," June 10, 2016, available at https://www.atomicheritage.org/history/limited-or-partial-test-ban-treaty-ltbtptbt.

163 The first paragraph of Article IV of the Outer Space Treaty reads as follows: "States Parties to the Treaty undertake not to place in orbit around the Earth any objects carrying nuclear weapons or any other kinds of weapons of mass destruction, install such weapons on celestial bodies, or station such weapons in outer space in any other manner."

164 Article I(1)(b) of the Partial Test Ban Treaty.

165 The Comprehensive Nuclear Test Ban Treaty, New York, on September 10, 1996; Cm. 3665; 35 ILM 1439; S. Treaty Doc. No. 105–28 (not yet in force).

forbids all nuclear explosions in all environments either for military or civilian purposes. The Treaty consists of the preamble, seventeen articles, a protocol, and two annexes. The preamble stresses the need for "continued systematic and progressive efforts to reduce nuclear weapons globally" with the ultimate goal of their elimination and of "general and complete disarmament under strict and effective international control."

Unlike the Partial Test Ban Treaty, the Comprehensive Nuclear Test Ban Treaty provides for an organization and a system in Articles II and IV, respectively, to verify compliance with its obligations set forth in the Treaty. The Treaty was opened for signature on September 24, 1996. However, it has not yet entered into force despite a large number of ratifications. Under Article XIV, all States with nuclear power or research reactors listed in its Annex 2 have to ratify the Treaty before it enters into force.[166] The majority of those States have ratified it accordingly, but the Treaty still needs to be ratified by China, North Korea, Egypt, Pakistan, India, Iran, Israel, and the United States to enter into force. As of November 2020, one hundred sixty-eight States have ratified the Treaty, and sixteen States have signed but not ratified it.[167]

A question may arise whether an international norm against nuclear weapon testing has achieved the status of customary international law through State practice and attendant *opinio juris*. While the Comprehensive Nuclear Test Ban Treaty has not yet gone into effect, scholars and experts generally agree that a global moratorium on nuclear testing exists.[168] This is evidenced by the official

166 The Comprehensive Nuclear Test Ban Treaty has relatively strict requirements for entry into force. Article XIV stipulates that the Treaty will enter into force 180 days after the date of deposit of the instruments of ratification by all States listed in Annex 2 to the Treaty. The list in Annex 2 comprises 44 States: Algeria, Argentina, Australia, Austria, Bangladesh, Belgium, Brazil, Bulgaria, Canada, Chile, China, Colombia, Democratic People's Republic of Korea, Egypt, Finland, France, Germany, Hungary, India, Indonesia, Iran (Islamic Republic of), Israel, Italy, Japan, Mexico, Netherlands, Norway, Pakistan, Peru, Poland, Republic of Korea, Romania, Russian Federation, Slovakia, South Africa, Spain, Sweden, Switzerland, Turkey, Ukraine, United Kingdom of Great Britain and Northern Ireland, United States of America, Viet Nam and Zaire.

167 The United Nations Treaty Collection, "Status of Treaties," accessed on November 15, 2020, available at https://treaties.un.org/pages/ViewDetails.aspx?src=TREATY&mtdsg_no=XXVI-4&chapter=26.

168 George Bunn, "The Status of Norms against Nuclear Testing," The Nonproliferation Review (1999), 29; David S. Jonas, "The Comprehensive Nuclear Test Ban Treaty: Current Legal Status in the United States and the Implications of a Nuclear Test Explosion," New York University Journal of International Law and Politics 39, no. 4 (2007), 1028–1046; David A. Koplow, "Nuclear Arms Control by a Pen: Effectuating the Comprehensive Test Ban Treaty without Ratification," Georgetown Journal of International Law 46, no. 2 (2015), 507; Daniel Rietiker, "The (Il)legality of Nuclear Weapons Tests Under International

statements from States and the resolutions of the UN Security Council condemning nuclear tests.

Nonetheless, opinions differ on the legal status of the norm and whether nuclear testing violates international law.[169] Some authors contend that "the relevant States seem not to believe that their respective declared testing moratoria are currently obligatory."[170] Moreover, they advocate that the fact that several States with nuclear weapons programs have not ratified the Treaty weighs "against a determination that the prohibition has developed into a rule of customary international law."[171] Indeed, the UN Security Council has strongly condemned nuclear tests but has refrained from suggesting that they violate international law. In comparison, with regard to Syria's use of chemical weapons, the UN Security Council used explicit language in Resolution 2118,[172] stating that "[t]he use of chemical weapons constitutes a serious violation of international law."

George Bunn, the first general counsel of the US Arms Control and Disarmament Agency, advocates that a norm banning nuclear test is at least "politically" binding. He adds that "there is a time when it has not become widely enough accepted to be called legally binding [...], yet it nevertheless seems to influence the conduct of many." He bases his conclusion on both State behavior in support of the norm and international condemnation of nuclear testing.[173] Apart from the strength of the norm, it is likely that any

---

Law: Filling the Possible Legal Gap by Ensuring the Comprehensive Test Ban Treaty's Entry into Force" American Society of International Law Insights (March 16, 2017), https://www.asil.org/insights/volume/21/issue/4/illegality-nuclear-weapons-tests-under-international-law%E2%80%94filling-possible.

169 *Cf.*, Jack M. Beard, "The Nuclear Nonproliferation Regime and Nuclear Realities: Repair or Reassessment," American Society of International Law Proceedings 101 (2007), 439.

170 *Ibid.* David A. Koplow; Jill M. Sheldon, "Nuclear Weapons and the Laws of War: Does Customary International Law Prohibit the Use of Nuclear Weapons in All Circumstances," Fordham International Law Journal 20, no. 1 (1996), 257.

171 Christopher J. LeMon, "International Law and North Korean Nuclear Testing," American Society of International Law Insights (October 19, 2006), https://www.asil.org/insights/volume/10/issue/27/international-law-and-north-korean-nuclear-testing#_edn6.

172 Adopted by the United Nations Security Council at its 7038th meeting on September 27, 2013, S/RES/2118 (2013), 1–2. *Supra* Chapter 1, n. 168, Daniel Rietiker; Sakif Alam, "Do North Korea's nuclear tests violate international law?" The Daily Star Opinion (October 03, 2017), https://www.thedailystar.net/opinion/global-affairs/do-north-koreas-nuclear-tests-violate-international-law-1470622.

173 Supra Chapter 1, n. 168, George Bunn at 21, 29.

further violation will have severe consequences to most of the world, and ultimately, global cooperation is essential to recognize the legally binding effect of the norm.

2.5.2 South Korea's Ratification of the Two Treaties

On August 30, 1963, South Korea signed the Partial Test Ban Treaty and ratified it on July 24, 1964, with prior consent from the National Assembly on May 28, 1964,[174] under domestic Treaty No. 127.[175] The Treaty entered into force for Korea on the day of ratification.

In addition, South Korea signed the Comprehensive Nuclear Test Ban Treaty on the opening day of signature and ratified it on September 24, 1999. However, the Treaty has not yet gone into effect, as mentioned above.

As a signatory to these treaties, South Korea is obligated to ensure that its space activities, both public and private, are consistent with the terms of the treaties. The Partial Test Ban Treaty prohibits nuclear weapons testing in outer space, while the Comprehensive Nuclear Test Ban Treaty prohibits all nuclear explosions, including those conducted in space. To achieve compliance with the Treaties, it is advisable for South Korea to consider measures to ensure that its private space sector does not engage in nuclear testing in outer space, and that its space legislation and policies align with these international obligations.

Furthermore, these Treaties have significant implications for inter-Korean relations, as Korea has been divided into two since World War II. South and North Korea are technically still at war since the Korean War ended with an armistice in 1953. Over the course of joining the Partial Test Ban Treaty, South Korea's government prudently consulted with the National Assembly and obtained its approval to ratify the Treaty. The government also transmitted a written statement to the United Nations as follows:

> The ratification by the Korean government of the Treaty does not in any way mean or imply the recognition of any territory or regime which has not been recognized by the Republic of Korea as a State or government.[176]

---

174 The Partial Test Ban Treaty was regarded to be relevant to national security which requires the prior consent of the National Assembly under Article 6(1) of the Constitution of the Republic of Korea.

175 UN Treaty Series, accessed on January 20, 2020, https://treaties.un.org/doc/Publication/UNTS/Volume%20510/volume-510-A-6964-English_French.pdf.

176 UN Treaty Series, volume 533, at 366, accessed on January 20, 2020, https://treaties.un.org/doc/Publication/UNTS/Volume%20533/v533.pdf.

This statement reflects South Korea's past political stance towards North Korea during the Cold War era, where it viewed North Korea as "any territory or regime which ha[d] not been recognized by South Korea."[177]

A similar position is found in Article 3 of the South Korean Constitution, which provides that "the territory of the Republic of Korea shall consist of the Korean peninsula and its adjacent islands." The majority of jurists construe this clause as South Korea's constitutional declaration that it is the only legitimate government on the Korean peninsula.[178]

The approach undertaken by South Korea as described above evinces its prudence in ratifying the Treaty and assessing the subsequent impact of such ratification on Korean society. Notwithstanding, the unresolved issues concerning North Korea's nuclear program persist, as exemplified by its continued testing of a range of missiles, including those armed with nuclear payloads.

3 A Member of the International Space-Related Organizations

3.1 *UNCOPUOS*

The United Nations (UN) officially came into existence in 1945 upon ratification of the Charter of the United Nations (UN Charter),[179] which aims to maintain international peace and security, develop friendly relations among nations, achieve international cooperation, and be a center for harmonizing the actions of nations.[180]

Shortly after Sputnik 1's launch in 1957, the UN General Assembly established an *ad hoc* Committee on the Peaceful Uses of Outer Space (UNCOPUOS)[181] in 1958 to govern space activities and codify international space law. A year later, the *ad hoc* committee soon developed into a permanent body. It was initially composed of eighteen members and has grown to include ninety-five

177 As to Korean National Assembly's perception of North Korea in the late 1940s, *see* National Archives of the Republic of Korea, "The Minutes of the National Assembly on December 12, 1948," accessed on January 20, 2020, https://dl.nanet.go.kr/SearchDetailView.do.

178 For more information about historical backgrounds, "The Problem of the Independence of Korea," United Nations General Assembly, Yearbook of the United Nations, 1947–48 (New York: Department of Public Information, United Nations, 1949), 290.

179 The Charter of the United Nations (hereinafter the "UN Charter"), signed on June 26, 1945, in San Francisco, came into force on October 24, 1945.

180 *Ibid.* Article 1 of the UN Charter.

181 Hereinafter referred to as "UNCOPUOS" or "COPUOS."

members as of 2019.[182] COPUOS has two subcommittees organized in 1961, the Scientific and Technical Subcommittee and the Legal Subcommittee. They have played an essential role in creating the five UN space treaties and other relevant principles.

South Korea was officially recognized by the UN General Assembly in 1948 under Resolution 195 and started participating in the General Assembly as an observer. In 1991, South Korea became a member of the United Nations and began to participate in COPUOS in 1994 as one of the nations that rotated seats every two years. After the practice of sharing seats terminated in 2001, South Korea finally became a full member State[183] and has been attending every year-session since then.

3.2 *The IADC*

The Inter-Agency Space Debris Coordination Committee (IADC)[184] is a forum of the European Space Agency (ESA) and twelve national space agencies founded in 1993,[185] coordinating activities related to space debris to mitigate its adverse effects.[186] The primary purposes of the IADC are to exchange information on space debris research activities, facilitate opportunities for cooperation in the area, review the progress of ongoing cooperative activities, and

182 Committee on the Peaceful Uses of Outer Space: Membership Evolution, accessed on March 3, 2020, https://www.unoosa.org/oosa/en/ourwork/copuos/members/evolution.html.

183 UNOOSA, "Committee on the Peaceful Uses of Outer Space: Membership Evolution," accessed on January 21, 2020, https://www.unoosa.org/oosa/en/ourwork/copuos/members/evolution.html.

184 Hereinafter the "IADC."

185 As of 2020, those twelve agencies are, in alphabetical order, Agenzia Spaziale Italiana (ASI), Centre National d'Études Spatiales (CNES), China National Space Administration (CNSA), Canadian Space Agency (CSA), Deutsches Zentrum für Luft- und Raumfahrt (DLR), Indian Space Research Organisation (ISRO), Japan Aerospace Exploration Agency (JAXA), Korea Aerospace Research Institute (KARI), National Aeronautics and Space Administration (NASA), Russian Federal Space Agency (ROSCOSMOS), State Space Agency of Ukraine (SSAU), United Kingdom Space Agency (UKSA).

186 As to the IADC in general, *see* Joanne Wheeler, "Space Debris: Legal Framework, Issues Arising and New ISO Guidelines," in 2010/2011, in Yearbook on Space Policy 2010/2011: The Forward Look (Eds. P. Hulsroj, S. Pagkratis & B. Baranes) (2013), 260; Joseph N. Pelton, Space Debris and Other Threats from Outer Space (2013), 31–32; Lotta Viikari, "Environmental Aspects of Space Activities," in Frans von der Dunk (ed.), Handbook of Space Law (2014), 749–751; *Supra* Chapter 1, n. 82, Francis Lyall and Paul B. Larsen, *Space law: A Treatise* (2009), 23, 38, 308, 493, 529, and 563.

identify debris mitigation options.[187] To that end, the IADC issued guidelines to address space debris on a worldwide basis that focus on the limitation of debris released during normal operations, the minimization of the potential for on-orbit break-ups, the post-mission disposal, and the prevention of on-orbit collisions.[188]

The guidelines reflect and consolidate mitigation measures developed by several national and international organizations. Although they are not legally binding, the guidelines have achieved wide international recognition.[189] They have been used by UNCOPUOS[190] and the International Organization for Standardization (ISO)[191] when developing new international standards as well as by national or regional organizations to identify their own standards.[192] This demonstrates the growing acceptance of these standards at the international level, which could eventually contribute to the creation of customary international law in the future.[193] In practice, some major spacefaring countries, such as the United States, the United Kingdom, France, Italy, and Japan, are using these guidelines in their domestic licensing procedures and imposing obligations on their private space operators.[194] This whole process that reflects the principles of the IADC and COPUOS guidelines will likely evolve into norms of international customary space law through State practice and attendant *opinio juris*.

South Korea joined the IADC in 2014, of which the Korea Aerospace Research Institute (KARI)[195] is a member agency in charge of undertaking space debris

187 Article 1 of the Terms of Reference of the Inter-Agency Space Debris Coordination Committee, available at https://www.iadc-home.org/terms_reference. *See also*, IADC, "What's IADC," accessed on January 26, 2020, https://www.iadc-home.org/what_iadc.

188 Section 5 of the IADC Space Debris Mitigation Guidelines; A/AC.105/C.1/L.260; available at https://www.unoosa.org/oosa/oosadoc/data/documents/2003/aac.105c.1l/aac.105c.1l.260_0.html. The guidelines were updated in 2007.

189 *Supra* Chapter 1, n. 186, Joanne Wheeler, 31–32.

190 Space Debris Mitigation Guidelines of the Committee on the Peaceful Uses of Outer Space; UNGA Res. 62/217 of December 22, 2007; UN Doc. A/RES/62/217, accessed on November 19, 2020, available at https://www.unoosa.org/pdf/publications/st_space_49E.pdf.

191 The International Organization for Standardization (ISO)is an international standard-setting body composed of representatives from 165 national standards organizations. *See*, as to the ISO in general, accessed on November 19, 2020, https://www.iso.org/about-us.html.

192 *Supra* Chapter 1, n. 186, Lotta Viikari, 751.

193 Frans von der Dunk, *Advanced Introduction to Space Law* (2020), 37–39.

194 Lotta Viikari, *The Environmental Element in Space Law: Assessing the Present and Charting the Future* (2008), 96; *Ibid*. Frans von der Dunk, 39.

195 For more details on KARI, *infra* Chapter 2 §3.1.

research and contributing to an increased understanding of space debris issues with the other member agencies.[196] In July 2020, South Korea issued its own Space Debris Mitigation Recommendations that apply to the whole phases of space mission planning, manufacturing and operating spacecraft, and post-mission disposal.[197] The purpose of the Recommendations is to provide guidelines to ensure that domestic entities involved in the Korean space industry carry out sustainable space development and operation in accordance with international standards such as the UN Space Debris Mitigation Guidelines.[198]

4 Intergovernmental Collaboration and Global Cooperation

During the 15th National Space Committee on January 7, 2019, the Korean government announced its strategy for space activities, emphasizing Korea's international cooperation and participation in global space missions.[199] Given South Korea's relatively smaller size in terms of territory, population, and finances, its participation in global space projects and cultivation of favorable relations with both established and emerging space-faring nations can be an ideal approach to expanding its space capabilities.

Through such inter-State cooperation and collaboration, South Korea, in tandem with its private space sector, can leverage the experiences of other nations, share the costs and risks of space missions, and access cutting-edge space technology and research institutes. This can facilitate the development

---

196 *See*, KARI & Korea Association for Space Technology Promotion (KASP), "우주산업실태조사 2017 (Survey on the Korea's Space Industry 2017 [English title added])," 167; IADC, "An overview of the IADC annual activities," 53rd Session of the Scientific and Technical Subcommittee United Nations Committee on the Peaceful Uses of Outer Space, February 22, 2016, available at https://iaaweb.org/iaa/Scientific%20Activity/debrisminutes09164.pdf.

197 "우주 쓰레기 경감을 위한 우주비행체 개발 및 운용 권고 (Recommendations for Space Debris Mitigation in the Course of Developing and Operating Spacecraft [English title added by the author])," press release by the Ministry of Science and ICT on July 24, 2020, at 11–12. For further discussion on the Recommendations in practice, *see infra* Chapter 4 §3.15 and Chapter 5 §3.10.

198 *Ibid*, the press release by the Ministry of Science and ICT states that the recommendations are based on the Space Debris Mitigation Guidelines of the Committee on the Peaceful Uses of Outer Space; UNGA Res. 62/217 of December 22, 2007; UN Doc. A/RES/62/217, accessed on November 19, 2020, available at https://www.unoosa.org/pdf/publications/st_space_49E.pdf.

199 The 15th National Space Committee, January 8, 2019, "Strategy for Space Industry by Ministry of Science and ICT [English title added]."

of a more comprehensive legal framework for regulating private space activities, thereby ensuring their safety and compliance with applicable laws at the international as well as national level.

4.1 *The Agreements with Russia in Space Activities*

After a series of negotiations beginning in 1998, South Korea and Russia signed the "Agreement Between the Government of the Republic of Korea and the Government of the Russian Federation on Cooperation in the Field of the Exploration and Use of Outer Space for Peaceful Purposes" on September 21, 2004, in Moscow. This was Korea's first bilateral treaty on space cooperation with another country.[200] The purpose of the Agreement is to promote mutually beneficial scientific, technological, industrial and economic cooperation related to the exploration and use of outer space.[201]

Based on this Agreement, South Korea initiated its first launch vehicle program in the mid-2000s as the two governments agreed to jointly develop and build a space booster complex. Their cooperation areas are extensive, including an exploration of outer space, remote sensing of the Earth, studies of space materials, satellite communications and navigation, spacecraft operation, development of launch vehicles and launch services.[202] A cross-waiver of liability is applied to their collaborative projects under the Agreement.[203]

Around two years after the first Agreement, a subsequent agreement and its protocol on technology safeguards were concluded and signed in Seoul.[204] Its purpose is to establish technology safeguards in connection with the implementation of joint projects and ensure the safety and security of protected items.[205] The Protocol to the Agreement primarily aims to facilitate cooperative activities concerning the development and operation of the Korea Space Launch System (KSLS).[206] This means that Russia was a key partner of

200 Came into force on September 5, 2006, as Treaty No. 1811.

201 Article 1 of the Agreement.

202 Article 3 of the Agreement.

203 Article 10 of the Agreement.

204 "Agreement Between the Government of the Republic of Korea and the Government of the Russian Federation on Technology Safeguards Associated with Cooperation in the field of the Exploration and Use of outer Space for Peaceful Purposes" and "Protocol to the Agreement between the Government of the Republic of Korea and the Government of the Russian Federation on technology Safeguards Associated with Cooperation in the field of the Exploration and Use of Outer Space for Peaceful Purposes of 17 October 2006," came into force on July 17, 2007, Treaty No. 1861.

205 *Ibid*, Article 3 of the Agreement.

206 *Supra* Chapter 1, n. 204, the preamble of the Protocol to the Agreement.

technological collaboration when South Korea was initially developing and building its space launch vehicle and spaceport.

4.2 *The Relationship with the United States in Space Cooperation*

The space cooperation agreement between South Korea and the United States, which had been suspended since around 2010, was finally signed on April 27, 2016, in Seoul.[207] This Framework Agreement marked the first comprehensive bilateral agreement between the United States and an Asian country on space cooperation. It was considered as a significant step towards opening up new horizons for the South Korea-US alliance.[208]

The Framework Agreement aims to closely cooperate in the use and exploration of air and outer space for peaceful purposes based on equal and mutual benefits.[209] The two countries further agreed to develop space programs in the areas of space and Earth science, Earth observation, and space exploration.[210] Concerning the registration of space objects, Article 7 of the Framework Agreement provides that both parties determine which agency shall request its government to register the space object in accordance with the Registration Convention, and their registration shall not affect the rights or obligations of either party under the Liability Convention. The Framework Agreement remains in force for ten years unless extended by written agreement of the parties[211] or terminated by written notice.[212] South Korea expects that the Framework Agreement will accelerate space cooperation between the two countries, including collaboration between KASI[213] and NASA on the solar and space environment.[214]

South Korea also joined the Artemis Accords on May 27, 2021, becoming the 10th signatory of the pact. The Artemis Accords are a set of principles for space exploration cooperation among nations participating in NASA's ambitions for

207 "Framework Agreement between the Government of the Republic of Korea and the Government of the United States of America for Cooperation in Aeronautics and the Exploration and Use of Airspace and Outer Space for Civil and Peaceful Purposes," entered into force on November 3, 2016, assigned domestic Treaty No. 2316.

208 Press release on November 4, 2016, by the Ministry of Science and ICT of the Republic of Korea, at 2.

209 *Supra* Chapter 1, n. 207, Article 1 of the Framework Agreement.

210 *Ibid*, Article 3 of the Framework Agreement.

211 *Ibid*, Article 16.1 of the Agreement.

212 *Ibid*, Article 16.3 of the Agreement.

213 Korea Astronomy and Space Science Institute (KASI), a government-funded institute, established in 1974. For further information, *see infra* Chapter §3.4.

214 *Supra* Chapter 1, n. 208, press release, at 3.

the Artemis Program.[215] The Minister of Science and ICT stated that "it is critical to implement space development activities in a transparent and responsible way with the international community." He further stated that "South Korea's participation in the Artemis Accords is expected to expand cooperation among the signatories in space exploration."[216] The signing of the Artemis Accords came as a follow-up to the summit on May 21, 2022, between the two presidents at the White House. During the summit, the two leaders agreed to strengthen bilateral partnerships in civil space exploration and astronautical research and develop cooperative responses to space security challenges.[217]

4.3 *Collaboration with Japan in Space Research*

Although there is not yet a treaty-level space agreement between the two countries, there have been various collaborations with JAXA.[218] These collaborations include the exchange of space experts and technologies, cooperation in Earth observation and satellite data utilization, collaborative development of satellites, and an annual KARI-JAXA joint seminar. In the private space sector, the world's first Digital Multimedia Broadcasting (DMB) satellite called Hanbyul was developed and launched by Korean and Japanese enterprises in 2004.[219]

4.4 *The Expansion of Space Cooperation with the United Arab Emirates*

On January 15, 2023, the Ministry of Science and ICT of South Korea and the United Arab Emirates (UAE) Space Agency signed a memorandum of understanding (MOU) for the expansion of space cooperation in conjunction with the leaders' summit of the two nations in Abu Dhabi.

This was an upgrade to the prior MOU signed in January 2017, under which the two nations focused on space science research, space technology

215 NASA, "Republic of Korea Joins List of Nations to Sign Artemis Accords," last accessed on October 3, 2022, available at https://www.nasa.gov/feature/republic-of-korea-joins-list-of-nations-to-sign-artemis-accords.

216 The Korea Herald, "S. Korea signs US-led moon exploration accord," last accessed on October 3, 2022, available at https://www.koreaherald.com/view.php?ud=20210527000099.

217 Space News, "South Korea signs Artemis Accords; Brazil, New Zealand likely next," last accessed on October 3, 2022, available at https://spacenews.com/south-korea-signs-artemis-accords/.

218 Japan Aerospace Exploration Agency (JAXA), formed in 2003 by merging three independent organizations. For more discussion on JAXA, *see infra* Chapter5 §3.6.4.2.

219 Mikyung Kim, "DMB Market and Audience Attitude," in Encyclopedia of Multimedia Technology and Networking, Second Edition 2009, 423.

development, and space-related regulations. In addition to the previous partnership, the 2023 MOU broadened the field of cooperation to cover space exploration, satellite communications and navigation, Earth observation, launch services, space situational awareness, and space traffic management.

The expanded space collaboration between the two nations is already in the works. The UAE's Mohammed Bin Rashid Space Centre (MBRSC) is considering carrying a payload of the Korea Astronomy and Space Science Institute (KASI) on its first lunar rover, "Rashid," which is scheduled to go to the Moon in 2026.[220]

4.5 *The Partnership with Thailand on the Establishment of Its Spaceport*

On February 13, 2023, the Ministry of Science and ICT of South Korea signed an "Implementation Agreement" with the Geo-Informatics and Space Technology Development Agency of Thailand concerning the "Feasibility Study on the Establishment of Spaceport in Thailand."[221] This Agreement marks a significant milestone in the development of a spaceport in Thailand and underscores the increasing cooperation between South Korea and Thailand in the field of space exploration and technology.

Through this partnership, South Korea stands to expand its reach and influence in the Southeast Asian space sector by sharing its experience and knowledge with Thailand. The Feasibility Study, which is estimated to span three years, will focus on crucial factors such as geographical suitability, environmental impact, infrastructure, and regulatory considerations. The Study will utilize South Korea's expertise in space programs, including the successful construction and launch of its homegrown space vehicle from its own spaceport.

Moreover, the partnership can create opportunities for South Korea's private sector to invest in Thailand's space industry, thus generating more revenue and increasing job opportunities in both countries.

220 Press release by the Ministry of Science and ICT on January 15, 2023, "South Korea-UAE's MOU for Space Cooperation," last accessed on January 17, 2023, available at https://www.msit.go.kr/bbs/view.do?sCode=user&mId=113&mPid=238&pageIndex=&bbsSeqNo=94&nttSeqNo=3182635&searchOpt=ALL&searchTxt=.

221 Press release by the Ministry of Science and ICT on February 13, 2023, "한-태국 우주 발사장 구축 타당성 조사 협력 이행약정 체결 (Implementation Agreement on Feasibility Study on the Establishment of Spaceport in Thailand)," last accessed on February 21, 2023, available at https://www.msit.go.kr/bbs/view.do?mId=113&bbsSeqNo=94&nttSeqNo=3182721.

4.6 *Cooperative Relationship with Global Community*

In addition to Russia, the United States, Japan, the United Arab Emirates, and Thailand, South Korea has been working with various countries, such as the United Kingdom, France, Germany, the Netherlands, Switzerland, Italy, Ukraine, Rumania, Kazakhstan, Seychelles, China, India, Taiwan, Mongolia, Pakistan, Peru, and South Africa.[222]

Since 2010, South Korea has been running the KARI International Space Training (KARIST) program that invites space researchers from emerging nations to share Korea's experiences on satellite production and remote sensing.[223] With this diverse approach, South Korea is contributing to international cooperation for the exploration and peaceful use of outer space.

5 Concluding Remarks

This chapter has provided an overview of South Korea's engagement with international space law by examining its membership in the four UN space treaties and other space-related legal instruments. It has also discussed South Korea's interaction with the global space community, including its participation in international organizations and cooperation with other countries. This involvement has significantly influenced South Korea's national space legislation, which plays a critical role in regulating its domestic space activities and private space sector.

South Korea has demonstrated its commitment to the global space community by implementing international legal norms within its national regulatory regime. The nation is a member of major international space treaties and organizations, and it has established partnerships with other countries in the space sector. These collaborations are essential as conducting space missions requires significant financial and technological resources.

The relevance of this chapter to South Korea's national space legislation and private space sector lies in the fact that it provides an understanding of the nation's legal framework and its adherence to international legal norms for

222 Ministry of Science and ICT, "International Space Cooperation," October 16, 2014, accessed on January 30, 2020, https://doc.msit.go.kr/SynapDocViewServer/viewer/doc.html?key=fa1aa5adfe3d4186bf924848e5dd49ea&convType=img&convLocale=ko_KR&contextPath=/SynapDocViewServer.

223 "Statement of Republic of Korea," accessed on January 30, 2020, https://www.unoosa.org/documents/pdf/copuos/2018/hls/04_02E.pdf.

subsequent chapters. This understanding is essential for the growth and development of South Korea's space activities and private space sector.

South Korea's adherence to international legal norms has enabled the nation to develop a national regulatory framework to address its space activities and regulate its private space participants. The next chapter will explore South Korea's national space activities and programs, which will provide further insights into the nation's space capability and potentiality.

CHAPTER 2

Korea's National Space Activities in the Past, Present, and Future

1 Introduction

Upon the advent of the Space Age with the launch of Sputnik 1 in 1957, South Korea was struggling to recover from the aftermath of colonial rule and war. For Koreans at the time, space development and research sounded like what was occurring on a different planet. Indeed, the Korean government's top priority was to reconstruct the nation's industrial infrastructure, which had been decimated. To achieve this, the government executed a Five-Year Economic Development Plan four times between 1962 to 1981. Subsequently, from 1982 to 1996, the Plan was rebranded as the Five-Year Economic and Social Advancement Plan to reflect its expanded scope beyond just economic development.

Meanwhile, as the domestic economy began to recover, the government shifted its focus towards investing in education. As part of this commitment, the Korea Advanced Institute of Science (KAIS), now known as the Korea Advanced Institute of Science and Technology (KAIST),[1] was established in 1971 under the special law – the Korea Advanced Institute of Science and Technology Act.[2] The institution was created to provide postgraduate training in engineering and applied sciences for the professional personnel.

With the economy prospering ahead of the 1988 Seoul Olympics, the National Assembly passed the Aerospace Industry Development Promotion Act in December 1987[3] to develop aerospace science and technology as well as to encourage the aerospace industry, which was the first explicit space-related law in South Korea.

1 For further discussion on KAIST, *see infra* Chapter 2 §3.3. When KAIS was merged with KIST in 1980, it changed its name to KAIST. Although they were separated in 1989, KAIST decided to keep the name. For more information about its history, https://www.kaist.ac.kr/_prog/history/?site_dvs_cd=en&menu_dvs_cd=010202&site_dvs_cd=en&menu_dvs_cd=010202, (accessed on November 19, 2019).

2 Enacted on December 31, 2019, Act No. 3310; partially amended on December 24, 2019, Act No. 16022.

3 For further discussion on the Aerospace Industry Development Promotion Act, *see infra* Chapter 3.

 | DOI:10.1163/9789004694743_004

Two significant accomplishments under the Aerospace Industry Development Promotion Act paved the way for South Korea's space development in its early stage. First, the Korea Aerospace Research Institute (KARI) was founded in 1989[4] as the Act stipulates that the government may have research institutes undertake aerospace projects such as the development of spacecraft and the training of the specialized personnel.[5] Second, South Korea's first space program was initiated in 1996, according to the provision referring to the establishment of aerospace development plans.[6]

In light of the country's historical background, this chapter will examine Korea's space-related institutions, private enterprises, and national space programs, tracing their development from the past toward the future.

2 National Space-Related Committees

2.1 *National Space Committee*

The National Space Committee was founded by the Space Development Promotion Act in 2005 to deliberate on matters concerning space activities.[7] The Committee is an inter-ministerial consultative body under the control of the President, which consists of sixteen members including the Prime Minister, who is the chairperson of the Committee, the Minister of Science and ICT, the vice-chairperson, as well as other relevant ministers and those who have expertise and experience in the space sector.[8]

Major matters deliberated by the Committee are reviewing national space plans, financing space developments, and issuing permits for launching space vehicles.[9] Among these, the Committee's most fundamental duty is to review and finalize national space plans announced every one/five/ten years, depending on the types of plans.[10]

4 For more information about KARI, *see infra* Chapter 2 §3.1.

5 Articles 4, 10 and 12 of the Aerospace Industry Development Promotion Act.

6 Article 3 of the Aerospace Industry Development Promotion Act.

7 Article 6(1) of the Space Development Promotion Act. Details will be discussed in Chapter 5 §3.4.

8 Articles 6(3) and (4) of the Space Development Promotion Act, partially amended on August 10, 2021, Act No. 18375, which entered into force November 11, 2021.

9 Article 6(2) of the Space Development Promotion Act.

10 Details of these national space plans will be discussed in Chapter 2 §6 and §7.

2.2 *Working Committee for the Promotion of Space Development*

The Working Committee for the Promotion of Space Development is comprised of up to twenty-five members, including a chairperson – the Vice Minister of Science and ICT.[11] The Working Committee serves to assist the aforementioned National Space Committee in carrying out its work efficiently.

2.3 *Working Committee for the Utilization of Satellite Data*

The Vice Minister of Science and ICT also chairs the Working Committee for the Utilization of Satellite Data with a maximum of twenty-one members in total.[12] This Working Committee deals with issues concerning the management of satellite systems and the use of satellite data acquired from government-led satellites developed and built under the national space programs.[13]

3 Space-Related Institutes and Facilities

3.1 *The Korea Aerospace Research Institute (KARI)*

The Korea Aerospace Research Institute (KARI) was established in 1989 as an affiliate of the Korea Institute of Machinery and Materials (KIMM), in order to efficiently implement the government's aerospace policies outlined in the Aerospace Industry Development Promotion Act.[14] In 1996, KARI gained independence from KIMM and became a government-funded research institution under the jurisdiction of the Ministry of Science and ICT. KARI's main laboratories are located in Daejeon, in the middle of South Korea.

KARI has contributed to developing space technologies and improving national competitiveness in the global space industry for over three decades.[15] In the field of satellites, KARI has developed the KOMPSAT series[16] for Earth

11 Article 6(5) of the Space Development Promotion Act and Article 6(1) of the Presidential Decree of the Space Development Promotion Act.

12 Article 6(5) of the Space Development Promotion Act and Article 6 *bis* (1) of the Presidential Decree of the Space Development Promotion Act.

13 For further information, *see infra* Chapter 2 §5.3 and Chapter 5 §3.8. Additionally, information on the newly established Working Committee for National Space Security can be found in *infra* Chapter 5 §3.9.

14 For further discussion on the Aerospace Industry Development Promotion Act, *see infra* Chapter 3.

15 KARI celebrated its 30th anniversary in October 2019. The anniversary statement by KARI's president is available at https://www.kari.re.kr/kor/sub01_10.do, (accessed on November 19, 2019).

16 *See, infra* Chapter 2 §5.3.

observation or meteorological purposes.[17] As part of its efforts to develop launch vehicles, KARI has achieved success in launching KSLV-I and KSLV-II from the Naro Space Center.[18] KARI's primary objectives include building up indigenous launch capabilities, commercializing satellite data applications, and utilizing domestic technologies to explore the Moon and other celestial bodies. These efforts demonstrate South Korea's commitment to fulfilling its aspirations towards outer space.[19]

In 2016, KARI was designated as a Specialized Institute of Space Development according to Article 7(1) of the Space Development Promotion Act, which allows the Minister of Science and ICT to designate a specialized institution to systematically and efficiently promote space development projects.[20] KARI is at the forefront of South Korea's space program, conducting comprehensive activities to develop, launch, and operate space objects, as well as performing the duties assigned to it by the Minister of Science and ICT.[21]

KARI announced, in its thirtieth anniversary in 2019, the "Future Vision 2050" for another thirty-year goals and strategies as a blueprint for the upcoming space development, which includes developing space transportation technology, securing South Korea's participation in lunar activities, and completing a satellite constellation for deep space research.[22]

3.2 *The Naro Space Center*

The Naro Space Center is a spaceport operated by KARI. It is situated on Naro Island, part of South Korea, which is about 485 km (300 mi) south of Seoul (see Figure 2). The government began to develop and build the center in 1996 according to the Mid-to Long-Term Basic Plan for the Promotion of Space Development.[23] This building project consists of two stages: The first stage was completed in 2009 with the construction of its first launch pad and infrastructure facilities. The second stage has since been ongoing with the aim of

---

17 KARI, "Welcome to KARI," accessed on July 29, 2020, https://www.kari.re.kr/eng/sub01_01.do.

18 *See, infra* Chapter 2 §3.2.

19 KARI, "2017 Korea Aerospace Research Institute Promising Technologies for Commercialization," at 6.

20 In-depth discussion on the Space Development Promotion Act will be made in Chapter 5.

21 Article 7(2) of the Space Development Promotion Act. For further discussion on KARI, *see infra* Chapter 5 §3.6.

22 For more information about KARI's goals and strategies, KARI, "Future Vision 2050," accessed on April 30, 2020, https://www.kari.re.kr/eng/sub01_06.do.

23 For more information about the Mid-to Long-Term Basic Plan for the Promotion of Space Development, *see infra* Chapter 2 §6.

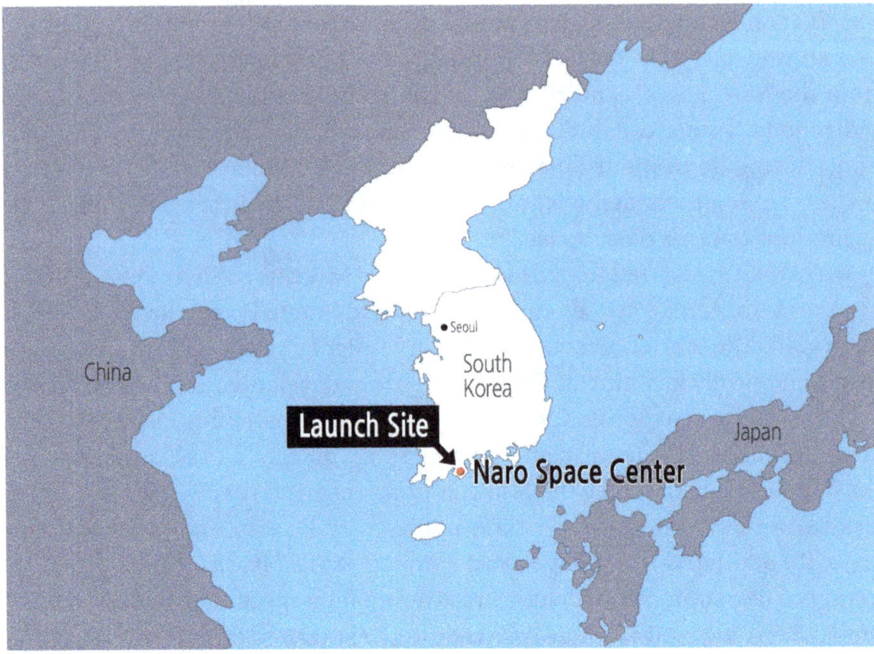

FIGURE 2 The Naro Space Center

completing its second launch pad and expanding test facilities. South Korea's first launch vehicle, KSLV-I, was successfully launched from the first launch pad in 2013, and KSLV-II lifted off in 2022 from the second launch pad.[24]

The Naro Space Center includes facilities for satellite and launch vehicle assembly, a control tower, an electric power station, a media center, and a space exhibition hall. In addition to these, there are two tracking stations outside the Naro Space Center. One of them is the Jeju Tracking Station located on Jeju Island, which is approximately 180 km (111 mi) southwest of the Naro Space Center. The Jeju Tracking Station is equipped with a set of tracking radar and two sets of telemetry systems to track launch vehicles departing from the Naro Space Center. It also collaborates with the French Centre National d'Études Spatiales (CNES) under a bilateral agreement to receive data and track launch vehicles during their flights over Northeast Asia after being launched from the Guiana Space Center.

The other tracking station is the Palau Tracking Station, located in the Republic of Palau in the South Pacific, which began operating in November

24 For more information about the KSLV program, *see infra* Chapter 2 §5.2.

2019. Its first mission was to receive flight data and satellite separation signals during the KSLV-II launch in 2022. The Palau Tracking Station operates exclusively during planned launches to minimize operating costs.[25]

3.3 *The Korea Advanced Institute of Science and Technology* (KAIST)

The Korea Advanced Institute of Science and Technology (KAIST)[26] is the nation's first research-focused science and engineering university established by the Korean government in 1971.[27] Its establishment is based on a special law – the Korea Advanced Institute of Science and Technology (KAIST) Act.[28] Article 1 of the KAIST Act stipulates that the purpose of KAIST is to train qualified scientific and engineering specialists in order to conduct mid- and long-term research and development as well as provide necessary assistance for other research institutes and space industries.

KAIST has been researching and developing satellites and remote sensing technologies mainly through its Satellite Technology Research Center (SaTRec) established in 1989 – KAIST SaTRec.[29] In the early 1990s, KAIST SaTReC, along with KARI, developed the first Korea Institute of Technology Satellite (KITSAT) -1[30] in collaboration with the University of Surrey in the United Kingdom. The KITSAT-1 program was a success as it drew public attention to space development for the first time in South Korea. Furthermore, its operational and technological performance was the driving force for further space research and development. Within a year after KITSAT-1, KITSAT-2 followed using full domestic technology. KAIST SaTRec has also been working on the Science and Technology Satellite (STSAT) series as well as performing the Next Generation Satellite (NEXTSat) project.[31]

25 KARI, "Naro Space Center," accessed on July 23, 2020, https://www.kari.re.kr/eng/sub03_03_04.do.

26 Formerly named Korea Advanced Institute of Science (KAIS).

27 Geunhong Park, "The Advance of a Korean Institute: A Brief History of KAIST," KAIST Herald, April 21, 2011, available at https://herald.kaist.ac.kr/news/articleView.html?idxno=158.

28 Enacted on December 31, 1980, Act No. 3310. The former Korea Advanced Institute of Science (KAIS) Act was repealed by the KAIST Act.

29 KAIST SaTRec, "History," accessed on July 1, 2020, http://satrec.kaist.ac.kr/e_01_02.php.

30 Also known as *Uribyol-1* (우리별) in Korean, meaning 'our star.'

31 For more information about the NEXTSat project, SaTRec, "Research and Development," accessed on May 1, 2020, http://satrec.kaist.ac.kr/e_02_08.php.

3.4 *The Korea Astronomy and Space Science Institute* (KASI)

In the beginning, the Korea Astronomy and Space Science Institute (KASI) was founded as a National Astronomical Observatory under the Ministry of Science and Technology in 1974 and now has become a government-funded independent research institute. The legal basis of KASI's current transformation is the Establishment, Operation, and Fosterage of Government-Funded Science and Technology Research Institutes Act.[32] Article 2 of the Act defines the term "government-funded science and technology research institute" as an institute funded by the government and primarily aimed at research in the field of science and technology. KASI is one of twenty research institutes under the Act.[33]

KASI has been conducting joint research on space science since it signed the cooperation agreement with NASA in 2010.[34] KASI also operates the National Space Situational Awareness Organization (NSSAO) designated by the Korean government for the nation's space risk management. It monitors space hazards and provides continuous information thereof.[35]

3.5 *The National Space Policy Research Center* (SPREC)

The Space Policy Research Center (SPREC) is a new government-funded think tank, established in August 2021.[36] SPREC conducts space-related research and analysis assigned by the Korean government to provide direction for the nation's space policies and private sector initiatives. Researchers and experts from KARI, KASI, and the Agency for Defense Development (ADD) constitute the majority of SPREC. SPREC regularly holds the Space Policy Forum and periodically produces its research and analysis publications on various domestic and global space issues.

---

32 Enacted on September 23, 2004, Act No. 7219.

33 Article 8(1) of the Establishment, Operation, and Fosterage of Government-Funded Science and Technology Research Institutes Act.

34 KASI, "Solar and Space Weather," accessed on May 5, 2020, https://www.kasi.re.kr/eng/pageView/73.

35 For more discussion about NSSAO, *infra* Chapter 5 §3.11.

36 The National Space Policy Research Center, available at https://stepi.re.kr/site/sprec/main.do.

4 Private Entities in the Space Industry

During the early stages of economic development, South Korea's major industries were primarily driven by government initiatives, but the space industry was not a priority until the early 1990s. Since its first space program in 1996, the space industry in South Korea has evolved to include participation by the private sector in government-led projects. While 58 companies are involved in the production of satellites and 68 companies in the production of launch vehicles,[37] the private sector's independent space activities are still in their infancy.

The activities conducted by private entities in the Korean space industry can be broadly classified into three categories: First, satellite production and export; second, satellite application through remote sensing; and third, launch vehicle manufacturing and launch activities.

The activities of the first category *per se* would hardly be considered "national activities in outer space" that give rise to international responsibility under Article VI of the Outer Space Treaty.[38] However, if such activities include operating and controlling satellites beyond merely building and exporting them, their operational activities would fall within the scope of space activities set out in the Outer Space Treaty, which is the case for Satrec Initiative (SI). SI is primarily a satellite manufacturing company founded in 1999 by the former KAIST engineers who developed South Korea's first satellite, KITSAT-1, at KAIST SaTRec.[39] SI's entry into the global market began with the launch of RazakSAT, a Malaysian Earth observation satellite, in 2009. Since then, SI has conducted space programs with international partners by building and controlling high-performing Earth observation satellites such as DubaiSat-2 for the United Arab Emirates, which was launched in 2013, and Deimos-2 for Spain, which was launched in 2014.[40] SI manages ground systems to operate multiple satellites, including South Korea's KOMPSAT series.[41] One of its subsidiaries, SI Imaging Service (SIIS),[42] provides image data services through remote sensing.[43] In

37 The Ministry of Science and ICT, "2019 우주산업실태조사 (Space Industry Survey 2019 [English title added])," 43.

38 *See, supra,* Chapter 1 §1.1.2 International Responsibility for "National Activities."

39 *See, infra,* Chapter 2 §3.3.

40 For more information about SI's products, *see* "World-leading solution provider for Earth observation missions," accessed on July 31, 2020, https://www.satreci.com/sub0101.

41 *See, infra,* Chapter 2 §5.3.

42 For more about SIIS, *see* https://www.satreci.com/sub0301.

43 SI commenced as a satellite manufacturer in 1999, which falls under the purview of the Aerospace Industry Development Promotion Act of 1987 (*see infra* Chapter 3). The company's operation of government-developed satellites, including the KOMPSAT series, is regulated by the Orders on the Dissemination and Utilization of Satellite Data, Orders

addition to SIIS, CONTEC[44] and InSpace[45] also operate ground stations for satellite utilization, which analyze and provide satellite data obtained through remote sensing.

Perigee Aerospace is a launch vehicle manufacturer that was founded by KAIST students and became a corporation in 2018. The company began by developing and launching sounding rockets and has since expanded its portfolio to include orbital launch vehicles, demonstrating its ability to innovate and adapt in the rapidly evolving launch vehicle industry. In 2018 and 2019, Perigee Aerospace secured two rounds of venture capital funding from South Korea's Samsung Venture Investments and LB Investment, a subsidiary of LG, to support the development of its launch vehicle, Blue Whale.[46] Blue Whale is planned to become the smallest launch vehicle in the world, designed to lift small satellites weighing up to 50 kilograms (110 lb) to a 500-kilometer (310 mi) sun-synchronous orbit.[47] In 2019, Perigee Aerospace signed a launch agreement with Southern Launch, an Australian firm that provided a unique facility for Perigee's micro-lift launch vehicle.[48] The pair committed to testing the launch facility in the second half of 2020 ahead of regular commercial launches.[49]

There may be different approaches in academia as to whether Perigee's procurement of launch should be considered "national activities" pursuant to Article VI of the Outer Space Treaty,[50] and furthermore, whether it should be regarded as launch activities to which Article VII of the Outer Space Treaty and the Liability Convention are applicable.[51] Given that the concept of "launching

---

on the Security Management of Satellite Data, and Guidelines for the Organization and Operation of the Consultative Body for the Utilization of Satellite Data (*see infra* Chapter 5 §4.8). However, as of February 2023, there exists no specific legislation in South Korea addressing private satellite operation and control.

44 CONTEC's subsidiary, CONTEC Space, is located in Luxembourg. For more about CONTEC, *see* http://contec.kr/index.

45 For more about InSpace, *see* https://www.inspace.co.kr/.

46 "South Korean rocket startup to launch from South Australia," accessed on August 3, 2020, https://studyadelaide.com/whats-happening/south-korean-rocket-startup-launch-south-australia.

47 Caleb Henry, Space News, "Backed by Samsung, South Korean startup Perigee aims for 2020 maiden launch," October 23, 2019, https://spacenews.com/backed-by-samsung-south-korean-startup-perigee-aims-for-2020-maiden-launch/.

48 Max Blenkin, "Southern Launch signs rocket launch deal with Korean space company," October 2, 2019, https://www.spaceconnectonline.com.au/launch/3783-southern-launch-signs-rocket-launch-deal-with-korean-space-agency.

49 *Supra* Chapter 2, n. 46.

50 *See, supra,* Chapter 1 §1.1.2.

51 *See, supra,* Chapter 1 §1.3.2.

State" includes the procurement of launch according to Article VII of the Outer Space Treaty and Article I(c) of the Liability Convention[52] and the activities are being conducted by Korean nationals (personal jurisdiction), the series of activities by Perigee Aerospace can amount to launch activities that may result in State's international liability for space damage.[53]

UNA STELLA Corporation is the latest space start-up established in 2022 that aims to create a human space flight platform and provide necessary services using its own launch vehicles.[54] The commercial space flight market in South Korea is relatively less researched and developed than other space sectors, and there is yet no domestic regulation directly addressing human space flight. UNA STELLA is currently building a launch vehicle, USB Bravo, focusing on developing a crew capsule and propulsion system that can accommodate 4 to 6 participants on a suborbital trip at a time, with the goal of providing complete flight services by 2027.

While the aforementioned companies engage in direct and independent space activities, these three private entities are primarily involved in South Korea's national space program, providing components for satellites or rockets. Hanwha Aerospace is an aerospace engine manufacturer, which built the main engines of KSLV-II[55] in collaboration with KARI under the Korean launch vehicle development program. SPACE SOLUTIONS, a spacecraft component producer, furnished KSLV-II with component parts.[56] Korea Aerospace Industries (KAI), which has long been involved in the research and development of Korean satellites and launch vehicles, manufactured KSLV-II's first-stage propellant tank and was involved in the whole assembly process.[57] KAI is also working with KARI to transfer satellite technologies obtained by the Korean government to private companies with the aim of establishing a mass-production infrastructure led by industry.[58]

52 Article I(c) of the Liability Convention defines the term "launching State" as follows: (i) A State which launches or *procures* the launching of a space object; (ii) A State from whose territory or facility a space object is launched. [Italics added].

53 For more discussion on launch procurement in relation to Korean space legislation, *see* Chapters 5 and 6.

54 For more about UNA STELLA, *see* https://www.unastella.co/.

55 Korea Space Launch Vehicle (KSLV)-II. *See infra* Chapter 2 §5.2.

56 For more about SPACE SOLUTIONS, *see* http://www.spacesolutions.co.kr/.

57 KAI, "Korea Space Launch Vehicle," accessed on August 2, 2020, https://www.koreaaero.com/EN/Business/KoreaSpaceLaunchVehicle.aspx.

58 KAI, "Compact Advanced Satellite," accessed on August 2, 2020, https://www.koreaaero.com/EN/Business/CAS500_01.aspx.

There are several other startups operating in the Korean space industry, although their activities are not considered space activities under the international responsibility and liability regime. These include NARA Space Technology, a CubeSat manufacturer;[59] Unmanned Exploration Laboratory (UEL), a developer of lunar and Martian rovers;[60] and UZURO Tech (우주로테크), a system developer focused on space debris removal technology.[61]

As the government announced a gradual transition from government-led to private sector-led space development in 2018,[62] it is expected that South Korea's space industry will become more prosperous in the foreseeable future.

5 Space Programs and National Space Activities

5.1 *The Korea Sounding Rocket (KSR) Program in the 1990s*

In the early 1990s, South Korea witnessed a shift from a military regime to a civilian government. As part of such a transition, the government selected KARI to be in charge of the Korea Sounding Rocket (KSR) program, replacing the former military efforts.

The development of KSR-I began in 1990 and was successfully launched in 1993, which was South Korea's first single-stage solid propellant rocket for scientific purposes.[63] Later in 1997 and 1998, KSR-II, a two-stage rocket, lifted off carrying an ultraviolet radiometer to measure vertical ozone distribution in the stratosphere over the Korean peninsula.[64] Furthermore, KSR-III, the first-ever liquid propellant rocket of South Korea, was built and launched in 2002.[65] KSR-III served as a testbed for the development of a satellite launch vehicle powered by a liquid fuel engine planned for KSLV-I.[66] It also demonstrated core technologies that would be used for KSLV-I in the propulsion, guidance, and control devices.[67]

59 For more about NARA Space Technology, *see* https://www.naraspace.com/.

60 For more about UEL, *see* https://www.facebook.com/unmannedexplorationlab.

61 For more about UZURO Tech (우주로테크), accessed on August 2, 2020, available at https://m.post.naver.com/viewer/postView.nhn?volumeNo=27197207&memberNo=6307839&vType=VERTICAL.

62 The Basic Plan for Promotion of Space Development in 2018. *Infra*, Chapter 2 §7.1.

63 For more specifics about KSR-I, *see* http://www.astronautix.com/k/ksr-i.html.

64 KSR-II, "Part of KSR," accessed on May 10, 2020, http://www.astronautix.com/k/ksr-ii.html.

65 KSR-III, "Part of KSR," accessed on May 10, 2020, http://www.astronautix.com/k/ksr-iii.html.

66 *Infra* Chapter 2 §5.2.

67 *Supra* Chapter 2, n. 65.

The entire KSR program, which involved the development of a single-stage solid propellant rocket to a two-stage liquid propellant rocket, was completed in 2002. This was followed by the development of a satellite launch vehicle.

5.2 *The Korea Space Launch Vehicle (KSLV) Program*

The KSLV program commenced in 2002 immediately after the KSR program, as was announced in South Korea's first national space plan in 1996.[68] The Korean government's ultimate goal at that time was to launch "our satellite" on board "our launch vehicle" from "our soil." To that end, the government built the Naro Space Center in 2009 while developing KSLV-I[69] in collaboration with Russia at the beginning.[70] KSLV-I's first stage was conducted by Russian Khrunichev State Research and Production Space Center,[71] and its second stage and payload were built and designed in South Korea led by KARI. KSLV-I is capable of launching a 100-kilogram (220 lb) payload into a low elliptical orbit with an altitude of 300 kilometers (186 miles) in perigee and 1500 kilometers (932 miles) in apogee, which is 33 meters (108 feet) long and 2.9 meters (9.5 feet) in diameter, with an overall mass of 140 metric tons.[72]

However, the first and second KSLV-I launch attempts in 2009 and 2010, respectively, had both failed. Finally on January 30, 2013, it lifted off successfully from the Naro Space Center, ushering in a new era of domestic space launch vehicles that goes beyond the period of sounding rockets.

After the success of KSLV-I, KARI focused on South Korea's second launch vehicle, KSLV-II,[73] applying indigenous technologies especially by using all domestically developed engines. KSLV-II is capable of launching a 1.5-ton (3,300 lb) utility satellite into the low Earth orbit of 600–800 kilometers (370–480 mils) above the Earth.[74] The KSLV-II program was comprised of three phases: In phase 1, ground tests for the liquid-fuel engines were conducted by July 2015; phase 2 was assigned for the tests of the launch vehicle by the end of 2018; on June 21, 2022, phase 3 culminated in the successful launch of

---

68 *Infra* Chapter 2 §6.

69 Also known as *Naro-ho* (나로호) in Korean. *Naro* is the name of the island where South Korea's spaceport is situated on.

70 *Supra* Chapter 1 §4.1.

71 Khrunichev State Research and Production Space Center, "Korea Space Launch Vehicle-KSLV (South Korea)," accessed on April 15, 2020, http://www.khrunichev.ru/main.php?id=73&lang=en.

72 *Ibid.*

73 Also known as *Nuri-ho* (누리호) in Korean, *Nuri* means 'the whole world.'

74 KARI, "Korea Space Launch Vehicle (Nuri)," accessed on March 17, 2020, https://www.kari.re.kr/eng/sub03_03_01.do.

KSLV-II, placing all the satellites on board into the 700 kilometers (435 miles) Sun-synchronous orbit (SSO).[75] This launch made South Korea the seventh country in the world to have the capability of putting satellites weighing a ton or heavier into orbit, joining the United States, Russia, France, China, Japan, and India.[76]

5.3 *The Satellite Development Program and Satellites in Orbit*

South Korea's first satellite, KITSAT-1,[77] was launched in 1992 on Ariane 4 from the Guiana Space Center.[78] At that time, although South Korea could have owned its first satellite just by purchasing one, the nation, instead, chose to acquire fundamental technology through the satellite development program in collaboration with the UK University of Surrey. These efforts led to the success of KITSAT-2 and -3 applied domestic technologies from design to production and operation independently.

With the technologies obtained by the KITSAT program, the field of satellite research and development began to grow rapidly. The following are the major satellite series that have come out since the KITSAT series:[79]

i. Koreasat – 1, 2, 3, 5, 5A, 6 and 7 for communications and broadcasting;
ii. STSAT (Science and Technology Satellite) – 1, 2A, 2B, 2C and 3;
iii. KOMPSAT (Korea Multi-Purpose Satellite) – 1, 2, 2A, 2B, 3, 3A, 5, 6, and 7 for Earth observation and meteorology; and
iv. NEXTSat (Next-Generation Satellite) -1 and 2 for scientific missions.

---

75 Stephen Clark, "South Korea's all-domestic satellite launcher reaches orbit for first time," Spaceflight Now, accessed January 21, 2023, available at https://spaceflightnow.com/2022/06/21/south-koreas-all-domestic-satellite-launcher-reaches-orbit-on-test-flight/.

76 Japan's Kyodo News on June 21, 2022, "South Korea succeeds in putting satellites into orbit, 7th in the world," accessed on January 21, 2023, available at https://english.kyodonews.net/news/2022/06/292e01462a69-update1-s-korea-succeeds-in-putting-satellites-into-orbit-7th-in-world.html?phrase=masks&words=; Dasol Kim, "S. Korea joins elite space club as 7th member," The Korea Herald, accessed on January 21, 2023, available at https://www.koreaherald.com/view.php?ud=20220621000810.

77 Korea Institute of Technology Satellite (KITSAT).

78 SaTRec, "Research and Development: KITSAT-1," accessed on November 19, 2019, http://satrec.kaist.ac.kr/e_02_01.php.

79 In Korean culture, number 4 is considered bad luck. As a result, satellite series in South Korea do not have a satellite No. 4. Similarly, many buildings in Korea do not have a 4th floor or label it as 'F' instead of number 4, due to the negative connotation associated with the number in Korean culture.

As of May 2020, thirty-two Korean satellites, excluding five decayed, are in orbit, thirty of which are registered with the United Nations pursuant to the Registration Convention.[80]

5.4 *The Korean Astronaut Program*

In the early 2000s, the Korean government initiated the Korean Astronaut Program, aiming to send the first Korean into space in collaboration with the Russian space program. The program was successful, with Dr. Soyeon Yi, a former researcher at KAIST, taking off from the Baikonur Cosmodrome in Kazakhstan aboard the Soyuz TMA-12 on April 8, 2008. During her nine-day stay on the International Space Station (ISS), Dr. Yi conducted valuable scientific experiments before returning on board Soyuz TMA-11.[81] Despite the success of the program and extensive media coverage with ardent support from the Korean public, there have been no further astronaut missions in South Korea to date.[82]

5.5 *The Korea Lunar Exploration Program (KLEP)*

South Korea commenced the Korea Lunar Exploration Program (KLEP) in 2016, recognizing that missions to the Moon would be a stepping stone for deep space exploration as well as a good opportunity to facilitate more rapid development of space technology.[83]

Under the program, the Korea Pathfinder Lunar Orbiter (KPLO) mission is South Korea's first lunar mission that is being carried out by KARI. KPLO[84] is equipped with six payloads – five from KARI[85] and one from NASA.[86] To this

80 UNOOSA, "Online Index of Objects Launched into Outer Space," accessed on May 6, 2020, https://www.unoosa.org/oosa/osoindex/search-ng.jspx#?c=%7B%22filters%22:%5B%7B%22fieldName%22:%22en%23object.launch.stateOrganization_s%22,%22value%22:%22Republic%20of%20Korea%22%7D%5D,%22sortings%22:%5B%7B%22fieldName%22:%22object.launch.dateOfLaunch_s1%22,%22dir%22:%22desc%22%7D%5D,%22match%22:%22%22,%22termMatch%22:%22korea%22%7D.

81 South Korean Scientist and Astronaut, accessed on April 24, 2020, https://www.britannica.com/biography/Yi-Soyeon.

82 *Supra* Chapter 1, n. 15, Youngshin Ahn, Air & Space Law 44, at 173.

83 KARI, "Lunar Exploration," accessed on May 7, 2020, https://www.kari.re.kr/eng/sub03_04.do.

84 Also known as "Danuri (다누리)," a combination of two Korean words meaning 'Enjoy the Moon.' "Danuri" was selected as the KPLO's name through the nationwide naming contest, where a total of 62,719 names were submitted for South Korea's first lunar orbiter.

85 Lunar Terrain Imager (LUTI), Wide-Angle Polarimetric Camera (PolCam), KPLO Magnetometer (KMAG), KPLO Gamma Ray Spectrometer (KGRS), and Delay-Tolerant Networking experiment (DTNPL).

86 ShadowCam.

end, KARI and NASA signed an "Implementing Arrangement between NASA and KARI for Cooperation on the Korea Pathfinder Lunar Orbiter (KPLO) Mission" in December 2016.[87] KPLO was launched on August 4, 2022[88] on board a SpaceX's Falcon 9 Block 5 launch vehicle in Cape Canaveral, Florida. KPLO took more than four months to reach the Moon because it used ballistic lunar transfer (BLT) to go to a Moon orbit to minimize its fuel consumption. Its mission period is planned for around a year.[89]

The next phase of the program involves a lunar lander mission that will build upon the achievements of the previous orbiter mission. The lander is planned to launch from South Korea on a Korean launch vehicle,[90] which will represent a significant milestone in South Korea's lunar exploration program. The nation's ultimate objective is to secure advanced technologies that will facilitate future deep-space exploration, while also integrating decades of accumulated space science and technology. South Korea expects to reap substantial benefits for the nation as a whole through this program.[91]

6 National Space-Related Plans

6.1 *The Basic and Action Plans for the Promotion of Space Development*

The Basic Plan for the Promotion of Space Development is a five-year plan published by the government which prescribes mid- and long-term space policy and sets the direction of space development under Article 5 of the Space Development Promotion Act. The basic plan includes strategies, financing, expert training, and international cooperation for space development as well as how to manage space objects and utilize such performance.[92] The National Space Committee[93] is in charge of deliberating on and finalizing the basic plan.[94]

---

87 *Supra* Chapter 2, n.83, KARI, "Lunar Exploration."

88 At 7:08 p.m. Eastern Daylight Time (EDT).

89 KARI, "Korea's first step toward lunar exploration," accessed on January 21, 2023, https://www.kari.re.kr/eng/sub03_07_01.do.

90 KARI, "Introduction to Korea Lunar Exploration Program and KPLO Mission," August 2016, at 2.

91 KARI, "Cooperative Convergence Research on Lunar Exploration," accessed on May 6, 2020, https://www.kari.re.kr/eng/sub03_04_02.do#link.

92 Article 5(2) of the Space Development Promotion Act.

93 *Supra* Chapter 2 §2.1.

94 Articles 5(3) and (4) of the Space Development Promotion Act.

Furthermore, the Minister of Science and ICT, in accordance with the basic plan, formulates and executes the Action Plan for the Promotion of Space Development every year in consultation with the heads of relevant administrative agencies.[95]

6.2 *The Master and Action Plans for the Utilization of Satellite Data*

Article 5-3 of the Space Development Promotion Act provides that the government shall formulate the Master Plan for the Utilization of Satellite Data every five years in order to promote the dissemination and utilization of satellite data. The master plan covers all aspects of satellite data policy, including how to train satellite data experts and develop relevant technologies.

The Action Plan for Utilization of Satellite Data is announced annually in the same procedure as the aforementioned Action Plan for Promotion of Space Development.

6.3 *The Basic and Action Plans to Prepare for Hazards in Space*

Every ten years, the Korean government formulates the Basic Plan to Prepare for Hazards in Space, which includes environmental protection of outer space, hazards predictions in outer space, research on the prevention of space hazards, and international cooperation in this respect.[96] The Basic Plan also covers issues involving collisions of space objects, ranging from artificial to natural, including near-Earth objects (NEOs).

Like the other action plans discussed above, the Action Plan to Prepare for Hazards in Space is announced annually by the Minister of Science and ICT.[97]

6.4 *The Basic and Action Plans for Aerospace Industry Development*

Unlike all of the aforementioned plans formulated according to the Space Development Promotion Act under the oversight of the Ministry of Science and ICT, the Basic and Action Plan for Aerospace Industry Development is based on the Aerospace Industry Development Promotion Act under the authority of the Ministry of Trade, Industry and Energy.

With the primary objective to foster and develop the aerospace industry for economic benefits, the basic plan is established every ten years, and its action plan is announced and executed every year.[98] The Aerospace

95 Article 5-2 of the Space Development Promotion Act.
96 Article 15 of the Space Development Promotion Act. Details will be addressed in Chapter 5.
97 Article 15-2 of the Space Development Promotion Act.
98 Article 3 of the Aerospace Industry Development Promotion Act.

Industry Development Policy Council deliberates on the drafts of such plans.[99]

7 An Overview of the Recent Major National Space Plans

7.1 *The Third Basic Plan for the Promotion of Space Development (2018–2022)*

The Third Basic Plan for Promotion of Space Development was announced on February 5, 2018, under the title of "Korea's New Challenge for Space" for the years 2018 to 2022.[100] The Korean government unveiled a new policy to reform the nation's space development system, expecting gradual growth in the domestic space industry.

The third basic plan includes six strategic targets of (i) achieving self-sufficiency of space launch vehicle technology, (ii) advancing satellite technology and relevant services, (iii) embarking on space exploration, (iv) establishing a Korea Positioning System (KPS), (v) creating a space innovation environment, and (vi) promoting the space industry and job creation. Details of each strategy are explored in the following subsections.

7.1.1 Self-Sufficiency of Space Launch Vehicle Technology

This first objective refers to the completion of the second Korean launch vehicle, KSLV-II,[101] and the launch service program thereafter. The government stated in the third basic plan that the mass production of launch vehicles would be ready through its follow-up research and development program so that launch services by private entities could be provided from 2026. The government further mentioned that private companies would lead and operate all launch service systems for small and medium satellites beginning in 2030.[102]

7.1.2 Initiation of Space Exploration

The current lunar exploration program, KLEP,[103] is in its phase 1 (Lunar Orbiter) scheduled to be completed by 2022. The preliminary task for phase

99 Article 14 of the Aerospace Industry Development Promotion Act.

100 Press release by the Ministry of Science and ICT on February 5, 2018, "우주를 향한 대한민국의 새로운 도전 (South Korea's New Challenge for Space [English title added])," available at https://www.msit.go.kr/web/msipContents/contentsView.do?cateId=_policycom2&artId=1374583.

101 Korea Space Launch Vehicle (KSLV)-II. *Supra* Chapter 2 §5.2.

102 *Supra* Chapter 2, n. 100, press release at 6.

103 Korea Lunar Exploration Program (KLEP). *Supra* Chapter 2 §5.5.

2 (Lunar Lander), meanwhile, began in 2019. According to phase 2 of KLEP, the lunar lander will lift off to the Moon in 2030, fly over to an asteroid, and return to the Earth by 2035. To that end, the government stated that it would commence the development of docking and re-entry technologies in 2021 to prepare for phase 2 beforehand.[104]

7.1.3 Enhancement of Satellite Utilization Service

This strategy focuses on advanced satellite services provided by national satellites to increase the utilization of satellite data. The service sectors under this strategy include the natural disaster response service, the reporting service to the public in agricultural and fishery industries, the navigation correction service, and the monitoring service of the Korean Peninsula. The government noted that the natural disaster response service, in particular, will be available in 2022 by reducing the current interval between images through more upgraded small satellites, the government mentioned. In addition, the navigation correction service will be executed by 2022, which provides more accurate data service with an error range of less than 1 meter (3 feet).[105]

7.1.4 Development of the Korea Positioning System (KPS)

South Korea has initiated the development of its own navigation system, the Korea Positioning System (KPS). Three GEO[106] satellites and five GIO[107] satellites, eight in total, will cover the vicinity of the Korean Peninsula (see Figure 3, the GEO satellites are in orange and the GIOs in yellow). The KPS expert group is conducting comprehensive research on the required technologies and resources as well as organizing international collaboration. The initial phase of the project that began in 2020 includes constructing the on-ground test center, building payloads, and securing necessary frequencies. The main project commenced in earnest in 2022. The government stated that the full service of KPS would be provided from 2035.[108]

7.1.5 Creation of Space Development-Friendly Environment

The Korean government is working to create an environment where various entities can participate in space development. As part of this effort, the

104 *Supra* Chapter 2, n. 100, press release at 7.
105 *Supra* Chapter 2, n. 100, press release at 8–9.
106 Geosynchronous Equatorial Orbit (GEO), also referred to as a geostationary orbit, which is a special type of geosynchronous orbit with an inclination of zero degrees.
107 Geosynchronous Inclined Orbit (GIO).
108 *Supra* Chapter 2, n. 100, press release at 9.

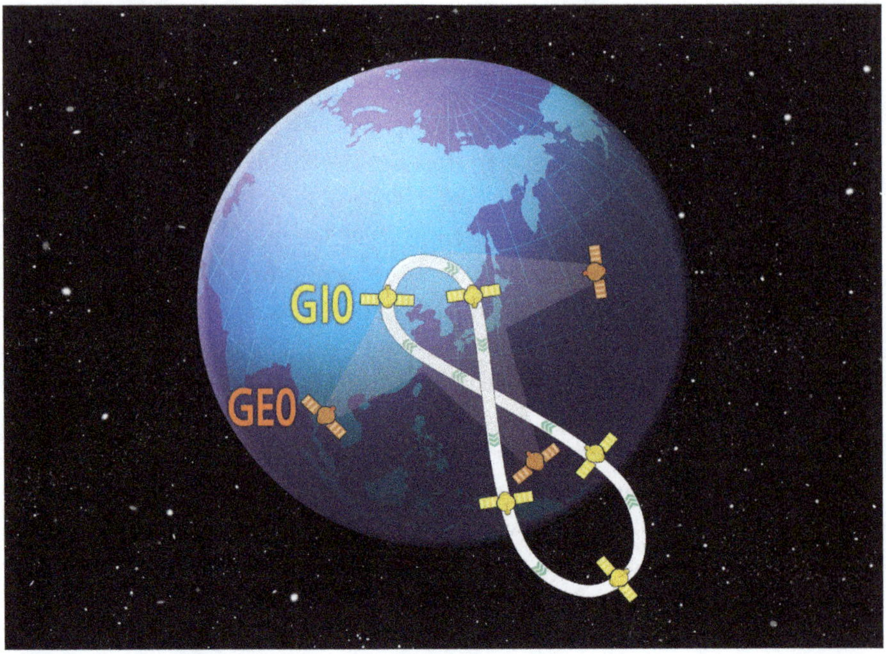

FIGURE 3 Schematic diagram of the Korea Positioning System (KPS)

government announced that KARI would gradually shift its role from what was implementing all national space projects into focusing on core technology developments that are difficult for the private sector to conduct. The government also added that it would expand global space cooperation in which South Korea and the countries concerned mutually complement each other's needs.[109]

7.1.6 Promotion of Space Industry and Job Creation

In order to reflect diverse opinions in promoting the space industry, the government has decided to actively involve the private sector in the National Space Council and the Space Development Promotion Working Committee. Besides, with regard to the development of national satellites, the private sector will be executing the next project beginning with the NEXTSat (Next-Generation Satellite)-2,[110] which was previously exclusive to KARI and KAIST. By shifting to

109 *Supra* Chapter 2, n. 100, press release at 9–10.

110 *Supra* Chapter 2 §5.3.

such an industry-led manufacturing system, the government expects to create new jobs in the space field.[111]

7.2 *The Basic Plan for Fosterage of Civil Space Industry* (2019–2023)

The Korean government finalized its plan to foster the civil space industry for the upcoming five years through the 15th National Space Committee on January 7, 2019.[112] This plan is based on Article 18 of the Space Development Promotion Act, which provides that the Minister of Science and ICT shall adopt measures to promote space development and expand investments in research and development for the private sector.

Until recently, South Korea's space industry – except for telecommunications, broadcasting, and navigation service sector – was in its early stages and mostly consisted of small and medium-sized businesses. To promote the industry, the government unveiled its plan to expand the space market's size to 3.7 trillion Korean Won (approximately USD 3.1 billion) by 2021. Mr. Yoo, the Minister of Science and ICT, remarked that "Outer space has been a dream of humanity and is an arena that will grow into a high value-added industry in the near future." He also assured that "The government will continue to foster a more dynamic and efficient space industry."[113]

7.3 *The Second Master Plan for Utilization of Satellite Data* (2019–2023)

The Second Master Plan for Utilization of Satellite Data was unveiled on January 7, 2019, together with the aforementioned Basic Plan for Fosterage of Civil Space Industry.[114] The government presented a new national strategy for utilizing satellite data and providing relevant services in the era of the fourth industrial revolution.

---

111 *Supra* Chapter 2, n. 100, press release at 10–11.

112 Press release by the Ministry of Science and ICT on January 10, 2019, "정부, 민간주도 우주개발 생태계조성으로 미래 혁신성장동력을 창출한다 (The government, creating innovative space environment led by the private sector [English title added])," available at http://www.korea.kr/news/pressReleaseView.do?newsId=156312526.

113 Yonhap News, January 9, 2019, "우주개발 민간주도 전환, 2021년 우주산업 3조7천억으로 확대 (Shift to private sector-led space development, economic expansion of space industry to 3.7 trillion Korean won by 2021 [English title added])," https://www.yna.co.kr/view/AKR20190109070300017?input=1195m.

114 *Supra* Chapter 2, n. 112, press release at 5–10; Press release by the Ministry of Science and ICT on February 28, 2019, "The Second Master Plan for Promotion of Utilization of Satellite Data [English title added]," available at http://www.korea.kr/archive/expDocView.do?docId=38652.

The Ministry of Science and ICT stated in its press release, "The government has already begun creating an integrated satellite data system in 2019 and will complete the establishment of a national center for satellite data operation by 2022." It further noted that each government department – including the Ministry of Environment, the Ministry of Maritime Affairs and Fisheries, and the Ministry of Land, Infrastructure and Transport – is working to develop ideas on how to utilize satellite data and promote the industry from their respective viewpoints. In addition, the government stated that it would increase the number of satellite images acquired from global satellites by building a satellite operating system in cooperation with South America, such as Peru and Argentina.[115]

8 Concluding Remarks

This chapter has explored South Korea's space activities from its early beginnings to the present and future outlook. South Korea's space program has come a long way since its inception in the 1990s, with a focus on developing and acquiring indigenous satellite technologies and launch capabilities led by the government. Currently, South Korea is transitioning towards a more private sector-led space development and activities while transferring the government-owned technologies to the private companies. This shift is expected to attract diverse entrants to space activities and bring about more innovative and dynamic developments in the industry.

Notably, South Korea's space program is characterized by its systematic implementation, with the government periodically announcing its new and/or revised space plans in accordance with relevant national space laws. This has enabled the country to make significant strides in the space sector over the past three decades.

The transition towards a private sector-led approach requires careful attention to the legal framework governing private space activities. As new players enter the market, it becomes increasingly crucial to ensure that national space laws keep pace with the evolving industry and effectively address legal challenges. This will promote safe, responsible, and sustainable space activities in South Korea.

115 *Ibid*, press release on February 28, 2019, at 10.

CHAPTER 3

An Analysis of the Aerospace Industry Development Promotion Act

1 Introduction

The "Aerospace Industry Development Promotion Act" was enacted on December 4, 1987, with the repeal of the 'Aviation' Industry Promotion Act of 1978,[1] and entered into force on December 5, 1988. The Act reflects South Korea's passions and commitments in the late 1980s to promote not only the aviation industry but also the space sector.

After a year since the Act's enforcement, the Presidential Decree of the Act was issued and came into force on December 13, 1989, followed by the Ordinance of the Ministry of Trade, Industry and Energy which became effective on March 8, 1990. These secondary regulations provide legally enforceable rules and procedures for implementing principles set out in the Act. Since their enactment, the Act and the secondary regulations have undergone several partial amendments.

In addition, the Administrative Rules and Municipal Ordinance pertaining to a specialized complex for the aerospace industry, which will be discussed in this chapter, were issued to establish internal guidelines and work standards within the administrative agencies.

The Aerospace Industry Development Promotion Act does not exclusively or specifically deal with space activities that squarely fall under international space law. However, national space legislation in the broadest sense could encompass "every legal or regulatory regime having a significant impact, even if implicitly or indirectly, on at least one type of space activity or major space application."[2] From this perspective, the Act establishing the nation's fundamental notion of space law and policy could be regarded as part of South Korea's space legislation. Indeed, the Act has paved the way for South Korea's current space development, which makes it meaningful to briefly explore the Act ahead of other laws.

1 Enacted and came into force on December 5, 1978, under Act No. 3124, abolished on December 5, 1988, under Act No. 3991.

2 *Supra* Chapter 1, n. 11, Frans von der Dunk, Handbook of Space Law, xxvi. *See* also, Frans von der Dunk, Advanced Introduction to Space Law (2020), 9, 115.

 | DOI:10.1163/9789004694743_005

1.1 *Legislative History*

A draft bill on the aerospace industry development was proposed on October 16, 1987, by members of the National Assembly.[3] Their proposal pointed out that the existing 'Aviation' Industry Promotion Act merely focused on aviation despite the fact that systematic and better-organized space research and development would be essential for the coming twenty-first century. It further emphasized that, by enacting a new law covering the space sector along with the aviation business, South Korea could establish a comprehensive industrial system in preparation for a rapidly changing aerospace era, with the aim of developing the aerospace industry into a new export business.[4]

The legislative process proceeded expeditiously in the National Assembly after the proposal. The Commerce and Industry Committee reviewed the draft bill's contents from an economic perspective, and then the Legislation and Judiciary Committee examined its phraseology from a legal point of view. The reviewed bill was submitted to the Plenary Session of the National Assembly and finally approved on October 30, 1987. The South Korean President promulgated the "Aerospace Industry Development Promotion Act" on December 4, 1987, which came into force a year later, on December 5, 1988, pursuant to Article 1 of its Addenda.

1.2 *The Structure and Purpose of the Act*

At the time of enactment, this Act had consisted of twenty-four articles, but currently, sixteen articles remain as some articles have been abolished (see Table 1) due to the achievements of its objectives or in line with the changes in the aerospace industry. The Act provides for the formulation of aerospace industry development policies and the adoption of policy measures to promote the industry. It also stipulates the designation of or support for the aerospace-specialized complexes as well as the performance and quality inspection of aerospace products such as aerospace craft and other related apparatuses.

Article 1 of the Act prescribes that "the purpose of this Act is to 'contribute to the sound development of the national economy and the improvement of people's lives' by rationally supporting and promoting the aerospace industry,

---

3 The National Assembly Bill Information, "The Draft of the Aerospace Industry Development Promotion Act (October 16, 1987) [English title added]," at 1, available at http://likms.assembly.go.kr/bill/billDetail.do?billId=010578&ageFrom=21&ageTo=2. In South Korea's legislative process, members of the National Assembly or ministries of the government can propose a bill. Either way, it is required to pass through the National Assembly in order to become law, and there is no difference in legal effect between the two.

4 The 137th minutes of the National Assembly, at 23.

TABLE 1 Contents of the Aerospace Industry Development Promotion Act

Articles	Contents
1	Purposes
2	Definitions
3	Establishment of a Basic Plan for Aerospace Industry Development
4	Fosterage of the Aerospace Industry
5 to 8 [a]	*Repealed* [b]
8 *bis*	Designation of and Support for a Specialized Complex for the Aerospace Industry
9 [c]	*Repealed* [d]
10, 11, 19, and 22	Performance and Quality Inspection, Delegation and Entrustment of Inspection Authority, Inspection Fees, Penalties
12 to 13	Financial Support and Lending of State-Owned Facilities
14 to 16	Establishment of Aerospace Industry Development Policy Council
17, 17 *bis*, and 18 [e]	*Repealed* [f]
23 to 24 [g]	*Repealed* [h]

a Those were provisions related to a designation of and support for a "Specified Business Entity." Once designated as a "Specified Business Entity," preferential support under the Act might be provided by the government.

b On January 28, 2015, by Act No. 13097. The reason for the abolishment is as follows: The system of a "Specified Business Entity," which allowed the government to provide various support for such entity, was originally established for the purpose of efficiently fostering industries and preventing duplicate investments. However, 1) now that the original purpose has been achieved, and 2) if the system continues to be maintained, there is a concern that fair competition in the market may be hindered.

c Article 9 was about a mandatory report by a business entity in advance of suspension and discontinuation of business.

d On February 5, 1999, by Act No. 5774, in order to enhance the competitiveness of the aerospace industry by removing the regulations.

e Those were about an establishment of research institution in the aerospace sector.

f On January 29, 1999, by Act No. 5733, because a special "Act on the Establishment, Operation and Fostering of Government-Funded Research Institutes" was enacted.

g Article 23 was about administrative fine related to a mandatory report. Article 24 provided that details necessary for the enforcement of the Act shall be determined by the Presidential Decree.

h On February 5, 1999, by Act No. 5774, in order to promote competition in a deregulated aerospace industry.

and efficiently researching and developing aerospace science and technology." In this regard, as far as the space sector is concerned, a question may arise as to whether the purpose of this Act overlaps with that of the Space Development Promotion Act of 2005,[5] since the two Acts contain the same ultimate goal set out in their Article 1, which is to "contribute to the sound development of the national economy and the improvement of people's lives." Indeed, there was such a discussion in the course of enacting the Space Development Promotion Act regarding how to establish a proper relation between the two Acts. Two significant features lie in distinguishing this Act from the Space Development Promotion Act. While the Space Development Promotion Act is solely dedicated to the space sector, this Act deals with not only the space sector but also the aviation sector. In addition, this Act focuses more on the industrial activities carried out on Earth. Specifically, this Act concentrates on the space-related manufacturing industry and its business aspects, whereas the Space Development Promotion Act pays special attention to the space activities and concomitant affairs that will directly lead to activities in outer space and their benefits.[6]

2 The Definitions of the Terms in the Act

Article 2 provides definitions of seven terms used in the Act, which include "aerospace industry," "business entity engaged in the aerospace industry," "aircraft," "spacecraft," "related accessory apparatus," "related materials," and "aerospace science and technology." Among these, terms and definitions associated with the space sector are as follows:

i. The term "aerospace industry" means a business of producing[7] aircraft, spacecraft, related accessory apparatus or materials and an application services business[8] using aircraft and spacecraft as

5 The Space Development Promotion Act was enacted and entered into force in 2005, which is considered South Korea's key national space law implementing international obligations. *See* further, Chapter 5.

6 Details will be addressed in Chapter 5.

7 Including manufacturing, processing, assembling, overhauling, modifying, or repairing them, but excluding such work as conducted by an operator for flight, such as maintenance, repair, and modification of aircraft under subparagraph 1 of Article 2 of the Aviation Safety Act.

8 Excluding air transportation business and aircraft-using business under the Aviation Business Act.

prescribed by Ordinance of the Ministry of Trade, Industry and Energy.[9]

ii. The term "spacecraft" means space launch vehicles, aerospace ships, artificial satellites, crewed or crewless spaceships flying in and outside the atmosphere of the Earth and other vehicles used for space flight prescribed by Presidential Decree.[10]

iii. The term "related accessory apparatus" means components of aircraft or spacecraft.

iv. The term "related materials" means materials used for the production of aircraft or spacecraft.

v. The term "aerospace science and technology" means the science and technology related to the aerospace industry or the flight in and outside the Earth's atmosphere, or the applied science and technology related to aircraft and spacecraft.

The terms defined above, along with Article 1 which lays down the Act's purposes, offer fundamental insights into the main focus of the Act, which is the aerospace industry, specifically its manufacturing aspect.

3 Major Provisions of the Act

3.1 *The Establishment of the Basic Plan for Aerospace Industrial Development*

According to Article 3(1) of the Act, the Korean government is required to formulate a plan for the development of the aerospace industry, which includes aims, implementation strategies, a comprehensive research system, budgets, financing, investment strategies, training for professionals, international cooperation, a specialized aerospace industrial complex, and "other matters prescribed by Presidential Decree." Under the aegis of this provision, Article 3(3) of the Presidential Decree provides that "other matters" in the Act mean matters concerning the dissemination of research results of the aerospace science and technology, protection and management of the relevant intellectual property rights thereof, and promotion for mutual exchange and understanding of such technologies.

---

9 Despite of this mandate saying "as prescribed by Ordinance of the Ministry of Trade, Industry and Energy" under Article 2(1) of the Act, no such detail can be found in the Ordinance.

10 Article 2 of the Presidential Decree stipulates that "other vehicles used for space flight" include a space station, a space ballistic missile, a transfer-orbit propellent rocket, an orbital vehicle, and a space flight training system.

In compliance with the framework above, the Korean government initiated a project to formulate a national space plan in July 1994, followed by a public hearing to discuss a draft on September 19, 1995. After considerable consultation with relevant ministries, South Korea's first space program, the "Mid-to Long-Term Basic Plan for the Promotion of Space Development," was finally released on April 30, 1996.[11] The government mentioned in a statement that it aimed to lay the groundwork for South Korea to become one of the world's space powers in the coming twenty-first century and to promote the efficient utilization of research and development resources by systematically facilitating technology development in the space sector. The plan presented four goals: i) to set up a system linking industries, universities, and research institutes in order to strengthen comprehensive coordination in space technology, ii) to develop satellites, sounding rockets and launch vehicles by employing domestic technology by 2010, iii) to place a total of nineteen satellites in orbit by 2015, and vi) to become one of the top ten countries in the global space industry by 2015.[12]

This initial plan was slightly modified to advance the target year after North Korea allegedly succeeded in launching its first satellite aboard a multi-stage rocket on August 31, 1998, which stimulated South Korea to secure its own launch capability. South Korea expedited the implementation of its space plan accordingly. Under the plan, the first outcome was a two-stage KSR-III rocket[13] launched in 2002 from Anheung Proving Ground of South Korea. With key technologies demonstrated during the KSR-III rocket project, the government immediately embarked on developing its first space launch vehicle, KSLV-I.[14] In addition, a science and technology satellite, STSAT-2, was developed in 2005, which was planned to be launched on KSLV-I from South Korean soil for the first time.[15]

Meanwhile, as the Space Development Promotion Act was enacted in 2005, the existing "Mid-to Long-Term Basic Plan for the Promotion of Space

11 The National Archives of Korea, "우주개발중장기기본계획 (the Mid-to Long-Term Basic Plan for the Promotion of Space Development [English Title added])," by the Minister of Science and Technology on April 30, 2019, p. 233, available at, https://www.archives.go.kr/next/search/showDetailPopup.do?rc_code=1310377&rc_rfile_no=200802067513&rc_ritem_no=000000000009.

12 *Ibid.* at 221.

13 *Supra* Chapter 2 §5.1.

14 *Supra* Chapter 2 §5.2.

15 Unfortunately, as the first and second launch attempts of KSLV-I in 2009 and 2010 failed, a STSAT-2 satellite could not be placed into orbit.

Development" was renamed the "Basic Plan for the Promotion of Space Development" under the new law.[16]

3.2 *The Promotion of the Aerospace Industry*

Article 4(1) of the Act stipulates that the government shall adopt policy measures to perform projects for the aerospace industry such as the development of spacecraft, the manufacturing of the performance and quality test equipment, the training of specialists, the advancement of spacecraft technology, and 'other projects' prescribed by Presidential Decree.[17] Article 7 *bis* (1) of the Presidential Decree provides that 'other projects' include international joint space development and improvement or remodeling of spacecraft.

Article 4(2) of the Act further stipulates that the government may have certain institutes conduct such projects,[18] which is a primary legal basis whereby KARI[19] was established in 1989 and selected as the leading research institute of

---

16 Details will be addressed in Chapter 5.

17 The author extracted projects relevant to the space sector from Article 4(1). The whole list of examples of projects provided by Article 4(1) is as follows:
1. Projects for the development of passenger aircraft, cargo aircraft, and unmanned aircraft;
2. Projects for the development of utility rotorcraft and attack rotorcraft;
3. Projects for the development of spacecraft;
4. Projects for the development of technologies available for apparatus and materials;
5. Projects for the development of equipment and training of specialized personnel necessary to test the performance and quality of aircraft, spacecraft, apparatus, and materials;
6. Projects for the advancement of test and assessment technology for aircraft, spacecraft, apparatus, and materials; and
7. Other projects prescribed by Presidential Decree to develop the aerospace industry.

18 Article 4(2) stipulates that the government may have any of the following persons perform the projects as referred to in paragraph (1):
1. National or public research institutes;
2. Specific research institutes under Article 2 of the Support of Specific Research Institutes Act, research institutes under Article 8 of the Act on the Establishment, Operation and Fostering of Government-Funded Research Institutes, research institutes under Article 8 of the Act on the Establishment, Operation and Fostering of Government-Funded Science and Technology Research Institutes and the Agency for Defense Development under Article 3 of the Act on Agency for Defense Development;
3. Universities, colleges, industrial colleges, junior colleges, or technical colleges under Article 2 of the Higher Education Act;
4. Specialized industrial technology institutes under Article 42 of the Industrial Technology Innovation Promotion Act; and
5. Institutions, organizations, or business entities in relation to the aerospace industry and related technologies, prescribed by Presidential Decree.

19 *Supra* Chapter 2 §3.1.

South Korea's space programs. It can be said that the history of Korean space development began in earnest from here.

3.3 *The Designation of and Support for Specialized Aerospace Industrial Complex*

The Act, as amended on April 5, 2013, introduced the concept of a specialized aerospace industrial complex to promote the aerospace industry. In terms of the purpose and relation between this Act and the Space Development Promotion Act of 2005 as mentioned earlier, the government's intention appears to support that this Act will still cover the development of the space industry even after the implementation of the Space Development Promotion Act in 2005, given that the government inserted a new provision in 2013 into this Act rather than the Space Development Promotion Act.

A specialized aerospace industrial complex is specified as follows. Pursuant to Article 8 *bis* (1), the Minister of Trade, Industry and Energy may designate an area in which enterprises related to the aerospace industry are collectively located or intend to be located as a specialized complex or may support such area. In addition, Article 8 *bis* (2) stipulates that the nation may financially support a local government having jurisdiction over the area in which a specialized complex is situated.

Details related to a specialized complex are set out in the Presidential Decree and the Administrative Rules of this Act. Article 9 *bis* of the Presidential Decree provides that at least ten business entities engaging in the aerospace industry are required to collectively move to or be scheduled to move to an industrial complex. The Administrative Rule of the Act elaborates on the requirements and guidelines for the designation and management of a specialized complex.

Accordingly, on August 7, 2014, the Minister of Trade, Industry and Energy designated a city called Sacheon as a specialized complex according to Article 8 *bis* (1) of the Act with government funding as outlined in Article 8 *bis* (2) of the Act.[20] In response to that, the city Sacheon promulgated the "Municipal Ordinance on the Management of Sacheon Specialized Aerospace Industrial Complex" on March 31, 2016, to efficiently and systematically develop and operate the complex. This whole process illustrates how the central and local governments of South Korea have been cooperating in promoting the private aerospace industry in accordance with the Act. The establishment of such

20 Sacheon, "Support for the specialized aerospace complex," accessed on September 28, 2020, https://www.sacheon.go.kr/aerospace/02811/02813.web.

a specialized complex will likely contribute to the concentration of South Korea's space development capacities.

3.4 *The Performance and Quality Inspection*

Business entities producing aerospace craft or other relevant apparatuses are subject to a performance and quality inspection directed by the Minister of Trade, Industry and Energy according to Article 10(1) of the Act. For such an inspection, the Minister of Trade, Industry and Energy may delegate or entrust the inspection affairs to another administrative agency or specialized inspection institution.[21] KARI was accordingly designated as a specialized institution in 1992.

Any products that have not been inspected as per Article 10 shall not be used except for testing purposes only.[22] In case of violating such obligation, fines are imposed not only on the violator[23] but also on the corporation to which the violator belongs.[24]

The aim of the inspection would be to ensure that a certain aerospace product manufactured in South Korea fulfills the required standards at an international level. This process appears to be necessary for the sustainable development of the Korean private space industry.

3.5 *Financial Support and Lending State-Owned Facilities*

The Korean government may provide long-term low-interest loans or research funds to foster the aerospace industry, develop aerospace science and technology, and hold aerospace science and technology exhibitions.[25] If necessary for the research, development, or production of aerospace craft or apparatuses, the government may, gratuitously or onerously, lend state-owned facilities to business entities engaged in the aerospace industry or have them use those facilities.[26] Conditions and procedures for the loan and usage are prescribed in Article 11 of the Presidential Decree.[27]

The aerospace industry has high entry barriers in terms of capital and technology, but once successfully entered, it can generate stable profits and create quality jobs in the long run. The market size of South Korea's aerospace

21 Article 10(2) of the Aerospace Industry Development Promotion Act.
22 Article 11 of the same Act.
23 Article 21 of the same Act.
24 Article 22 of the same Act.
25 Article 12 of the same Act.
26 Article 13(1) of the same Act.
27 Article 13(2) of the same Act.

industry is still significantly smaller than that of its other manufacturing industries, such as automobiles and general machinery, despite its steady growth since the 1980s. Besides, investment in space research and development is not yet sufficient. In this regard, the provisions mentioned above could serve as a legal basis for governmental supports for South Korea's aerospace industry, given that the aerospace industry is characterized by a long payback period with massive investment, and thus governmental supports in this sector are not uncommon worldwide.

3.6 *The Establishment of the Aerospace Industry Development Policy Council*

The Aerospace Industry Development Policy Council, established under the Minister of Trade, Industry and Energy, comprises no more than fifteen members, including a chairperson.[28] The Council deliberates on matters concerning the formulation of the aforementioned basic plan for aerospace industry development,[29] as well as the policy coordination between the government and the relevant ministries, budgeting for the execution of the plan, and the general control of the aerospace research and development.[30]

However, since the "Space Development Promotion Act" entered into force in 2005, the role of the Aerospace Industry Development Policy Council has somewhat diminished as a dedicated space plan by the "National Space Committee" has been implemented under the new Act of 2005. Indeed, as far as space planning is concerned, there seems to be some overlap of role between the Council under this Act and the "National Space Committee" under the "Space Development Promotion Act." Despite the fact that this Act deals with the aerospace industry in general whereas the "Space Development Promotion Act" addresses space activities under international space law, the complete separation of industrial aspects from space planning conducted under the "Space Development Promotion Act" is unlikely to be easy in light of the nature of space development. In this regard, it seems inevitable to adjust or rearrange their role in order to prevent duplication of work and achieve efficiency moving forward.

---

28 Articles 14 and 16 of the same Act.

29 *Supra* Chapter 3 §3.1.

30 Article 15 of the same Act.

4 An Assessment of the Act

The Aerospace Industry Development Promotion Act is mostly silent when it comes to international obligations under the four UN space treaties of which South Korea is a member State. Specifically, as discussed in Chapter 1, South Korea is required to implement the core principles set forth in the international space treaties – most notably, such as the norm of "international responsibility for national activities in outer space" pursuant to Article VI of the Outer Space Treaty[31] and the concept of the "launching State" bearing international liability for damage caused by space objects under both Article VII of the Outer Space Treaty and the Liability Convention.[32]

Nonetheless, the Aerospace Industry Development Promotion Act does not explicitly deal with the activities in outer space or with the general launch activities. This is perhaps partly because, by the time of the Act's enactment, South Korea failed to thoroughly contemplate what the nation's space development would be like in the coming decades and/or what international obligations under the UN space treaties should be entailed in conducting space activities.

It was not until 1996 that South Korea planned its first space program, at which point the nation lacked the necessary infrastructure to execute it. Thus, constructing essential facilities with advanced technologies and trained personnel might have been the nation's priority, as evidenced by some provisions of the Aerospace Industry Development Promotion Act. This explains why the Space Development Promotion Act of 2005[33] was necessary to advance South Korea's space missions and to commence its domestic launch activities in the 2000s.

5 Concluding Remarks

This chapter examined the space-related provisions of the Aerospace Industry Development Promotion Act primarily from South Korea's policymaking perspective.

Under this Act, South Korea's first space program commenced in the mid-1990s with the establishment of the Korea Aerospace Research Institute (KARI), which was pivotal in the nation's space missions.

---

31 *Supra* Chapter 1 §1.1.2.

32 *Supra* Chapter 1 §1.1.3 and §1.3.2.

33 The "Space Development Promotion Act" will be examined in detail in Chapter 5.

In order to promote South Korea's space industry as a whole, the government has implemented policy measures based on the Act's guidelines, including financial support, lending government-owned facilities, and fostering a specialized complex to concentrate the nation's human resources and space capabilities.

The beauty of this Act is that it laid the foundation for South Korea's current space activities in terms of national policymaking and infrastructure setting. It has served as a platform for the nation to continue developing its space industry, leading to the implementation of a national space law to fulfill obligations under the international space law regime, as will be discussed in the subsequent chapters.

CHAPTER 4

An Analysis of the Radio Waves Act

1 Introduction

The telecommunications industry around the globe has been growing rapidly with the increasing demand for satellite-based services that are indispensable in our daily lives. The telecommunications sector in South Korea is mostly governed by two Acts: the first Act is the Telecommunications Business Act as explored in Chapter 1 in relation to the ITSO and the WTO regimes,[1] and the second Act is the Radio Waves Act that mainly deals with the fundamentals of frequencies and satellite communications in accordance with the ITU regime.[2]

The Radio Waves Act was enacted on December 30, 1961, and commenced enforcement on January 1, 1962. After several minor revisions, the Act was completely amended in 2000,[3] instituting new chapters regarding spectrum management and space communications. The 2000 Amendments aimed to better

1 *See supra* Chapter 1 §2.2.2.2. and §2.4.2.

2 Other Korean national laws relevant to the telecommunications sector are as follows:

i. The Broadcasting Act: enacted on December 16, 1963, entered into force on January 1, 1964 (Act No. 1535) as partially amended on December 8, 2020 (Act No. 17632). This Act addresses license, approval, registration concerning the operation of a terrestrial broadcasting business.

ii. The Internet Multimedia Broadcasting Business Act: enacted on January 17, 2008, entered into force on April 18, 2008 (Act No. 8849) as partially amended on December 29, 2020 (Act No. 17799). The purpose of this Act is to ensure the proper operation of broadcasting business using internet multimedia where broadcasting and telecommunications are converged.

iii. The Promotion of Communications Network Utilization and Information Protection Act: enacted on May 12, 1986 (Act No. 3848), as partially amended on June 9, 2020 (Act No. 17358). As indicated by its title, this Act focuses on facilitating the sound utilization and protection of information via communications networks.

iv. The Broadcasting Communications Development Framework Act: enacted on March 22, entered into force on September 23, 2010, (Act No. 10165) as partially amended on December 10, 2019, (Act No. 16751). The purpose of this Act is to contribute to the development of broadcasting communications, in response to a new communications environment in which broadcasting and telecommunications are merged, by prescribing such matters as the promotion of broadcasting communications and technical standards for broadcasting communications. Broadcasting communications is governed by this Act unless provided otherwise in other statutes (Article 6 of the Broadcasting Communications Development Framework Act).

3 Additional minor revisions have also been made since 2000.

 | DOI:10.1163/9789004694743_006

implement the ITU principles and requirements as its member State.[4] Notably, the introduction of the space communications chapter makes it clear that the Radio Waves Act applies to space telecommunications as well.

The latest Radio Waves Act[5] consists of ten chapters with one hundred thirty articles (see Table 2).[6] The Act's purpose is to facilitate the efficient and safe utilization of frequency bands by developing technologies and promoting related industries.[7]

The Radio Waves Act is supplemented by a Presidential Decree[8] and the Administrative Rules of the Radio Waves Act,[9] as well as the Regulations on Technical Standards of Broadcasting and Communications Facilities[10] and the Ordinance for Technical Standards of Radio Facilities.[11]

2 The Definitions of the Terms in the Act

Article 2 of the Radio Waves Act provides definitions for the terms that help to explain the overall contents of the Act. To begin with, the term "radio waves," the primary and fundamental concept in the Act, which also appears in its title, is defined in subparagraph 1 of Article 2 as "electromagnetic waves which propagate in space without any artificial guidance *within the range of frequency spectrum determined by the International Telecommunication Union*."[12] In comparison, the Radio Regulations, which complement the ITU Constitution and the Convention,[13] define "radio waves" as "[e]lectromagnetic waves of frequencies arbitrarily lower than 3000 GHz, propagated in space without any artificial guide."[14] Given that the definition provided by the Act does not fix the scope

---

4 *See* Chapter 1 §2.1.2.2.

5 As of August 2022.

6 Act No. 17355, partially amended on June 9, 2020, entered into force on December 10, 2020.

7 Article 1 of the Radio Waves Act.

8 Enacted and entered into force on March 10, 1962, Presidential Decree No. 531, partially amended on January 5, 2021, Presidential Decree No. 31380.

9 Enacted and entered into force on May 23, 2014, Administrative Rules No. 19, partially amended on December 24, 2020, Administrative Rules No. 60.

10 Enacted and entered into force on February 29, 2008, Presidential Decree No. 20664, partially amended on January 5, 2021, Presidential Decree No. 31380.

11 Enacted on August 12, 2016, Administrative Rules No. 78 (by the Ministry of Future Creation and Science), partially amended on December 24, 2020, Administrative Rules No. 63 (by the Ministry of Science and ICT).

12 Italics added.

13 *Supra* Chapter 1 §2.1.2.

14 No. 1.5 of the Radio Regulations.

TABLE 2 The composition of the Radio Waves Act

Chapters	Titles and contents
1	General Provisions: Purposes, Terms, and Definitions
2	Securing Spectrum Resources: Master Plan for the Utilization of Frequencies
3	Allocation, Assignment, and Designation of Spectrum Resources
4	Use of Spectrum Resources – Section 1 Authorization for and Operation of Stations – Section 2 Authorization to Establish Broadcasting Stations and Operation Thereof – Section 3 Operation of Space Communications
5	Preservation of Spectrum Resources: Master Plans for Space Weather Disaster Management
5 *bis*	Management of Broadcasting and Communications Equipment – Section 1 Conformity Assessment of Broadcasting and Communications Equipment – Section 2 International Cooperation and Follow-Up Management of Broadcasting and Communications Equipment
6	Promotion of Spectrum Resources: Research, Development, and Standardization of Technologies, and Facilitation of International Cooperation.
7	Operators: Qualifications and Posting of Operators at Stations
8	Supplementary Provisions: Revocation of Authorization or Qualification, Hearings, and Delegation or Entrustment of Authority
9	Penalties

of the frequency spectrum at the national level but rather refers to the scope determined by the ITU regime, it seems to be flexible and properly set within the ITU framework.

Subparagraphs 2 to 4 of Article 2 define the "allocation," "assignment," and "designation" of frequencies, respectively. Such definitions were added to the 2000 Amendments.

First, the definition of "allocation of the frequencies" is "determining the purpose and usage of specified frequencies." When interpreted in conjunction with Article 9(3) of the Act, the term "allocation of frequencies" ultimately appears to indicate the process of entering a given frequency in the 'Table of Frequency Allocations of the Republic of Korea.'[15] Specifically, Article 9(3) of the Act stipulates the Minister of Science and ICT's obligation to announce the results of the allocation of frequencies.[16] In practice, the Minister publishes the 'Table of Frequency Allocations of the Republic of Korea' every time after the allocation. This interpretation is further supported by No. 1.16 of the ITU Radio Regulations which defines the "allocation (of a frequency band)" as an "[e]ntry in the Table of Frequency Allocations of a given frequency band for the purpose of its use by one or more terrestrial or space radiocommunication services" In other words, the allocation process set out in the Radio Waves Act is a domestic version modeled after the ITU Radio Regulations which deals with the international allocation of a frequency band.

Second, both "assignment" and "designation" of frequencies pertain to Article 4 of the ITU Radio Regulations which govern member States' assignment and use of frequencies. The ITU Radio Regulations broadly define "assignment" of frequencies as member States' authorization that allows a station to use a frequency.[17] In contrast, the Radio Waves Act classifies such authorization into two categories – "assignment" and "designation" – based on to whom the right of use is granted. Specifically, the "assignment" of frequencies means to bestow "a specific person" the right to use a specified frequency, whereas the "designation" of frequencies aims to allow a certain frequency to be utilized by "a specific station."[18]

Aside from the aforementioned concepts, another way of using frequencies, which was introduced in the Act's partial revision in 2014, is the government's "approval for use of frequencies" for temporary/particular purposes. This is defined as "approving the use of specific frequencies for security or diplomatic purposes or for international or national events."[19]

South Korea's own terms and definitions regarding its frequency usage system above illustrate to what extent the nation has implemented international principles under the ITU regime[20] and how those principles have been

15 *See* Table 3 in *infra* Chapter 4 §3.3.

16 *Infra* Chapter 4 §3.3.

17 No. 1.18 of the ITU Radio Regulations.

18 According to Articles 19 and 19 *bis* of the Radio Waves Act, any person who intends to establish a radio station must obtain authorization from or must file a report to the Minister of Science and ICT. Details will be addressed in the following sections.

19 Subparagraph 4 *bis* of Article 2 of the Radio Waves Act.

20 *See* Chapter 1 §2.1.2.3.

adapted and modified to suit the nation's own needs and domestic communications environment.

Third, the Act also provides the definition of "radio communication" as 'any transmission or reception of all types of information such as signs, signals, words, images, and sounds' 'by means of radio waves.'[21] According to No. 1.6. of the Radio Regulations, the term "radio communication" is defined as "telecommunication by means of radio waves." The Radio Regulations further define "telecommunication" in No. 1.3. as "any transmission, emission or reception of signs, signals, writings, images and sounds."[22] Thus, the definition of "radio communication" in the Act appears to combine the two clauses from the Radio Regulations, which is in line with how the Radio Regulations define the term.

Finally, other key terminologies added to the 2000 Amendments are related to space communications as follows: i) "space station," a station established in a satellite;[23] ii) "Earth station," a station established on Earth to communicate with a space station;[24] iii) "satellite network," a whole communications network (including satellite frequencies and orbits) comprised of a space station and an Earth station;[25] and iv) "satellite orbit," the location or path of a space station.[26] These definitions provided by the Act are more succinct than those provided by the ITU Radio Regulations which delineate each term in more detail and technicality.[27] Nonetheless, the Act's definitions still fall under the purview of the ITU Radio Regulations.

---

21 Subparagraph 5 *bis* of Article 2 of the Radio Waves Act.

22 The full language of No. 1.3. of the Radio Regulations is "any transmission, emission or reception of signs, signals, writings, images and sounds or intelligence of any nature by wire, radio, optical or other electromagnetic systems."

23 Subparagraph 10 of Article 2 of the Radio Waves Act.

24 Subparagraph 11 of Article 2 of the Radio Waves Act.

25 Subparagraph 12 of Article 2 of the Radio Waves Act.

26 Subparagraph 13 of Article 2 of the Radio Waves Act.

27 The definitions prescribed by the ITU Radio Regulations are as follows:

i) No. 1.64 "space station," a radio station located on an object which is beyond, is intended to go beyond, or has been beyond, the major portion of the Earth's atmosphere;

ii) No. 1.63 "earth station," a station located either on the Earth's surface or within the major portion of the Earth's atmosphere and intended for communication with one or more space stations or with one or more stations of the same kind by means of one or more reflecting satellites or other objects in space;

iii) No. 1.112 "satellite network," a satellite system or a part of a satellite system, consisting of only one satellite and the cooperating earth stations; and

iv) No. 1.184 "orbit," the path, relative to a specified frame of reference, described by the center of mass of a satellite or other object in space subjected primarily to natural forces, mainly the force of gravity.

3 Major Provisions of the Act

3.1 *Securing and Facilitating the Utilization of Spectrum Resources*

The definition clause is followed by the Korean government's declaration of its own duty to formulate and implement policy measures to maximize "limited" spectrum resources for public welfare.[28] This recalls one of the main principles of the ITU regime, which states that "[i]n using frequency bands for radio services, Member States shall bear in mind that radio frequencies [...] are 'limited' natural resources and that they must be used rationally, efficiently and economically."[29]

To that end, more specific obligations are laid upon the Minister of Science and ICT which prescribes that the Minister must establish the following strategies in detail:[30]

i. promoting technologies for the use of new frequencies;
ii. enhancing efficiency in using current frequencies;
iii. developing technologies for the joint use of frequencies;[31]
iv. instituting a process for recording satellite networks and their particulars in the ITU's Master International Frequency Register;[32] and
v. coordinating efforts to avoid and eliminate harmful interference between nations.

Furthermore, for the equitable and efficient use of spectrum resources, the Minister of Science and ICT executes necessary measures such as i) an alteration to the allocation of frequencies, ii) a withdrawal or reallocation of frequencies, iii) conversion to new technical methods, and/or iv) joint use of frequencies.[33] These domestic measures are essentially in line with the ITU principles of equitable access to frequencies and efficient operation of communications services.[34]

28 Article 3 of the Radio Waves Act.

29 Article 44(2) of the ITU Constitution and reiterated in the Preamble of the Radio Regulations. *See supra* Chapter 1 §2.1.2.2.

30 Article 5(1) of the Radio Waves Act.

31 The joint use of frequencies is defined in Article 2(1) 4–5 of the Radio Waves Act as the use of the same frequency range by two or more users without mutual exclusion. Article 6-3(1) of the Act further stipulates that the Minister of Science and ICT may require a person who has been granted the assignment, designation, or approval for the use of frequencies to provide all or part of the frequencies for the joint use.

32 Details on the recording process under the ITU Radio Regulations will be discussed in Chapter 4 §3.10.

33 Article 6 of the Radio Waves Act.

34 *See supra* Chapter 1 §2.1.2.2.

3.2 *Master Plan for Frequency Spectrum Promotion*

A master plan by the Minister of Science and ICT is issued every five years to promote the effective utilization of spectrum frequency and to develop new technologies in the broadcasting equipment industry.[35] The Minister holds hearings to seek opinions from both telecommunications experts and the general public over the formulation of the master plan.[36] The master plan must include matters such as a medium- and long-term scheme for the use of frequencies, development of new spectrum resource, support for the advancement of technologies and facilities, development of space communications, standardization of spectrum operation, and improvement of the spectrum environment.

The latest Master Plan for Frequency Spectrum Promotion (2019–2023) was announced on January 25, 2019,[37] after South Korea's first (2009–2013) and second (2014–2018) master plans. Prior to these master plans, the nation initially had the Medium- and Long-Term Plan for Frequency Spectrum *Utilization* focused on the use of frequencies as indicated by its title, which covered the following ten years since 1996. However, with an amendment to the Act's original provision in 2008,[38] the medium- and long-term plan was transformed into the master plan by elaborating on its previous content as well as by adding new subjects such as a program for space communications development.

The principal strategies of the 2019–2023 master plan include streamlining the regulatory process,[39] promoting the spectrum-related industry,[40] strengthening international cooperation,[41] improving space communication technologies,[42] training and securing professional personnel in the telecommunications sector.[43]

35 Article 8(1) of the Radio Waves Act.

36 Article 8(2) of the Radio Waves Act.

37 The Ministry of Science and ICT, "The Establishment of the Five-Year Master Plan for Radio Waves Promotion (2019–2023) [English title added]," accessed on January 20, 2021, available at https://www.msit.go.kr/publicinfo/view.do?sCode=user&mPid=62&mId=63&publictSeqNo=19&publictListSeqNo=2&formMode=R&referKey=19,2.

38 Partially revised on June 13, 2008, Act No. 9128, entered into force for the revision on December 14, 2008.

39 *Supra* Chapter 4, n. 37, at 14 and 28.

40 *Ibid.* at 25–26 and 30.

41 *Ibid.* at 29.

42 *Ibid.* at 35.

43 *Ibid.* at 38.

3.3 *The Allocation of Frequencies*

Under the Radio Waves Act, the first step toward the actual use of frequencies is for the Minister of Science and ICT to domestically allocate frequency bands for services in accordance with the Table of Frequency Allocations defined in Article 5 of the Radio Regulations,[44] where South Korea is part of Region 3.[45]

When allocating frequencies, the Minister of Science and ICT considers the following factors:[46]

i. the necessity for national security, maintenance of order, or safety of life such as national defense, public safety, and rescue of persons in distress;
ii. domestic conditions for the spectrum utilization such as the current status of using frequencies;
iii. trends in the international use of frequencies;
iv. trends in the development of communications technologies; and
v. demand for communications services.

The public is notified of the allocation by the Minister of Science and ICT[47] and, if applicable, with a period for that usage.[48] The same requirement of public notice applies where the Minister alters the allocation of frequencies.[49] In practice, the Minister notifies the Table of Frequency Allocations of the Republic of Korea following an allocation or its alteration.[50] The table indicates the international frequency allocations by the ITU in the first three columns and illustrates South Korea's in the next two columns (see Table 3).

3.4 *The Regime of the Spectrum Use*

3.4.1 Introductory Remarks

Once allocated, frequencies are allowed to be employed by way of assignment or designation of frequencies, or approval for the use of frequencies (see Table 4). The Radio Waves Act stipulates the conditions and considerations

44 *See supra* Chapter 1 §2.1.2.3.

45 No. 5.2. of the Radio Regulations, "For the allocation of frequencies, the world has been divided into three Regions."

46 Article 9(1) of the Radio Waves Act.

47 The first sentence of Article 9(3) of the Radio Waves Act.

48 Article 9(4) of the Radio Waves Act.

49 The second sentence of Article 9(3) of the Radio Waves Act.

50 As of February 2021, the latest Table of Frequency Allocations of the Republic of Korea is Notification No. 2020-11 issued on January 6, 2021. Available in Korean at https://www.law.go.kr/LSW/conAdmrulByLsPop.do?&lsiSeq=218931&joNo=0009&joBrNo=00&datClsCd=010102&dguBun=DEG&lnkText=%25EA%25B3%25A0%25EC%258B%259C%25ED%2595%2598%25EC%2597%25AC%25EC%2595%25BC %2520%25ED%2595%259C%25EB%258B%25A4 &admRulPttninfSeq=6256#AJAX, accessed on February 4, 2021.

TABLE 3 An excerpt of the Table of Frequency Allocations of the Republic of Korea. [translated into English by the author]

International			Republic of Korea	
(1)	(2)	(3)	(4)[a]	(5)[b]
Region 1	**Region 2**	**Region 3**	**Bands**	**Notes**
70–72 RADIONAVIGATION 5.60	70–90 FIXED MARITIME MOBILE 5.57 RADIONAVIGATION 5.60 Radiolocation 5.61	70–72 RADIONAVIGATION 5.60 Fixed Maritime Mobile 5.57 5.59	70–72 RADIONAVIGATION 5.60	Restricted to Hyperbolic Curve Radionavigation (DECCA)
72–84 FIXED MARITIME MOBILE 5.57 RADIONAVIGATION 5.60 5.56		72–84 FIXED MARITIME MOBILE 5.57 RADIONAVIGATION 5.60	72–84 FIXED MARITIME MOBILE 5.57	Ship Station for Radiotelegraphy
84–86 RADIONAVIGATION 5.60		84–86 RADIONAVIGATION 5.60 Fixed Maritime Mobile 5.57 5.59	84–86 RADIONAVIGATION 5.60 Maritime Mobile 5.57	Restricted to Hyperbolic Curve Radionavigation (DECCA) Ship Station for Radiotelegraphy
86–90 FIXED MARITIME MOBILE 5.57 RADIO NAVIGATION 5.56		86–90 FIXED MARITIME MOBILE 5.57 RADIONAVIGATION 5.60	86–90 FIXED MARITIME MOBILE 5.57 RADIONAVIGATION	Ship Station for Radiotelegraphy

[a] Column (4) describes South Korea's frequency allocation based on the international allocation for Region 3.
[b] Column (5) explains specific frequency usages or services related to the allocation in Column (4).

TABLE 4 Current frequency usage system

	Frequency assignment	**Frequency designation**	**Frequency usage approval**
Concepts	Granting a person the right to use specified frequencies	Designating frequencies to be used by an individual radio station	Approving the use of specific frequencies for security or diplomatic purposes or for international or national events
Main Services	Mobile communications	Broadcasting	Event purposes relating to security or diplomacy

that must be taken into account over the process of assignment, designation, or approval of which the Minister of Science and ICT is in charge. Essentially, the process applies to both radio and satellite frequency usage. Anything particular that only applies to satellites is specifically indicated in the Radio Waves Act and/or the Presidential Decree.

3.4.2 The Assignment of Frequencies

The frequency assignment process begins with the Minister of Science and ICT's public announcement including the range of persons eligible to apply for the assignment as well as the purposes and technical modes of the frequencies to be assigned.[51] Any person who intends to be assigned such frequencies is required to apply with the Minister of Science and ICT.[52] The Presidential Decree of the Radio Waves Act provides for the details of the public announcement procedures and the application for the assignment of frequencies in Articles 11 and 12, respectively.[53]

51 Article 10(1) of the Radio Waves Act.

52 Article 10(3) of the Radio Waves Act.

53 The full language of Article 11 of the Presidential Decree is as follows:

(1) The Minister of Science and ICT shall publicly announce the following matters in order to assign frequencies pursuant to Article 10(1) of the Act: Provided, That subparagraph 3 shall only apply to the assignment of frequencies at a price calculated under the

The main process of assigning radio or satellite frequency spectrum is classified into two different categories depending on whether prices for such assignments excluding fees are paid by recipients or not. The first category essentially goes through a price competition among applicants[54] – a spectrum auction. Nonetheless, in cases where there is no competitive demand for the

---

proviso to Article 11(1) of the Act, and subparagraphs 6-2 and 6-3 shall only apply to the assignment of frequencies through an auction under the main sentence of Article 11(1) of the Act (hereinafter referred to as the "frequency assignment through an auction")

1. Frequency and bandwidth subject to an assignment;
2. Methods and timing of an assignment;
3. Prices for an assignment of frequencies;
4. Timing of the use of frequencies;
5. Matters concerning the use of frequencies and technical methods;
5-2. Scope of persons eligible to apply for the assignment of frequencies;
6. Conditions imposed under Article 13(2);
6-2. Methods and procedures for the frequency assignment through an auction;
6-3. The reserve price provided for in Article 11(2) of the Act; and
7. Other matters necessary for the frequency assignment.

(2) Paragraph (1), *mutatis mutandis*, shall apply to the public announcement of an assignment of satellite frequency and orbit prescribed in Article 10(2) of the Act (hereinafter referred to as a "satellite frequency, *et cetera*"). In such cases, "frequency and bandwidth subject to an assignment" referred to in paragraph (1) 1 shall be construed as "satellite frequency, *et cetera* subject to an assignment."

(3) The public announcement referred to in paragraphs (1) and (2) shall be made by no later than one month prior to the scheduled date for the frequency assignment.

The full language of Article 12 of the Presidential Decree is as follows:

(1) A person who applies for the assignment of frequencies pursuant to Article 10(3) of the Act shall submit the following documents (including electronic documents): 1. Articles of incorporation of the corporation (including a corporation to be established; hereafter the same shall apply in this Article, Articles 17 and 19); 2. A list of stockholders of the corporation and documents concerning the ownership of stocks; 3. Plans to use frequencies; 4. Documents determined by the public announcement of the frequency assignment pursuant to Articles 10(1) or (2) of the Act.

(2) Upon receipt of an application for the assignment of frequencies filed under paragraph (1), the Minister of Science and ICT shall verify the corporate registration certificate by sharing administrative information under Article 36(1) of the Electronic Government Act.

(3) Except as otherwise expressly prescribed in paragraphs (1) and (2), the procedures and methods for filing applications for the assignment of frequencies and other necessary matters shall be determined and publicly announced by the Minister of Science and ICT.

54 The first sentence of Article 11(1) of the Radio Waves Act provides that "[t]he Minister of Science and ICT may assign, for a consideration, any frequencies publicly notified under Articles 10(1) or (2) through a price competition."

spectrum concerned, it can be assigned at a calculated price[55] in consideration of the frequency's economic value.[56]

A spectrum auction is a primary means of assigning frequencies whereby the Korean government applies an auction system to grant companies the right to use scarce spectrum resources. The first spectrum auction in South Korea was conducted in August 2011, with a winning bid of approximately USD 1 billion, where South Korea's two giant telecommunication companies at the time competed for the 1.8 GHz band over 83 rounds. Since August 2011, the government has conducted an additional 11 spectrum auctions,[57] of which the auction for fifth generation (5G) drew the most attention in June 2018,[58] leading to South Korea's first introduction of 5G networks to the world.[59] With the engagement of private enterprises in the process of assigning and using public resources, spectrum auctions appear to be an effective approach toward market-based frequency management.[60]

The second category, on the other hand, is subject to being assigned through the examination of the following criteria: i) the efficiency of the use of spectrum resources, ii) applicants' financial and technical capabilities, and iii) the characteristics of frequencies to be assigned.[61] The administrative process requires applicants to submit a proposal as to how they aim to use it. This approach is commonly referred to as a beauty contest.[62] After examining all the applications, the Minister of Science and ICT awards frequencies to those with the most suitable proposals.

One of the major distinctions between the two categories according to the Radio Waves Act is that a person who has been awarded frequencies via the first category process holds the right to *exclusively* use the frequencies,[63] and

---

55 The second sentence of Article 11(1) of the Radio Waves Act provides that "the Minister of Science and ICT may assign frequencies at calculated price pursuant to the latter part of paragraph (3) where exceptional circumstances are deemed to exist such as lack of competitive demand for the frequency spectrum."

56 For instance, the turnover or revenue expected from the business for which frequencies are assigned according to the second sentence of Article 11(3) of the Radio Waves Act.

57 As of February 2021.

58 Press release on June 18, 2018, by the Ministry of Science and ICT, the Results of the 5G Spectrum Auction, accessed on February 7, 2021, available at https://www.msit.go.kr/bbs/view.do?sCode=user&mId=113&mPid=112&bbsSeqNo=94&nttSeqNo=1386500.

59 *Supra* Chapter 1 §2.1.1.

60 Countries that have conducted spectrum auctions for their frequency assignment include, but not limited to, the United States, Canada, the United Kingdom, Germany, Sweden, and India.

61 Article 12 of the Radio Waves Act.

62 Peter Cramton, "Spectrum Auctions," in Martin Cave, Sumit Majumdar, and Ingo Vogelsang (Eds) *Handbook of Telecommunications Economics* (2002), 607.

63 Article 14(1) of the Radio Waves Act.

thus the person is allowed to transfer or lease such right to others.[64] Another distinction is that the maximum period of using assigned frequencies also depends on which category process it falls into. More specifically, frequencies under the first category can be used for up to twenty years, whereas the second category is not to exceed more than ten years. Nonetheless, the Minister of Science and ICT may reassign expired frequencies to incumbent users.[65] The specific usage period for each user is determined by the Minister within the scope of the maximum period in consideration of circumstances surrounding the use of frequencies.[66]

The Minister of Science and ICT *may* revoke frequency assignments in the following cases: Where the person is subject to a revocation of a communications business license under the Telecommunications Business Act[67] or to a revocation of a broadcasting business license under the Broadcasting Act,[68] where the person violates the usage or technical mode of frequencies, where the person fails to comply with attached conditions, or where the person fails to pay the aforementioned price for an assignment. However, if a person has been assigned frequencies by fraud or other improper means, the Minister *must* revoke such assignment.[69]

3.4.3 The Designation of Frequencies

Another method of allowing spectrum utilization as introduced in the 2015 partial amendments is to designate frequencies that will be used by a station to be established.[70] Thus, this method is essentially combined with the process of establishing a station,[71] which increases the diverse and efficient utilization of frequencies by streamlining administrative procedures.[72]

---

64 Article 14(2) of the Radio Waves Act.

65 Article 16(1) of the Radio Waves Act.

66 Article 15(1) of the Radio Waves Act.

67 *Supra* Chapter 1 §2.2.2.2. and §2.4.2. Enacted on December 30, 1983 (Act No. 3686), as partially amended on December 24, 2018 (Act No. 16019).

68 *Supra* Chapter 3, n. 2. Enacted on December 16, 1963, entered into force on January 1, 1964 (Act No. 1535), as partially amended on December 8, 2020 (Act No. 17632). Article 1 of the Broadcasting Act provides that the purpose of this Act is "to promote the protection of the rights and interests of the viewers, the formation of the democratic public opinion and the improvement of national culture, and to contribute to the development of broadcasting and advancement of public welfare, by guaranteeing the freedom and independence of broadcasting and by enhancing public responsibilities of broadcasting."

69 Article 15 *bis* (1) of the Radio Waves Act.

70 Article 18-4 of the Radio Waves Act.

71 Details on a radio station establishment will be addressed in Chapter 4 §3.7.

72 The National Law Information Center, "Reasons for the Partial Revision," accessed on January 25, 2021, https://www.law.go.kr/LSW/lsInfoP.do?lsiSeq=177652&ancYd=20151222&ancNo=13588&efYd=20160623&nwJoYnInfo=N&efGubun=Y&chrClsCd=010202&ancYnChk=0#0000.

3.4.4 The Approval for Use of Frequencies

The frequency usage approval has a slightly different nature compared to the assignment or designation of frequencies. The Minister of Science and ICT may approve the use of frequencies (in cases of satellite frequencies, the approval includes the use of satellite orbits), where the Minister deems it necessary to use specific frequencies for security or diplomatic purposes or for international or national events.[73] In this respect, approving the use of frequencies for a particular purpose is distinct from allocating, assigning, or designating frequencies as discussed earlier.

To initiate the approval process, the Radio Waves Act requires any person who intends to obtain such approval to apply with the Minister of Science and ICT.[74] Upon receipt of an application, the Minister examines the efficiency in using spectrum resources, the availability of frequencies, and the possibility of causing harmful interference. If the results of the examination are acceptable, the Minister issues an approval certificate which includes the type of radio waves, bandwidth and frequency as well as the configuration of the antenna and its supply power (the electronic power supplied to antenna feeders).[75] In instances where a person who secured approval discontinues using the specified frequencies, the person must return the frequencies to the Minister without delay.[76]

3.4.5 The Assessment of the Current Frequency Usage Regime

Since its enactment in 1961, the Radio Waves Act has been partially amended nearly 40 times as well as the full amendments in 2000 as new telecommunications technologies are developed and the business environment continually changes. The current frequency usage system is not an exception; part of the system was introduced each time as needed. Specifically, the concept of frequency assignment was added to the 2000 amendments while the approval for frequency usage was adopted in 2014 and the frequency designation entered into force in 2016. This has resulted in a complicated and hard-to-understand frequency usage system. It would be desirable to have a single overarching license regime that integrates each concept of spectrum use, thus making it easier to facilitate the overall frequency management.

73 Article 18 *bis* (1) of the Radio Waves Act.
74 Article 18 *bis* (2) of the Radio Waves Act.
75 Article 18 *bis* (3) of the Radio Waves Act.
76 Article 18 *bis* (4) of the Radio Waves Act.

3.5 *National Register of Frequency Usage Rights*

The rights to use frequencies are registered and managed electronically by the Minister of Science and ICT.[77] The register contains information relating to assigned frequencies and usage right holders, bandwidth, usage periods, condition terms, and frequency transfer or leasing if applicable.[78] This information is available to the public by filing an application with the Minister for browsing or obtaining a copy of it.[79] This centralized registry system allows existing and prospective spectrum users to conveniently ascertain frequency availabilities and other associated rights that they need to know about for their business.

3.6 *The Management of Public Purpose Frequencies*

Public sector agencies are also substantial users of frequencies. They deliver services at the national or local levels for defense, public safety, public broadcasting and transport, and scientific research. In order to efficiently manage these public purpose frequencies, the Minister of Science and ICT establishes a frequency supply and demand plan every year.[80] Relevant administrative agencies submit their own plans for the public frequency use to the Minister for a nationwide annual plan.[81] The Policy Council for Public Purpose Frequencies, with the Vice Minister of Science and ICT as a chairperson, consults and coordinates affairs related to formulating the nationwide plan.[82]

3.7 *Authorization or Report for the Establishment of a Station*

The Radio Waves Act provides for three different methods or categories of establishing a station depending on the type or purpose of the station. First of all, any person who intends to establish a station is, in principle, required to obtain authorization from the Minister of Science and ICT[83] by filing an application.[84] The Minister, upon receipt of such an application, examines the following criteria:[85]

---

77 Articles 18(1) and (3) of the Radio Waves Act.

78 Article 20(1) of the Presidential Decree and Article 6(1) of the Administrative Rules of the Radio Waves Act. For more discussion on the frequency transfer or leasing, *see infra* Chapter 4 §3.12.

79 Article 18(2) of the Radio Waves Act, Article 20(2) of its Presidential Decree, and Article 6(2) of its Administrative Rules.

80 Article 18-6(1) of the Radio Waves Act.

81 Article 18-6(2) of the Radio Waves Act.

82 Article 18-9 of the Radio Waves Act.

83 Article 19(1) of the Radio Waves Act.

84 Article 21(1) of the Radio Waves Act.

85 Article 21(2) of the Radio Waves Act.

i. whether the designation of frequencies is possible;
ii. whether the facilities to be installed or operated are in conformity with technical requirements;[86]
iii. whether a personnel arrangement plan for wireless work meets the qualification standards;[87] and
iv. whether the establishment of a station is in conformity with the establishment requirements under Article 20 *bis*.[88]

Second, in cases where a station to be established has no need to restrict its frequencies or antenna supply power to avoid interference between nations or regions, the person establishing such a station is merely required to report to the Minister of Science and ICT for the following stations:[89] i) a station with weak radio waves or with no need to install radio facilities, ii) a station exclusively used for a reception, iii) a station established by a person who has been assigned frequencies with payment or through examination under Article 11

86 Article 45 of the Radio Waves Act stipulates that "[a]ny radio facilities (excluding those used only for the purpose of receiving broadcasts) shall conform with technical standards such as those for the *frequency tolerance** and the antenna supply power, determined by the Ordinance of the Ministry of Science and ICT." [Italics added]. Accordingly, the detailed technical standards are prescribed in the Ordinance for Technical Standards of Radio Facilities, (*supra* Chapter 4, n. 11, enacted on August 12, 2016, partially amended on December 24, 2020, Administrative Rules No. 63). **Frequency tolerance* is defined in No. 1.151 of the Radio Regulations as "[t]he maximum permissible departure by the center frequency of the frequency band occupied by an emission from the assigned frequency or, by the characteristic frequency of an emission from the reference frequency."

87 Article 71 of the Radio Waves Act stipulates that "[e]very authorized person shall place operators at his/her radio station according to the standards for qualification and number of operators prescribed by the Presidential Decree," and Article 117 of the Presidential Decree, accordingly, specifies the standards based on each type of radio station.

88 Article 20 *bis* of the Radio Waves Act sets out requirements for establishing a station as follows:
i. The content of communications shall be appropriate for the purpose of establishment;
ii. The radio facilities shall not be provided to persons other than the authorized person;
iii. No purpose of establishment, content of communications, nor selection of correspondents shall violate any statute or regulation;
iv. The minimum radio frequencies and antenna supply power necessary for the achievement of the purpose of establishment shall be used;
v. The radio facilities shall be installed at a place that does not cause any impediment to the human life, property, and safety of aircraft; and
vi. No radio station shall cause any inference to the operation of other radio stations already established.

89 Article 19 *bis* (2) of the Radio Waves Act.

or 12,[90] or iv) a station established for digital multimedia broadcasting under the Broadcasting Act.[91] The Minister of Science and ICT, in response, issues a certificate of report on the establishment of such a station.[92]

Lastly, there are cases where even a report to the Minister of Science and ICT is not required.[93] The Presidential Decree of the Radio Waves Act specifies that stations using particular types of equipment fall under this no-need-to-report category. Such equipment includes small electric power generators for measurement, individuals' daily life equipment with open usage frequency, and other receive-only equipment.[94]

From the above, it appears that the two non-authorization ways which are less burdensome for applicants are meant to streamline the overall administrative procedures so that the private sector can efficiently and conveniently use spectrum resources in cases where there is little concern about harmful interference with other stations.

However, establishing or operating a station without obtaining the required authorization or filing a report constitutes a criminal offense. Punishments for those offenses vary from imprisonment to fines depending on the types of stations.[95]

---

90 *Supra* Chapter 4 §3.4.2.

91 *Supra* Chapter 4, n. 2. Subparagraph 1(d) of Article 2 of the Broadcasting Act provides for the definition of "digital multimedia broadcasting" as follows: broadcasting which transmits television broadcasting, radio broadcasting, and datacasting in complexity using multi-channels for the main purpose of receiving while moving.

92 Article 22 *bis* (2) of the Radio Waves Act.

93 Article 19 *bis* (2) of the Radio Waves Act.

94 Article 25 of the Presidential Decree of the Radio Waves Act, the full language of which is as follows:

"Radio station specified by Presidential Decree" in Article 19 *bis* (2) of the Act means a radio station using any of the following radio equipment:

i. A standard field strength generator, heterodyne-radio frequency measuring instrument, and other small electric power generators for measurement;

ii. Radio equipment for a citizen band station which has undergone conformity assessment under Article 58 *bis* (1) of the Act (hereinafter referred to as "conformity assessment") and is established using radio frequencies determined by the Minister of Science and ICT for free use by individuals in their daily lives;

iii. Receive-only radio equipment other than the radio equipment referred to in Article 24(1)-2; and

iv. Radio equipment which has undergone conformity assessment, and the Minister of Science and ICT determines and publicly notifies the use, radio frequencies, antenna power, electric field strength, and suchlike for use within the scope of output that does not obstruct communications among other radio stations.

95 Articles 84 and 87 of the Radio Waves Act.

In operating a station, the Radio Waves Act explicitly stipulates that each station must be operated "in a manner that does not interfere with, impedes, or obstructs the operation of other stations,"[96] which demonstrates that the international principle to minimize harmful interference between stations of different countries under the ITU regime[97] is also being applied domestically under national law.

3.8 *Examination of Permission for Establishment of Broadcasting Stations*

The Minister of Science and ICT does not have any authority to permit the establishment of broadcasting stations under the Broadcasting Act but has the authority conferred by the Radio Waves Act to examine whether it fulfills the requirements of spectrum usage under the Radio Waves Act. In other words, according to the Broadcasting Act, any person who intends to obtain or renew permission for a broadcasting business is required to submit an application to the Korea Communications Commission (KCC).[98] In response to the application, the KCC requests the Minister of Science and ICT to examine the following matters:[99]

i. whether it is possible to designate frequencies within the frequency range allocated for broadcasting;
ii. whether the facilities to be installed or operated meet the technical requirements;[100]
iii. whether a personnel arrangement plan for wireless work meets the qualification standards;[101] and
iv. whether the conditions for establishing a broadcasting station under Article 35 are fulfilled;[102]

---

96 Article 29 of the Radio Waves Act.

97 *Supra* Chapter 1 §2.1.2.2. Article 1 of the ITU Constitution and the Preamble of the Radio Regulations.

98 Article 34(1) of the Radio Waves Act.

99 Article 34(2) of the Radio Waves Act.

100 *Supra* Chapter 4, n. 89, Article 45 of the Radio Waves Act.

101 *Supra* Chapter 4, n. 90, Article 71 of the Radio Waves Act.

102 Article 35 of the Radio Act provides that a broadcasting station must be installed in a manner that does not cause any harmful interference with the reception of other broadcasts concerning such conditions as the location of the station, the height, output, directional characteristics of a transmission antenna.

The Minister of Science and ICT then sends the examination results to the KCC,[103] and the KCC decides whether to grant or renew permission based on the Minister's examination report.[104]

The KCC is a central administrative agency established by the Act on Establishment and Operation of the Korea Communications Commission in 2008,[105] under the control of the South Korea's President. It was formed by reorganizing a former Broadcasting Commission and is responsible for regulating and governing broadcasting and communications while protecting the rights and interests of users.[106]

The Radio Waves Act appears to recognize the different roles of the Minister of Science and ICT and the Korea Communications Commission. In the process of granting permission to establish a broadcasting station, the Korea Communications Commission retains the authority, while the examination of frequency-related operation is conducted by the Minister of Science and ICT. The Commission makes its decision based on the examination report. This demonstrates the recognition and respect for the expertise of each government agency involved in the process.

3.9 *A Duty to Secure and Manage Satellite Frequencies for Space Communications*

The terms "satellite frequencies" and "space communications" were first introduced into the Radio Waves Act in 2000 when the "Operation of Space Communication" section was inserted. The first clause of the section states that the Minister of Science and ICT is required to devise policies to secure and manage satellite frequencies and other relevant natural resources for space communications.[107] As part of such efforts, the Ministry of Science and ICT holds a bi-monthly frequency policy advisory meeting to help formulate and promote better policies on space communications.[108] This provision does not merely reiterate the Minister's general policymaking duty but emphasizes satellite-related resource management specifically for space communications.

---

103 Article 34(3) of the Radio Waves Act.

104 Article 34(4) of the Radio Waves Act.

105 The Establishment and Operation of the Korea Communications Commission Act, enacted and entered into force on February 29, 2008 (Act No. 8867).

106 Article 3 of the Establishment and Operation of the Korea Communications Commission Act.

107 Article 38 of the Radio Waves Act.

108 Press release by the Ministry of Science and ICT on May 30, 2019, "Launch of the Radio-Frequency Policy Advisory Meeting [English title added]," available at https://www.msit.go.kr/bbs/view.do?sCode=user&mId=113&mPid=112&bbsSeqNo=94&nttSeqNo=1994901.

3.10 *International Recording of Satellite Networks*

The Radio Waves Act prescribes the domestic procedures prior to initiating international recording of satellite networks under the ITU Radio Regulations, which commences with an applicant's request for the recording to the Minister of Science and ICT. In other words, any person who intends to secure frequencies for satellite networks to establish a space station must submit an application to the Minister of Science and ICT[109] with the information required by the Radio Regulations[110] as well as its satellite communication business plan.[111] It is noteworthy that the Radio Waves Act does not enumerate exactly which information needs to be furnished; rather it stipulates that an application containing the required information under the Radio Regulations must be submitted to the Minister. A benefit of this approach is that even if the information listed on the Radio Regulations is amended, national legislation does not have to be amended accordingly just to include the new list.

With such application, the Minister of Science and ICT adheres to the international procedures in accordance with the Radio Regulations[112] in cases where i) it is possible to designate frequencies for the space station to be established by the applicant, ii) the suggested business plan is acceptable and appropriate, and iii) the applicant has the capability to adjust interference of satellite networks. However, if the application does not fulfill such conditions, the request is returned to the applicant, or the Minister may require the applicant to supplement or modify the application within a specified period.[113]

Once the above domestic process is complete, the Minister of Science and ICT submits a notice with all the required information to the Radio communication Bureau for advance publication under the Radio Regulations[114]

109 Article 39(1) of the Radio Waves Act.

110 Appendix 4 of the Radio Regulations, "Consolidated list and tables of characteristics for use in the application of the procedures of Chapter III (notification and recording of frequency assignments and plan modifications)," enumerates information that needs to be furnished including, but not limited to, satellite name, responsible administration and operating agency, location of the station, antennas, nature of service, power levels, and necessary bandwidth.

111 Article 63(1) of the Presidential Decree of the Radio Waves Act.

112 *See supra* Chapter 1 §2.1.2.3.

113 Article 39(2) of the Radio Waves Act.

114 No. 9.1 of the Radio Regulations stipulates that "an administration, or one acting on behalf of a group of named administrations, shall send to the Bureau a general description of the network or system for advance publication in the International Frequency Information Circular (BR IFIC) not earlier than seven years and preferably not later than two years before the planned date of bringing into use of the network or system. The characteristics to be provided for this purpose are listed in Appendix 4."

via the Bureau's online submission system.[115] The Bureau examines the notice for completeness and correctness before officially publishing it in a Special Section of its International Frequency Information Circular.[116] Regarding this publication phase, the Radio Waves Act stipulates that a person who has requested the Minister of Science and ICT to file such an application has to bear costs involved in satellite network filings as prescribed by the International Telecommunication Union.[117] Details on processing charges are specified in the ITU Administrative Council Decision 482.[118]

Given the ITU's essential objectives to harmonize international telecommunications practices and minimize harmful interference between stations globally,[119] the above process at the national law level seems to serve as a useful preliminary before entering into the international procedures with the ITU. Over the course of the ITU coordination[120] and if appropriate, the Minister of Science and ICT may request the applicant to furnish relevant data necessary to avoid or eliminate interference.[121] Furthermore, the applicant may be required by the Minister to adjust satellite network interference that is under the jurisdiction of a foreign country.[122]

Ultimately, these domestic procedures are intended to ensure that the Minister of Science and ICT, who is in charge of submitting such information in accordance with the Radio Regulation,[123] completes all possible examinations in advance and implements the ITU principles as much as possible, from advance publication[124] to notification and frequency recording in the Master International Frequency Register.[125]

---

115 ITU, "E-Submission of Satellite Network Filings," accessed on February 1, 2021, available at https://www.itu.int/en/ITU-R/space/e-submission/Pages/default.aspx.

116 No. 9.2B of the ITU Radio Regulations.

117 Article 39(3) of the Radio Waves Act.

118 ITU, "Cost Recovery for Satellite Network Filings," accessed on February 1, 2021, available at https://www.itu.int/ITU-R/go/space-cost-recovery/en.

119 *See supra* Chapter 1 §2.1.2.1.

120 *See supra* Chapter 1 §2.1.2.3.

121 Article 40(2) of the Radio Waves Act.

122 Article 63(4) of the Presidential Decree of the Radio Waves Act.

123 *Supra* Chapter 4, n. 114, No. 9.1 of the Radio Regulations provides that "an 'administration' [...] shall send to the Bureau a general description of the network or system." Regarding the term 'administration,' No. 1.2 of the Radio Regulations defines it as "[a]ny governmental department or service responsible for discharging the obligations undertaken in the Constitution of the International Telecommunication Union, in the Convention of the International Telecommunication Union and in the Administrative Regulations."

124 Article 9 of the Radio Regulations.

125 Article 11 of the Radio Regulations. *See* also *supra*, Chapter 1 §2.1.2.3.

3.11 *The Establishment of a Space Station*

A requirement for the establishment of a space station that the Radio Waves Act mentions is that any space station must be capable of immediately halting the emission of radio waves and of changing its orbit by means of remote control.[126] This requirement concerns the maneuverability of satellites whereby the Minister of Science and ICT may order orbit alterations if necessary to minimize interference or to assure efficient spectrum utilization, to the extent that such alteration does not cause serious impediments to their purpose.[127]

3.12 *The Transfer or Lease of Satellite Frequency Usage Rights*

Spectrum trading is a market-based mechanism that enables the transfer or lease of frequency usage rights from one user to another at a certain price. The Radio Waves Act allows for spectrum trading which permits incumbent users to transact after a certain period of use.[128] This period is defined in the Presidential Decree as three years after the date of frequency assignment or designation. Nonetheless, in cases of an incumbent user's bankruptcy, business merger, satellite defect, and other sudden changes, spectrum trading is allowed even before the three-year period.[129] Both parties to the trade are required to obtain prior approval from the Minister of Science and ICT.[130] The trading regulation was introduced in 2015 after South Korea's largest telecommunications company, Korea Telecommunication Corporation (KT),[131] sold its satellites, including frequencies and orbits, which were originally developed by the government prior to the company's privatization,[132] to Asia Broadcast Satellite (ABS), a global satellite operator in Hong Kong.[133]

Generally, spectrum trading is considered to contribute to more efficient use of frequencies by facilitating trades between incumbent and prospective users. It also makes it easier for companies to enter the market or expand their

126 Article 42 of the Radio Waves Act.

127 Article 43 of the Radio Waves Act.

128 Article 41(2) of the Radio Waves Act.

129 Article 64 *bis* of the Presidential Decree of the Radio Waves Act.

130 Article 41(3) of the Radio Waves Act.

131 *Supra* Chapter 1 §2.2.2.1. and §2.2.2.2. The Korea Telecommunication *Public* Corporation was privatized and renamed Korea Telecommunication Corporation in 2002. [Italics added].

132 *Supra* Chapter 2 §5.3. The satellites at issue were Koreasat-2 and 3.

133 ABS, "Asia Broadcast Satellite Acquires Koreasat-2," accessed on February 13, 2021, available at https://absatellite.com/asia-broadcast-satellite-to-acquire-koreasat-2/, also "Asia Broadcast Satellite Acquires Koreasat-3," https://absatellite.com/asia-broadcast-satellite-acquires-koreasat-3/.

business by acquiring spectrum. Such trades are registered in the national register mentioned earlier,[134] which enables potential traders to access information pertaining to the frequencies concerned.

3.13 *The Transfer or Lease of a Space Station's Facility*

In addition to spectrum trading, the Radio Waves Act provides for facility trading of a space station. The space station facilities can either be fully or partially transferred or leased under the approval of the Minister of Science and ICT.[135] The transferee who has obtained such trading approval succeeds the status of the transferor,[136] which means not only are the rights but also obligations are transferred for the purpose of the trading. In this regard, where the transferee fails to comply with rules and conditions in operating transferred facilities, the Minister may command corrections or revoke the approval.[137]

3.14 *The Registration of Satellites with the United Nations*

As discussed in Chapter 1, Article VIII of the Outer Space Treaty establishes a legal link between an object launched into outer space and a State on whose registry the object is carried, by granting jurisdiction and control over such an object.[138] The Registration Convention further stipulates an obligation for a launching State to nationally register the space object[139] and to furnish the required information to the Secretary-General of the United Nations.[140] These obligations motivate member States to enact certain kinds of national regulations at their discretion.

The Radio Waves Act first introduced a registration provision in its 2000 amendments,[141] which provides for the Minister of Science and ICT's duty to register a *satellite* launched by a *South Korean national* with the United Nations.[142] In other words, the scope of registration set out in the Radio Waves

134 *Supra* Chapter 4 §3.5.

135 Article 42(1) *bis* of the Radio Waves Act.

136 Article 42(3) *bis* of the Radio Waves Act.

137 Article 42(4) *bis* of the Radio Waves Act.

138 *Supra* Chapter 1 §1.4.1.

139 Paragraph 1 of Article II of the Registration Convention.

140 Paragraph 1 of Article IV of the Registration Convention.

141 *Supra* Chapter 4 §1, as amended on January 21, 2000, under Act No. 6197, entered into force on April 1, 2000.

142 Italics added. Article 44(1) of the Radio Waves Act stipulates that "[t]he Minister of Science and ICT shall register an artificial satellite launched by a citizen of the Republic of Korea with the United Nations in accordance with the Convention on Registration of Objects Launched into Outer Space."

TABLE 5 The application scope of each Act regarding the registration of a space object

	Radio Waves Act	**Space Development Promotion Act**
National Registration	N/A	Applicable to space objects including satellites
International Registration	Applicable to any type of satellites launched by Korean nationals	Applicable to space objects excluding satellites launched by Korean nationals

Act is limited to the *international* registration of *satellites* including satellites for communication, Earth observation, and navigation.[143] This indicates that the Act does not encompass the whole range of registration principles under the Registration Convention. As a result, those not covered by the Radio Waves Act – namely, the national registration of space objects as well as the international registration of space objects excluding satellites launched by Korean nationals– are governed by the Space Development Promotion Act enacted in 2005 (see Table 5).[144] The only difference in procedures depending on whether the Radio Waves Act is applied or the Space Development Promotion Act is applied is as follows: Under the Radio Waves Act, satellites launched by Korean nationals are registered directly by the Minister of Science and ICT with the United Nations. Other space objects are also registered by the Minister of Science and ICT but through the Minister of Foreign Affairs under the Space Development Promotion Act.

Throughout the history of the multiple amendments of the Radio Waves Act, the current term "satellite" of the registration provision is the result of being amended from the term "satellite, *et cetera*."[145] in 2005 when the Space

143 On May 25, 2022, Hancom InSpace, a private South Korean aerospace technology company, launched Sejong-1, the nation's first commercial Earth observation satellite from the Kennedy Space Center at Cape Canaveral, Florida. In this case, the international registration of Sejong-1 is subject to the regulations outlined in the Radio Waves Act.

144 The Space Development Promotion Act will be addressed in detail in Chapter 5.

145 According to the Radio Waves Act as amended on January 21, 2000, Article 44(1) stipulated that "[t]he Minister of Science and ICT shall register an artificial satellite, *et cetera* launched by a citizen of the Republic of Korea with the United Nations in accordance

Development Promotion Act was enacted.[146] This indicates that the then-existing Radio Waves Act turned its attention more to utilizing spectrum or managing satellites as the Space Development Promotion Act has initiated regulating the overall matters of space activities since 2005. Indeed, according to the Space Development Promotion Act, the Radio Waves Act is considered as a special law rather than a basic space law in terms of the management of space objects.[147]

With regard to the term "launched by a South Korean national" in the provision, a question may arise as to whether the international satellite registration under the Radio Waves Act includes any procured launch. The Act does not explicitly mention anything about this, nor does it specify any territorial jurisdiction that may imply an application scope. One possible answer is that since the registration provision does not restrict its applicability, it applies regardless of whether the launch is procured. It should be also noted that around the time this provision was introduced in the 2000 Amendments, satellites owned by Koreans were mostly launched by foreign launching service providers from outside Korea. In practice, regardless of from where and by whom satellites were launched, the Minister of Science and ICT has furnished the Secretary-General of the United Nations with the information required by the Registration Convention. In order to complete the international registration, the Minister may request a person launching a satellite to provide him or her with the information of a satellite concerned.[148]

Besides the initial international registration, the Radio Waves Act requires the Minister of Science and ICT to notify the Secretary-General of the United Nations of any changes after launch to the previously registered satellite.[149] This appears to be more stringent than the approach taken by the international space law, given that the Registration Convention stipulates in Paragraph 2 of Article IV that "[e]ach State of registry may, from time to time, provide the Secretary-General of the United Nations with additional information concerning a space object carried on its registry." Furthermore, Paragraph 3 of Article IV merely refers to each State's obligation to notify space objects that no longer

with the Convention on Registration of Objects Launched into Outer Space." [Italics added].

146 The Radio Waves Act as amended on May 31, 2005, under Act No. 7559, entered into force on December 1, 2005.

147 Article 4 of the Space Development Promotion Act. Details will be discussed in Chapter 5.

148 Article 44(2) of the Radio Waves Act.

149 Article 44(3) of the Radio Waves Act provides that "[i]f any change is made to the matters registered with the United Nations [...], the Minister of Science and ICT *shall* notify the United Nations thereof." [Italics added].

exist in Earth's orbit after transmitting the information concerning the space objects.[150] In contrast to the Registration Convention, the language of the Radio Waves Act, "any changes to the satellite after launch," includes not only the existence of the satellite but also any transferring of satellite ownership or operator. As such, the Act's notification system can bring more transparency in maintaining the international register up to date.

3.15 *The Submission of a Satellite Operation Plan by the Satellite Operator*

In the course of administering and maintaining satellite networks internationally registered by the Minister of Science and ICT under the ITU Radio Regulations,[151] the Minister may request a satellite operator using such networks to submit a plan to secure and operate a subsequent satellite.[152] The request is made five years prior to the estimated end of the lifetime of the satellite concerned,[153] based on the operator's business plan filed earlier for the international registration of the satellite networks.[154]

The satellite operation plan must be submitted to the Minister of Science and ICT within six months upon receipt of such request.[155] It must contain details about the subsequent satellite such as its orbit and frequency, its production schedule and launch date, estimated lifetime in service, as well as the operator's business plan.[156] In the operator's business plan, it is strongly recommended – though not required – that measures for space debris mitigation be included in accordance with the Recommendations for Space Debris Mitigation issued by the Korean government in 2020.[157] The measures for space debris mitigation are advised to include the operator's endeavors to employ the best satellite manufacturing technologies, to address the probability of an

150 The full language of Paragraph 3 of Article IV the Registration Convention is as follows: "Each State of registry shall notify the Secretary-General of the United Nations, to the greatest extent feasible and as soon as practicable, of space objects concerning which it has previously transmitted information, and which have been but no longer are in Earth orbit."

151 *Supra* Chapter 4 §3.9.

152 Article 44(1) *bis* of the Radio Waves Act.

153 Article 64-6(1) of the Presidential Decree of the Radio Waves Act.

154 *Supra* Chapter 4 §3.9.

155 Article 44(2) *bis* of the Radio Waves Act.

156 Article 64-6(2) of the Presidential Decree of the Radio Waves Act.

157 *Supra* Chapter 1 §3.2, the Recommendations for Space Debris Mitigation in the Course of Developing and Operating Spacecraft of 2020. The Recommendations consist of six Articles, and Article 1(2) states that the main principles of the UN COPUOS Space Debris Mitigation Guidelines of 2007 shall be applicable *mutatis mutandis*.

accidental collision or explosion, and to maneuver satellites for post-mission disposal.[158]

If there is any alteration to the submitted satellite operation plan, the operator must immediately notify the Minister of Science and ICT thereof.[159] These follow-up measures regarding satellite networks are a national-level management to maintain such networks that were internationally registered and secured to be used.

3.16 *A Master Plan for Severe Space Weather Management*

Space weather refers to dynamic conditions in the space environment that can disrupt satellite operations, communications, and navigation, leading to extreme socio-economic losses. The growing importance of space security and economy as well as the increasing reliability of space-borne technological systems requires the government's response to develop capabilities of mitigating the deleterious effects of severe space weather.[160] Accordingly, the Minister of Science and ICT formulates and implements a master plan every five years to prepare for any severe space weather and to rapidly control such conditions.

The master plan includes, but is not limited to, matters concerning the observation and monitoring of any change to electromagnetic fields outside the atmosphere, the severe space weather forecast and alert, research on space weather, and international cooperation to manage such space weather.[161] The first master plan was established in December 2012 followed by the second in December 2018.[162] As part of an effort to cooperate internationally as prescribed by the master plan, South Korea is a member of the International Space Environment Service (ISES), a collaborative network of space weather service-providing organizations, where nineteen States and the European Space Agency (ESA) are members.[163] South Korea runs the Korean Space Weather

158 Articles 5 and 6 of the Recommendations for Space Debris Mitigation in the Course of Developing and Operating Spacecraft.

159 Article 44(3) *bis* of the Radio Waves Act.

160 The Subcommittee on Disaster Reduction of the US National Science and Technology Council, accessed on February 23, 2021, https://www.sdr.gov/docs/185820_Space_FINAL.pdf.

161 Article 51 of the Radio Waves Act.

162 The Korean Space Weather Center, "Introduction," accessed on February 23, 2021, https://spaceweather.rra.go.kr/eng/Survey.do.

163 Those members include China, the United States of America, India, Canada, Republic of Korea, Czech Republic, Japan, Australia, Sweden, Belgium, Poland, South Africa, Brazil, Austria, the United Kingdom, Mexico, Russia, Norway, and Indonesia. Accessed on February 23, 2021, available at http://www.spaceweather.org/ISES/rwc/rwc.html.

Center, which plays a role as one of the regional warning centers of the ISES[164] and provides real-time data of space weather on its online dashboard.[165]

3.17 *International Spectrum Monitoring*

Spectrum monitoring is one of the essential processes of spectrum management. Article 16 of the ITU Radio Regulations contains provisions concerning international spectrum monitoring.[166] No. 16.1 stipulates that "[t]o assist to the extent practicable in the implementation of these Regulations, in particular to help ensure efficient and economical use of the radio-frequency spectrum and to help in the prompt elimination of harmful interference, administrations agree to continue the development of monitoring facilities and, to the extent practicable, to cooperate in the continued development of the international monitoring system."[167] No. 16.3 further provides that "[e]ach administration [...] participating in the international monitoring system, shall designate a centralizing office to which all requests for monitoring information shall be addressed and through which monitoring information will be forwarded to the Bureau."

Under these international principles, the Radio Waves Act requires the Minister of Science and ICT to perform international spectrum monitoring, which includes monitoring frequencies emitted by foreign stations as well as analyzing and removing harmful interference.[168] To execute such duty, the Act stipulates that the Minister shall install or operate necessary facilities.[169]

In accordance with the provisions of both the international and national law above, South Korea has the Central Radio Management Service in Seoul as a designated "centralizing office" and also operates eleven regional offices nationwide.[170] The Central Radio Management service conducts international spectrum monitoring and notifies the ITU Radiocommunication Bureau of

---

164 The International Space Environment Service, "Organization," accessed on February 23, 2021, https://spaceweather.rra.go.kr/eng/Survey.do.

165 The Korean Space Weather Center, "Space Weather Information," accessed on February 23, 2021, https://spaceweather.rra.go.kr/eng/spaceenvsun.do.

166 ITU, "International monitoring," accessed on February 24, 2021, https://www.itu.int/en/ITU-R/terrestrial/monitoring/Pages/default.aspx.

167 No. 16.1 of the ITU Radio Regulations.

168 Article 50(1) of the Radio Waves Act.

169 Article 50(2) of the Radio Waves Act.

170 The Central Radio Management Service, "Organization," accessed on February 24, 2021, https://www.crms.go.kr/en/lay1/S192T196C199/contents.do.

its monitoring results, and the Bureau publishes reports of monitoring data received from participating administrations on the ITU website.[171]

3.18 *International Cooperation to Improve Spectrum Usage Technologies*

The significance of international cooperation among States cannot be overemphasized given the nature of spectrum resources. In addition to the aforementioned cooperation for the management of space weather as well as the spectrum monitoring around the globe, the Radio Waves Act also highlights international cooperation to improve spectrum usage technology,[172] stating that the Minister of Science and ICT may support international cooperative programs designed for the exchange of personnel and technology, international standardization, and joint research and development.[173] Although the general principle of international cooperation does not directly impose a specific obligation at the national level, the exercise of such cooperation would be mutually beneficial in the telecommunication sector with a strong international aspect.

3.19 *Disclosure of Current Use of Spectrum Resources*

Paragraph 1 of Article 60 of the Radio Waves Act stipulates that the Minister of Science and ICT shall make public the current status of spectrum use in order to facilitate efficient frequency utilization.[174] Paragraph 2 states that the scope of disclosed information and the publication procedures and timing shall be prescribed by the Presidential Decree of the Act. Following the mandate of the Radio Waves Act, the Presidential Decree provides for three main parameters: First, any information referred to as being subject to nondisclosure per Article 9 of the Official Information Disclosure Act[175] may not be

---

171 ITU, "Regular Monitoring Program in frequency bands between 2 850 kHz and 28 000 kHz," https://www.itu.int/en/ITU-R/terrestrial/monitoring/Pages/Regular.aspx and "Monitoring Program band 406–406.1 MHz," https://www.itu.int/en/ITU-R/terrestrial/monitoring/Pages/Res205.aspx, accessed on February 24, 2021.

172 The other two types of international cooperation that the Radio Waves Act refers to pertain to the technical standards for the manufactured or imported equipment that cause electromagnetic interference in Article 47-3(7) and the conformity assessment of broadcasting and communications equipment that need mutual recognition between States in Articles 58-8 and 58-9. These norms, however, appear to exceed the scope of the present discussion as they specifically focus on the technical requirements for equipment.

173 Article 65 of the Radio Waves Act.

174 Article 60(1) of the Radio Waves Act.

175 The Official Information Disclosure Act aims to ensure people's rights to know and to secure the transparency of national affairs by stipulating matters necessary for the disclosure of information kept and controlled by public institutions, and for the obligations of public institutions to disclose such information. Article 9 of the Act provides

disclosed.[176] Second, the Minister of Science and ICT shall establish and operate an information system to disclose the status of spectrum use, and third, the Minister shall update the information system without delay where such status has changed.[177]

Accordingly, an online system for spectrum use has been maintained on a dedicated website which is updated regularly.[178] To provide total information, the Minister of Science and ICT conducts the investigation and confirmation of the following matters each year: The allocation, assignment, and designation of frequencies, and approval for the use of frequencies; socioeconomic indicators relating to the use of frequencies; trends in the development of technologies and related industries; and the status of use and operation of facilities and equipment.[179] This system appears to not only promote equitable and efficient spectrum utilization but also give transparency to the general public regarding the overall spectrum information.

3.20 *Other Authorities Concerned*

3.20.1 The Korea Communications Commission (KCC)

The Ministry of Science and ICT is of course the most relevant authority under the Radio Waves Act. However, as technical developments are weakening the distinction between telecommunications and broadcasting, the Korea Communications Commission (KCC)[180] is getting involved in dealing with broadcasting issues pertaining to frequency management at the same time.

The KCC is a presidential commission founded pursuant to the Act on the Establishment and Operation of the Korea Communications Commission,[181] which is responsible for regulating broadcasting and communications services

"[a]ll information kept and managed by public institutions shall be subject to disclosure to the public," except information classified as non-disclosure such as confidential information pertaining to the national security and defense, a trial in progress, *et cetera*.

176 Article 85(1) of the Presidential Decree of the Radio Waves Act.

177 Article 85(2) of the Presidential Decree of the Radio Waves Act.

178 The Total Spectrum Information System, accessed on February 26, 2021, available at http://spectrummap.kr.

179 Article 4(1) of the Presidential Decree of the Radio Waves Act.

180 Its full name in Korean is 방송통신위원회. If translated word for word, 방송 means broadcasting, 통신 communications, and 위원회 commission. Although the English name "Korea Communications Commission (KCC)" does not include the meaning of 방송 broadcasting, it is the official name which appears on its official English website at https://kcc.go.kr/user/ehpMain.do.

181 The Act on the Establishment and Operation of the Korea Communications Commission, enacted and entered into force on February 29, 2008, Act No. 8867.

and protecting users thereof to maintain the independence of such services.[182] The KCC is composed of five standing commissioners including a chairperson and a vice-chairperson.[183] South Korea's President directly appoints two of the five commissioners including a chairperson. The other three commissioners are nominated by the National Assembly and then appointed by the President.[184] The KCC deliberates and resolves key issues based on the consent of a majority of all the incumbent commissioners.[185]

The KCC's tasks and roles referred to in the Radio Waves Act are where spectrum management and broadcasting are intertwined. For instance, the KCC has the authority to approve the Minister of Science and ICT's decision to make broadcasting frequencies available for their joint use.[186] The Radio Waves Act further states that frequencies used in the broadcasting business under the Broadcasting Act[187] shall be managed by the KCC.[188] In addition, while the KCC permits the establishment of broadcasting stations pursuant to the Broadcasting Act, the Minister of Science and ICT examines whether such permission fulfills spectrum usage requirements stipulated in the Radio Waves Act.[189] Furthermore, it is noted that not only the Minister of Science and ICT but also the KCC has the authority to revoke permissions for the establishment of radio stations,[190] impose or collect

182 Article 3(1) of the Act on the Establishment and Operation of the Korea Communications Commission.

183 Article 4(1) of the Act on the Establishment and Operation of the Korea Communications Commission.

184 Article 5 of the Act on the Establishment and Operation of the Korea Communications Commission.

185 Article 13(2) of the Act on the Establishment and Operation of the Korea Communications Commission. For more information, visit the English website of the Korea Communications Commission at https://kcc.go.kr/user/ehpMain.do, accessed on March 1, 2021.

186 Article 6-3 of the Radio Waves Act. The joint use of frequencies is discussed in *Supra* Chapter 4 §3.1. Article 2(1) 4-5 of the Radio Waves Act defines it as the use of the same frequency range by two or more users without mutual exclusion.

187 *Supra* Chapter 4, n. 2.

188 Article 6-4 of the Radio Waves Act.

189 *Supra* Chapter 4 §3.7. Article 34 of the Radio Waves Act.

190 Article 72(2) of the Radio Waves Act provides that "[w]here an authorized person falls under any of the following, the *Minister of Science and ICT* or the *Korea Communications Commission* may revoke the authorization to establish the relevant radio station, or issue an order discontinuing operation of the radio station, the establishment of which has been filed or the suspension of operation thereof or the restriction on the authorized operational hours, radio frequencies or the antenna supply power of the radio station for a given period not exceeding six months: Provided, That in cases falling under subparagraph 1 or 2, the *Minister of Science and ICT* or the *Korea Communications Commission*

penalties[191] and administrative fines,[192] and conduct hearings.[193]

3.20.2 The Frequency Deliberation Committee

The Frequency Deliberation Committee, chaired by the Minister of the Office for Government Policy Coordination, deliberates over matters where frequencies are allocated, withdrawn, or reallocated.[194] The Radio Waves Act does not further provide for the Committee apart from stating that details concerning the composition and operation of the Committee shall be determined by the Presidential Decree.[195] Accordingly, under Article 7 *bis* 2 of the Presidential Decree, the Frequency Deliberation Committee is comprised of not more than seven members including a chairperson.[196] A majority of its members constitutes a quorum, and any decision thereof requires the concurring votes of a majority of those present.[197] In practice, the Frequency Deliberation Committee has deliberated over the agendas submitted by the Minister of Science and ICT or the Korea Communications Commission (for broadcasting spectrum) and resolved to allocate frequencies each time following the

---

shall order the revocation or the discontinuation of the operation of the radio station." [Italics added].

191 Article 73(1) of the Radio Waves Act stipulates that "[t]he *Minister of Science and ICT* or the *Korea Communications Commission* may, in cases where it must issue an order to suspend operation of a radio station or limit the use of radio frequencies, *et cetera* in accordance with Article 72(2) and such suspension or limit is likely to cause severe inconvenience to the users of such radio station or harm the public interest, impose and collect a penalty surcharge not exceeding 30 million won in lieu of such suspension or limit." Article 73(3) also provides that "[t]he *Minister of Science and ICT* or the *Korea Communications Commission* shall, when a person liable to pay a penalty surcharge under paragraph (1) fails to pay such penalty surcharge, urge him/her to make the payment by a given period, and, if he/she fails to pay the penalty surcharge within the given period, collect it in the same manner as delinquent national taxes are collected." [Italics added].

192 Article 93 of the Radio Waves Act stipulates that "[t]he administrative fines prescribed in Articles 89-2, 89-3 and 90 through 92 shall be imposed and collected by the *Minister of Science and ICT* or the *Korea Communications Commission*, as prescribed by Presidential Decree." [Italics added].

193 Article 77 of the Radio Waves Act states that "[t]he *Minister of Science and ICT* or the *Korea Communications Commission* shall hold a hearing if he/she or it intends to take any of the following dispositions." [Italics added].

194 Article 6 *bis* (3) of the Radio Waves Act.

195 Article 6 *bis* (4) of the Radio Waves Act.

196 Article 7 *bis* 2(1) of the Presidential Decree of the Radio Waves Act.

197 Article 7 *bis* 2(6) of the Presidential Decree of the Radio Waves Act.

ITU's World Radiocommunication Conference, withdraw particular frequency bands, or reallocate them for efficient use.[198]

3.20.3 The National Radio Research Agency (RRA)

The National Radio Research Agency (RRA), established in 1966 by the Presidential Decree on the National Frequency Management,[199] is a governmental research agency under the Ministry of Science and ICT designed to conduct in-depth research of spectrum resources and develop innovative technologies of broadcasting and communications equipment.[200]

Although the Radio Waves Act does not explicitly refer to the Agency, Article 78(1) of the Act allows the Minister of Science and ICT to delegate part of his/her authority granted under the Act to the heads of institutions affiliated therewith as per Presidential Decree. Accordingly, Article 123(1) of the Presidential Decree specifies that the Minister shall delegate such authority to the Agency's Director-General as to register satellite networks with the ITU,[201] analyze harmful interference to determine whether to approve a certain frequency use,[202] examine applications in the process of authorizing the establishment of stations,[203] and publicly notify technical standards and requirements of facilities and equipment.[204] Thus, some of the Minister of Science and ICT's main duties are conducted by the Director-General of the National Radio Research Agency under the delegation of authority by law.

3.20.4 The Korea Communications Agency (KCA)

The Korea Communications Agency (KCA)[205] is a juridical person[206] founded by the Radio Waves Act in order to efficiently manage frequencies, perform

198 Press release on August 24, 2016, by the Ministry of the Office for Government Policy Coordination, Deliberation and Resolution of the Fourth Frequency Deliberation Committee, accessed on March 3, 2021, available at https://www.korea.kr/news/pressReleaseView.do?newsId=156151354.

199 As amended and entered into force on February 5, 1966. 2. 5, Presidential Decree No. 2397.

200 For more information, visit https://www.rra.go.kr/en/intro/object.do, National Radio Research Agency, "Introduction," accessed on March 3, 2021.

201 *Supra* Chapter 4 §3.10.

202 *Supra* Chapter 4 §3.4.4.

203 *Supra* Chapter 4 §3.7.

204 *Supra* Chapter 4, n. 86.

205 Its full name in Korean is 한국방송통신전파진흥원, if translated word for word, 한국 means Korea, 방송broadcasting, 통신 communications, 전파 radio waves, 진흥 promotion, and 원 agency. Its English name "Korea Communications Agency (KCA)" comes from its official English website https://www.kca.kr/eng/, although it does not include all the meaning of its original Korean name.

206 Article 66(2) of the Radio Waves Act.

affairs for the promotion of broadcasting, telecommunications, and radio waves, as well as execute tasks entrusted by the Korean government.[207] Specifically, the Agency researches the promotion of frequency spectrum utilization, analyzes information and supports education on domestic and overseas technology related to broadcasting, telecommunications, and radio waves, as well as discharges its duties entrusted by statutes or the Minister of Science and ICT.[208] Most of the entrusted duties pertain to the qualification examination of facilities or equipment[209] such as the technical standards inspection,[210] the measurement of the electromagnetic field strength,[211] and the issuance of certificates of technical qualification.[212] Expenses incurred in operating the Agency are primarily covered by the fees earned by conducting such entrusted duties,[213] and the Agency is under the supervision of the Minister of Science and ICT who may issue instructions, dispositions, or orders to the Agency regarding its affairs if deemed necessary.[214]

3.20.5 The Korea Radio Promotion Association (RAPA)

The last institution the Radio Waves Act prescribes for is the Korea Radio Promotion Association (RAPA)[215] established under Article 66 *bis* (1) of the Act. Unlike the Korea Communications Agency above, the Association is comprised of various private members such as broadcasting and telecommunications companies, authorized facility operators, and equipment manufacturers relating to radio waves[216] to strengthen cooperation, build relationships, standardize technologies, and internationalize their industries. The Association is aimed at serving as a bridge between the government and the industrial sector by gathering opinions from its members, suggesting policies to the government, and supporting radio wave broadcasting businesses.[217]

---

207 Article 66(1) of the Radio Waves Act.
208 Article 66(4) of the Radio Waves Act.
209 Articles 78(2) and (3) of the Radio Waves Act.
210 Article 24 of the Radio Waves Act.
211 Article 47 *bis* 2(4) of the Radio Waves Act.
212 Article 70(2) of the Radio Waves Act.
213 Article 66-3(1) of the Radio Waves Act.
214 Article 87(1) of the Presidential Decree of the Radio Waves Act.
215 The abbreviation RAPA is from the Association's official English website at https://www.rapa.or.kr/en/uc/uc01/list.do, accessed on March 4, 2021.
216 Article 66 *bis* (3) of the Radio Waves Act.
217 Korea Radio Promotion Association, "Business," accessed on March 4, 2021, available at https://www.rapa.or.kr/en/un/un01/list.do.

4 Concluding Remarks

The Radio Waves Act has a relatively long history compared to other space-related laws in South Korea. The Act reflects South Korea's effort to comply with its international obligations related to spectrum management and other telecommunications activities.

As explored, the Act closely mirrors both the explicit and implicit purposes of the ITU regime as well as part of the Outer Space Treaty and the Registration Convention, by declaring the Korean government's duty to formulate and implement policy measures in order to maximize the use of limited spectrum resources for public welfare. In this regard, the master plan for spectrum promotion issued every five years by the Minister of Science and ICT serves as a framework for South Korea's regulations and policies concerning frequencies and the communications industry.

The current spectrum utilization system in South Korea is governed by i) assigning specified frequencies to a person, ii) designating an individual station to use frequencies, or iii) approving the use of frequencies for particular purposes. However, as discussed, an *ad hoc* patchwork of different objectives and methods made it complicated to understand and manage the spectrum use overall. While such a manner worked immediately when the need arose, it is recommended that now is the time to restructure the existing system into an organized, unified licensing regime given that it has been over twenty years since the Radio Waves Act was fully amended in line with the ever-changing telecommunications market trends.

The Radio Waves Act allows spectrum or relevant facility trading whereby the right to use frequencies or the ownership of facilities can be transferred or leased based on the needs of the market. This trading system appears to contribute to more efficient use of natural or artificial resources for private entities in the telecommunications business. In this regard, the national register of frequency usage rights and other associated information, as well as the disclosing system of spectrum use by the Minister of Science and ICT, provides more increased transparency in the market-based telecommunications sector.

The Radio Waves Act also implements the obligation of international registration of satellites regardless of their types including communication, Earth observation, and navigation satellites. Even though international space law – Article VIII of the Outer Space Treaty and the Registration Convention – requires both national and international registration of space objects, the Radio Waves Act, does not fully cover the entire scope of registration obligations.

The Radio Waves Act emphasizes international cooperation among States regarding spectrum management as well as research and development of telecommunications technologies. Such cooperation ranges from spectrum interference monitoring under the Radio Regulations of the ITU regime to space weather monitoring under the collaborative network with other countries, which meets the general purpose of international space law.

The supervisory authority over the frequency-related activities in the Radio Waves Act is the Ministry of Science and ICT, and the Act confers powers to the Minister of Science and ICT to grant permission or approval for the use of frequencies. While the Minister is essentially in charge of implementing most of the legal obligations, the Radio Waves Act also allows other governmental agencies or private associations to get involved in their relevant or technical affairs, which helps the Minister to efficiently carry out the missions stipulated in the Act.

Given the history of amendments to the Radio Waves Act as discussed, there seems to be little consideration for space-related or satellite activities from the Act's initial enactment in 1961 until its entire amendments in 2000. However, the Act expeditiously adopted what was required under the ITU regime and other international space law. In particular, the Act reflects the fundamental purpose of the ITU Constitution, which highlights that frequencies and associated orbits are limited natural resources and that they must be used rationally, efficiently, and economically in conformity with the provisions of the Radio Regulations. Besides, the Radio Regulations further stipulate that administrations of member States are obliged not to assign to a station any frequency in derogation of either the Table of Frequency Allocations or the other provisions of the Radio Regulations. In response, the Radio Waves Act establishes the Minister of Science and ICT's duty to comply with the Table of Frequency Allocations as well as the provisions of the Radio Regulations. South Korea's national table of frequency allocations is a good demonstration of how sufficiently South Korea has carried out its international commitments under the ITU regime.

The principles and obligations set out in the UN space treaties but not covered by the Radio Waves Act pertain to i) the launch activities and the authorization and continuous supervision thereof, ii) the national and international registration of space objects – the Radio Waves Act only addresses the international registration of satellites launched by Korean nationals –, iii) international liability for national activities, and iv) other obligations related to the rescue and return of personnel and space objects. In order to implement these still remaining international requirements, South Korea has legislated additional space laws, which will be explored in the following chapters.

CHAPTER 5

An Analysis of the Space Development Promotion Act

1 Introduction

As discussed in the prior two chapters, despite the fact that the Aerospace Industry Development Promotion Act and the Radio Waves Act contributed to South Korea's early space (-related) development, both Acts are almost silent on the international principles and obligations regarding space activities that South Korea is required to fulfill. The "Space Development Promotion Act" was enacted on May 31, 2005, in response to these demands.

1.1 *Legislative History*

In the early 2000s, South Korea was passionate about establishing new space legislation with which to govern diverse space activities implementing international requirements, as the nation's first space launch vehicle, KSLV-I, was being developed enthusiastically pursuant to the national space program initiated in 1996.[1] In addition to reorganizing the legal framework, the Korean government launched a series of public relations efforts to explain its ambitious space plan. With the commencement of the campaign in 2003, the government began working on drafting a bill regarding space development promotion,[2] which was then made public in July 2004 to seek comments from interested individuals and groups.

The draft bill, in compliance with internal procedures of the government, was reviewed for its contents and examined for its phraseology prior to the President's signature. On December 29, 2004, the bill was submitted to the National Assembly and then referred to the Science, Technology, Information and Telecommunications (STIT) Committee under the National Assembly on the following day. This government-initiated bill clearly shows in its proposal that the reason for proposing the bill is to systematically promote space

1 *Supra* Chapter 3 §3.1.

2 According to Article 52 of the Constitution of the Republic of Korea, members of the National Assembly or ministries of the government can propose a bill, either of which is required to pass through the National Assembly to become law, and there is no difference in legal effect between the two.

 | DOI:10.1163/9789004694743_007

development, to establish a legal and institutional framework for the efficient use and management of space objects, and to provide a legal basis for fulfilling the obligations stipulated in the international treaties as a space developing country.[3]

After a public hearing and deliberations held at the STIT Committee, the modified bill was forwarded to the Plenary Session of the National Assembly and finally approved on May 3, 2005. The President promulgated the Act on May 31, 2005, which, pursuant to Article 1 of the Act's Addenda,[4] began enforcement six months later, on December 1, 2005. For South Korea, the year 2005 marks a turning point in its space development and national space legislation, as the government proclaimed 2005 as the new beginning of space development under the motto "Space Korea."[5]

1.2 *The Structure and Purpose of the Act*

The Space Development Promotion Act post enactment underwent nineteen amendments in total and is comprised of forty-five articles as of August 2022, which is supplemented by the Presidential Decree and the Administrative Rules of the Act. The Act addresses a wide range of matters, including the development of a national space program, the formation of a national space committee, the registration of space objects, launch permission, liability for damages caused by space accidents, and the rescue and return of astronauts and space objects (see Table 6). The Act aims to facilitate the peaceful use and scientific exploration of outer space, as well as to contribute to national security, economic growth, and the betterment of citizens' lives by systematically promoting the development of outer space and efficiently using and managing space objects.[6]

During the review process by the Science, Technology, Information and Telecommunications (STIT) Committee of the National Assembly, there was a brief discussion about whether to retain the term 'national security' in Article 1 of the government bill as one of the Act's purposes. The rationale behind this discussion was that, even if Article 1 does not explicitly refer to 'national security,' the purpose of space development inherently involves national security,

3 The Bill on Space Development Promotion, at 1, December 29, 2004. Since the bill proposal was written in Korean, it is translated into English by the author.

4 Article 1 of the Addenda provides that the Act comes into force six months after its promulgation.

5 Then Ministry of Science and Technology (current Ministry of Science and ICT), "2005 과학기술연감, Science and Technology Annual" (2006), 117–118.

6 Article 1 of the Space Development Promotion Act.

TABLE 6 Main contents of the Space Development Promotion Act

Articles	Contents
1	Purposes
2	Definitions
3	Government's Obligations and Commitments
4	Relation with other Acts
5	Formulation of National Space Programs and Other Related Plans
6 to 7	National Space Committee and Other Institutions
8 to 10	Registration of Space Objects
11 to 13	Launch Permission
14	Liability for Damages Caused by Space Accidents
14-2 to 14-3	Rescue and Return of Astronauts and Space Objects
15	Formulation of Plans to Prepare for Hazards in Space and Designation of Space Environment Surveillance Institutes and suchlike
16	Space Accident Investigation Committee
17	Dissemination and Utilization of Satellite Data
18	Promotion of Private Sector-led Space Development
19 to 21	Orders for Suspension or Rectification of Space Development and National Security and Safety
22 to 23	Designation of and Financial Support for Space Industry Clusters
24	Survey on the Current Status of Space Development and Space Industry
25	Confidentiality
26	Entrustment of Authority
27 to 29	Penalty and Administrative Fine

and the term 'national security' is merely a descriptive expression that proclaims the peaceful development of outer space.[7] Although no further details about the discussion are available, it is confirmed that the government draft,

7 Science, Technology, Information and Telecommunications (STIT) Committee of the National Assembly, "우주개발진흥법안 심사보고서(Review of the Bill on the Space Development Promotion [English title added])," April 22, 2005, at 13.

which contains 'national security' as one of the Act's purposes, was ultimately accepted in Article 1 of the passed bill.[8]

2 The Definitions of the Terms in the Act

Article 2 of the Space Development Promotion Act provides definitions clarifying the meanings of the terminology used in the Act. The first term is "space development," which refers to activities such as research and development of the design, manufacturing, launch and operation of artificial space objects[9] as well as the exploration and use of outer space and other related operations to enable such activities.[10] The second term "space development project" means a project to advance space development, including other relevant projects to promote the development of space education, technology, informatization and industry,[11] based on the prior definition of "space development."[12]

The term "space object" is defined in a slightly unique manner, comprised of three subparagraphs as follows:

(a) The term "artificial space object" means an object designed and manufactured for use in outer space (including a space launch vehicle, artificial satellite, spaceship, and the components thereof);[13]

(b) The term "natural space object" means an object (including a meteorite) formed naturally in outer space;[14]

(c) The term "meteorite" means a solid piece of debris from outer space, which has fallen to the Earth's surface attracted by the gravity of Earth.[15]

In other words, a "space object" in this Act is essentially classified into two main categories depending on whether it is artificial or natural: An "artificial space object" and a "natural space object." Compared to the Liability Convention and the Registration Convention both containing the same definition of a "space object," which "includes component parts of a space object as well as its launch vehicle and parts thereof,"[16] what is referred to as an "artificial space object" in the Act is basically equivalent to the term "space object" in the two treaties.

8 *Supra* Chapter 5, n. 6.
9 Subparagraph 1(a) of Article 2 of the Space Development Promotion Act.
10 Subparagraph 1(b) of Article 2 of the Space Development Promotion Act.
11 Subparagraph 2 of Article 2 of the Space Development Promotion Act.
12 Subparagraph 1 of Article 2 of the Space Development Promotion Act.
13 Subparagraph 3(a) of Article 2 of the Space Development Promotion Act.
14 Subparagraph 3(b) of Article 2 of the Space Development Promotion Act.
15 Subparagraph 3(c) of Article 2 of the Space Development Promotion Act.
16 Article I(d) of the Liability Convention and Article I(b) of the Registration Convention.

According to the revision records of the Act, the terms and the definitions of a "natural space object" and a "meteorite" were added to Article 2 of the 2015 Amendments,[17] in order to deal with "natural" objects that originate in outer space by applying the Act.[18]

The term "space accident," which appears in relation to liability for damages and the Space Accident Investigation Committee, is defined as "a breakdown, crash, collision, explosion, and suchlike of an artificial space object, which occurs in the course of launching (including preparation for launch, test launch, and unsuccessful launch) and operating the space object."[19]

In addition, as the Act covers some aspects of the dissemination and utilization of satellite information, it also provides a definition of "satellite information," which refers to "information processed with images, voice, sound, data, or combinations thereof acquired using a satellite (including those obtained by processing or utilizing such information)."[20]

The last term "hazards in space" is defined as "risks of a crash, collision, and suchlike of space objects in outer space,"[21] which was introduced into the 2014 Amendments as the Act added provisions relating to space situational awareness and space environment surveillance.[22]

As observed from the terms and definitions discussed above, the Act does not include the definition or delimitation of the term "outer space." Historically, the question of demarcating the boundary between the upper limit of airspace and the beginning of outer space is older than the history of human space exploration itself.[23] Nonetheless, there has yet to be any international consensus on the subject matter, which also pertains to the vertical limit of the sovereignty of States and the application of air law versus space law.[24] While certain States such as Australia and Denmark explicitly refer to 100 kilometers above

17 Amended on January 20, 2015, went into force on July 21, 2015, Act No. 13009.

18 Details of the provisions on such natural space objects will be examined in the subsections of 5.3.

19 Subparagraph 4 of Article 2 of the Space Development Promotion Act.

20 Subparagraph 5 of Article 2 of the Space Development Promotion Act.

21 Subparagraph 6 of Article 2 of the Space Development Promotion Act.

22 Amended on June 3, 2014, went into force on December 4, 2014, Act No. 12723. The provisions concerned will be discussed in more detail in Chapter 5 §3.10.

23 UNCOPUOS Scientific and Technical Subcommittee, Report of the Scientific and Technical Sub-Committee on the Work of its Fifth Sessions (1967) UN Doc A/AC.105/39, at 2.

24 For more discussions, *see* Frans von der Dunk, "International Space Law," in Frans von der Dunk (ed.), *Handbook of Space Law* (2014), at 60–72.

sea level as the beginning of outer space in their national space laws,[25] some other States adopt more vague or functional approaches; the United States, for example, rejects the idea of creating a firm demarcation line for outer space[26] and merely mentions "outside the Earth's atmosphere" in its national legislation.[27]

The Korean government's approach to the question of legally delimitating outer space is currently more of a "wait-and-see" attitude from a functionalist perspective, while some domestic scientists theoretically acknowledge or refer to the Kármán Line.[28] After examining prior discussions on this issue at the United Nations as well as the national space laws of other States, South Korea concluded that, at least for the time being, it is not urgent or necessary to define the explicit boundary between air space and outer space in its national space law,[29] while keeping track of the international discussion towards a potential global consensus.

Recently, however, the Act newly added the definition of a "space launch vehicle" right next to the existing definition of a "space object," while delegating details of its definition to the Presidential Decree of the Act. As a result, a remarkable clause concerning the aforementioned boundary issue

25 Section 8 of the Australian Space Activities Act (Act No. 123 of 1998 as amended Act No. 8 of 2010) provides that "launch a space object means launch the object into an area beyond the distance of 100 km above mean sea level, or attempt to do so."

Section 4 (4) of the Danish Outer Space Act (Act No. 409 of May 11, 2016) defines "outer space" as "space above the altitude of 100km above sea level."

26 The US Statement, "Definition and Delimitation of Outer Space And The Character And Utilization Of The Geostationary Orbit," Legal Subcommittee of the United Nations Committee on the Peaceful Uses of Outer Space at its 40th Session in Vienna from April 2001, last accessed on October 24, 2022, available at https://2009-2017.state.gov/s/l/22718.htm. The US Statement reads that "[w]ith respect to the question of the definition and delimitation of outer space, we have examined this issue carefully and have listened to the various statements delivered at this session. Our position continues to be that defining or delimiting outer space is not necessary. No legal or practical problems have arisen in the absence of such a definition. On the contrary, the differing legal regimes applicable in respect of airspace and outer space have operated well in their respective spheres. The lack of a definition or delimitation of outer space has not impeded the development of activities in either sphere."

27 Sec. 103(1)(A), of the National Aeronautics and Space Act of 1958.

28 The Fédération Aéronautique Internationale (FAI), "100km Altitude Boundary for Astronautics," last accessed on October 24, available at https://www.fai.org/page/icare-boundary.

29 The Ministry of Foreign Affairs, "우주활동의 자유와 국가주권관련 국제법적 문제에 대한 연구 (A Study on the International Legal Issues Regarding Space Activities and National Sovereignty [English title added])" conducted by Wonwha Park, September 25, 2009, at 13–20 and 44–45.

was adopted in the Presidential Decree following the Cabinet meeting on November 29, 2022.

Specifically, Subparagraph 3 *bis* of Article 2 of the Act, which entered into force on December 11, 2022, reads: The term "space launch vehicle" means an artificial space object that launches a satellite, spacecraft, and suchlike into outer space by its own propulsion or booster/engine system, including a 'suborbital launch vehicle' with the particular performance prescribed by the Presidential Decree of the Space Development Promotion Act, but excluding weapons such as missiles.

Accordingly and interestingly, the term 'suborbital launch vehicle' is defined in Article 1 *bis* of the Presidential Decree as:[30]

> An artificial space object that ascends and descends by its own propulsion or booster/engine system and is designed and manufactured to 'have a performance that can ascend to more than 100 kilometers above sea level.'

It should be noted that although the Presidential Decree does not explicitly and directly provide for the definition of outer space, it requires a suborbital launch vehicle to have a performance enough to ascend to 100 kilometers. In other words, it can be understood that, by setting the 100-kilometer-performance requirement for a suborbital launch vehicle, the Presidential Decree implies how and where South Korea sees the boundary between air space and outer space; yet, South Korea officially sticks to its "wait-and-see" attitude by avoiding expressly demarcating outer space in the Act.

3 General Provisions on National Space Policies and Organizations

The Space Development Promotion Act not only provides for the implementation of international obligations in accordance with the UN space treaties but also contains domestic space policies and strategies to develop South Korea's space sector. Before analyzing the Act from the perspective of international space law, this section will examine the national aspects that the Act addresses such as the Korean government's stance on space-related activities, national

30 Presidential Decree No. 33016, partially amended on December 6, 2022, and entered into force on December 11, 2022.

space plans, the National Space Committee, space organizations, and other domestic space policies.

3.1 *Government's Declaration of Its Fundamental Obligations*

Article 3 of the Act articulates the Korean government's obligations and commitments, stating that the government must "observe any space-related treaties it has entered into with other countries and/or international organizations" and "pursue the peaceful exploration and use of outer space."[31] This provision underscores a general obligation to comply with international space law[32] and reiterates one of the key principles as stipulated in the preamble and Article IV of the Outer Space Treaty.[33] The phrase "any space-related treaties" refers to the four UN space treaties that South Korea is a party to, as well as any future space-related treaties that may be signed.

Article 3 further provides that the government should "establish and promote a comprehensive policy for space development."[34] By emphasizing the significance of space policy-making, the Korean government affirms its overarching commitment to ensure steady and sustainable progress in the space sector.

3.2 *The Relationship with Other Acts*

Pursuant to Article 4 of the Space Development Promotion Act, "the promotion of space development and the use and management of space objects" are governed by this Act *unless* otherwise provided in any other laws. This indicates that if there is a special provision in another Act, such provision shall prevail over the Space Development Promotion Act in terms of space development and administration of space objects.

A question can be raised as to whether it is appropriate for the Act to have lower status than other laws in relation to the application and scope of

---

31 Article 3(1) of the Space Development Promotion Act.

32 Matthew Schaefer, "What Level of Detail in National Commercial Space Legislation Is Ideal for the Harmonization and Enforcement of Such Legislation and Outer Space Treaty?" in Proceedings of the International Institute of Space Law 62 (2019), 239–241.

33 The preamble of the Outer Space Treaty includes the following phrases: "Recognizing the common interest of all mankind in the progress of the exploration and *use of outer space for peaceful purposes*," and "[d]esiring to contribute to broad international cooperation in the scientific as well as the legal aspects of the *exploration and use of outer space for peaceful purposes*" (Italics added). Paragraph 2 of Article IV of the Outer Space Treaty states that "[t]he Moon and other celestial bodies shall be used by all States Parties to the Treaty exclusively for peaceful purposes."

34 Article 3(2) of the Space Development Promotion Act.

space-related matters. Three current Acts, in particular, may be pertinent to this question.

One is the Aerospace Industry Development Promotion Act examined in Chapter 3. However, such a situation where there is a conflict over the application and scope is unlikely to occur in practice because, as discussed in Section 1.2 of Chapter 3, the Aerospace Industry Development Promotion Act focuses on the manufacturing activities conducted on Earth, specifically, more on the aviation industry than on the space industry, while the Space Development Promotion Act applies solely to the space sector and aims to promote space development and manage space objects as stipulated in Article 1 of the Act.

Another law concerned is the Radio Waves Act explored in Chapter 4 that governs activities related to satellite communications and frequency bands under the ITU regime. Prior to examining what the Radio Waves Act specifies, it is worth noting that the first sentence of Article 9(1) of the Space Development Promotion Act provides for the Minister of Science and ITC's international obligation to register "artificial space objects" with the UN, and "artificial space objects," as detailed Article 2(3)(a) of the Act, includes artificial *satellites* by definition.[35] Nonetheless, Article 9 of the Act further stipulates in its second sentence that the foregoing does *not* apply to artificial *satellites* registered with the United Nations pursuant to Article 44(1) of the Radio Waves Act. As examined earlier,[36] Article 44(1) of the Radio Waves Act provides for the international registration of artificial *satellites* including those for communication, navigation, and Earth observation.[37] In other words, the UN registration of artificial satellites is governed by the Radio Waves Act, while other space objects than artificial satellites are regulated by the Space Development Promotion Act. It can be understood that this was the result of a compromise between the then existing Radio Waves Act which already had the regulation on the satellite registration and the newly enacted Space Development Promotion Act. Since the Space Development Promotion Act clarifies the application scope on the international registration of space objects, there appears to be no conflict of interpretation between the two laws in that regard.

The other law that can be related to the issue on which law takes precedence is the Space Damage Compensation Act[38] enacted in 2007 in accordance with

35 *See supra* Chapter 5 §2. *See* also *infra* Chapter 5 §4.3 for more details on Article 9 of the Space Development Promotion Act.

36 *See supra* Chapter 4 §3.14, especially Table 5.

37 It provides that "[t]he Minister of Science and ICT shall register an artificial satellite launched by a citizen of the Republic of Korea with the United Nations in accordance with the Convention on Registration of Objects Launched into Outer Space."

38 The Space Damage Compensation Act will be examined in detail in Chapter 6.

Article 14 of the Space Development Promotion Act, which provides "[a]ny person who has launched a space object [...] shall hold the liability for damages arising from space accidents caused by the artificial space object. In such cases, the scope of compensation for damages, limitation of liabilities and other relevant matters shall be prescribed by a separate law." Therefore, regardless of the appropriateness of Article 4 of the Space Development Promotion Act, matters on compensation for space damage are governed by the Space Damage Compensation Act, which can be considered as a special law in such matters.

3.3 *The Formulation of the Basic Plan and the Action Plan for the Promotion of Space Development*

The Basic Plan for the Promotion of Space Development is South Korea's fundamental and comprehensive space development program which is established every five years pursuant to Article 5 of the Space Development Promotion Act. The Basic Plan presents the government's mid- to long-term vision for the space sector and sets goals to promote space development and manage space objects.

The Basic Plan features various aspects of South Korea's space ambitions including:[39]

i. Objectives and directions of space policies;
ii. Space development systems and strategies;
iii. Expanding necessary infrastructure;
iv. Financing and investment in space development;
v. Space research and development;
vi. Strengthening professional human resources;
vii. International cooperation;
viii. Supporting space development programs;
ix. Promoting private space development and business;[40]
x. The development and operation of the satellite navigation system;[41]
xi. The Management of space objects;
xii. The utilization of the outcomes of space development; and
xiii. 'Other matters' related to the promotion of space development and the management of space objects prescribed by the Presidential Decree.

39 Article 5(2) of the Space Development Promotion Act.

40 Article 5(2) 9 *bis* of the Space Development Promotion Act, which was newly inserted under Act No. 18867.

41 Article 5(2) 9 *ter* of the Space Development Promotion Act, which was newly inserted under Act No. 18867.

The Presidential Decree specifies that such 'other matters' encompass policy-making on the protection and management of intellectual property rights, facilitating active information exchange among space industries, academia, and research institutes, as well as commercializing space technologies.[42]

Notably, two subject matters from the list above were recently added to the Act and took effect on December 11, 2022. The first subject matter pertains to promoting private space development and business. It is significant that the term "private" space development is now legally and officially included in the Basic Plan under the Act. Accordingly, it is anticipated that the upcoming five-year Basic Plan will present a substantial framework for the private space sector. Discussions such as the contract types between the government or its agencies and the private sector are ongoing. The second subject matter added to the Act concerns the development and operation of the satellite navigation system. Although the Act does not explicitly mention its name, what it refers to is the Korea Positioning System (KPS), which is expected to commence its full service in 2035.[43]

The Basic Plan is formulated by the Minister of Science and ICT in consultation with the heads of related central administrative agencies including the National Intelligence Service,[44] to whom the Minister notifies the schedule and guidelines for the formulation prior to the planning process. If necessary, the Minister may request the heads of agencies to submit information and data needed to draft a plan.[45] A final draft is confirmed through the deliberation of the National Space Committee,[46] which is announced to the public by the Minister of Science and ICT without delay. Nevertheless, matters concerning national security may not be open to the public in consultation with the heads of relevant administrative agencies and the Director of the National Intelligence Service.[47]

---

42 Article 2(3) of the Presidential Decree of the Space Development Promotion Act.

43 *Supra* Chapter 2 §7.1.4.

44 Article 5(5) of the Space Development Promotion Act, Article 2(1) of the Presidential Decree of the Space Development Promotion Act.

The National Intelligence Service was established in 1961 to protect society, guarantee national security, and promote national interests, under which there are five divisions: the National Cyber Security Center, the National Industrial Security Center, National Counterintelligence Integration Center, the Transnational Crime Information Center, and the Terrorism Information Integration Center.

45 Article 5(5) of the Space Development Promotion Act and Article 2(2) of the Presidential Decree of the Space Development Promotion Act.

46 Article 5(3) of the Space Development Promotion Act.

47 Article 5(4) of the Space Development Promotion Act.

In order to efficiently execute the Basic Plan, the Minister of Science and ICT also formulates the Action Plan for the Promotion of Space Development every year in accordance with the Basic Plan (see Table 7).[48] The Action Plan includes an overview of each project, a report on performance results from the preceding year as well as a detailed implementation plan for the pertinent year.[49] The Action Plan is finalized by the end of February following deliberation of the Working Committee for the Promotion of Space Development chaired by the Vice Minister of Science and ICT. The Minister of Science and ICT notifies the finalized Action Plan to the heads of relevant central administrative agencies. If necessary for national security, the Minister of Science and ICT may establish a separate Action Plan in consultation with the Minister of National Defense and the Director of the National Intelligence Service.[50] As such, the Korean government acknowledges that space is becoming the dominant domain for national security, thus taking this into special consideration during the process of making both the Basic and Action Plans.[51]

Both the Basic and Action Plans would be revised if necessary to meet continuing developments and changes in the space sector. Such revisions to the original Basic or Action Plan are also deliberated and finalized by the National Space Committee[52] or the Working Committee for the Promotion of Space Development,[53] respectively.

One of the noticeable revisions to the Basic Plan of 2018 to 2022 was made in June 2021 following the South Korea-US summit during the preceding month. During the summit, the South Korean and US leaders agreed to significantly enhance space cooperation by announcing the termination of missile guidelines imposed on South Korea in 1979. Lifting the 42-year-old restriction on South Korea's missile development program indicates that South Korea can now develop ballistic missiles capable of reaching targets far beyond the Korean Peninsula, with a maximum range of 1,000 to 5,000 kilometers.[54]

---

48 Article 5-2(1) of the Space Development Promotion Act.

49 Article 5-2(2) of the Space Development Promotion Act and Article 3(1) of the Presidential Decree of the Space Development Promotion Act.

50 Article 5-2 of the Space Development Promotion Act, Articles 3(2) and (3) of the Presidential Decree of the Space Development Promotion Act.

51 A discussion on national security will be addressed in Chapter 5 §4.6.

52 Article 5(3) of the Space Development Promotion Act.

53 Articles 2(1) and 3(3) of the Presidential Decree of the Space Development Promotion Act.

54 Brian Kim, "US lifts missile restrictions on South Korea, ending range and warhead limits," Defense News, May 25, 2021, available at https://www.defensenews.com/global/asia-pacific/2021/05/25/us-lifts-missile-restrictions-on-south-korea-ending-range-and-warhead-limits/.

About a year before this missile range restriction was lifted, there was another significant agreement between the two nations that allowed South Korea to use solid fuel for space launch vehicles. A solid-propellant can offer greater missile and launch vehicle mobility than a liquid one and reduces launch preparation time.[55] To incorporate and embody such crucial changes in the national space program, the Minister of Science and ICT revised the Basic Plan by adding a goal of private-led development of a small launch vehicle using solid fuel and its launch by 2024. The revision was deliberated and finalized by the Nineteenth National Space Committee held in June 2021.[56]

3.4 *The Establishment of the National Space Committee*

The National Space Committee is a non-permanent body established in 2005 pursuant to Article 6 of the Space Development Promotion Act. As the nation's top deliberation body in the space sector, the Committee examines various matters related to space development, such as deliberation on major space programs, granting launch permission, space affairs coordination between relevant central administrative agencies, evaluation on the management of space development projects, and the designation and operation of institutions specialized in space development.[57]

The National Space Committee, while organizationally under the purview of the President,[58] was originally chaired by the Minister of Science and ICT until August 2021 when the Space Development Promotion Act underwent partial amendment. Prior to the 2021 Amendment, the Committee was composed of fifteen members, including vice-ministers of relevant central administrations[59] and civilian space experts. However, there were concerns regarding the Committee's status and composition, given its pivotal role in South Korea's space development. The appointment of the Minister of Science and ICT as the chair of the Committee was deemed inadequate, and there was a growing

---

55 Hyungjin Kim, "South Korea to have solid-fuel rockets in major deal with US," Defense News, July 28, 2020, available at https://www.defensenews.com/global/asia-pacific/2020/07/28/south-korea-to-have-solid-fuel-rockets-in-major-deal-with-us/.

56 Press release by the Ministry of Science and ICT, June 10, 2021, "한미 정상회담을 통한 우주개발 성과의 실현을 위한 '제19회 국가우주위원회 개최' (The Nineteenth National Space Committee Held to Fulfill the Achievements of Space Development Following the Korea-US Summit) [English title added by the author]."

57 Article 6(2) of the Space Development Promotion Act.

58 Article 6(1) of the Space Development Promotion Act.

59 They included the Vice Minister of Strategy and Finance, the Vice Minister of Foreign Affairs, and the Vice Minister of Trade, Industry, and Energy, as stipulated in Articles 6(3) and (4) of the Space Development Promotion Act before its amendment.

TABLE 7 Comparison between the Basic Plan and the Action Plan for the Promotion of Space Development

	The Basic Plan for the Promotion of Space Development	**The Action Plan for the Promotion of Space Development**
Authority	Minister of Science and ICT	Minister of Science and ICT
Features	Comprehensive space development policies and a framework for mid to long term goals and strategies	Specific execution methods
Deliberation	National Space Committee	Working Committee for the Promotion of Space Development
Duration	Every five years	Each year
Announcement	A public announcement without delay	Notification to the ministers of relevant central agencies
Matters concerning national security	May not be published	May be formulated as a separate plan

consensus that the President or the Prime Minister of South Korea should take the helm. Additionally, criticism was leveled against the Committee's composition of relatively lower-level representatives, such as vice-ministers, who lacked the requisite authority to negotiate or commit to critical decisions.

In response to these concerns, the National Assembly revised Article 6 pertaining to the National Space Committee (see Table 8).

Essentially, as of November 11, 2021,[60] the National Space Committee is chaired by the *Prime Minister*, and the Minister of Science and ICT is now a vice president of the Committee. In addition, instead of vice-minister level officials, the Amendment precisely specifies that the Committee's members

60 The Addenda to the Amendment to the Space Development Promotion Act provides that the Amendment shall enter into force three months after the date of its promulgation. The Amendment was promulgated on August 10, 2021.

TABLE 8 Comparison between the original Article 6 and the amendment to Article 6 of the Space Development Promotion Act. [Italics added]

Original	Amended
Article 6 [(1) and (2) omitted] (3) The Committee shall be comprised of no more than ***fifteen*** members including one chairperson. (4) The ***Minister of Science and ICT*** shall take the ***chair*** of the Committee, and the following persons shall become the members thereof: 1. The ***Vice Minister*** of Strategy and Finance, the ***Vice Minister*** of Foreign Affairs, the ***Vice Minister*** of Trade, Industry and Energy, and ***public officials of the vice-minister level of relevant central administrative agencies*** prescribed by the Presidential Decree; and 2. Persons with abundant knowledge and experience [...]. [(5) and (6) omitted]	Article 6 [(1) and (2) omitted] (3) The Committee shall be comprised of no more than ***sixteen*** members including one chairperson. (4) The ***Prime Minister*** shall take the ***chair*** of the Committee, the ***Minister of Science and ICT*** shall take the ***vice-chair*** of the Committee, and the following persons shall become the members thereof: 1. The ***Minister*** of Strategy and Finance, the ***Minister*** of Foreign Affairs, the ***Minister*** of Trade, Industry and Energy, the ***Minister of National Defense***, and the ***Director of the National Intelligence Service***; and 2. Persons with abundant knowledge and experience [...]. [(5) and (6) omitted]

include the *Minister* of Strategy and Finance, the *Minister* of Foreign Affairs, the *Minister* of Trade, Industry and Energy as well as the *Minister of National Defense* and the *Director of the National Intelligence Service*.[61] The latter two members are newly added into Article 6 of the Act in order to clarify who are the concerned minister-level officials.

Given the inter-ministerial characteristic in implementing space development programs and the significant growth in the space sector since the Committee was established in 2005, it seems opportune to have upgraded the

61 Italics added.

Committee by being chaired by the Prime Minister and consisting of minister-level officials. Similarly, some Space-faring countries such as the United States and the United Kingdom also have an organization in their governmental system, the National Space Council, to improve the clarity and efficiency of space policy across governments.[62]

The US National Space Council chaired by the US Vice President coordinates space policy as an interagency forum in order to assure rapid and coherent federal decision making, which consists of the Secretaries of State, Defense, Commerce, Transportation, and Homeland Security along with the Director of National Intelligence, Director of the Office of Management and Budget, National Security Advisor, Assistant to the President for Economic Policy, Assistant to the President for Domestic Policy, Administrator of NASA, the Director of the Office of Science and Technology Policy, and the Chairman of the Joint Chiefs of Staff.[63] Likewise, the UK National Space Council led by the UK Prime Minister was established in 2020 as a cabinet committee, a group of ministers that can take collective decisions that are binding across government,[64] which develops the nation's space framework and provides strategic direction to the cross-government approach to space.[65] Both the US and the UK National Space Councils therefore seem to be equivalent to South Korea's National Space Committee with a similar role and organization, chaired by the Vice President and the Prime Minister, respectively.

Meanwhile, the explicit inclusion of the Minister of National Defense and the Director of the National Intelligence Service in the National Space Committee as mentioned above manifests the growing importance of using space to enhance military capabilities and national security. As the space applications for the defense industry are proliferating and space is becoming a vital domain for national security, South Korea started seeing the space domain as not only a scientific/economic development arena but also a valuable asset for national defense and security.

---

62 The UK Department for Business, Energy & Industrial Strategy and Ministry of Defense, "National Space Strategy," 40, September 27, 2021, available at https://www.gov.uk/government/publications/national-space-strategy.

63 The White House, "Presidential Executive Order on Reviving the National Space Council," June 30, 2017, available at https://www.federalregister.gov/documents/2017/07/07/2017-14378/reviving-the-national-space-council.

64 The UK Government, "List of Cabinet Committees," https://www.gov.uk/government/publications/the-cabinet-committees-system-and-list-of-cabinet-committees, accessed on October 14, 2021.

65 Supra Chapter 5, n. 62, the UK "National Space Strategy."

3.5 *The Establishment of the Working Committee for the Promotion of Space Development*

The Working Committee for the Promotion of Space Development was set up along with the National Space Committee in 2005. Article 6(5) of the Space Development Promotion Act provides that the Working Committee is established under the National Space Committee in order to efficiently conduct the Committee's affairs. The Act leaves details on the composition and operation of the Working Committee to the Presidential Decree.[66]

The Working Committee is chaired by the Vice Minister of Science and ICT, which consists of no more than twenty-five members in total[67] who are in charge of space-related affairs in the upper echelons of the Civil Service or have considerable expertise and experience in the space field commissioned by the Working Committee.[68]

The Working Committee's primary task is to formulate the aforementioned annual space development implementation scheme, known as the Action Plan for the Promotion of Space Development.[69] However, it may also organize and operate subcommittees to conduct expert reviews on specific topics such as space object management and international cooperation.[70] Accordingly, the Subcommittee on International Space Cooperation was launched in January 2019, chaired by the Director-General of the Policy and Research Department of the Ministry of Science and ICT, with eight Directors from the Ministry of National Defense, the Ministry of Foreign Affairs, the Ministry of Land, Infrastructure and Transport, the Ministry of Environment, the Ministry of Trade, Industry and Energy, the Ministry of Oceans and Fisheries, the Ministry of the Interior and Safety, and the Korea Meteorological Administration.[71]

The Subcommittee on International Space Cooperation is meeting regularly at least twice a year and may have additional meetings at any time if necessary. The Subcommittee reviews international cooperation matters on the agenda

---

66 Article 6(6) of the Space Development Promotion Act. Articles 3(2) and (3) of the Presidential Decree of the Space Development Promotion Act.

67 Article 6(1) of the Presidential Decree of the Space Development Promotion Act.

68 Article 6(2) of the Presidential Decree of the Space Development Promotion Act.

69 *Supra* Chapter 5 §3.3.

70 Article 6(7) of the Presidential Decree of the Space Development Promotion Act.

71 Press release by the Ministry of Science and ICT, "글로벌 우주 이슈, 범부처 공동 대응 강화 – 국가우주위원회 우주개발국제협력소위원회 출범 (Reinforcing Cross-Ministerial Responses to Global Space Issues – the Launch of the Subcommittee on International Space Cooperation [English title added by the author])," January 25, 2019, available at https://www.msit.go.kr/bbs/view.do?sCode=user&mId=113&mPid=112&bbsSeqNo=94&nttSeqNo=1502086.

provided by the Working Committee and discusses and coordinates responses to international space-related issues including sharing satellite images, developing the Korea Positioning System (KPS),[72] enhancing space situational awareness, and deregulating the space industry. If necessary for in-depth discussion, civilian experts may be invited to the Subcommittee.[73] Given that space activities and related issues inherently transcend national boundaries, international cooperation is imperative and crucial. Therefore, the creation of such a subcommittee dedicated to these matters will enhance collaborative efforts among ministries and establish an integrated working framework across the government.

3.6 *The Designation of Space Development Specialized Institutes*

3.6.1 General Norms of the Act

Article 7(1) of the Space Development Promotion Act provides that the Minister of Science and ICT may designate and support specialized institutions in order to systematically and efficiently facilitate space development programs. Each designated institution executes national space projects under the Basic Plan,[74] performs the development, launch, and operation of space objects,[75] as well as promote international space cooperation, and assists in investigating space accidents.[76] The Presidential Decree sets the standards for the selection and government support of designated institutions.[77] Specifically, to qualify for designation, an institution must fulfill one of the following requirements:[78]

i. It must retain human resources and facilities capable of designing and producing space objects;
ii. It must have a record of achievement and experience in space research and development or executing a space project;

---

72 *Supra* Chapter 2 §7.1.4.
The Korea Positioning System (KPS) is an independent navigation satellite system, with a regional focus on the Korean peninsula, which is aimed at establishing South Korea's own system without relying on other Global Navigation Satellite Systems (GNSS) s such as Global Positioning System (GPS) and Galileo. Separately, South Korea is operating the Korea Augmentation Satellite System (KASS) to improve the accuracy of GPS signals and to better ensure flight safety. South Korea officially registered KASS with the International Civil Aviation Organization (ICAO), becoming the seventh space power of its kind after the United States, the European Union, India, Japan, Russia, and China.

73 *Supra* Chapter 5, n. 71, Press release at 4.

74 *Supra* Chapter 5 §3.3.

75 Article 7(2) of the Space Development Promotion Act.

76 Article 7 of the Presidential Decree of the Space Development Promotion Act.

77 Article 7(3) of the Space Development Promotion Act.

78 Article 8(1) of the Presidential Decree of the Space Development Promotion Act.

iii. It must have human resources and facilities needed to launch, track, and operate space objects (hereinafter referred to as "space center"); or

iv. It must have human resources and facilities capable of performing support tasks for the establishment of space policies.[79]

In particular, an entity designated as a specialized institute according to the criteria under iii above is required to formulate an annual "space center" operation plan by the end of January each year and obtain approval for the plan from the Minister of Science and ICT.[80] In return, the government establishes and implements various supporting policies, including manpower supply and government grants to efficiently operate such an institution.[81] Furthermore, the Minister of Science and ICT may subsidize the "space center" for its operating expenses.[82]

3.6.2 The Practice of the Norms and Concerns about the Status of KARI

In 2016, the Minister of Science and ICT designated the Korea Aerospace Research Institute (KARI), founded in 1989, as a special institution for space development, which has been the only such designation under the Act so far.[83] KARI has continued developing indigenous launch capabilities and industrializing satellite application technology with goals to strengthen national safety and public services as well as explore the Moon and beyond in the foreseeable future. KARI also operates the nation's "space center," Naro Space Center. As a leading institute in South Korea's space sector, KARI undoubtedly fulfills each of the requirements from i to iv above although meeting any of the four requirements is sufficient according to the Presidential Decree.

While KARI is arguably the most significant space research and development institute conducting South Korea's space programs, it does not have the authority to represent the Korean government on the international stage. In other words, KARI is not a government agency. It is merely a designated institution by the Minister of Science and ICT as being specialized in space development under Article 7 of the Space Development Promotion Act; no provision in the Act directly mentions the name of KARI or specifies its legal status or roles.

79 On November 9, 2021, Paragraph iv was newly added to Article 8(1) of the Presidential Decree of the Space Development Promotion Act.

80 Article 8(2) of the Presidential Decree of the Space Development Promotion Act.

81 Article 9(1) of the Presidential Decree of the Space Development Promotion Act.

82 Article 9(2) of the Presidential Decree of the Space Development Promotion Act.

83 As of October 2021.

In this regard, questions arise as to the need for an official national space agency representing South Korea both at the national and international level: Is the current rank or status of KARI sufficient, given that KARI plays a critical role in the nation's space research and development? Is it necessary to establish an independent space agency, as the world's major space-faring countries have done? Before delving into the search for answers, it should be noted that South Korea is neither a newcomer to the space arena nor a fully-fledged, leading space-faring nation. Therefore, it would be beneficial to examine both the space agencies of the classic and the emerging countries.

3.6.3 A General Assessment of the Establishment of National Space Agencies

Technical advancements and relatively lower launch costs than ever before have reduced traditional obstacles to access outer space, allowing a more diverse space community throughout the world. Along with this, the number of national space agencies has steadily increased in recent years.[84] While there are benefits to creating a new space agency, emerging space nations confront distinct challenges as the space environment becomes more congested and competitive.

There are elements for emerging space-developing countries to consider when establishing their space agency, as well as rationales for existing space-faring countries to contemplate when creating a new sort of space agency. While their motivations may vary depending on each nation's history or ambition, they nonetheless share several fundamental characteristics.

First of all, nations establish space agencies for economic or socioeconomic reasons. In this context, space agencies are a means of supporting national space industries and fostering the private space sector. Space agencies can assist in tapping opportunities that can create a better way of life for the well-being of their society, such as combating climate change via Earth observation capabilities.

Another reason lies in coordinating or consolidating the administration of their existing space programs that were previously distributed across several

84 According to the research conducted by the George Washington University, between 2014 and 2019, sixteen national space agencies, including one continental entity, were established by African Union, Australia, Bahrain, Egypt, Greece, Kenya, Luxembourg, New Zealand, Paraguay, the Philippines, Poland, Portugal, Saudi Arabia, Turkey, the United Arab Emirates, Zimbabwe in alphabetical order. *See*, Renata Knittel Kommel *et al.*, "Exploring Insights from Emerging Space Agencies," the George Washington University Elliott School of International Affairs, October 2020, at 1 and 8.

governmental departments. On this occasion, they have already been involved with a certain degree of space activities. By centralizing their space endeavors, they anticipate that they would be able to encourage civilian participation and make better use of human resources as well as decrease administrative redundancy.

In addition, nations can use their space agency to better engage in the global space community by creating stronger and broader international relations. They can present and position themselves with distinct plans and policies through their national space agencies.

Last but not least, governments with a thriving space industry typically establish space agencies to oversee their national space activities, particularly those involving commercial entities. These space agencies serve as regulatory authorities, streamlining national legal procedures while upholding international space law commitments.[85]

3.6.4 An Analysis of National Space Agencies in Other Nations

The space development system may take different shapes based on each nation's unique governmental system as well as its space development level and environment. However, there are certain similarities in the rationales for the establishment and operation of the space agencies in both the major space-faring and emerging space developing nations. In this regard, South Korea can draw ideas to establish a suitable and realistic space development system by looking into the national space agencies of the United States and Japan, which have a long history of space development, as well as Luxembourg and the United Arab Emirates as passionate, rising nations.

3.6.4.1 *The United States*

The National Aeronautics and Space Administration (NASA) is an independent federal government agency of the United States in charge of the civilian space program including aeronautics and space research. NASA was founded in 1958, the year following the launch of the Soviet Union's Sputnik that accelerated the idea of establishing an American national space agency.

Prior to the formation of NASA, several key factors were considered: i) Should it be a new space agency, or should it be built based on an existing organization? ii) Should it be a military or a civilian agency? iii) Should the

85 For more information, *Ibid.*, Renata Knittel Kommel *et al.*, "Exploring Insights from Emerging Space Agencies," at 9–15.

agency encompass aeronautical activities? iv) Should it be given the authority to execute international agreements?[86]

The then-newly established NASA turned out to be a civilian-controlled agency, succeeding the National Advisory Committee for Aeronautics (NACA) founded in 1915. NACA's assets and personnel formed the nucleus of NASA. The National Aeronautics and Space Act of 1958 was the federal statute that authorized the creation of NASA, drafted by the United States House Select Committee on Astronautics and Space Exploration and signed by President Eisenhower on July 29, 1958.[87] Congress highlighted the nation's devotion of space activities to peaceful purposes for the benefit of all humankind.[88] It also emphasized the importance of commercial space activities, declaring that "the general welfare of the United States requires that the Administration seek and encourage, to the maximum extent possible, the fullest commercial use of space."[89] The National Aeronautics and Space Act (NASA Act) identifies the objectives for NASA, which include:

i. The expansion of human knowledge of the Earth and of phenomena in the atmosphere and space;
ii. The improvement of the usefulness, performance, speed, safety, and efficiency of aeronautical and space vehicles, as well as the development and operation of vehicles capable of carrying instruments, equipment, supplies, and living organisms through space;
iii. The establishment of long-range studies of the potential benefits to be gained from, the opportunities for, and the problems involved in the utilization of aeronautical and space activities for peaceful and scientific purposes;
iv. The preservation of the role of the United States as a leader in aeronautical and space science and technology;
v. Cooperation by the United States with other nations and groups of nations; and

86 NASA, "The Birth of NASA," March 28, 2008, last accessed on December 13,2021, available at https://www.nasa.gov/exploration/whyweexplore/Why_We_29.html.

87 More information about the early history of NASA, *see* National Archives, Dwight D. Eisenhower, Presidential Library, Museum & Boyhood Home, last accessed on December 13, 2021, available at https://www.eisenhowerlibrary.gov/research/online-documents/early-history-and-development-national-aeronautics-and-space.

88 51 USC 20102(a). For full language, *see* https://uscode.house.gov/view.xhtml?path=/prelim@title51/subtitle2/chapter201&edition=prelim.

89 51 USC 20102(c).

vi. The most effective utilization of the scientific and engineering resources of the United States, with close cooperation among all interested agencies to avoid unnecessary duplication of effort, facilities, and equipment.[90]

The National Aeronautics and Space Act enumerates NASA's powers to perform its functions. NASA is authorized to acquire, construct, improve, operate, and maintain laboratories, research and testing facilities, aeronautical and space vehicles, and other real and personal property.[91] NASA also has the authority to perform contracts, leases, cooperative agreements, or other transactions necessary in the conduct of its work.[92] This enables a smoother combination of public and private funding while also accelerating the development of new capabilities. In addition, NASA is authorized to provide liability insurance to any user of a space vehicle to compensate all or a portion of third-party claims for death, bodily injury, or loss or damage to property resulting from activities carried out in connection with the launch, operations, or recovery of the space vehicle.[93] As such, NASA has been operating with defined objectives and authorities within the scope of the National Aeronautics and Space Act. Notably, private/commercial space activities by non-governmental entities pursuant to Article VI of the Outer Space Treaty are regulated by other federal agencies. The primary agencies include the Federal Aviation Administration (FAA), which issues licenses for launch, re-entry, and spaceport operations; the Federal Communications Commission (FCC), which governs requirements for frequency operations and licenses satellite communication activities; and the National Oceanic and Atmospheric Administration (NOAA) granting licenses for remote sensing activities.

3.6.4.2 *Japan*

The Japan Aerospace Exploration Agency (JAXA) is the Japanese national aerospace agency, responsible for government-wide aerospace research and technology development, space object launches, and a variety of space missions.

JAXA was formed on October 1, 2003, by the merger of three organizations: Japan's Institute of Space and Astronautical Science (ISAS), the National Aerospace Laboratory of Japan (NAL), and the National Space Development Agency of Japan (NASDA).[94] The three prior agencies, founded through the 1950s and 60s, focused on different aspects of Japan's national aerospace

90 51 USC 20102(d).

91 51 USC 20113(c)(1).

92 51 USC 20113(e).

93 51 USC 20138(b).

94 JAXA, "About JAXA," last accessed December 15, 2021, https://global.jaxa.jp/about/.

research and development. ISAS pursued space and planetary research, while NAL focused on aviation research. NASDA developed and launched the nation's home-grown launch vehicles and satellites.

JAXA began as an independent administrative institution overseen by the Ministry of Education, Culture, Sports, Science, and Technology, as well as the Ministry of Internal Affairs and Communications.[95] In April 2015, JAXA was transformed from an independent administrative institution to a National Research and Development Agency, and its leadership was restructured to reflect the shift accordingly.[96]

Pursuant to the Act on the Japan Aerospace Exploration Agency, National Research and Development Agency (JAXA Act), the purpose of JAXA is to facilitate academic research, improve aeronautical and space science and technology, and promote the development and use of outer space in collaboration with universities and other research institutes, all while adhering to the basic principles of peaceful use of outer space.[97] Under its purpose, one of the JAXA's duties is to provide assistance and advice in response to requests from private enterprises concerning the development, launch, tracking, and operation of space objects.[98] JAXA's tasks and roles are explicitly stipulated in the aforementioned Act, which validates JAXA's legal status within the Japanese government as well as its representation in the global space community. However, like NASA in the United States, JAXA does not have the authority to license and supervise private space activities. Permissions for launch, satellite operations, and remote sensing businesses are granted by the Prime Minister of Japan.[99] The Prime Minister also continually supervises private space activities, which

95 Article 26 of the Law Concerning the Japan Aerospace Exploration Agency, Law No. 161 of 2002, December 13, 2002, available at https://global.jaxa.jp/about/law/index.html. Prior to 2004, the English name of the Ministry of Internal Affairs and Communications was the Ministry of Public Management, Home Affairs, Posts, and Telecommunications.

96 Article 4-2 of the Act on the Japan Aerospace Exploration Agency, National Research and Development Agency, as amended Act No. 76 of 2016, available at http://www.japaneselawtranslation.go.jp/law/detail/?id=3194&vm=02&re=.

97 Article 4 of the Act on the Japan Aerospace Exploration Agency, National Research and Development Agency.

98 Article 18(vi) of the Act on the Japan Aerospace Exploration Agency, National Research and Development Agency.

99 Articles 4 to 12 of the Japanese Act concerning the Launch and Control of Spacecraft, so-called the Space Activities Act (人工衛星等の打上げ及び人工衛星の管理に関する法律, Act No. 76 of 2016); Articles 4 to 17 of the Japanese Act concerning Adequate Handling of Satellite Remote Sensing Records, so-called the Remote Sensing Act (衛星リモートセンシング記録の適正な取扱いの確保に関する法律, Act No. 77 of 2016).

includes on-site inspection, correction orders, and conditions attached to the permitted activities.[100]

3.6.4.3 *Grand Duchy of Luxembourg*

The Luxembourg Space Agency (LSA) was founded on September 12, 2018, under Luxembourg's broader economic diversification agenda. The LSA, unlike the other conventional space agencies previously noted, was not designed to focus on conducting its own space exploration and scientific research. Rather, the agency's primary goal is to encourage economic growth in Luxembourg's space sector by creating a supportive and welcoming environment for current and future space enterprises. The private sector is required to obtain authorization for space activities from the minister in charge of space policy and legislation, who is currently the Minister of the Economy.[101] The operators authorized to perform space activities are under continuing supervision of the Minister.[102]

Prior to the agency's establishment, space activities were being conducted under the auspices of the Department of Space Affairs in the Ministry of the Economy. However, the government concluded that creating a space agency would better serve the nation's objectives. Luxembourg has now become a particularly attractive destination for space startups since it does not restrict foreign investment and extends legal protections to companies funded by international markets.[103] For example, CONTEC, an up-and-coming space company originally founded in South Korea in 2015, was fascinated by the agency's streamlined and accessible investment policy. Accordingly, CONTEC decided to have a subsidiary in Luxembourg and finally established CONTEC Space in 2019. It provides space ground station and satellite image processing services globally, including Northern Europe and North and South America. CONTEC Space is also introduced on the official website of the Luxembourg Space Agency.[104]

---

100 Articles 31 to 34 of the Japanese Space Activities Act and Articles 27 to 30 of the Japanese Remote Sensing Act.

101 Articles 5 to 10 of the Luxembourgian Law of 15 December 2020 on Space Activities (loi du 15 décembre 2020 portant sur les activités spatiales).

102 Article 11 of the Luxembourgian Law of 15 December 2020 on Space Activities.

103 *Supra* Chapter 5, n. 85, Renata Knittel Kommel *et al.*, "Exploring Insights from Emerging Space Agencies," the George Washington University Elliott School of International Affairs, October 2020, at 20.

104 Luxembourg Space Agency, "Expertise," last accessed December 15,2021, https://space-agency.public.lu/en/expertise/space-directory/contec.html.

The agency, housed under the Ministry of Economy, is organized into two primary teams: One for Economic Development and the other for International Affairs and Space Resources.[105] The Economic Development team facilitates and endorses individual projects through collaboration with commercial enterprises, whereas the International Affairs and Space Resources team manages international partnerships with other nations' space agencies as well as assists with regulatory and financial matters and coordinates tasks related to space resources.[106]

As the agency's establishment was primarily driven by economic motives, it prioritizes the economic aspects of space development more than traditional space agencies. The agency's objectives include i) promoting the nation's space ecosystem and generating synergies with enterprises and organizations outside the space sector, ii) assisting in job creation and increasing the space sector's contribution to the Luxembourg economy, and iii) encouraging the development of human resources and the attractiveness of space and its potential, particularly among the young generation.[107] The agency also leads the "SpaceResources.lu initiative," which presents Luxembourg as a pioneer in the exploration and utilization of space resources. Its mission is to guarantee that space resources explored under its authority serve a peaceful purpose compliant with international law. To that end, Luxembourg provides a legal framework, the Law of 2017 on the Exploration and Use of Space Resources which ensures that commercial operators have confidence in their rights to resources extracted in space.[108] Overall, the Luxembourg Space Agency implements its space economic development strategy and policy at the national level as well as internationally representing Luxembourg within the European Space Agency, space programs of the European Union, and the United Nations.[109] Within a few years of its establishment, Luxembourg has been attracting a variety of space companies by providing accessible funding opportunities, making it an attractive nation in Europe, especially in relation to space resource utilization.

---

105 Luxembourg Space Agency, "Our Team," last accessed December 22, 2021, https://space-agency.public.lu/en/expertise/space-directory.html?r=f%2Faem_theme%2Ftags_theme%3Aspace_agency%5Cearth_observation&.

106 *Supra* Chapter 5, n. 85, Renata Knittel Kommel *et al.*, at 21.

107 Luxembourg Space Agency, "The Agency," last accessed December 15,2021, https://space-agency.public.lu/en/agency/lsa.html.

108 Luxembourg Space Agency, "Space Resources," last accessed December 16,2021, https://space-agency.public.lu/en/space-resources/the-initiative.html.

109 Luxembourg Space Agency, "International Collaboration," last accessed December 22, 2021, https://space-agency.public.lu/en/agency/international-collaboration.html.

3.6.4.4 *The United Arab Emirates*

The United Arab Emirates Space Agency (UAESA) is a federal agency established under Federal Law by Decree No. 1 of 2014. The UAE President announced the decree, which states that the agency operates in accordance with the Council of Ministers and has an independent legal status to direct activities necessary to accomplish its objectives, with financial and administrative independence. All initiatives, operations, and programs relating to outer space are included in its space sector. The Board of Directors has the authority to create branches or other offices both inside and outside of the United Arab Emirates.[110]

Prior to the founding of the UAE Space Agency, the Emirates Institution for Advanced Science and Technology (EIAST) served as a federal government actor in the UAE space sector. It was established in 2006 to help the United Arab Emirates further develop and utilize space science and technologies.[111] The EIAST cooperated with South Korean engineers to launch DubaiSat-1 and DubaiSat-2 in 2007 and 2013, respectively,[112] marking the first two Earth observation satellites launched by a UAE government institution. The satellites were designed and developed by Satrec Initiative, a satellite manufacturing company in South Korea.[113] In 2015, the EIAST was reformed as the Mohammed bin Rashid Space Centre (MBRSC), an official organization of the Government of Dubai. Currently, the MBRSC continues to manage the development and operation of space science and technology programs funded by the UAE federal government.[114]

Meanwhile, the government recognized various motives for establishing the centralized UAE Space Agency to regulate and support the burgeoning space industry. Above all, like Luxembourg, the UAE government sought to diversify its economic activities by recognizing the space industry as a one-of-a-kind economic opportunity. The government identified the potential to stimulate new businesses to participate in domestic space activities, which would have

---

110 UAE Space Agency, "About UA Space Agency," last accessed on December 17, 2021, https://space.gov.ae/Page/20120/20230/About-UAE-Space-Agency.

111 Government of Dubai, "Mohammed Bin Rashid Space Centre," November 15, 2017, last accessed December 23, 2021, available at https://www.unoosa.org/documents/pdf/hlf/HLF2017/presentations/Day4/high_level_panel/4th/Presentation7.pdf.

112 Mohammed bin Rashid Space Centre (MBRSC), "DubaiSat-1," available at https://www.mbrsc.ae/satellite-programme/dubai-sat-1, and "DubaiSat-2," available at https://www.mbrsc.ae/satellite-programme/dubai-sat-2, last accessed December 23, 2021.

113 Adnan Al Rais *et al.*, "DubaiSat-1: Mission Overview, Development Status and Future Applications," 2009 IEEE International Geoscience and Remote Sensing Symposium, 2009, at V-196.

114 *Supra* Chapter 5, n. 111, Government of Dubai.

a positive impact on the UAE economy. In the global context, the UAE government considered space programs as an additional chance to enhance its geopolitical position. It envisioned that if the United Arab Emirates establishes itself as a worldwide leader in space, it will be able to use its position to contribute to the stability of the broader Arab region. Furthermore, the government anticipated that the UAE's engagement in the space sector, through its space agency, could assist to promote and strengthen effective international relationships in the global space community.[115]

With such consideration, the federal UAE Space Agency aims at regulating and developing the national space sector in a way that contributes to supporting a sustainable national economy, nurturing human resources, and strengthening the UAE's role in the regional and global space community. To that end, the agency formulates space policies, strategies, and programs authorized by the Council of Ministers. Other responsibilities of the agency include issuing a license in the space sector in accordance with rules and mechanisms approved by the Council of Ministers. In international space conventions and forums, the agency represents the United Arab Emirates. It is also in charge of overseeing businesses in the space industry, ensuring safe and proper activities in the space sector. The agency is entrusted with providing technical and advisory support to the competent authorities, as well as any additional tasks allocated by the Council of Ministers.[116]

The chairperson of the UAE Space Agency serves on the Board of Directors, which governs the agency and is comprised of representatives from the federal government, state-owned commercial businesses, military organizations, and academia, providing for cross-sector collaboration and policy coordination.[117] In addition to the Board of Directors, the agency has the Advisory Committee composed of international civil specialists from the United States, Europe, Russia, China, India, Japan, Saudi Arabia, and South Korea.[118] The Advisory Committee was instrumental in the establishment of the agency and has provided strategic insight and counsel to the agency since.

115 *Supra* Chapter 5, n. 84, Renata Knittel Kommel *et al.*, 28–29.

116 UAE Space Agency, "About UAE Space Agency," last accessed January 7, 2022, available at https://space.gov.ae/Page/20120/20230/About-UAE-Space-Agency.

117 UAE Space Agency, "Chairperson of Board of Directors," last accessed January 7, 2022, available at https://space.gov.ae/Page/20120/20126/CHAIRPERSON.

118 As of January 2022, there are ten international individuals consisting of the Advisory Committee. The South Korean specialist is a former president of the Korea Aerospace Research Institute (KARI). For more information, *see* UAE Space Agency, "Advisory Committee," last accessed January 7, 2022, available at https://space.gov.ae/AdvisoryCommittee.

The UAE government has a significant influence over the national space sector's financial objectives and investments. The government's active involvement and support led to the quick decision-making to expedite the execution of major space programs. Since the establishment of its space agency, the UAE government has formulated defined strategies for its space activities, outlining clear objectives and purposefully implementing them. During the seven years since its foundation, the UAE Space Agency has established innovative policies and an adaptive regulatory framework as well as a comprehensive Mars exploration program.[119]

3.6.5 Current Space Governance in South Korea

Space development in South Korea has been conducted under a dispersed system with no integrated and centralized governmental body. The National Space Committee, comprised of the ministers of relevant administrative agencies, is recognized as the top authority that primarily deliberates national space policy and grants launch permission, as well as overseeing the inter-government formulation of the space development plan. However, being a non-permanent entity, the committee has limitations of its ongoing oversight. Regarding launch permission, in particular, it would be preferable to ultimately have a permanent decision-making body for continuous supervision.

Under the National Space Committee as a deliberative body, the Ministry of Science and ICT is the most relevant government ministry in the space sector. Main space-related tasks, including the implementation of the space development plan, are delegated to this ministry or minister by the Space Development Promotion Act. However, because there are only a few public officials in charge of space affairs, who rotate to different departments every one to two years, the task of addressing professional space issues on a consistent basis can be challenging. Moreover, in the absence of an absolutely dedicated ministry in charge of space affairs, other governmental administrations, such as the Ministry of Foreign Affairs, the Ministry of Trade, Industry and Energy, the Ministry of National Defense, and the Director of the National Intelligence Service, are also dealing with their own space-related issues and further executing each project separately. Thus, South Korea's capacity for space development is spread among various ministries, resulting in redundancy and inefficiency.

---

119 UAE Space Agency, "Agency Achievements," last accessed January 7, 2022, available at https://space.gov.ae/Page/20120/20161/Achievements.

While the Ministry of Science and ICT is the primary government body responsible for establishing space policy, it is the Korea Aerospace Research Institute (KARI) that actually conducts space research and development. KARI, a government-funded institute founded in 1989, has been leading South Korea's space programs which includes the development of Korea Space Launch Vehicles (KSLVs) I and II, the lunar mission, and numerous satellite series to name a few. It also promotes the utilization and application of collected satellite data and the commercialization of acquired space technologies. Over the course of completing its assigned tasks, KARI collaborates with other government-funded institutes or academic research organizations, including the Electronic Telecommunication Research Institute (ETRI), the Korea Astronomy and Space Science Institute (KASI), and the Korea Advanced Institute of Science and Technology (KAIST).

Although KARI has played a pivotal role, as a *de facto* national space agency, by developing innovative technologies and enhancing domestic space capabilities, it does not have *de jure* representativeness of the Korean government in the international space community. Furthermore, KARI has no discretionary authority to make decisions for the Korean government's space aspirations.

In 2016, the Minister of Science and ICT designated KARI as a specialized space development institute under Article 7 of the Space Development Promotion Act. However, this designation has no additional significance for KARI; rather, it just validates what KARI has meant for South Korea's space development thus far. Therefore, it is hard to conclude that the designation added extra meaning to KARI as no provision of the Act specifies the legal standing of the designated institute or KARI's duty in particular.

3.6.6 Summary and Need for a National Space Agency

Approximately forty nations have listed their space agencies on the United Nations Office for Outer Space Affairs (UNOOSA).[120] In the past decade alone, over fifteen governments established national space agencies: Bahrain, Paraguay, Poland, Syria, and the United Arab Emirates in 2014; New Zealand in 2016; Kenya in 2017; Australia, Greece, Luxembourg, Saudi Arabia, and Zimbabwe in 2018; Egypt, the Philippines, Portugal, and Turkey in 2019; and Costa Rica 2021. According to the general analysis in Section 3.6.3 of Chapter 5, the primary impetus for the creation of space agencies by emerging space nations was economic considerations, indicating the growing importance of

120 UNOOSA, "Our Work: Worldwide Space Agencies," last accessed January 15, 2022, available at https://www.unoosa.org/oosa/en/ourwork/space-agencies.html.

commercial space activities in the "NewSpace" era.[121] Nations that have been carrying out existing space programs, on the other hand, decided to coordinate and centralize their space activities via a space agency. Regardless of whether it concerns emerging or well-established space-faring nations, their space agencies function as a platform to develop a domestic regulatory framework as well as comply with international principles in the space sector. They further interact with other space-faring nations and participate in the global space community through their space agencies.

As outlined in Section 3.6.4 of Chapter 5, the United States, a traditional space powerhouse, carefully considered a range of detailed factors when it founded NASA in 1958, such as the specific form and nature of the agency, as well as the scope of its authority. Notably, even during the Cold War era, the United States recognized the potential for commercial use of outer space and cooperation with private enterprises. To further clarify the status and position of NASA, Congress passed the NASA Act, which outlines the purpose of NASA's establishment and specifies its authority. This legislation has helped to alleviate controversy over the division of tasks in the course of NASA's operations. Overall, the founding of NASA reflects a thoughtful and strategic approach to space development that has contributed to the United States' continued leadership in this field.

Japan, a space superpower in Asia and globally, created JAXA by merging three existing space-related institutions. Like the United States, Japan also clarifies major matters concerning JAXA's operation, by stipulating the agency's purpose and role under the JAXA Act. In addition, according to the Act, one of the agency's tasks is to cooperate and collaborate with the private sector for better space development. This reflects the current trend of expanding private companies' participation in space development as well as increasing public-private partnerships for national space missions.

In recent years, Luxembourg has demonstrated its ambition to become a global hub for the exploration and commercialization of space resources by leveraging its combined financial and competent space experiences. Unlike traditional space powers such as the United States and Japan noted previously,

121 For example, the National Congress of Costa Rica clearly shows its economic consideration for the establishment of a space agency in 2021, announcing that it "passed a law that created the Costa Rican Space Agency to promote space exploration as a development tool for the country's industry and economy." *See* Steve Colantuoni, the Central American Group, "The Costa Rican Space Agency has been created," June 3, 2021, last accessed January 13, 2022, available at https://www.thecentralamericangroup.com/costa-rican-space-agency-has-been-created/.

the Luxembourg Space Agency was established in 2018 with a strong focus on economic benefits, providing government support to commercial space enterprises, rather than on space research and exploration itself. This was Luxembourg's strategy to diversify its economic opportunities and promote industrial growth. Although Luxembourg was already conducting space-related activities under the aegis of the Ministry of Economy before the agency's foundation, the nation concluded that establishing a dedicated space agency would be more beneficial in creating an appealing environment to achieve its goals.

Another rising space power, the United Arab Emirates, created the UAE Space Agency in 2014 separately from its existing federal government body, the Emirates Institution for Advanced Science and Technology (EIAST). Like Luxembourg, the UAE government also sought to diversify and stimulate its economic environment by pursuing potential benefits from new opportunities in the international space industry. The government recognized that the United Arab Emirates could strengthen its geopolitical position in the Middle East and beyond while consolidating and regulating space activities through its space agency.

South Korea's national space governance is slightly different as discussed in Sections 3.6.2 and 3.6.5 of Chapter 5: i) There is no independent, central space agency; ii) Although the Korea Aerospace Research Institute (KARI) plays a pivotal role in space development, it does not have the legal authority to make decisions or represent the Korean government on the global stage. Technically, KARI is one of the government-funded institutes, focusing on space-related research and development. In fact, on the UNOOSA website, the Korea Astronomy and Space Science Institute (KASI), as well as KARI, is also listed as South Korea's space agency,[122] which implies that there is no single centralized governmental body in South Korea (see Table 9).

In the early space age, a national space agency may not have been necessary for a nation to carry out its space program; diffused decision-making and the absence of centralized agency may not have impeded achievements in space activities when governments were primary actors in the exploration and use of outer space, emphasizing scientific research and technology development rather than social and economic value. However, the space sector has significantly evolved over time. In the last decade, in particular, there has been a tremendous increase in the number and variety of space activities, as well as the establishment of national space agencies across the world.

---

122 *Supra* Chapter 5, n. 120, UNOOSA, "Our Work: Worldwide Space Agencies," last accessed January 15, 2022, available at https://www.unoosa.org/oosa/en/ourwork/space-agencies.html.

TABLE 9 Features of selected nations' space agencies

	USA	Japan	Luxembourg	UAE	South Korea
Space Agency	NASA	JAXA	LSA	UAESA	KARI (and KASI)
Year of the Establishment	1958	2003	2018	2014	1989 (and 1974, respectively)
Main Rationales for the Establishment of the Agency	Geopolitical, Efficiency, Coordination, Centralization	Economic, Centralization	Economic	Economic, Coordination, Centralization, Geopolitical, Regulatory	Research
Legal Authority	Decision-making, Representativeness	Decision-making, Representativeness	Decision-making, Representativeness	Decision-making, Representativeness	No discretionary authority

Essentially, it appears that South Korea's current approach to space governance is outdated. While traditional objectives of space research and development are still relevant, the motivation to establish a modern space agency is closely linked to the increasing commercialization of space activities. Therefore, South Korea needs to scrutinize its current space management system and restructure its space development organizations. To achieve this, it is imperative for South Korea to create a centralizing agency that coordinates space research and development currently dispersed across various organizations. An ideal national space agency for South Korea should have the authority to make decisions and represent the country both domestically and internationally. The space agency should have discretionary power in terms of budgeting, technology development, and space policy-making, including coordination with other government departments. Preferably, it is desirable to enact a specific law, similar to NASA and JAXA, that clarifies the basis for the establishment of the space agency and its roles and authority.[123]

3.7 *The Formulation of the Master Plan and the Action Plan for the Utilization of Satellite Data*

Articles 5-3 and 5-4 on the formulation of satellite data utilization plans were inserted into the 2014 Amendments of the Space Development Promotion Act, as the data application acquired via satellites became increasingly important. The Master Plan, established every five years by the Minister of Science and ICT in consultation with the heads of relevant central administrations,[124] outlines the government's mid- to long-term strategies to disseminate and better utilize satellite data, which includes: Matters concerning objectives and direction of policies; satellite data acquisition; a system for the data dissemination; the nurturing of professionals in the satellite data field; demand for and technologies of utilizing satellite data and developing satellites for data collecting purposes; the prevention of duplicate investments in satellite data

123 In 2021, one of members of the National Assembly Science and Technology Committee rendered a bill concerning promotion of South Korea's space development, which includes launching an independent national space agency as well as elevating the legal status of the National Space Committee by being chaired by the Prime Minister. Whereas the suggestion concerning the National Space committee was accepted immediately, leading to the amendment of the Space Development Promotion Act as discussed in Chapter 5 §3.4, the agenda on the establishment of a new space agency is still pending as of January 2022, with no significant progress.

124 Article 5-2(1) of the Space Development Promotion Act and Article 3-2(1) of the Presidential Decree of the Space Development Promotion Act.

related equipment or facilities; and the promotion of the dissemination and utilization of satellite data.[125]

The Presidential Decree stipulates more detailed procedures for planning, stating that the Minister of Science and ICT must inform the heads of relevant central administrations of the timeline for the formulation of the Master Plan, as well as the guidelines for its preparation. If necessary, the Minister of Science and ICT may request heads of relevant central administrations to submit the data required to establish the plan.[126] A final draft is confirmed through the deliberation of the National Space Committee,[127] which is promptly announced to the public by the Minister of Science and ICT. However, subjects of national security may not be presented to the public.[128]

In order to effectively implement the Master Plan, the Minister of Science and ICT annually develops the Action Plan for the Utilization of Satellite Data in compliance with the Master Plan.[129] The Action Plan comprises an overview of each project, a report on last year's performance outcomes, and a comprehensive execution plan for the pertinent year.[130] The Minister of Science and ICT finalizes the Action Plan by the end of February following deliberation of the Working Committee for the Utilization of Satellite chaired by the Vice Minister of Science and ICT. The approved Action Plan is notified to the heads of relevant central administrations by the Minister of Science and ICT.[131]

The First Master Plan of the years 2014 to 2018 and its annual Action Plan of the year 2014 were released in May and September 2014, respectively,[132] following the 2014 Amendments of the Act. The First Master Plan and its Action Plan outlined the government's strategies to utilize value-added satellite data to improve public safety and quality of life as well as distribute satellite images to meet national demand and promote the satellite image processing industry.

---

125 Article 5-2(2) of the Space Development Promotion Act. *See supra* Chapter 2 §7.3 for the Master Plan of the year between 2019 to 2023.

126 Article 5-2(5) of the Space Development Promotion Act, Article 3-2(2) of the Presidential Decree of the Space Development Promotion Act.

127 Article 5-2(3) of the Space Development Promotion Act.

128 Article 5-3(4) of the Space Development Promotion Act.

129 Article 5-4(1) of the Space Development Promotion Act.

130 Article 5-4(2) of the Space Development Promotion Act, Article 3-3(1) of the Presidential Decree of the Space Development Promotion Act.

131 Article 3-3(2) of the Presidential Decree of the Space Development Promotion Act.

132 Press release by the Ministry of Science and ICT on May 30, 2014, "The First Master Plan for Promotion of Utilization of Satellite Data [English title added]" and on September 30, 2014 "The 2014 Action Plan for Promotion of Utilization of Satellite Date [English title added]," available at https://www.korea.kr/archive/expDocView.do?docId=35262 and https://www.korea.kr/archive/expDocView.do?docId=35723, respectively.

Moreover, for international cooperation, the government began contributing to the International Charter Space and Major Disasters as one of the Charter Members by providing satellite imagery for disaster monitoring purposes.[133]

The Second Master Plan of the years 2019 to 2023, announced in January 2019, presented the government's plan to create an integrated satellite data system and build a national center for satellite data operation. The Second Master Plan also outlined the government's expansion of international collaboration with South America by establishing a joint operation system of satellite data.[134] In the annual Action Plan of 2021, the government emphasized that it would continue to develop the Korea Positioning System (KPS),[135] provide more daily life-related satellite data, and expand the disaster monitoring system.[136]

Overall, this periodic planning for satellite data utilization enables South Korea to take full advantage of the unique vantage point for observing the Earth as well as exploring outer space, which seeks to maximize the use of satellite data and develop innovative applications in order to monitor and safeguard the Earth's environment and improve the quality of life.

3.8 *The Establishment of the Working Committee for the Utilization of Satellite Data*

The Working Committee for the Utilization of Satellite Data was established under the National Space Committee in order to efficiently conduct the Committee's affairs, following the 2014 Amendments to Space Development Promotion Act.[137] Aside from the clause on the Working committee's establishment itself, the Act defers to the Presidential Decree on how the Working Committee is to be formed and operated.[138]

The Working Committee is chaired by the Vice Minister of Science and ICT, with no more than twenty-one members in total including the Vice Minister.

---

133 As of January 2022, there are seventeen Charter Members, including The European Space Agency (ESA), the Japan Aerospace Exploration Agency (JAXA), the United States Geological Survey (USGS), and the UK Space Agency and DMC International Imaging (DMCii). For more information, *see* the International Charter Space and Major Disasters, "Charter Members," last accessed January 19, 2021, available at https://disasterscharter.org/web/guest/home;jsessionid=B5E7A1D8FB97850C79683D1D84615350.APP1#portlet-wrapper-56_INSTANCE_NqTgFexnyH9p.

134 *Supra* Chapter 2 §7.3.

135 *Supra* Chapter 2 §7.1.4.

136 Press release by the Ministry of Science and ICT on January 29, 2021, "The 2021 Action Plan for Promotion of Utilization of Satellite Date [English title added]," available at https://www.korea.kr/archive/expDocView.do?docId=39358.

137 Article 6(5) of the Space Development Promotion Act.

138 Article 6(6) of the Space Development Promotion Act.

The members are either higher echelons of the Civil Service in charge of space-related affairs or have significant competence and experience in the space area as appointed by the chairperson of the Working Committee.[139] By having practitioners with satellite-related expertise in the Working Committee under the National Space Committee, the government is able to conduct a more professional examination of satellite operating and data utilization, as well as the creation of associated policies.

3.9 *The Establishment of the Working Committee for National Space Security*

The 2021 Amendments to the Space Development Promotion Act stipulated that the National Space Committee would have the Working Committee for National Space Security, co-chaired by the Vice Minister of Defense and one of the Deputy Directors of the National Intelligence Service.[140] This is consistent with the explicit inclusion of the Minister of National Defense and the Director of the National Intelligence Service as members of the National Space Committee in the 2021 Amendments, demonstrating that the government views space as an increasingly significant domain for defense and national security operations.

The Working Committee consists of no more than fifteen members, who are high-ranking government officials in charge of space development for national security or civilians with considerable expertise and experience in the field of national security. The Working Committee deliberates on matters promoted by the heads of relevant central administrative agencies in terms of national security. It also addresses matters agreed upon by both the chairperson of the Working Committee for the Promotion of Space Development and the co-chairs of the Working Committee for National Security in Space Development to be reviewed in the Working Committee.[141]

This increased emphasis on national defense and security in space development is related not only to the fact that space is becoming an important domain, but also to geopolitics on the Korean peninsula. Particularly, on May 21, 2021, both Presidents of South Korea and the United States agreed to entirely abolish the 42-year-old bilateral missile guidelines, allowing South Korea to

139 Article 6-2 of the Presidential Decree of the Space Development Promotion Act, as amended on December 3, 2014.

140 Article 6(5) of the Space Development Promotion Act, as amended on August 10, 2021, entered into force on November 11, 2021.

141 Article 6-3 of the Presidential Decree of the Space Development Promotion Act, as amended on November 9, 2021, entered into force on November 11, 2021.

build and possess any type of missile, including intercontinental ballistic missiles (ICBMs) and advanced submarine-launched ballistic missiles (SLBMs).[142]

In 2020, a year prior to the complete termination of the guidelines, both nations already agreed to lift the ban on using solid fuel for space launch vehicles, which now allows South Korea to develop solid-fuel space launch vehicles with no restrictions on range and payload.[143] These series of changes affected South Korea's current standing by stimulating its ambition for space development and appears to be the actual impetus for the 2021 Amendments that reinforced national defense and security aspects of space development; in other words, the Korean government is escalating and integrating space as part of national defense and security to ensure that they are interconnected and interoperable for capacity-building in the space domain.

3.10 *The Formulation of the Basic Plan and Action Plan to Prepare for Hazards in Space*

Article 15(1) of the Space Development Promotion Act stipulates that the Korean government shall establish the Basic Plan to Prepare for Hazards in Space every ten years, which specifies mid- and long-term policy objectives and strategies for ensuring space safety preparedness. To better understand what the plan is for, it is first necessary to be reminded of the concept of "hazards in space" described in Section 2 of Chapter 5.

According to Article 2(6) of the Space Development Promotion Act, "hazards in space" are more of a collective term defined as "risks of a crash, collision, and suchlike of 'space objects' in outer space." Then what exactly is 'space objects'? Is it inclusive of natural objects like meteorite crashes? Or does it only cover manufactured objects such as satellite collisions? Or both?

The answer is found in Article 2(3) of the Act, which states that 'space objects' include both 'artificial' and 'natural' objects. More specifically, 'artificial space objects' mean objects designed and manufactured for use in outer space including space launch vehicles, artificial satellites, spaceships, and their components, while 'natural space objects' are objects formed naturally in outer space including meteorites. It further defines "meteorites" as solid pieces

142 Seokmin Oh, Yonhap News Agency, May 22, 2021, "Lifting of US missile restrictions signifies Seoul's missile sovereignty, Washington's China strategy: experts," last accessed January 22, 2022, available at https://en.yna.co.kr/view/AEN20210522003900325.

143 Previously limited to the range of less than 800 kilometers with a 500-kilogram warhead. For more information, Felix Kim, Indo-Pacific Defense Forum, "South Korea accelerates space defense program," November 14, 2021, last accessed January 21, 2022, available at https://ipdefenseforum.com/2021/11/south-korea-accelerates-space-defense-program/.

of debris from outer space that have fallen to the Earth's surface attracted by the Earth's gravity. Therefore, it can be understood that the plan on "hazards in space" will essentially present the government's strategies concerning the preparation for crashes or collisions of artificial and natural space objects, including current and future issues pertaining to space debris and near-Earth objects (NEOs).

Along with that, the Basic Plan broadly addresses environmental protection and surveillance of outer space, forecasts and alarms of space hazards, research and development for the prevention of space hazards, and international cooperation in that regard.[144] Like other plans discussed above, the Minister of Science and ICT is in charge of formulating the Basic Plan following the National Space Committee's deliberation,[145] as well as the annual Action Plan in consultation with the central administrative agencies concerned.[146] The detailed procedures are prescribed by the Presidential Decree of the Act, and the procedures are not much different from those of the other plans.[147]

All provisions regarding the formulation of those plans were added for the first time to the 2014 Amendments, together with the definition clause of "hazards in space." Accordingly, the First Basic and the Action Plans were both announced in 2014.

The First Basic Plan to Prepare for Hazards in Space is a ten-year plan that runs from 2014 to 2023. The First Basic Plan states that the rationale for this space hazard-dedicated initiative was the increasing probability of space risks such as satellite crashes to Earth and collisions between space assets and space debris due to the continuous development of space activities and the growing number of space assets. In addition, given South Korea's high population density, the government deemed it necessary to establish a systematic method of response to space hazards to protect people and national space assets from such risks.

In line with the First Basic Plan, the First Action Plan of 2014 was focused on establishing key infrastructure such as a space hazard response system and acquiring essential surveillance capabilities. Through the implementation of several subsequent annual Action Plans, South Korea has now established a robust system to enhance its resilience to space hazards: South Korea runs a space situational awareness organization which continually updates a manual

144 Article 15(2) of the Space Development Promotion Act.

145 Article 15(3) of the Space Development Promotion Act.

146 Article 15-2 of the Space Development Promotion Act.

147 Article 15(5) of the Space Development Promotion Act. Articles 13-2 and 13-3 of the Presidential Decree of the Space Development Promotion Act.

on what action people need to take in case of an incident and regularly holds an exercise drill with the public; South Korea joined the Inter-Agency Space Debris Coordination Committee (IADC) in 2014, contributing to member agencies efforts for space debris mitigation; and South Korea also issued its own Space Debris Mitigation Recommendations applicable to the domestic space industry and research institutes to ensure a sustainable space for all in accordance with international standards and guidelines outlined by the United Nations and the IADC,[148] to name a few.

These periodical Basic and Action Plans are comprehensive and beneficial in enhancing the awareness of and resilience to severe space hazards. Although there are annual Action Plans announced every year, the ten-year Basic Plan seems rather long-term compared to other Basic Plans explored earlier. Considering the rapidly changing space environment, it is recommended that the Basic Plan should be set up every five years, preferably from the Second Basic Plan in 2024 now that South Korea has essential response systems and facilities related to space risks through its first ten-year plan.

3.11 *The Designation of a Space Environment Surveillance Institute and Suchlike*

Article 15-3(1) of the Space Development Promotion Act provides for the efficient establishment and operation of space hazard preparedness systems. To this end, the Minister of Science and ICT may designate a Space Environment Surveillance Institute responsible for the following affairs:

i. Establishing and operating a system to issue forecasts, warnings, and alerts of space hazard events;
ii. Establishing and enhancing an international cooperation system to prepare for space hazards; and
iii. Undertaking any affairs related to space hazards as prescribed by the Presidential Decree.

Accordingly, Article 13-5 of the Presidential Decree further elaborates on the designated affairs, including i) research and development of risk response technology and ii) establishment and operation of an integrated response system consisting of civilian institutions, government, and military authorities. Additionally, Article 13-4(1) of the Presidential Decree specifies the eligibility and requirements for an organization to be designated as such.

Pursuant to the provisions above, in January 2015, the Minister of Science and ICT designated the Korea Astronomy and Space Science Institute

148 *Supra* Chapter 1 §3.2.

(KASI),[149] founded in 1974, as the Space Environment Surveillance Institute. Its key roles include monitoring and analyzing potential space hazards, forecasting and predicting consequential risks and impacts, performing space hazard research and development programs, and expanding and enhancing international cooperation concerning space situational awareness.

In addition to such designation, according to Article 15-3(3) of the Space Development Promotion Act, the Minister of Science and ICT may also establish and operate Headquarters for Space Hazard Countermeasures where necessary to prevent and prepare for space hazards. Its composition and the operating occasions are detailed in the Presidential Decree of the Act. More specifically, the Headquarters is comprised of government officials in the Senior Civil Service appointed by the heads of the relevant central government agencies as well as civilian experts commissioned by the Minister of Science and ICT.[150] The Headquarters is established and operated in cases where situations falling under the following take place:[151]

i. Where damage to the Korean Peninsula and adjacent waters is predicted due to the fall of an object from outer space;
ii. Where solar activity is deemed to have a significant impact on South Korean artificial space objects; and
iii. Where a South Korean satellite is expected to be destroyed or its serious malfunction is anticipated due to a collision of space objects.

Under KASI, two monitoring rooms are operated separately, one is for artificial space objects such as satellites, the other is for near-Earth objects such as asteroids. The monitoring rooms provide analyzed information to the relevant authorities, and if the object is predicted to crash into South Korea within seventy-two hours, the real-time situation is monitored and alerted to people according to the Korea Space Hazard Response Protocol Manual. When China's Tiangong-1 and 2 were re-entering the Earth's atmosphere in 2018 and 2019, respectively, although the objects were not expected to pose a severe threat to South Korea, KASI operated an around-the-clock monitoring room analyzing the trajectories and announcing the real-time status in case of emergency.

Since Russia's anti-satellite test on November 15, 2021, space debris-related issues have been drawing more attention. Across the globe, Space-faring nations and private space companies spoke out about Russia's test. In an official statement, South Korea's Ministry of Foreign Affairs stated, "we are concerned about the anti-satellite weapon test that occurred on November 15, in

149 *Supra* Chapter 2 §3.4. and Chapter 5 §3.6.6.
150 Article 13-6(1) of the Presidential Decree of the Space Development Promotion Act.
151 Article 13-6(2) of the Presidential Decree of the Space Development Promotion Act.

particular, the numerous pieces of debris generated in space as a result of the test." The Ministry of Foreign Affairs added that "all states must act responsibly to ensure peaceful and sustainable use of outer space and work together to establish international rules and norms of behavior in this regard."

As the designated Space Environment Surveillance Institute, KASI also performs space science research and monitors severe space weather that could have a significant impact on our infrastructure or vital services. Since signing a Letter of Agreement in 2010, KASI has been collaborating with NASA on solar and space physics research, as well as forecasting and responding to catastrophic space weather events. Again, however, since there is no single, centralized space agency in South Korea, roles and duties related to space research and development are being assigned and performed by two different institutes – KARI and KASI, one as a designated space development specialized institute and the other as a designated space environment surveillance institute –[152] whereas NASA is responsible for what KARI and KASI separately perform. Indeed, KASI plays an important role in space research and development as KARI does. However, in order to promote more systematic and efficient space development, it is necessary to reorganize the current organizational structure, for example, by placing such research institutes under a single, centered national space agency with discretionary authority.

3.12 *Executive Summary of the General Provisions of the Act*

Overall, South Korea's space governance is characterized by its periodic, comprehensive yet specific planning of space development (see Table 10) and various organizations dispersed throughout the government or government-funded institutes (see Table 11).

As examined in this Section 3 of Chapter 5, provisions of the Act regarding national space plans and organizations seem scattered and complicated because they have been revised or inserted whenever necessary since the Act's enactment in 2005. Therefore, the tables below might assist in understanding and summarizing the key aspects of the Act thus far.

In short, the fundamental space development plans are formulated by the Ministry of Science and ICT in consultation with the heads of relevant central administrations, which are deliberated and finalized by the National Space Committee. All major plans are complemented and/or supplemented by annual action plans which specify yearly objectives and what to execute each year. While the National Space Committee and the Ministry of Science

152 As discussed in Chapter 5 §3.6.6.

TABLE 10 National space development plans based on the Space Development Promotion Act

Title of major plan	Date of first formulation	Period	Content
Basic Plan for the Promotion of Space Development	2005 [a]	Every 5 years	Comprehensive national space policy including space development and application, financing, nurturing human resources, and international cooperation.
Master Plan for the Utilization of Satellite Data	2014	Every 5 years	Strategies related to the promotion of dissemination and better utilization of satellite data.
Basic Plan to Prepare for Hazards in Space	2014	Every 10 years	Strategies to ensure space safety preparedness, including forecasting and responding to severe space weather, satellite collision or reentry, and space debris.

a Prior to the enactment of the Space Development Promotion Act in 2005, there were national space plans called the Mid-to Long-Term Basic Plans for the Promotion of Space Development beginning in 1996 under the Aerospace Industry Development Promotion Act.

TABLE 11 Major space-related organizations based on the Space Development Promotion Act

Entity		Date of establishment	Primary functions	Features
National Space Committee	Working Committee for the Promotion of Space Development	2005	Deliberation of overall space development plans; grant launch permission; financing in space development programs; space tasks coordination and suchlike	Chaired by the Prime Minister, vice-chaired by the Minister of Science and ICT, comprised of the Ministers of the relevant central administrations and civilian space experts; emphasis on national space security by establishing a security-dedicated working committee
	Working Committee for the Utilization of Satellite Data	2014		
	Working Committee for National Space Security	2021		
Ministry of Science and ICT		Evolved by merging former Ministry of Post Office of 1948 and former Ministry of Science and Technology of 1967	Decision-making; establish space policies; formulate national space plans	Usually, one or two departments of the Ministry are involved in space-related tasks, where government officials rotate around different departments.
Korea Aerospace Research Institute (KARI)		1989	Space research and development; implement national space programs	Designated as a space development specialized institute in 2016
Korea Astronomy and Space Science Institute (KASI)		1974	Space science research; predict and respond to space hazards	Designated as a space environment surveillance institute in 2015

and ICT have decision-making power, KARI and KASI are two main institutes that actually conduct space research and development by implementing those national space plans.

4 Major Provisions on Space Activities

As examined in Section 3 of Chapter 5, a significant part of the Space Development Promotion Act is devoted to the establishment of domestic space policies and organizational aspects of South Korea's space governance in order to promote and encourage national space activities. Based on the prior analysis of the general provisions, this section will explore the Act's main provisions from the viewpoint of international space law such as international responsibility for national activities, liability as a launching State, and registration of space objects outlined in Chapter 1, as well as taking a comparative legal approach when necessary. In general, the analysis will also be related to the eight elements, adopted by the UN General Assembly in 2013, for consideration when establishing national regulatory frameworks:[153] i) the scope of space activities targeted by national space law; ii) national jurisdiction over space activities; iii) authorization by a competent national authority; iv) conditions for authorization; v) procedures for continuing supervision and monitoring of authorized space activities; vi) establishment of a national registry of space objects; vii) insurance requirements and indemnification procedures for damage claims; and viii) continuing supervision of space activities conducted by non-governmental entities in the event of the transfer of ownership or control of a space object in orbit.

Through this in-depth analysis, this section will demonstrate how effectively South Korea's fundamental space law implements international obligations and complies with the international principles set out in the UN space treaties. It will also disclose what should be required for improved national space legislation that can bring together South Korea's strengths in science and technology, defense, and diplomacy to pursue a bold national space ambition.

153 "Recommendations on National Legislation relevant to the Peaceful Exploration and Use of Outer Space," *supra* Chapter 1, n. 18, UNGA Res. 68/74 of December 11, 2013; UN Doc. A/RES/68/74.

4.1 *Jurisdiction*

4.1.1 Jurisdiction under International Space Law

In international law, jurisdiction generally refers to the power a State can exercise over persons, property, or events. While jurisdiction is typically associated with sovereignty and is inextricably related to its territory, it can also exist without such connection. In other words, jurisdiction can be classified based on territory, nationality of the actor, the nature of the act in question, and possibly the victim's nationality.[154] Ships and aircraft are subject to the jurisdiction of the State under whose flag they sail or in which they are registered. Specifically, Articles 17 and 18 of the Convention on International Civil Aviation state that "aircraft have the nationality of the State in which they are registered" and that "an aircraft cannot be validly registered in more than one State."[155]

When it comes to space activities, jurisdiction has distinctive implications. In outer space, the non-appropriation principle prevails, stating that outer space is not subject to national appropriation by claim of sovereignty[156] and that the exploration and use of outer space is the province of all mankind.[157] In essence, the Outer Space Treaty designates outer space as an extra-jurisdictional territory over which no State has sovereign authority. However, it does not preclude States from exercising jurisdiction and control over objects and personnel in outer space. For example, Article VIII of the Outer Space Treaty explicitly allows for the State of registry of a space object to retain jurisdiction over the registered object and personnel thereof, while in outer space or on a celestial body. In the areas other than those specified, general rules of jurisdiction will be applicable to persons, property, or events, to the extent permissible under international law.[158]

154 Malcolm Shaw, "International Law," last accessed February 3, 2022, available at https://www.britannica.com/topic/international-law/Jurisdiction; Donald R. Rothwell, "International Law," last accessed February 3, 2022, available at https://www.cambridge.org/core/books/international-law/jurisdiction/D939F2DB09A600497960EC1A362057BD#.

For more about international jurisdiction, *see* Peter Malanczuk, "Akehurst's Modern Introduction to International Law," Seventh Edition 1997, 109–117; Malcolm Shaw, "International Law," Ninth Edition 2021, 555–600.

155 Also known as the 1944 Chicago Convention, signed at Chicago on December 7, 1944, came into force on April 4, 1947.

156 Article II of the Outer Space Treaty.

157 Article I of the Outer Space Treaty.

158 Regarding the application of international law to outer space and space activities, Resolution 1721 A (XVI), which was adopted by the UN General Assembly on December 20, 1961, stipulates as follows: "International law, including the Charter of the United Nations, applies to outer space and celestial bodies." This principle, which was subsequently enshrined in Article III of the Outer Space Treaty, has been widely accepted by

4.1.2 National Jurisdiction of the Act

The South Korean Space Development Promotion Act does not have a general, blanket provision on the jurisdictional scope, but instead establishes separate applicable criteria for each subject matter, such as launch permission, space object registration, and liability for damage caused by space objects.

Specifically, first, while the permission mechanism of the Act is focused on regulating a launch of a space launch vehicle only, it applies to any person intending to launch a space launch vehicle from the territory of South Korea or the areas/facilities under the jurisdiction of South Korea.[159] It further applies to a person intending to launch a space launch vehicle from outside Korea in cases where the vehicle is owned by the Korean government or a Korean national.[160]

Second, the registration mechanism of the Act applies to any Korean natural and juridical person regardless of where the object is launched from, inside or outside of South Korea.[161] As for non-Koreans, however, it only applies to cases where the object is launched from the territory of South Korea or the areas/ facilities under the jurisdiction of South Korea, or the launch vehicle is owned by the Korean government or a Korean national.[162] The Act excludes space launch vehicles from registration. Therefore, space objects except for launch vehicles, primarily satellites and other spacecraft are subject to national registration, which leads to international registration with the United Nations.[163]

Third, the provision of liability for damage simply states that any person who has launched a space object pursuant to the provisions of launch permission and space object registration is liable for damage caused by the space object.[164] Thus, the applicable scope of both launch permission and the registration of space objects combined fall within South Korea's liability system. This means that the Korean liability regime applies to those who obtained launch permission and/or registered a space object. In other words, the launch licensees and/or the space object registrants are liable for damage caused by the space object.[165]

---

the international community and is now recognized as part of customary international space law.

159 Article 11(1) i of the Space Development Promotion Act.

160 Article 11(1) ii of the Space Development Promotion Act. Details will be discussed in Chapter 5 §4.2.

161 Article 8(1) of the Space Development Promotion Act.

162 Article 8(2) of the Space Development Promotion Act.

163 For more details, *see* Chapter 5 §4.3.

164 Article 14 of the Space Development Promotion Act.

165 For more details, *see* Chapter 5 §4.4. and Chapter 6.

Last but not least, two other provisions on space accident investigation and suspension or rectification of space development are governed based on (quasi-) territorial and/or personal jurisdiction. As such, since the Space Development Promotion Act sets the application scope for each subject matter, it is necessary to examine each provision individually and combine them together for better understanding. From this context, further details of the jurisdictional scope of the Act will be discussed in each of the following relevant sections.

4.2 *Authorization and Supervision*

4.2.1 The Authorization and Supervision Regime of the Act

One of the most pivotal aspects of the Space Development Promotion Act is essentially its authorization system, which states that anyone who falls within specified categories must obtain permission from the Korean government. This demonstrates how South Korea interprets and implements the international principle of authorization and continuing supervision over national space activities enshrined in Article VI of the Outer Space Treaty. The government administration in charge of oversight is the Ministry of Science and ICT, and its Minister grants permission following deliberation by the National Space Committee.

As to authorization targets, the Act regulates a person who intends to launch a space launch vehicle.[166] More specifically, a person planning on launch must apply for launch permission in the following cases:

i. Where a space launch vehicle lifts off from South Korean territory or areas/facilities under South Korean jurisdiction;[167] or
ii. Where a space launch vehicle is owned by the Korean government or a Korean national despite being intended to launch outside of Korea.[168]

In other words, the Act requires any natural or juridical person who meets prescribed criteria, whether Korean or non-Korean, to obtain launch permission. This implies that the Korean government is more concerned with where the launch activity occurs and whose launch vehicle it is than with who conducts such activities (see Table 12).

In addition, if a person who has obtained launch permission intends to change the permitted matters, the person must request approval for the modification from the Minister of Science and ICT as in the case of launch permission.[169] However, if a person only modifies the applicant's name and address

---

166 The first Sentence of Article 11(1) of the Space Development Promotion Act.
167 Article 11(1) i of the Space Development Promotion Act.
168 Article 11(1) ii of the Space Development Promotion Act.
169 The second sentence of Article 11(1) of the Space Development Promotion Act.

TABLE 12 The scope of launch permission: when is launch permission required?

1. Who	2. Type of activity	3. Launching from where?	
		From Korea	Outside of Korea
Any natural and juridical person regardless of nationality	Launch a space launch vehicle	Permission is always required	Permission is required only in a case where the launch vehicle is under Korean ownership

or the payload usage period in its payload operation plan, such modification simply needs to be reported within thirty days after the modification.[170] Thus, although minor changes still have to be notified to the authority, the reporting procedure is streamlined, as the requirement to obtain strict modification permission is not required, which results in maximized efficiency. A person who launches a space launch vehicle without obtaining launch permission or approval for changes to the permitted matters faces a criminal penalty of imprisonment for no more than five years with prison labor or a fine not to exceed fifty million Korean won (approximately forty thousand US dollars).

The applicant for launch permission has to submit a launch plan to the Minister of Science and ICT that includes a safety analysis report,* a payload operation plan,** and a compensation plan.***[171] The details required to be contained in the launch plan are enumerated in the Notice of the Ministry of Science and ICT[172] as outlined below (see Table 13). The rationale for providing this information is primarily to assure the safety of launch activity.

When granting launch permission, the Minister of Science and ICT considers the appropriateness of the purpose of using the launch vehicle, safety management for the launch, and the transportation plan of the launch vehicle, as well as circumstances in the vicinity of the launch site during the scheduled launch window and the applicant's financial ability such as whether to

170 The proviso of Article 11(1) of the Space Development Promotion Act, Article 12 of the Presidential Decree of the Space Development Promotion Act.

171 Article 11(2) of the Space Development Promotion Act.

172 Article 13 of the Presidential Decree of the Space Development Promotion Act; The Notice on the Details of the Launch Plan by the Ministry of Science and ICT, enacted on October 31, 2006, Notice No. 2006-27, amended on August 1, 2008, Notice No. 2008-127.

take out third party liability insurance.[173] The Minister of Science and ICT may attach necessary conditions to such launch permission.[174]

In addition to the above requirements, any of the following persons are not eligible for launch permission:[175]

i. A person who is incompetent under the adult guardianship;
ii. A person who is bankrupt and not yet reinstated;
iii. A person who was sentenced to imprisonment with prison labor for violating this Act and for whom three years have not passed since the execution of such punishment was terminated or exempted including cases where the execution is deemed to be terminated;
iv. A person who is under suspended sentence of imprisonment with prison labor for violating this Act; or
v. A corporation whose representative falls under any of subparagraphs i through iv.

Thus, if the eligibility criteria are not fulfilled, the Minister of Science and ICT will not be able to grant launch permission to an applicant. This reflects the minimum requirements to ensure that an applicant is a fit and proper person who has the legal ability, the perception and understanding of the launch activity, and adequate financial resources.

The Minister of Science and ICT has the authority to revoke launch permission in the cases specified in the Space Development Promotion Act.[176] Even if a case falls under those categories, revocation of launch permission is not compulsory but at the discretion of the Minister. The feasible revocation circumstances include cases where the launch is being delayed for more than a year from the scheduled date of the permitted launch without justifiable grounds,[177] where the permission is obtained by deceit or other fraudulent ways,[178] and where prior to the permitted launch, an abnormality is detected in the safety management of the space launch vehicle, such as fuel leakage and a defect in the communication system.[179] Launch permission can also be revoked in a case where the head of a central relevant agency requests

173 Article 11(3) of the Space Development Promotion Act, Article 8 of the Ministerial Decree of the Space Development Promotion Act.
174 Article 11(4) of the Space Development Promotion Act.
175 Article 12 of the Space Development Promotion Act.
176 Article 13(1) of the Space Development Promotion Act.
177 Article 13(1) i of the Space Development Promotion Act.
178 Article 13(1) ii of the Space Development Promotion Act.
179 Article 13(1) iv of the Space Development Promotion Act.

TABLE 13 Example of the kinds of information to be included in a launch plan

Content	Description
Projected launch date and planned Trajectory	(1) Projected launch window in both Korea Standard Time (KST) and Greenwich Mean Time (GMT) (2) Planned trajectory in the atmosphere and outer space (3) The sequence of events from lift-off to final orbital injection – separation, ignition, reorientation, ejection, and deorbit (4) Staging and impact locations
Information and performance of the launch vehicle	(1) Launch vehicle specifications including physical dimensions and mass (2) Details of the launch vehicle performance (3) Launch campaign schedule that identifies each review, rehearsal, and safety-critical launch
*Safety analysis report	(1) Organizational structure and personnel responsible for launch safety (2) Flight safety analysis (3) Ground safety analysis (4) Safety operations manual (5) Operator's safety duty and safety management system (6) Specific safety roles: safety manager, accountable manager, launch director, and flight termination personnel (7) Risk assessments (8) Identification of major accident hazards (9) Assessment of the likelihood of each major accident hazard arising (10) Assessment of the foreseeable consequences of the major accident hazards (11) Identification of contingency operations (12) Emergency response (13) Security management

TABLE 13 Example of the kinds of information to be included in a launch plan (*cont.*)

Content	Description
**Payload operation plan	(1) Payload name
	(2) Payload manufacturer, manufacturing number, and manufactured date
	(3) Payload specifications including lifetime
	(4) Physical dimensions and mass of the payload
	(5) Payload owner and operator
	(6) Intended payload operations during the life of the payload
	(7) End-of-life operational concept for the payload
	(8) Hazardous materials carried by the payload, radioactive materials, and the amounts of each
***Compensation plan	(1) Estimated situation and evaluation of damage – death, injury, or property loss – to a third party over the launch process
	(2) Methods of compensation for the estimated damage such as insurance or direct payment

its revocation due to the likelihood of a serious threat to national security.[180] These grounds are based mainly on concerns that the continuance of launch permission may jeopardize the safety of people and property and the protection of public order or national security.

Furthermore, if the permit holder fails to obtain approval for changes to the permitted matter in violation of the modification permission clause,[181] the Minister of Science and ICT may revoke the launch permission.[182] However, this does not apply to changes to minor matters which simply need to be reported to the regulator.[183] The last legitimate ground for revocation of launch permission is where the permit holder ends up falling within one of the eligibility failures listed in subparagraphs i to v as detailed above. This means in essence that the eligibility criteria must be met through the entire process, not only when launch permission is granted, but also after it is obtained. In the case of subparagraph v, however, if the corporate representative is replaced by a qualified person within three months from the date on which the representative falls under the grounds for disqualification, the launch permission is not subject to revocation.[184] In this manner, revocation of launch permission is handled flexibly rather than being unduly strict.

When deciding whether to revoke launch permission, the Minister of Science and ICT is required to hold a hearing.[185] Through this procedure, the permit holder has the opportunity to explain, while allowing for the Minister to make a rational decision. The hearing may be omitted, however, if the head of a relevant central agency requests permission revocation owing to the likelihood of a serious threat to national security, or if there is an abnormality in the safety management of the space launch vehicle.[186] In short, the hearing is mandatory in principle, but the Minister has discretion when it comes to national safety and security.

Moreover, the Space Development Act provides for suspension or rectification of "space development" under certain circumstances. Specifically, when the Minister of National Defense, for the purpose of military operations in wartime or other comparable emergencies, requests to suspend space

180 Article 13(1) iii of the Space Development Promotion Act.

181 *Supra* Chapter 5, n. 169, the second sentence of Article 11(1) of the Space Development Promotion Act.

182 Article 13(1) v of the Space Development Promotion Act.

183 *Supra* Chapter 5, n. 170, the proviso to Article 11(1) of the Space Development Promotion Act and Article 12 of the Presidential Decree of the Space Development Promotion Act.

184 Article 13(1) vi of the Space Development Promotion Act.

185 Article 13(2) of the Space Development Promotion Act.

186 Proviso to Article 13(2) of the Space Development Promotion Act.

development conducted by a Korean national, the Minister of Science and ICT must order the Korean national to do so.[187] In addition, the Minister of Science and ICT may order a Korean national to rectify space development after deliberation by the National Space Committee, when the head of a relevant central administrative agency, in the interest of maintaining public order or national security, requests such rectification of space development performed by a Korean national.[188] Since "Space development," as defined in this Act,[189] is close to a generic term that includes the exploration and use of outer space as well as activities that facilitate such exploration and use of outer space, launch activities conducted by a launch permit holder are therefore subject to the suspension or rectification order. In this broad sense of space development, it is also noteworthy that such an order only applies to Korean nationals as the Act explicitly states.

In summary, South Korea implements a single permission system aimed at regulating the launch of a space launch vehicle based on the territorial jurisdiction and the ownership of a launch vehicle. The applicant for a launch permission must fulfill specified eligibility criteria as well as provide detailed information regarding its launch activities with the authority. As a means of continuing supervision, the permit holder must obtain approval for changes to the permitted launch or report minor changes to the authority. The launch permission can be revoked primarily for safety or security reasons in cases where requirements are not fulfilled, or the permit holder breaches regulations. More broadly, launch activities by a Korean national can be suspended or rectified following requests from the head of a relevant administrative agency.

4.2.2 An Observation from the International Space Law Perspective

Article VI of the Outer Space Treaty is the first and foremost rationale for the enactment of national space legislation, which provides for the fundamental principle of international responsibility for national activities in outer space, whether such activities are conducted by governmental agencies or non-governmental entities. The activities of non-governmental entities, in particular, require authorization and continuing supervision by the appropriate State. Therefore, from this principle, States identify their need to regulate national activities in order to ensure that they adhere to the provisions of the Outer

187 Article 19(1) of the Space Development Promotion Act.

188 Article 19(2) of the Space Development Promotion Act.

189 *Supra* Chapter 5 §2; Article 2 i of the Space Development Promotion Act.

Space Treaty while authorizing and continually supervising activities by private entities for which States are responsible.

Article VI of the Outer Space Treaty not only creates a direct connection between the State and private entities, but it also provides a practical motivation for national space legislation as a means to regulate activities carried out by private entities, which stems from a logical consequence that a private entity's violation of international space law gives rise to the State's international responsibility.[190] Although enacting a national space law is not the only method to guarantee international responsibility, such legislation is indeed a clear instrument for complying with these international obligations.

However, while the Outer Space Treaty imposes international responsibility on States for national activities in outer space, relevant terminologies in the treaty are not explicitly defined, nor is the applicable extent of responsibility fully articulated. This ambiguity leads to a question as to which State is responsible for which activity.

Specifically, since there is no definition of "national activities" or "appropriate State" in the treaty, it is not undoubtedly clear what activities are considered as national activities and which State is confirmed to be the appropriate State that has to authorize and supervise such activities. Although there is no single consensus on the interpretation of "national activities," it is widely agreed that national activities over which the State can exercise legal power or control are those for which the State is internationally responsible.[191] Such legal power or control can be determined on the basis of territorial and/or personal jurisdiction, and/or the State of registry of space objects.

The term "appropriate State" can also be interpreted in various ways, especially in reference to i) the definition of 'launching State' prescribed in the Liability Convention, ii) the exercise of State's jurisdiction or control, or iii) the responsible State for national activities.[192] However, for the purposes of authorization and supervision for national activities, those interpretations do

190 *Supra* Chapter 1, n. 14, Bin Cheng, "Article VI of the 1967 Space Treaty Revisited: 'International Responsibility,' 'National Activities' and 'The Appropriate State,'" 15; *Supra* Chapter 1, n. 17, Frans von der Dunk, "Private Enterprise and Public Interest in the European 'Spacescape': towards harmonized national space legislation for private space activities in Europe" 18; Matthew Schaefer, "The Contours of Permissionless Innovation in the Outer Space Domain," University of Pennsylvania Journal of International Law, Vol. 39, Fall (2017), 140–143; Mark J. Sundahl, "Regulating Non-Traditional Space Activities in the United States in the Wake of the Commercial Space Launch Competitiveness Act," Air and Space Law 42, no. 1 (February 2017), 29–30.

191 For details on the interpretation of "national activities," *see supra* Chapter 1 §1.1.2.

192 For details on the interpretation of "appropriate State," *see supra* Chapter 1 §1.1.3.

not appear to be mutually exclusive, and thus it is preferable for each State concerned to establish its own regulating system as long as the relevant State is responsible for national activities under the first sentence of Article VI of the Outer Space Treaty.

Nonetheless, Article VI of the Outer Space Treaty provides neither substantive criteria for authorization nor specific requirements for supervision of national activities, apart from the continuation of such supervision. As a result, States have the discretion to authorize and supervise national activities based on how they interpret the Outer Space Treaty. This indicates that the scope of activities governed by national space legislation may differ from nation to nation. From this viewpoint, the following section will examine to what extent South Korea implements the international obligation of authorization and supervision by analyzing South Korea's approach.

4.2.2.1 *Territorial and Personal Scope of Authorization*

As outlined in Table 12, the territorial and personal scope of launch permission is clearly stated in the Korean Space Development Promotion Act. Regardless of nationality, a person who intends to launch a space launch vehicle from South Korea has to obtain launch permission from the Minister of Science and ICT. The territorial scope set out in the Act includes a launch carried out not only from the Korean territory but also from areas/facilities such as ships or platforms under Korean jurisdiction (quasi-territorial jurisdiction). The Act further extends the authorization scope to a launch conducted outside of Korea if the launch vehicle is owned by the Korean government or a Korean national.

The Act's approach based on territorial jurisdiction appears reasonable for safety considerations and efficient management of launch activities taking place within Korean territory. However, the extended application to outside of Korea relying on ownership of a launch vehicle may raise the question of whether it is beneficial and effective to oversee operations that occur outside of Korea.

The rationale for Korea extending its jurisdiction to such a case appears to be that, according to Article VI of the Outer Space Treaty, Korea may be responsible for activities conducted by non-governmental entities, specifically in cases where a Korean company launches from abroad a launch vehicle that it owns. These activities also require authorization and supervision by the Korean government. Furthermore, depending on the circumstances, Korea may be held liable for damage caused by the launch vehicle owned by a Korean company under Article VII of the Outer Space Treaty.

Nevertheless, absolute adherence to the Korean-owned-launch vehicle rule may be questioned in terms of practicality. It remains debatable how effectively the Korean government can enforce its authorization regime to non-Koreans being outside of Korea, given the fact that the launch activity occurs outside of Korea and is not under Korean territorial jurisdiction. A Korean citizen, on the other hand, who launches a non-Korean-owned launch vehicle outside of Korea, does not even fall under the Act's authorization scope. This appears insufficient in terms of excluding its nationals from its personal jurisdiction. In such a case, the scope of launching permission is not broad enough to cover potential situations for which South Korea may be held responsible and/or liable under the Outer Space Treaty.

4.2.2.2 *Material Scope of Authorization*

As discussed in Section 4.2.1 of Chapter 5, the Korean Space Development Promotion Act limits activities that require authorization to the launch of space launch vehicles. However, this narrow scope may not be sufficient to adequately govern all conceivable space activities occurring within South Korea's jurisdictional reach.

Although the Outer Space Treaty does not specify which activities require State authorization, a general approach is ascertained in the UN General Assembly's "Recommendations on national legislation relevant to the peaceful exploration and use of outer space."[193] According to Article 1 of the Recommendations, the scope of space activities targeted by national space legislation may include the launch and return of objects into and from outer space, the operation of a launch or re-entry site, and the operation and control of space objects in orbit.[194] As such, national activities that possibly require State authorization are not restricted only to launching a launch vehicle. Indeed, it is a legal loophole to exclude all activities other than launching a launch vehicle from appropriate control.

Given South Korea's international obligations as a launching State[195] and as the responsible State for national activities under the UN space treaties, the activities falling within South Korea's jurisdiction or control should be incorporated into its authorizing system. The applicable scope should include space

193 For more details, *supra*, Chapter 1 §1.1.2.

194 UNGA Res. 68/74 of December 11, 2013; UN Doc. A/RES/68/74. Article 1 of the Recommendations further states that "other issues for consideration may include the design and manufacture of spacecraft, the application of space science and technology, and exploration activities and research".

195 *Supra* Chapter 1 §1.3.2.

activities carried out from the Korean territory, and/or elsewhere by Korean nationals, and/or in relation to space objects registered by South Korea.[196]

Among the space activities suggested in the Recommendations above, activities that are not fully regulated under South Korea's current authorizing system are as follows:

First of all, South Korea lacks a launch site licensing system. This may be due to the fact that the existing launch sites in Korea were built and have been operated and managed by the Korean government or KARI, as part of the government-led space development program. However, it will be necessary to introduce a licensing system for launch sites, as private enterprises in Korea become increasingly involved throughout the entire launch-related operations, and commercial space launches are expected to expand rapidly.

Furthermore, even though a significant number of private enterprises are currently operating and controlling satellites in orbit, there is no regulatory framework for on-orbit activities. In light of South Korea's space capabilities to date – satellite technologies and operations are more advanced and active than those of launch, – it is worthwhile to consider broadening the scope of regulation for satellite-related activities including post-launch activities.

While the operation of a re-entry site and the return of a space object from outer space have not happened yet in South Korea, those activities may also require regulations in the foreseeable future. In February 2018, South Korea announced its first-ever, long-term asteroid mission, in which an orbiter/rover will return to Earth after collecting a sample of materials.[197] To that end, technologies specifically for the return of a space object are undergoing research and development. In addition, a project to develop a reusable launch vehicle was laid out in November 2021, which will be conducted in collaboration with the government and the private sector from 2022.[198] Once a reusable launch vehicle is successfully developed, there may be a need for a licensing system for its re-entry related activities including the operation of a re-entry site.

---

196 Article 2 of the Recommendations suggests that "[t]he State, taking into account its obligations as a launching State and as a State responsible for national activities in outer space under the United Nations treaties on outer space, should ascertain national jurisdiction over space activities carried out from territory under its jurisdiction and/or control; likewise, it should issue authorizations for and ensure supervision over space activities carried out elsewhere by its citizens and/or legal persons established, registered or seated in territory under its jurisdiction and/or control."

197 *Supra* Chapter 2 §7.1.2, "The Third Basic Plan for Promotion of Space Development."

198 Sisoo Park, "South Korea to develop reusable rocket with 100-ton thrust engines," last accessed February 12, available at https://spacenews.com/south-korea-to-develop-reusable-rocket-with-100-ton-thrust-engines/.

Lastly, aside from the arguments presented above, there still remains the question of permission for the launch of space objects except for a space launch vehicle, since the language of the Act's provision clearly states that a person who intends to "launch a space launch vehicle" has to obtain permission (see Table 14). This appears to be because the Act provides for the registration of space objects – here, however, except for a launch vehicle – with strict procedures. For such registration, a person who intends to launch a space object (again, except a launch vehicle) must furnish a launch plan and relevant information with the Minister of Science and ICT almost equivalent to those of launch permission for launching a launch vehicle,[199] which may amount to the government's control to a certain point. However, registration itself still falls short of the authorization level. Specifically, while a person has to complete preliminary registration of a payload, usually a satellite, as well as after-launch registration by submitting a launch plan, the Minister of Science and ICT has no power to permit or prohibit the launch or operation of the payload itself. This could lead to a situation in which South Korea may be liable for damage caused by registered space objects but has no sufficient legal control under the Act in advance.

4.2.2.3 *The Content of Supervision*

The Outer Space Treaty, like the State's international obligation to authorize non-governmental activities discussed above, lacks specifics on continuing supervision leaving it to the discretion of each State. South Korea's supervising mechanism is achieved by requiring a launch permit holder to obtain separate approval for major changes to permitted matters and to report minor changes to the regulator, revoking launch permission, and suspending or ordering rectification of the permitted launch activities. However, the same question as in the prior section may arise as to whether the current supervision system fully covers the scope of possible space activities. This is because activities that do not require permission are automatically not included in subsequent supervision.

Furthermore, regarding the provision on suspension or rectification order in a war-like emergency or for national security, the jurisdictional scope of the provision appears too narrow, compared to other provisions examined above, in that the provision applies to Korean nationals only. As long as the requirement for such suspension or rectification is fulfilled, there is no reason

199 Details on the registration for space objects will be examined in Chapter 5 §4.3.

for South Korea not to exercise its territorial jurisdiction over non-Koreans for military purposes during wartime or for national security and public order.

4.2.3 A Comparison with Select Other States' National Space Legislation

As examined in Section 4.2.2 of Chapter 5, States are required to authorize and continually supervise space activities conducted by private entities in accordance with Article VI of the Outer Space Treaty. However, due to the lack of a clear definition or specifics on such international obligations, States are allowed to establish a range of authorization and supervision systems in their national space legislation. While States have discretion over how to comply with the obligations, there may also be common approaches to their national authorization regime. A brief comparison below in this regard will provide the commonality and differences of the licensing systems in the United States, Japan, and France, which have been actively engaged in launch activities for decades, and will ultimately help to identify what can be introduced and adopted for the betterment of the existing Korean authorization regime.

4.2.3.1 *The United States*

With its extensive history in space exploration, the United States has a robust and detailed national space legislation. The majority of laws concerning the commercial use of outer space are contained in Title 51 of the United States Code (USC), titled National and Commercial Space Programs. Commercial space launch activities are governed by the Commercial Space Launch Act enacted in 1984[200] and its accompanying regulations. The Commercial Launch Act requires a license for:[201]

(1) a person to launch a launch vehicle, operate a launch or reentry site, or reenter a reentry vehicle inside the United States;
(2) a US citizen to launch a launch vehicle, operate a launch or reentry site, or reenter a reentry vehicle outside the United States;
(3) a US citizen to launch a launch vehicle, operate a launch or reentry site, or reenter a reentry vehicle outside the United States and outside the territory of a foreign country unless there is an agreement between the two governments that the foreign country has jurisdiction over the launch or operation or reentry; and

200 Commercial Space Launch Act, as amended and recodified in Title 51 USC Chapter 509 §§ 50901 to 50923.
201 Title 51 USC § 50904(a).

(4) a US citizen to launch a launch vehicle, operate a launch or reentry site, or reenter a reentry vehicle in the territory of a foreign country if there is an agreement between the two governments that the United States has jurisdiction over the launch or operation or reentry.

Essentially, the Commercial Space Launch Act regulates the launch of a launch vehicle, the operation of a launch or reentry site, and the reentry of a reentry vehicle, based on both territorial and personal jurisdiction as well as certain situations involving a foreign government. In addition, its implementing regulations in Title 14 of the Code of Federal Regulations (CFR)[202] establish separate procedures depending on the type of activity the applicant will perform: i) launch;[203] ii) operation of a launch site;[204] iii) launch and reentry of a reusable launch vehicle;[205] iv) operation of a reentry site;[206] and v) reentry of a vehicle other than a reusable launch vehicle.[207] An applicant must furnish the required information to the Federal Aviation Administration (FAA), and the FAA conducts policy, safety, payload, and environmental reviews for a proposed activity. Through such reviews, the FAA determines whether an applicant is capable of carrying out a proposed activity without jeopardizing public health and safety, the safety of property, national security, or international obligations of the United States, depending on a specific type of activity. Requirements for approval of human space flights are also detailed in the regulations.[208] While the Commercial Space Launch Act and its implementing regulations apply to the various launch-reentry activities, there is no regulation of on-orbit operations.

Commercial remote sensing operations are governed by the Land Remote Sensing Policy Act[209] and its implementing regulations.[210] It is illegal for any person who falls under the jurisdiction or control of the United States to operate a private remote sensing space system without a license.[211] Operating

202 Title 14 CFR Chapter III, Subchapter C, Parts 400 to 460.
203 Title 14 CFR Chapter III, Subchapter C, Part 415.
204 Title 14 CFR Chapter III, Subchapter C, Part 420.
205 Title 14 CFR Chapter III, Subchapter C, Part 431.
206 Title 14 CFR Chapter III, Subchapter C, Part 433.
207 Title 14 CFR Chapter III, Subchapter C, Part 435.
208 Title 14 CFR Chapter III, Subchapter C, Part 460.
209 The Land Remote Sensing Policy Act, as amended and recodified in Title 51 USC Chapter 601 §§ 60101 to 60162.
210 Title 15 CFR Part 960.
211 Title 51 USC § 60122(a).

TABLE 14 The scope of permission vs. registration

Permission	Registration
Launch a space launch vehicle	Launch a space object except for a launch vehicle
A launch plan including a safety analysis report, a payload operation plan, and a compensation plan	A launch plan including a compensation plan
Permission under conditions, modification, revocation	N/A

requirements of licensees include i) preserving national security and observing international obligations of the United States,[212] ii) making disposition of any satellites in space in a manner satisfactory to the President upon the termination of operations under the license,[213] and iii) furnishing complete orbit and data collection characteristics of the remote sensing system, and immediately providing notification of any deviation.[214] The Land Remote Sensing Policy Act authorizes the Secretary of Commerce to license private remote sensing satellite systems, the authority of which was delegated to the National Oceanic and Atmospheric Administration (NOAA).

As for satellite communications, the Communications Act of 1934, which has subsequently been amended by many acts of Congress, regulates commercial satellite activities by non-governmental entities.[215] The Communications Act created the Federal Communications Commission (FCC), the primary function of which is to grant licenses and supervise communications activities. In order to implement the Communications Act, the FCC establishes regulations that include requirements for licensing, technical standards for satellite communication facilities, procedures for filing an application with the FCC, and the practice of submitting an orbital debris mitigation plan.

For the continuing supervision of launch and reentry activities, the Secretary of Transportation has the power to monitor the activities of the licensees by placing a designated observer at a launch or reentry site used by the licensee,

212 Title 51 USC § 60122(b)(1).
213 Title 51 USC § 60122(b)(4).
214 Title 51 USC § 60122(b)(5).
215 The Communications Act of 1934, as amended, Title 47 USC §§ 151 *et sequens* (Pub. L. No. 416).

at a production facility or assembly site used by a licensee's contractor to produce or assemble a launch vehicle or reentry vehicle, at a site where a payload is integrated with a launch vehicle or reentry vehicle, or at a site not owned or operated by the US government or a foreign government for the crew, government astronaut, or space flight participant training.[216]

A license may be suspended or revoked if the licensee of launch and reentry activities has not complied with prescribed requirements or to protect the public health and safety, the safety of property, or national security or foreign policy interests of the United States.[217] Furthermore, the Secretary of Transportation may prohibit, suspend, or end immediately the launch of a launch vehicle or the operation of a launch site or reentry site, or reentry of a reentry vehicle if such activities are deemed detrimental to the public health and safety, the safety of property, or national security or foreign policy interests of the United States.[218] In short, under the US authorization regime, each activity of launch, operation, or reentry may be monitored, prohibited, suspended, or terminated. A license itself may also be suspended or revoked due to a violation of requirements or for the public safety or national security in a broad sense. Separately from this, communication satellite activities are supervised by the FCC, while remote sensing activities are monitored by NOAA within the US Department of Commerce.

4.2.3.2 *Japan*

Given its long history of space exploration, the Japanese Space Activities Act was enacted relatively late in 2016, which entered into force in 2018.[219] The Act establishes a Japanese authorization system for space activities conducted by private entities. It provides that any person who intends to launch "an artificial satellite, *et cetera*" from a launch facility located in Japan or on a ship or aircraft of Japanese nationality must obtain permission from the Prime Minister.[220] Thus, a launch from outside Japanese (quasi-) territorial jurisdiction does not require such permission. Also, a suborbital flight that does not involve any space object deployment into orbit or beyond is not within the scope of the

216 Title 51 USC § 50907(a).

217 Title 51 USC § 50908(c).

218 Title 51 USC § 50909(a).

219 人工衛星等の打上げ及び人工衛星の管理に関する法律 (平成二十八年法律第七十六号), [The Japanese Space Activities Act No. 76 of 2016, also known as the "Act concerning Launch and Control of Satellites, *et cetera*"].

220 Article 4(1) of the Japanese Space Activities Act.

Space Activities Act,[221] because the term "an artificial satellite, *et cetera*" under the Japanese space laws is defined as an artificial space object placed into orbit or on any celestial body *and* a launch vehicle for such deployment.[222]

In addition to permission for launch, the Prime Minister, upon application, approves the design of a launch vehicle and issues a type certification accordingly.[223] In the same manner, the Prime Minister also approves the conformity of a launch facility located in Japan or on a ship or aircraft of Japanese nationality.[224] This streamlines the permission procedures by not repeating reviews of the launch vehicle or the launch facility that has already been approved by the Prime Minister.

Furthermore, any person who intends to operate and control space objects using a facility located in Japan or on a ship or aircraft of Japanese nationality must obtain permission.[225] A space object operated and controlled outside Japanese (quasi-) territorial jurisdiction, therefore, does not fall within the Japanese authorization system even though such space object is managed by a Japanese national or corporate entity.

Permission to launch or control a space object above is granted following an evaluation of public safety and conformity with the fundamental principles of international and national space legislation. The purpose and use of a space object, in particular, are required to fulfill the principles of the Japanese Basic Space Law,[226] which includes the peaceful use of outer space, the improvement of people's lives, the advancement of space industries, the development of human society, the expansion of international cooperation, and environmental considerations.[227]

In addition to the general authorization rules under the Space Activities Act, Japan also enacted an Act to govern remote sensing activities. Under the Japanese Remote Sensing Act,[228] any person who intends to use a satellite

---

221 Setsuko Aoki, "Space Legislation in Japan" at 5, last accessed February 25, 2022, available at https://www.unoosa.org/documents/pdf/copuos/lsc/2019/tech-05E.pdf; Hiroko Yotsumoto *et al.*, "The Space Law Review: Japan," last accessed February 25, 2022, available at https://thelawreviews.co.uk/title/the-space-law-review/japan.

222 Article 2(3) of the Japanese Space Activities Act. Also, Article 2(2) iii of the Japan Aerospace Exploration Agency Act.

223 Article 13(1) of the Japanese Space Activities Act.

224 Article 16(1) of the Japanese Space Activities Act.

225 Article 20(1) of the Japanese Space Activities Act.

226 Law No. 43 of 2008, enacted on May 21, 2008, promulgated on May 28, 2008, entered into force on August 27, 2008.

227 Articles 2 to 7 of the Japanese Basic Space Law.

228 衛星リモートセンシング記録の適正な取扱いの確保に関する法律, Law No. 77 of 2016.

remote sensing device with a certain level of resolution located in Japan is required to obtain permission from the Prime Minister.[229] Thus, a remote sensing device controlled outside Japanese territory and with a low resolution does not fall within the scope of the Remote Sensing Act, regardless of who operates such a device or if a device detects Japanese territory.

Like in South Korea and the United States, an applicant under the Japanese authorization system also has to furnish information with the Prime Minister, such as the design of a space object, the location of launch, the location of a facility for space object control, and/or a launch or operation plan.[230]

The Prime Minister supervises activities conducted under the Space Activities Act in three main ways: First, the Prime Minister has the authority for on-site inspection to the extent necessary for the enforcement of the Act;[231] Second, in order to ensure the accurate and effective implementation of international space law and secure public safety, the Prime Minister may provide administrative guidance, advice, and recommendation to the person who has obtained permission or certificate pursuant to the Act;[232] Finally, the Prime Minister may issue a correction order in compliance with safety standards and take necessary measures to rectify any violation of the Act.[233]

Furthermore, the Prime Minister may revoke the permission or certificate if it was obtained by deception or other wrongful means, if the permit holder no longer complies with the requirements or safety standards, or if the permit holder violates attached conditions or the Prime Minister's correction order and suchlike.[234]

As such, the Japanese Space Activities Act governs launch activities and control over space objects through a well-established authorization system ranging from application for permission to continuous supervision and revocation of permission. It is noticeable that the Japanese Space Activities Act expressly stipulates that the provisions of launch permission do not apply to activities conducted by the Japanese government.[235] It also acknowledges an exception for JAXA, particularly stating that when JAXA asks for approval of

229 Articles 2 and 4 of the Japanese Remote Sensing Act.

230 Articles 4(2) and 20(2) of the Japanese Space Activities Act; Article 4 of the Japanese Remote Sensing Act.

231 Article 31 of the Japanese Space Activities Act.

232 Article 32 of the Japanese Space Activities Act.

233 Article 33 of the Japanese Space Activities Act.

234 Articles 12, 15, 18, and 30 of the Japanese Space Activities Act.

235 Article 57 of the Japanese Space Activities Act.

launch site or type certificate of a launch vehicle, the permission process can be streamlined.[236]

4.2.3.3 *France*

With its long history in space exploration, the French space sector has been active, especially in launch services and satellite manufacturing. France maintains a space launch facility in its territory, French Guiana, which serves as a major spaceport for current European launch operations. The French Space Operations Act, adopted in 2008 and entered into force in 2010,[237] established the essential principles for authorization and supervision of launch and on-orbit space activities.

In terms of the territorial, personal, and material scope, the Space Operations Act applies to:[238]

(1) any space operator, regardless of nationality, who intends to launch or return a space object from or to the French territory or facilities placed under French jurisdiction;
(2) any French space operator who intends to launch or return of a space object from or to the territory of a foreign State or facilities placed under the jurisdiction of a foreign State or an area that is not subject to the sovereignty of a State;
(3) any French natural or legal person, regardless of whether such person is a "space operator" falling within the meaning of the Act, who intends to launch a space object; and
(4) any French space operator who intends to control a space object in outer space.[239]

Essentially, the French authorization system adopted a combination of territorial and quasi-territorial jurisdiction as well as personal jurisdiction. The applicable activities are the launch, return, and control of a space object depending on where and who conducts such activities. It is also worth noting that the French Space Operations Act uses its unique term "space operator" defined as

236 Article 19 of the Japanese Space Activities Act.
237 LOI n° 2008-518 du 3 juin 2008 relative aux opérations spatiales [The French Space Operations Act No. 2008-518 of June 3, 2008].
238 Article 2 of the French Space Operations Act.
239 According to Article 3 of the French Space Operations Act, this authorization system also applies to any person previously authorized under the Act who wants to transfer control or command of a space object.

any natural or legal person who is responsible for independently conducting a space operation,[240] rather than referring to the conventional term 'citizen' or 'national.' The Act does not explicitly cover human space flights or suborbital flights.

Over the course of the authorizing process, France requires the applicant to furnish the authorities with detailed information specified in its implementing Ministerial Order,[241] such as a description of the space operation, a risk management plan and an assessment of the environmental impact. In essence, the candidate must demonstrate moral, financial, and professional guarantees, as well as fulfill technological, security, and safety criteria.[242] These requirements are aimed to ensure protection of national defense interests and compliance with France's international commitments. Space activities are required to be conducted in the interests of the safety of persons and property and the protection of public health and the environment.[243]

The license or authorization issued pursuant to the Act may be revoked or suspended if the holder fails to comply with the requirements or compromises the interests of national defense or France's international obligations. In the event of revocation or suspension of authorization to control a space object, the authorities may order the holder to take appropriate measures to reduce any potential damage to a space object.[244]

As part of supervision, designated agents can access premises and facilities where space activities are carried out. The agents are entitled to inspect operation sites and to request information and documents in order to ensure that space operators comply with their obligations.[245] Essentially, requirements and criteria examined during the authorizing process remain under continuous supervision, which includes moral, financial, and professional guarantees in the interests of national security and defense, France's international commitments, and safety of public health and the environment.

While the licensing and authorization requirements are stringent, such a system does not apply to activities carried out by the National Center for Space Studies (CNES)[246] for a public mission or by the nation in the interest

240 Article 1(2) of the French Space Operations Act.

241 Ministerial Order of March 31, 2011 (The Technical Regulation).

242 Article 4 of the French Space Operations Act.

243 Article 5 of the French Space Operations Act.

244 Article 9 of the French Space Operations Act.

245 Article 7 of the French Space Operations Act.

246 Centre National d'Etudes Spatiales, Loi n° 61-1382 du 19 dicembre 1961 instituant un centre national d'etudes spatiales [established on December 19, 1961, Law No. 61-1382].

of national defense. The technical regulations may also be derogated to the extent strictly necessary for national defense.[247] Like Japan discussed above, the French Space Operations Act also demonstrates that the Act's requirements are substantially applied to activities conducted by private entities.

4.2.4 Concluding Remarks

This section explored South Korea's authorization and supervision framework for national space activities in terms of the scope of the Space Development Promotion Act as well as how South Korea approaches international principles stipulated in Article VI of the Outer Space Treaty in comparison to the three selected nations – the United States, Japan, and France.

South Korea's approach to complying with international obligations of authorization and supervision is on the whole within the realm of allowable interpretation and State discretion under international space law. The requirements for obtaining launch permission as well as the conditions for maintaining such status are reasonable and thoroughly specified in the Act along with its Presidential Decree and implementing regulations.

The scope of the Act regarding permission, however, may be considered rather excessive or not broad enough in terms of the Act's jurisdictional scope, depending on the situation. For example, it may be too much to require non-Koreans abroad to obtain a launch permission just because they use a Korean-owned launch vehicle even though such a launch operation is performed outside of Korean (quasi-) territorial jurisdiction. On the other hand, it appears insufficient that the Korean launch permission system does not apply to even a Korean citizen if he/she launches a non-Korean-owned launch vehicle abroad. To have legal means of control over activities conducted by Koreans that may result in South Korea's international liability, South Korea may consider including its Korean national into the Act's personal scope of the launch permission like the United States and France do through their authorization regimes.

In addition, since the Act requires permission only for launching a space launch vehicle, there is a legal loophole in coverage of various other space operations that can be considered as South Korea's national activities under Article VI of the Outer Space Treaty. Comparing the three nations discussed above and garnering examples from their applicable activities, the possible scope of activities that can likely be regulated by Korean space legislation would be the operation of a launch site, the control over space objects in orbit, and the launch of space objects in a broad sense. The operation of a re-entry

247 Article 11 of the French Space Operations Act.

site or the return of a space object may also be included in the scope of the Act in the foreseeable future as South Korea is improving its space capabilities in that regard.

4.3 *Registration*

4.3.1 The Registration Regime of the Act

4.3.1.1 *National Registration of Artificial Space Objects*

South Korea has a unique national registration system in that the Space Development Promotion Act adopts a two-step approach to registering artificial space objects: i) the preliminary registration by no later than 180 days before the scheduled date of launch and ii) the formal registration within 90 days after a space object is successfully placed into orbit.

More specifically, Article 8 of the Act provides that:

(1) a Korean citizen who intends to launch an artificial space object (excluding a launch vehicle) in and outside of Korea shall file a preliminary registration with the Minister of Science and ICT by no later than 180 days before the scheduled date of launch; and[248]

(2) a person who is not a citizen of the Republic of Korea and falls under any of the following subparagraphs shall file a preliminary registration in accordance with paragraph (1):
   i. where an artificial space object is intended to be launched from South Korean territory or areas/facilities under South Korean jurisdiction; or[249]
   ii. where an artificial space object is intended to be launched outside of Korea aboard a space launch vehicle owned by the Korean government or a Korean citizen.[250]

Therefore, Korean citizens, regardless of where their artificial space objects are launched, have to register them, whereas non-Koreans are required to do so only in cases where a space object is launched from Korean territorial jurisdiction or where a launch vehicle to be used is under Korean ownership (see Table 15).

Like the process for launch permission discussed above, an applicant who intends to file preliminary registration must submit a launch plan. Article 8(3) of the Act and Article 10(3) of its Presidential Decree enumerate what needs

248 Article 8(1) of the Space Development Promotion Act.
249 Article 8(2) i of the Space Development Promotion Act.
250 Article 8(2) ii of the Space Development Promotion Act.

TABLE 15 In situations where domestic registration is required

	Korean citizen	Non-Korean citizen
Launching from Korea including area/facilities under Korean jurisdiction	Required	Required
Launching outside of Korea	Required	Required only if a launch vehicle is owned by the Korean government or a Korean citizen

to be included in the launch plan: The purpose of use of the artificial space object; its owner and/or usage right holder; its lifespan and/or usage period; its manufacturer and manufacturing number and date; its general function; data such as its weight, size, produced power, consumed power, and suchlike; the launching site and the projected launch date; the launch service provider and the specification and performance of the launch vehicle to be used; the planned trajectory of the artificial space object; basic orbital parameters; matters concerning security for the use and management of the artificial space object; and matters concerning the discharge of liability for damages in the event of a space accident. If, after reviewing the launch plan, the Minister of Science and ICT determines that the applicant is insufficient to bear such liability, the Minister may require the applicant to rectify or remedy the launch plan.[251] In practice, it is highly recommended to purchase third-party liability insurance when applying for preliminary registration.

A person who has completed preliminary registration is further required to file formal registration within 90 days after the date on which the artificial space object is successfully placed into orbit.[252] However, this formal registration process does not apply to an artificial space object registered with a foreign country under an agreement with the foreign government of the launching State pursuant to the Registration Convention.[253] Given that the Space

251 Article 8(4) of the Space Development Promotion Act.

252 The first sentence of Article 8(5) of the Space Development Promotion Act.

253 The second sentence of Article 8(5) of the Space Development Promotion Act.

Development Promotion Act mandates that the Korean government should proceed to internationally register the 'formal-registered' space object,[254] this exception, which is based on an intergovernmental agreement, appears reasonable in that it prevents unnecessary duplicate international registration by two or more States concerned. In this regard, Paragraph 2 of Article II of the Registration Convention provides that, in the case of a launch event wherein two or more launching States are involved, those States "shall jointly determine which one of them shall register the object [...] without prejudice to appropriate agreements concluded or to be concluded among the launching States." The Space Development Promotion Act adequately implemented this principle in the national 'formal registration' process.[255]

With regard to changes in registered matters, the Act adopted a type of continuing supervisory mechanism comparable to that of the launch permission system: If the submitted launch plan is changed, the person who completed preliminary registration or who acquired formal registration of an artificial space object shall report to the Minister of Science and ICT within 15 days of becoming aware of such a change.[256] If such a report is not submitted on time or is false, an administrative fine will be imposed.[257]

The Minister of Science and ICT is in charge of maintaining and managing national registries of both preliminary and formal registration of artificial space objects.[258] The national registries contain information such as the type, name, and purpose of a space object, the applicant's name, the registration number and date, and the (projected) location and date of launch.[259]

4.3.1.2 *International Registration of Artificial Space Objects*

Article 9 of the Space Promotion Development Act provides that the Minister of Science and ICT is required to register a space object with the United Nations pursuant to the Registration Convention. More specifically, space objects that have completed formal domestic registration are eligible for international registration via the Minister of Foreign Affairs.[260] Therefore, space objects that have been preliminarily registered but not yet formally registered cannot

254 Article 9 of the Space Development Promotion Act.

255 *See, supra,* Chapter 5, n. 253.

256 Article 8(6) of the Space Development Promotion Act.

257 Article 29(2) i of the Space Development Promotion Act. In such a violation, the maximum fine is 5 million Korean won, approximately 5,000 US dollars.

258 Article 10(1) of the Space Development Promotion Act.

259 Article 4(1) of the Ministerial Order of the Space Development Promotion Act.

260 First Sentence of Article 9(1) of the Space Development Promotion Act.

proceed to international registration. It is also noteworthy that the Minister of Foreign Affairs is involved in the registration process in consideration of the characteristics of the UN registration work.

International registration of satellites, however, is regulated by the Radio Waves Act.[261] This is because the Space Development Promotion Act provides for an exception that the Act's international registration rule does not apply to satellites falling under Article 44(1) of the Radio Waves Act.[262] Prior to the enactment of the Space Development Promotion Act, satellite-related matters including their international registration were already being governed by the Radio Waves Act. Thus, even post the Space Development Promotion Act, the Radio Waves Act continues to be applied to the international registration of satellites. According to Article 44(1) of the Radio Waves Act, the Minister of Science and ICT is required to register an artificial satellite launched by a Korean citizen with the United Nations in accordance with the Registration Convention.

Therefore, space objects falling under the scope of the international registration under the Space Development Promotion Act are those excluding i) launch vehicles – since launch vehicles are not even eligible for preliminary domestic registration according to the Act – and ii) satellites launched by a Korean citizen – since satellites launched by Korean citizens are supposed to be registered under the Radio Waves Act. In short, space objects likely to be internationally registered under the Space Development Promotion Act are indeed limited to such as domestically registered satellites launched by non-Koreans, rovers, landers, and orbiters.

4.3.1.3 *National Registration for Meteorites*

In 2015, the Space Development Promotion Act instituted a unique system of national registration for meteorites. Two provisions (Articles 8-2 and 8-3) were inserted in between the provisions of national (Article 8) and international (Article 9) registration of artificial space objects.

The rationale behind the introduction of this unusual system is that in March 2014, several meteorites were discovered for the first time in Jinju, Southern South Korea. As those meteorites were confirmed to have considerable research value, the Korean government attempted to purchase them from the discoverers for study and scientific purposes. The media covered this event nationwide, drawing public interest in space science and history, as well as attracting meteorite hunters to that location. Upon this opportunity, the

261 *See, supra* Chapter 4 § 3.14.

262 Second sentence of Article 9(1) of the Space Development Promotion Act.

government decided to operate a meteorite registry, similar to the registration system for artificial space objects, in order to better manage such valuable natural space objects.[263] This is nicknamed 'the Jinju meteorite registration system' after the location where those meteorites were first discovered.

Article 8-2 of the Act provides for the owner's right to apply for registration of a meteorite discovered in or brought to South Korea.[264] Compared to the language used for the registration of artificial space objects discussed above, this provision uses "may" instead of "shall."[265] Thus, registration of a meteorite under the Act is not an obligation but a right to be verified as the owner of an authentic meteorite. When applying for registration, the applicant is required to submit the relevant meteorite, and, if it holds, an appraisal or data analysis of the meteorite.[266] However, if the Minister of Science and ICT deems it difficult to move or transport the relevant meteorite in consideration of its size and characteristics, the meteorite does not need to be submitted at the request of the applicant. In such a case, the Minister of Science and ICT may have a public official concerned or an employee of the entrusted agency check, inspect, or analyze the meteorite at the site.[267] The Minister of Science and ICT must ascertain the authenticity of a meteorite within 30 days from the date of receiving the application and must issue a registration certificate where it is proven to be authentic.[268]

Although the application for the initial registration of a meteorite is optional, once a registration certificate has been issued, the holder is required to report any changes to the registered information, such as the transfer of ownership due to the sale, transfer, or division of the meteorite.[269] Upon receipt of the report, the Minister of Science and ICT will reissue a registration certificate

---

263 Reason for the Amendments to the Space Development Promotion Act, Act No. 13009, partially amended on January 20, 2015, entered into force on July 21, 2015, last accessed on March 22, 2022, available at https://www.law.go.kr/LSW/lsInfoP.do?efYd=20150721&lsiSeq=167384&ancYd=20150120&nwJoYnInfo=N&ancNo=13009&chrClsCd=010202&efGubun=Y#0000.

264 Article 8-2(1) of the Space Development Promotion Act.

265 Article 8-2(1) of the Space Development Promotion Act provides that "[t]he owner of a meteorite [...] *may* file an application for registration of the relevant meteorite," whereas Article 8(1) stipulates that "[a]ny citizen [...] *shall* file a preliminary registration." [Italics added].

266 Article 10-2(1) of the Presidential Decree of the Space Development Promotion Act.

267 Article 10-2(2) of the Presidential Decree of the Space Development Promotion Act.

268 Article 8-2(2) of the Space Development Promotion Act and Article 10-2(3) of the Presidential Decree of the Space Development Promotion Act.

269 Article 8-2(3) of the Space Development Promotion Act.

that reflects the changes.[270] The Minister is in charge of managing the national meteorite registry and recording the details of the issuance or reissuance of registration certificates.[271]

In addition, Article 8-3 of the Act stipulates that meteorites discovered in South Korea shall not be taken out of the nation, except for academic research purposes approved by the Minister of Science and ICT. This provision applies regardless of whether the meteorite has been registered or not. Therefore, anyone intending to take a meteorite found in South Korea outside of the nation must obtain the Minister's approval for academic research purposes. The procedures for obtaining such approval are specified in the Presidential Decree of the Act.[272]

Overall, South Korea's meteorite management system is one of a kind in that the Space Development Promotion Act addresses not only artificial space objects but also natural space objects including meteorites. On the other hand, however, questions may arise as to whether it is appropriate to deal with meteorites under the Space Development Promotion Act. If laws concerning space resource management are enacted in the future, it would be suggested that matters related to natural space objects may be transferred and incorporated into such laws.

4.3.2 An Observation from an International Space Law Perspective

Article VIII of the Outer Space Treaty implicitly refers to the registration of space objects, stating that the State of registry retains jurisdiction and control over the objects and personnel while in outer space. Further, the Registration Convention elaborates upon the State's obligation to maintain a national registry of space objects and to furnish information about the space objects to the UN Secretary General.[273]

4.3.2.1 *Territorial and Personal Scope of Registration*

Whether or not the scope of Korea's registration system under the Space Development Promotion Act is appropriate can be examined by analyzing the concepts enshrined in the Registration Convention. According to Paragraph 1 of Article II of the Registration Convention, the "launching State" is obliged to register a space object launched into Earth orbit or beyond. The term

270 Article 10-2(5) of the Presidential Decree of the Space Development Promotion Act.

271 Article 10(2) of the Space Development Promotion Act and Article 10-2(6) of the Presidential Decree of the Space Development Promotion Act.

272 Article 10-3 of the Presidential Decree of the Space Development Promotion Act.

273 *Supra* Chapter 1 §1.4.

"launching State" is defined in Article I(a) of the Registration Convention as (i) a 'State which launches or procures the launching of a space object' or (ii) a 'State from whose territory or facility a space object is launched.'[274]

To begin with, as demonstrated in Table 15, the Space Development Promotion Act requires the registration of space objects launched from South Korea or Korean jurisdiction, regardless of nationality. This is identical to the definition of "launching State" set by Article I(a)(ii) of the Registration Convention above, and thus there is no problem with the scope of the registration system. In addition, the Space Development Promotion Act mandates Korean citizens to register space objects even if they launch from outside of Korea. This falls under the interpretation of the definition of "launching State" outlined in Article I(a)(i) of the Registration Convention above, in that South Korea is considered as a "launching State" for the launch activities of its nationals. The most common example of Koreans launching space objects outside of Korea is likely to be when they purchase launch services abroad. According to the wording and interpretation of the Act, the registration system is applicable to the procurement of the launching of space objects, and the Korean government's practice is the same.

Concerns may arise, however, as to whether applying South Korea's registration procedure to non-Koreans outside of Korea is appropriate in some instances. This comes as the Space Development Promotion Act also imposes the registration obligation if a non-Korean entity launches a space object using a launch vehicle owned by the Korean government or a Korean national. A possible scenario would be when a non-Korean client who intends to launch a satellite outside of Korea procures a launch service provided by a Korean national company on board a Korean-owned launch vehicle.

Presumably, the rationale for Korea's willingness to extend its registration procedure to such a case appears to be that Korea may be liable for damage caused by the payload in accordance with Article VII of the Outer Space Treaty and the Liability Convention. Nonetheless, this may amount to an excessive reach in terms of personal jurisdiction. This may also be questioned since it inherently embraces a broad interpretation of 'procurement.'[275] Although the Act does not explicitly refer to the term 'procurement,' the Korean registration regime appears to be premised on the assumption of procurement of launch services. In interpreting so, it should also be considered that the registration

274 For more discussion of the term "launching State" in the Liability Convention, *supra* Chapter 1 §1.3.2. Both the Liability Convention and the Registration Convention share the same definition of the term "launching State."

275 *See*, *supra* Chapter 1 §1.3.2.

provision has been applied even before South Korea acquired launch capability and the same is true of the government's practice. As for the aforementioned scenario, when a foreign customer intends to launch a payload on a Korean-owned launch vehicle, preliminary registration of the payload is required under the Act. During this process, the Korean government can look into the specifications of the payload in terms of safety and other requirements. Further, when it proceeds to the formal registration, the question of which State should register the payload would be determined between the two States based on their agreement pursuant to Article 8(5) of the Act, as previously discussed.[276] Therefore, there would be no actual conflict in that regard.

While there has yet to be a real case of Koreans providing launch services to non-Korean clients outside of Korea, it is still worth discussing because such a case is highly likely to occur in the near future. It is also questionable what benefits South Korea would have by applying the Korean registration procedure to non-Korean people overseas just because they use a Korean-owned launch vehicle. Rather, the Korean government would only bear the burden to maintain such registration records and to keep tracking any changes to them. Perhaps, some of the potential issues pertaining to preliminary registration may be alleviated through individual contracts between Korean launch service providers and abroad service users. Also, as for formal registration, the second sentence of Article 8(5) of the Act may dilute some complicated situations since the obligation of formal registration does not apply to a space object registered with a foreign State under an agreement between the Korean and the foreign governments pursuant to the Registration Convention.[277] However, these do not solve fundamental concerns related to the scope of personal jurisdiction.

4.3.2.2 *Material Scope of Registration*

Another concern that may arise is whether South Korea's registration system adequately accommodates various space objects in terms of what types of space objects should be registered in the national registry.

---

276 *See, supra* Chapter 5 §4.3.1.1.

277 Article 8(5) of the Space Development Promotion Act does not specify exactly which provision of the Registration Convention it relates to. Given the aim and intent of the clause, it appears to refer to Article II(2) of the Registration Convention, which provides that "[w]here there are two or more launching States in respect of any such space object, they shall jointly determine which one of them shall register the object." Thus, Article 8(5) of the Act can be understood as an acknowledgement and reiteration of the meaning of Article II(2) of the Registration Convention.

Since Paragraph 1 of Article II of the Registration Convention mandates the registration of a "space object," the meaning of a "space object" needs to be confirmed prior to assessing the scope of the Korean registration under the Space Development Promotion Act. While the Registration Convention and other space treaties do not specifically define the term "space object," Article I(b) of the Registration Convention mentions that it "includes component parts of a space object as well as its launch vehicle and parts thereof."[278] This provides the foundation for a broad interpretation of the term "space object,"[279] which is used as the generic term to cover any object that human beings launch, attempt to launch, or have launched into outer space, including spacecraft, satellites, launch vehicles, and their components parts.[280]

The Space Development Promotion Act, on the other hand, adopts an atypical approach to national registration in that it confines the obligation to domestically register space objects to those other than launch vehicles. In other words, launch vehicles are expressly excluded from the scope of the registration under Article 8 of the Act.[281] More specifically, whereas the original meaning of "artificial space object" according to Article 2(3)(a) of the Act is defined as objects designed and manufactured for use in outer space – including space launch vehicles, artificial satellites, spaceships, and their components parts –,[282] Article 8 of the Act makes an exception to such definition by limiting its scope to space objects "excluding space launch vehicles," and the same exception applies to Articles 9 (International Registration of Artificial Space Objects) and 10 (Management of Registers of Artificial Space objects). As a result, launch vehicles are neither required to be registered with the Minister of Science and ICT nor the United Nations, while they must obtain permission to launch. This may result in a situation where a launch vehicle is authorized and launched by South Korea but is not registered internationally, even though South Korea is regarded as a launching State that is liable for damage caused by the space object.

In summary, given the meaning of "space object" set out in the Registration Convention, the registration system under South Korea's Space Development

278 The definition of a "space object" in Article I(b) of the Registration Convention is the same as in Article I(d) of the Liability Convention as follows: The term "space object" includes component parts of a space object as well as its launch vehicle and parts thereof.

279 Lesley Jane Smith and A. Karrest, "Article I (Definitions) LIAB," in Stephan Hobe, Bernhard Schmidt-Tedd and Kai-Uwe Schrogl (eds.), *Cologne Commentary on Space* Law, Vol. II (2013), 115.

280 Bin Cheng, "International Responsibility and Liability for Launch Activities," in Air and Space Law, vol. 20, no. 6 (1995), 297–298.

281 *See supra* Chapter 5 §4.3.1.1.

282 *See supra* Chapter 5 §2.

Promotion Act is not in line with the scope of the Registration Convention, which explicitly includes launch vehicles in its definition. The Act leaves launch vehicles outside of its registration system for no rational reason. While launch vehicles are regulated by South Korea's authorization system, which is regarded as more stringent in terms of governmental control over space objects, it does not play the same function as the treaty's national and international registration, nor does it serve the same purpose.

Although the National Assembly provided no official explanation for the exclusion of launch vehicles, it might be related to a desire to reduce excessive or duplicate government control over the private sector. As previously noted, the requirement for registering space objects, such as submitting a launch plan including a compensation plan for a potential accident, is not completely dissimilar to the requirement for obtaining launch permission although the latter is, of course, more thorough and inclusive. Back in the legislative process, registration would have been considered as a form of governance, and thus requiring both registration and permission for a launch vehicle would have been viewed as redundant/duplicate, since the majority of the requirements overlap with each other, imposing a double burden on the private sector. Based on this reasoning, the Act may have concluded that the categories of registration vs. permission should be differentiated; space objects other than launch vehicles are under the registration system whereas launch vehicles are under the permission regulation. Nonetheless, it appears evident that in terms of the purpose and role, registration of space objects is not the same as launch authorization. Of course, as a party to the Registration Convention, South Korea would be able to register a launch vehicle with the United Nations in compliance with the Registration Convention, independent of its national space legislation. It should be noted that Article 3(1) of the Space Development Promotion Act stipulates the obligation of the Korean government to comply with space-related treaties.

4.3.2.3 *The Contents and Conditions of Registration*

While the Registration Convention requires States to establish and maintain an appropriate national registry, it does not provide internationally uniform requirements for such obligation. Paragraph 3 of Article II of the Registration Convention states that the contents of each registry and the conditions under which it is maintained are determined by the State of registry concerned. As a result, the specific method of managing the domestic registry including what information to be registered therein is at the discretion of each State.[283]

283 *See, supra* Chapter 1 §1.4.2.

TABLE 16 Two-step registration procedure and timeframe

	Preliminary (pre-launch) registration	Formal (after launch) registration
Deadline for filing an application	180 days before the scheduled launch date	90 days after the launch
Deadline for reporting changes	15 days after the awareness	15 days after the awareness

In line with the intent of the Registration Convention, South Korea has developed its unique national registry. The Korean registration system is characterized by its two-step procedure of preliminary and formal registration as well as the timeframe established for registration application, among other things (see Table 16).

More specifically, the registration procedure begins with filing an application for preliminary registration together with a detailed launch plan, during the launch preparation phase. The deadline for the preliminary registration is no later than 180 days before the scheduled launch date. In this manner, the Korean government can examine relevant information and a launch plan in advance. If there is any concern over the submitted documents, the Minister of Science and ICT may direct the applicant to amend and/or supplement such matters prior to the preliminary registration. Once preliminary registration is completed, it is ready to proceed to the formal registration; nevertheless, preliminary registration does not necessarily mean that it leads to actual launch and gets formally registered. The launch may be postponed indefinitely or canceled forever. In the latter scenario, the registration process ends at the phase of preliminary registration. In either case, any changes must be reported to the Minister of Science and ICT within 15 days from the date of awareness. Once the pre-registered object is successfully launched, it must be formally registered within 90 days after the date of being placed into orbit. As with preliminary registration, any modification made after formal registration must also be notified within 15 days so that the national registry can always be maintained up to date.

With respect to the information transmitted to the UN Secretary General, Paragraph 1 of Article IV of the Registration Convention enumerates a list of specifics; they are the name of the launching State, an appropriate designator of the space object or its registration number, the date and location of launch, basic orbital parameters, and general function of the space object. Accordingly, although each State is free to determine the contents and conditions of its national registry, at least the aforementioned categories must be furnished to the UN "as soon as practicable."[284]

As for South Korea's national registration, on the other hand, the Space Development Promotion Act and its implementing Presidential Decree mandate applicants to submit more detailed and comprehensive information concerning the space object, as well as the intended launch plan (see Table 17). For instance, in addition to the standard information, South Korea requires information on the manufacturer, owner, and operator of the satellite, the life span or usage period of the satellite, the launching entity, the specification of the launch vehicle to be used, the security and safety information in relation to potential liability for damages and suchlike. Furthermore, Article 9(2) of the Space Development Promotion Act requires the Minister of the Science and ICT to notify any changes in the registered information to the UN Secretary General such as the decommissioning of the space object, whereas the transmission of additional information concerning a space object carried on its national registry is not an obligation but a recommendation, as Paragraph 2 of Article IV of the Registration Convention states that "Each State of registry may, from time to time, provide the Secretary General of the United Nations with additional information." Although the Registration Convention itself does not specify what the "additional information" is, the UN Resolution, "Recommendations on Enhancing the Practice of States and International Intergovernmental Organizations in Registering Space Objects,"[285] calls upon states to provide a list of additional information such as any change of status in operations when a space object is no longer functional, any change of orbital position, and the identification of the new owner or operation. Since South Korea maintains its national registry up to date by making it an obligation at the national level to be notified of any changes to the space object and launch plan, as well as requiring such changes to be furnished to the UN Secretary General, it appears that the additional information prescribed in the Resolution is also fully covered by the Korean national law.

In summary, the Korean registration system is well organized in stages with the timeframe for each registration of space objects and notification of changes. In addition, the range of information being recorded in the registry is broader and more detailed than the requirement of the Registration

---

284 *See, supra* Chapter 1 §1.4.3.

285 UNGA Res. 62/101, December 17, 2007.

TABLE 17 Information to be notified: Registration Convention vs. South Korean national space law

	Registration Convention	Korean Space Development Promotion Act
Standard Information	Information required by Article IV(1) of the Registration Convention: – The name of the launching state or states; – An appropriate designator of the space object or its registration number; – The date and territory or location of the launch; – The basic orbital parameters, including the nodal period, inclination, apogee, and perigee; and – The general function of the space object	Same as all the information required by Article IV(1) of the Registration Convention pursuant to Article 8(3) of the Act and Article 10(3) of its Presidential Decree
Additional Information	No specific obligation but recommended by Article IV(2) of the Registration Convention, and the Resolution 62/101 demonstrates example information	More comprehensive information required: – The purpose of the space object; – The owner and/or usage right holder; – The lifespan and/or usage period; – The manufacturer and manufacturing number and date; – The weight, size, produced power, consumed power, and suchlike of the space object; – The launching entity; – The specification and performance of the launch vehicle to be used; – A security plan concerning the use and management of the space object; and – A compensation plan concerning the discharge of liability for damages in the event of a space accident.
Changes in Transmitted Information	Recommended to notify	Required to notify within the specified timeframe

Convention. Further, the notification of changes is mandatory under the Space Development Promotion Act, although it is just a recommendation by international space law. Consequently, South Korea appears to maintain a meticulous and stringent registration system, given its compulsory registration and notification procedures combined with the timeframe and requirements outlined above.

4.3.3 Korea's Practice of International Registration and Notification

Since the obligation to register space objects and the information necessary to be furnished to the United Nations are explicitly specified by the Registration Convention, States' practices in terms of their international registration may be consistent up to a certain point.

South Korea informed the UN Secretary General in a note verbale dated January 15, 2009,[286] that it had established a national registry of space objects in conformity with Article II of the Registration Convention as well as its national space law, Articles 8 (Domestic Registration of Artificial Space Objects) and 10 (Management of Registry of Artificial Space Object) of the Space Development Promotion Act. The national registry is regularly updated and managed by the Minister of Science and ICT in accordance with the Ministry's Ordinance.[287] The Ordinance provides for each application form of the preliminary and formal registration of space objects as well as the notification form for modified matters thereof.[288] Upon each registration pursuant to the Act, the Minister issues a certificate of preliminary/formal registration.[289]

Although South Korea only informed the United Nations of the establishment of its national registry in 2009, following the enactment of the Space Development Promotion Act, South Korea had already been fulfilling its international obligation under the Registration Convention by transmitting the required information about space objects. South Korea's first notification to the United Nations is dated January 4, 1995, containing "information concerning space objects launched during the period 1992–1993," in its annex.[290] Those are

286 UN Doc. ST/SG/SER.E/INF.23, April 16, 2009, "Note verbale dated 15 January 2009 from the Permanent Mission of the Republic of Korea to the United Nations (Vienna) addressed to the Secretary-General," last accessed on April 8, 2022, available at https://www.unoosa.org/oosa/en/spaceobjectregister/national-registries/index.html.

287 The Ordinance of the Ministry of Science and ICT, Ordinance No. 78, enacted on November 30, 2005, entered into force on December 1, 2005.

288 Articles 2(1) and 3 (1) of the Ordinance of the Ministry of Science and ICT.

289 Article 2(2) of the Ordinance of the Ministry of Science and ICT.

290 UN Doc. ST/SG/SER.E/297, January 16, 1995, "Note verbale dated 4 January 1995 from the Permanent Mission of the Republic of Korea to the United Nations (Vienna) addressed

TABLE 18 An example of additional information submitted to the United Nations concerning changes in the status of a space object

	Initial	**Current**
Ownership	Korea Telecom Corp. (Republic of Korea)	Asia Broadcast Satellite Ltd. (Bermuda)
Geostationary orbit	Over 113 degrees East	Over 74.8 degrees East

South Korea's first-ever and second-built satellites, KITSAT-1 and 2,[291] placed into orbit aboard Arianespace's launch vehicles in 1992 and 1993, respectively. This demonstrates that South Korea has complied with its international obligation to register space objects ever since the beginning of its space program.

In practice, the information that South Korea transmits to the United Nations is more than the aforementioned basic data required by paragraph 1 of Article IV of the Registration Convention. For instance, South Korea's recent notification dated May 4, 2021, contains further information such as the type of orbit ("sun-synchronous orbit"), the outline of performing missions ("combustion experiments and biology experiments"), and the name and size of satellites ("CANYVAL-C Timon [1U] and CANYVAL-C Pumbaa [2U]").[292]

Moreover, pursuant to paragraph 2 of Article IV of the Registration Convention, South Korea provides additional information at its discretion concerning changes in the status of space objects listed in its national registry and previously registered with the United Nations. One example is KOREASAT-1, launched in 1995, with its mission suspension reported by South Korea in 2005.[293] Another instance involves the transfer of ownership and a change in the orbital position of KOREASAT-2, launched in 1996, for which South Korea furnished the relevant information as follows (Table 18):

to the Secretary-General," last accessed on April 11, 2022, available at https://www.unoosa.org/oosa/en/spaceobjectregister/national-registries/index.html.

291 *See, supra* Chapter 2 §3.3 and §5.3.

292 UN Doc. ST/SG/SER.E/990, October 7, 2009, "Note verbale dated 24 September 2009 from the Permanent Mission of the Republic of Korea to the United Nations (Vienna) addressed to the Secretary-General," last accessed on April 11, 2022, available at https://www.unoosa.org/oosa/en/spaceobjectregister/national-registries/index.html.

293 UN Doc. ST/SG/SER.E/304/Add.1, January 13, 2014, "Note verbale dated 13 December 2013 from the Permanent Mission of the Republic of Korea to the United Nations (Vienna)

Additionally, in compliance with paragraph 3 of Article IV of the Registration Convention, South Korea notified the United Nations on September 24, 2009, that its satellite, STSAT-1, was deactivated on May 31, 2009.[294] South Korea's notice to the United Nations took approximately four months, which appears to be within an acceptable time frame considering the phrasing used in paragraph 3, "to the greatest extent feasible and as soon as practical."

4.3.4 Concluding Remarks

As discussed in the preceding sections, Articles 8 to 10 of the Space Development Promotion Act and its implementing regulations specify the content and procedural aspects of South Korea's registration system. Domestically, space objects are registered twice, before and after launch within a set period. Meanwhile, the Korean government conducts supervision throughout the course of each initial registration and afterwards: the applicant for each registration or the registration certificate holder must notify the status change of space objects; if a launch plan submitted by the applicant does not meet the requirements, the Minister of Science and ICT may issue an order of rectification or supplementation of such plan; the administrative fine is imposed on those who fail to file preliminary and/or formal registration, fail to notify the status change of space objects, or submit a false notification of such change.

Overall, the applicable scope of South Korea's registration system is within the extent permitted by international space law. However, some criteria may be deemed excessive or insufficient: imposing the registration obligation on non-Koreans outside of Korea in cases where their satellite is launched via a Korean-owned launch vehicle appears excessive. On the other hand, the exclusion of a launch vehicle from the domestic registration system seems insufficient in that the term "space object" under the Registration Convention does not exclude a launch vehicle. Although the aforementioned issues have not yet occurred in reality, it is nonetheless imperative to review and address such challenges given that private launch businesses in South Korea are on the verge of providing commercial launch services in and outside of Korea using their own launch vehicles.

---

addressed to the Secretary-General," last accessed on April 11, 2022, available at https://www.unoosa.org/oosa/en/spaceobjectregister/national-registries/index.html.

294 UN Doc. ST/SG/SER.E/580, May 21, 2021, "Note verbale dated 4 May 2021 from the Permanent Mission of the Republic of Korea to the United Nations (Vienna) addressed to the Secretary-General," last accessed on April 11, 2022, available at https://www.unoosa.org/oosa/en/spaceobjectregister/national-registries/index.html.

The information that South Korea transmits to the United Nations concerning space objects as well as maintains in its national registry is not limited to the basic data outlined in Article IV of the Registration Convention. The Space Promotion Development Act requires an applicant to submit a detailed launch plan when filing for a domestic preliminary registration, making a notice of any modification also mandatory. However, not every detail is officially provided to the United Nations. Nonetheless, it is still broader than the international requirements. In practice, the additional information provided voluntarily by South Korea includes the mission outline, orbital location, operational change, and ownership change. Apart from the registration of space objects, it is rather unique that South Korea established its national registry of meteorites, which is maintained by the Minister of Science and ICT in the same way as that of space objects.

4.4 *Liability*

Since South Korea has a dedicated space law that deals with liability issues,[295] the Space Development Promotion Act does not specifically address them. Article 14 of the Space Development Promotion Act stipulates that a person who launches an artificial space object in accordance with Articles 8 and 11 of the Act is liable for damages resulting from "space accidents" caused by the space object. It also states that the scope of compensation for damages, limitations of liability, and other relevant matters are prescribed by separate legislation. This led to the promulgation of the Space Damage Compensation Act in 2007, which will be discussed in detail in the following Chapter 6.

Prior to the enactment of the Space Damage Compensation Act, the Space Development Promotion Act had included a provision on liability insurance, which was removed in 2007[296] as the Space Damage Compensation Act directly came to address such matters. Consequently, only the principle of liability remains in the Space Development Promotion Act.

To further analyze Article 14 of the Act, it is essential to break down its provisions. First, Article 14 references Articles 8 and 11 with respect to those who are subject to liability for damages. This indicates that the liability regime under Article 14 applies to those who comply with the obligations established in Articles 8 and 11, which respectively require the domestic registration of

295 The Space Damage Compensation Act enacted on December 21, 2007, Act No. 8714, entered into force on June 22, 2008, *see supra* Chapter 5 §3.2.

296 The deleted provision stipulated that a person who intends to obtain launch permission is obliged to take out a liability insurance in compliance with the minimum amount of insurance set out in the Ordinance of the Ministry of Science and ICT.

artificial space objects and obtaining permission to launch space launch vehicles. Thus, such registrants and licensees fall under this liability regime.[297]

Second, Article 14 stipulates that these registrants and licensees are liable for damages arising from "space accidents." The term "space accident" is defined in Article 2 of the Act as a breakdown, crash, collision, explosion, or other occurrence of an artificial space object during its launch and operation, including preparation for launch, test launch, and unsuccessful launch.[298] This definition provides clarity on what types of incidents fall under the liability regime set forth in Article 14.

In summary, Article 14 of the Act outlines South Korea's domestic legal stance on the principle of liability regarding space activities, indicating who is liable under what circumstances. The liability regime applies to those who comply with the domestic registration and launch permission requirements and covers a range of incidents defined under Article 2 as "space accidents."

4.5 *Rescue and Return*

Unlike the principles and obligations set forth in the Outer Space Treaty, the Liability Convention, or the Registration Convention, those under the Rescue Agreement do not necessarily incentivize States to draft national legislation on the subject matter. In other words, it is uncommon for national law to specifically incorporate what the Rescue Agreement enshrines. Nonetheless, the Korean Space Development Promotion Act contains two provisions, Articles 14-2 and 14-3, which address the rescue and return of astronauts and space objects.

4.5.1 The Rescue and Return System of the Act

Article 14-2 of the Act stipulates that in cases where astronauts aboard an artificial space object of a "foreign country" have made an emergency landing or are in distress or have suffered an accident in the territory of the Republic of Korea or the "adjacent high seas," the Korean government shall render them (all) possible assistance[299] and return them to the "launching State, the State

297 This liability rule outlined in the Space Development Promotion Act only provides for who is liable under what circumstances. Details such as obligations for reimbursement and insurance are stipulated in a separate law, the Space Damage Compensation Act, which will be addressed in Chapter 6.

298 *Supra* Chapter 5 §2.

299 While Article 2 of the Rescue Agreement mentions "all possible steps" and "all necessary assistance," the Space Development Promotion Act adopted the term "possible assistance." It seems that the Korean legislators avoided using the word "all" although there

of registry, or an international organization whichever is responsible for the launching of the artificial space object."

Furthermore, according to Article 14-3 of the Act, if an artificial space object of "a foreign country" "crashes or makes an emergency landing," the Korean government is required to safely return the artificial space object to the "launching State or the State of registry or to an international organization, whichever is responsible for launching the artificial space object."

These two provisions, in conjunction with Article 3(1) of the Act which declares the Korean government's duty to comply with international space-related treaties to which it is a party, demonstrate South Korea's commitment to explicitly implement the international principles of the Outer Space Treaty and the Rescue Agreement, as well as to domestically underscore the government's obligations to rescue and return astronauts and space objects under those treaties.

4.5.2 An Observation from an International Space Law Perspective

While the intention of Articles 14-2 and 14-3 of the Space Development Promotion Act appears to be the same as the international principles of rescue and return of astronauts and space objects, the terminology employed in the Act is not identical to that in the space treaties. In this regard, examining parallels and differences between South Korean national legislation and international law would thus be useful for a better understanding of the Act's two provisions.

4.5.2.1 *The Rescue and Return Principle under the Outer Space Treaty*

Articles V and VIII of the Outer Space Treaty address the humanitarian aspects of protecting astronauts and the return of space objects, respectively.

Essentially, Article V of the Outer Space Treaty consists of three paragraphs with the notable phrase in the first paragraph referring to "astronauts as envoys of mankind in outer space." According to paragraph 1 of Article V, States Parties shall render to astronauts "all possible assistance in the event of accident, distress, or emergency landing on the territory of another State Party or on the high seas." When astronauts make such a landing, they shall be "safely and promptly returned to the State of registry of their space vehicle." In short, this paragraph addresses the obligations of State Parties for astronauts and emergencies that occur somewhere on Earth.

---

seems to be no significant difference in interpreting the meaning between "all possible assistance" and "possible assistance."

Paragraph 2 of Article V, on the other hand, stipulates the obligation of the astronauts from one State Party to render "all possible assistance to the astronauts of other States Parties," "[i]n carrying on activities in outer space and on celestial bodies."

Aside from such obligations, paragraph 3 of Article V requires States Parties to immediately inform the other States Parties or the UN Secretary General of "any phenomena" discovered in outer space that may endanger the lives or health of astronauts.

In addition, while Article VIII primarily provides for the core principles of registration, jurisdiction and control, and ownership of space objects, it also establishes in its third sentence an obligation to return space objects found beyond the limits of the State Party to the "State of registry," as well as, "upon request, to furnish identifying data prior to their return."[300]

The term "astronaut," as used in Article V, is not explicitly defined in the Outer Space Treaty or any other international legal instruments. Historically, when the Outer Space Treaty was drafted in the 1960s, there was no need to discuss private individuals traveling to outer space. In the absence of a precise definition, and given the intention of the drafters, the meaning of "astronaut" in the treaty should be understood as those who fundamentally travel into outer space for professional reasons, as opposed to solely commercial spaceflight participants or space tourists who are not part of the crew and whose primary reason for the flight is for leisure purposes.[301]

Another term that may generate interpretative concerns is "all possible assistance," which appears in both paragraphs 1 and 2 of Article V of the Outer Space Treaty. What is the scope of "all possible assistance"? Although there is no definitive explanation in the treaty, it should be essentially understood in relation to the wording in paragraph 1 that presents the situation where such assistance is required, which is "in the event of accident, distress, or emergency landing on the territory of another State Party or on the high seas." In

300 The full language of Article VIII the Outer Space Treaty is as follows: "A State Party to the Treaty on whose registry an object launched into outer space is carried shall retain jurisdiction and control over such object, and over any personnel thereof, while in outer space or on a celestial body. Ownership of objects launched into outer space, including objects landed or constructed on a celestial body, and of their component parts, is not affected by their presence in outer space or on a celestial body or by their return to the Earth. Such objects or component parts found beyond the limits of the State Party to the Treaty on whose registry they are carried shall be returned to that State Party, which shall, upon request, furnish identifying data prior to their return."

301 Bernhard Schmidt-Tedd and Kai-Uwe Schrogl (eds.), *Cologne Commentary on Space Law*, Vol. I (2013), 96–97.

paragraph 2, however, there is no such reference to the extent of assistance. Does this imply an extensive obligation to render all kinds of assistance in any circumstances? Perhaps, the obligation enshrined in paragraph 2 is more comprehensive than that of paragraph 1, as it refers to the obligation of astronauts of one States Party to another State Party in carrying on activities in outer space. Nonetheless, given the intention of Article V overall, it should be construed as a comprehensive obligation but within the reasonable scope of the humanitarian and international cooperation purposes.[302]

Lastly, it should be also noted that under both Articles V and VIII of the Outer Space Treaty it is the "State of registry" to which astronauts in distress and space objects found beyond the limits of the State Party have to be returned. According to the definition in Article I(c) of the Registration Convention, "State of registry" means a launching State on whose national registry a space object is carried. Ultimately, launching States that ideally carry such objects on their registry are entitled to claim the return of their astronauts and/or space objects.

4.5.2.2 *The Rescue and Return Principle under the Rescue Agreement*

The Rescue Agreement elaborates on the general principles of assistance and return enshrined in Articles V and VIII of the Outer Space Treaty. Articles 1 through 4 of the Rescue Agreement address the "personnel of a spacecraft" regarding the obligations to notify information on accidents, distress, emergency or unintended landings, assist such personnel in distress, and return the personnel to the "launching authority." Further, concerning "a space object or its component parts," Article 5 of the Rescue Agreement covers the obligations to notify information, recover and return space objects, and reimburse expenses incurred in fulfilling such obligations.

While the Preamble of the Rescue Agreement clearly states that one of its purposes is to "develop and give further concrete expression" to the Outer Space Treaty's rescue and return duties, the terms used in the two treaties are not identical, leaving room for interpretation. Thus, depending on the interpretation or different terminology employed, the scope of the duties under the Outer Space Treaty may be enlarged or decreased to some extent under the Rescue Agreement.

Above all, the term "personnel of a spacecraft" stands out in Articles 1 to 4 of the Rescue Agreement as compared to "astronauts" in the Outer Space Treaty. Notably, Article 1 provides for the notification obligation as follows:

302 *Ibid.*, Bernhard Schmidt-Tedd and Kai-Uwe Schrogl (eds.), 98–100.

> Each Contracting Party which receives information or discovers that the *personnel of a spacecraft* have suffered an *accident* or are experiencing conditions of *distress* or have made an *emergency or unintended landing* in territory under its *jurisdiction* or on the *high seas* or in any other place *not under the jurisdiction of any State* shall immediately:
> (a) Notify the *launching authority* or, if it cannot identify and immediately communicate with the launching authority, immediately make a public announcement by all appropriate means of communication at its disposal;
> (b) Notify the Secretary-General of the United Nations, who should disseminate the information without delay by all appropriate means of communication at his disposal. [Italics added]

Given that the term "astronauts" appears in both the title and the Preamble of the Rescue Agreement,[303] and that it makes little sense if the rest of the Rescue Agreement refers to the "personnel of a spacecraft" in a different meaning, it can thus be submitted that the two terms are not mutually exclusive and that the meaning of "personnel of a spacecraft" should preferably be understood in relation to the interpretation of "astronauts" as discussed in the previous section despite the different wording.[304]

It should also be noted that the provisions concerning the "personnel of a spacecraft" in the Rescue Agreement are based on a situation where an "accident," "distress," or "emergency or unintended landing" has occurred. Although none of the international space treaties contain a definition of each term, it does not seem difficult to understand the meaning of such terms through their ordinary or dictionary meanings. Especially, since the term "distress" is generally defined as "a feeling of great worry or unhappiness; great mental pain; severe problems caused by not having enough food and suchlike; a situation in which a ship, plane, and suchlike is in danger or difficulty and needs help; a state of physical pain and effort,"[305] accordingly "distress" seems to include situations in which the persons involved are in trouble even if there is no actual accident. Thus, the term "distress," which is not strictly limited to a specific

303 The full title of the Rescue Agreement is the "Agreement on the Rescue of Astronauts, the Return of Astronauts and Return of Objects Launched into Outer Space," and its Preamble refers to the text of the Outer Space Treaty using the term "astronauts."

304 *Supra* Chapter 1 §1.2.2; Bernhard Schmidt-Tedd and Kai-Uwe Schrogl (eds.), *Cologne Commentary on Space* Law, Vol. II (2013), 41.

305 Oxford University Press, *Oxford Learner's Dictionaries*, last accessed on April 29, 2022, available at https://www.oxfordlearnersdictionaries.com/definition/english/distress_1.

"accident" or an "emergency or unintended landing," should be construed as the broadest conception of the situations described in the Rescue Agreement.[306]

Notably, the obligations specified in Articles 1 to 5 of the Rescue Agreement apply to a "Contracting Party" only if the event occurs "in territory under its jurisdiction or on the high seas or in any other place not under the jurisdiction of any State." This indicates the territorial scope of the obligations, or to what extent the obligations apply from a territorial sovereignty standpoint, while also emphasizing that the obligations are required to be fulfilled by the "Contracting Party."

Specifically, Article 1 requires each Contracting Party to notify the launching authority and the UN Secretary-General of any distress, regardless of whether the event occurs within the territory of a Contracting Party. Article 4 similarly requires the return of a spacecraft's personnel to the launching authority, regardless of where they have been found.[307] However, Articles 2 and 3 are confined to a certain territorial scope that applies exclusively to one another. Article 2 addresses events that occur within the territory of a Contracting Party, which is required to immediately take all possible steps to rescue and render all necessary assistance to the personnel of a spacecraft, whereas Article 3 covers events that occur on the high seas or in any place not under its jurisdiction. In the latter case, the obligation to extend assistance is limited to the condition that the Contracting Party be "in a position to do so" and "if necessary."[308]

Article 5, which deals with space objects or their component parts that have landed on Earth, also classifies States' obligations according to the territorial areas, as do Articles 1 through 4. The notification obligation under Paragraph 1 of Article 5 applies regardless of where the objects have landed. The recovery obligation, however, applies only if each Contracting Party has jurisdiction over the territory where the objects have been discovered "upon the request of the launching authority" and if "practicable."[309] The return obligation under

---

306 *Supra* Chapter 5, n. 304, Bernhard Schmidt-Tedd and Kai-Uwe Schrogl (eds.), 44–45.

307 Article 4 of the Rescue Agreement reads in full: "If, owing to accident, distress, emergency or unintended landing, the personnel of a spacecraft land in territory under the jurisdiction of a Contracting Party or have been found on the high seas or in any other place not under the jurisdiction of any State, they shall be safely and promptly returned to representatives of the launching authority."

308 For more discussion especially on Articles 1 through 4 and 5 of the Rescue Agreement, *see* Frans von der Dunk, "A Sleeping Beauty Awakens: The 1968 Rescue Agreement after Forty Years," Journal of Space Law 34, No. 2 (Winter 2008), 422–425.

309 Paragraph 2 of Article 5 reads in full: "Each Contracting Party having jurisdiction over the territory on which a space object or its component parts has been discovered shall, upon the request of the launching authority and with assistance from that authority

Paragraph 3 applies in any case if the objects have been found beyond the launching authority's territory upon request.[310] Nonetheless, Paragraph 4 of Article 5 allows a Contracting Party to notify the launching authority of any objects that are discovered within its territory or recovered elsewhere and are believed to be "hazardous or deleterious." The launching authority is then required to take immediate "effective steps" to eliminate any "possible danger of harm."[311] Notably, the expenditures for recovery and return of a space object are imposed on the launching authority in Paragraph 5, but there is no comparable clause for the rescue and return of the personnel of a spacecraft.[312]

Last but not least, it is unique that Article 1 and subsequent provisions of the Rescue Agreement adopted the term "launching authority" to indicate to whom the obligations must be fulfilled, such as to whom information must be notified or the personnel of a spacecraft must be returned. Article 6 of the Rescue Agreement defines the "launching authority" as the "State responsible for launching, or, where an international intergovernmental organization is responsible for launching, that organization." The distinctiveness here stems from its explicit inclusion of international organizations. In contrast, the Liability Convention and the Registration Convention, both concluded after the Rescue Agreement, do not use the term; instead, they refer to the "launching State," which is defined identically in their respective Article 1.[313]

---

if requested, take such steps as it finds practicable to recover the object or component parts."

310 Paragraph 3 of Article 5 reads in full: "Upon request of the launching authority, objects launched into outer space or their component parts found beyond the territorial limits of the launching authority shall be returned to or held at the disposal of representatives of the launching authority, which shall, upon request, furnish identifying data prior to their return."

311 Paragraph 4 of Article 5 reads in full: "Notwithstanding paragraphs 2 and 3 of this article, a Contracting Party which has reason to believe that a space object or its component parts discovered in territory under its jurisdiction, or recovered by it elsewhere, is of a hazardous or deleterious nature may so notify the launching authority, which shall immediately take effective steps, under the direction and control of the said Contracting Party, to eliminate possible danger of harm."

312 Paragraph 5 of Article 5 reads in full: "Expenses incurred in fulfilling obligations to recover and return a space object or its component parts under paragraphs 2 and 3 of this article shall be borne by the launching authority."

313 Article 1(c) of the Liability Convention and Article 1(a) of the Registration Convention, where the term "launching State" is defined as: i) a State which launches or procures the launching of a space object or ii) a State from whose territory or facility a space object is launched. However, it should be noted that these two treaties identically provide that "In this Convention, [...] references to States shall be deemed to apply to any international intergovernmental organization which conducts space activities if the organization

4.5.2.3 *A Comparison between the Act and the International Space Treaties*

Essentially, Articles 14-2 and 14-3 of the Space Development Promotion Act, which primarily requires the Korean government to comply with the rescue and return obligation, succinctly address the fundamental principles enshrined in both the Outer Space Treaty and the Rescue Agreement. The Act's terminology, however, is not completely the same as that of the treaties; the Act adopted specific terms selectively from the Outer Space Treaty, the Rescue Agreement, or both by combining them, while employing its own lexicon allowing it to expand the scope of the international obligation at the national level (see Table 19).

More specifically, whether or not the nation is a party to the treaties, the Act mandates the Korean government to fulfill such an obligation. The Act makes no mention of the terms "State Parties to the Treaty" or "Each Contracting Party" found in each treaty. Rather, it refers to "astronauts aboard 'a foreign country's artificial space object" to whom the Korean government must render possible assistance. This is significant because it extends South Korea's obligation beyond signatory States to all nations from a humanitarian perspective. In other words, regardless of other nations' signatory status, such domestic obligation is imposed on the Korean government as long as the emergency described in the Act occurs in the 'Korean territory or the adjacent high seas,' which serves as the territorial scope of the obligation.

The "astronauts" who would be rendered assistance under the Act are prescribed as 'those on board an artificial space object,' which implies that the Act fundamentally incorporates both terms from the Outer Space Treaty's "astronauts" and the Rescue Agreement's "personnel of a spacecraft" in a broad sense.

There is another notable expression found in Articles 14-2 and 14-3 of the Act that combines terminology from both treaties, which concerns 'to whom the astronauts and space objects should be returned.' The wording of the Act is that the government must safely return them to the "launching State, the State of registry, or the international organization, whoever is responsible for the launch of the artificial space object." In contrast, as examined in the prior sections, Articles V and VIII of the Outer Space Treaty merely refer to the "State of registry," while the Rescue Agreement mentions the "launching authority," which is defined as the 'State or international organization responsible for

declares its acceptance of the rights and obligations [...] if a majority of the States members of the organization are States Parties to this Convention" in Article XXII of the Liability Convention and Article VII of the Registration Convention, respectively. As a result, those intergovernmental organizations that meet the requirements can be qualified as the "launching States" for the purposes of these treaties.

TABLE 19 Comparison of terminology between the Act and the space treaties

	Korean Space Development Promotion Act	**Outer space treaty**	**Rescue agreement**
Who	Korean government for a foreign country	Among State Parties to the Treaty	Between Each Contracting Party
Where: (Extra) terrestrial scope	In the territory of the Republic of Korea or adjacent high seas	On the territory of another State Party or the high seas, or in outer space	In territory under the jurisdiction of a Contracting Party or on the high seas or in any other place not under the jurisdiction of any State
Situation	An emergency landing, distress, or an accident	An accident, distress, or an emergency landing	An accident, distress, an emergency or unintended landing
Render assistance to	Astronauts aboard an artificial space object of a foreign country	Astronauts	The personnel of a spacecraft
Return to	The launching State, the State of registry, or the international organization, whichever is responsible for the launch of the artificial space object	The State of registry	The launching authority

launching' under Article 6 of the Rescue Agreement. Ultimately, it appears that the Korean legislators included both returning options from the two treaties so that there is no potential controversy in interpretation.

Although there is no additional provision in the Act other than the obligation to rescue and return astronauts and space objects, South Korea as a party to the Outer Space Treaty and the Rescue Agreement is bound to abide by detailed international obligations such as notification to the concerned State and the United Nations. Furthermore, Article 3(1) of the Act reaffirms the Korean government's adherence to the international principles embodied in the space treaties that South Korea has joined.[314]

In essence, the significance of Articles 14-2 and 14-3 of the Act in comparison with the two international space treaties is that the Act, from the sentiment of humanity, domestically requires the Korean government to bear the rescue and return obligation regardless of whether the State in issue is a party to the treaties. And it is unquestionable that the government must and will fulfill the remainder of the obligations that are not specified in its national law but contained in Articles V and VIII of the Outer Space Treaty and the Rescue Agreement in order to promote international cooperation in the peaceful exploration and use of outer space.

4.5.3 A Comparison with Other States' National Space Legislation

Given the fact that the underlying spirit and duties to cooperate in rescue and return efforts on Earth or in outer space are primarily based on humanitarian considerations, such duties do not necessarily need to be codified in national space law as each Member State is required to comply with the treaties anyhow. In this sense, like South Korea, Belgium is unique in that its national space legislation includes a clause that addresses at least one of the aspects obliged by the Rescue Agreement.

The Belgian Law on the Activities of Launching, Flight Operations or Guidance of Space Objects provides that any space object found on the Belgian territory or in Belgian jurisdiction shall be returned to the competent Belgian authorities and it shall be informed to the authorities immediately so that they may arrange for the said object to be returned to its State of registry in accordance with the Rescue Agreement.[315] This clause is noticeable in that it states

---

314 *Supra* Chapter 5 §3.1, Article 3(1) provides that the Korean government must "observe any space-related treaties it has entered into with other countries or international organizations" and "pursue the peaceful exploration and use of outer space."

315 Section 1 of Article 17 of the Law of 17 September 2005 on the Activities of Launching, Flight Operation or Guidance of Space Objects, as revised by the Law of 1 December 2013 (Belgian Official Journal of 15 January 2014), available at https://www.belspo.be/belspo/space/doc/beLaw/Loi_en.pdf.

TABLE 20 Comparison between the provisions of South Korea and Belgium

	South Korea	**Belgium**
Regulation for the rescue and return of astronauts	Yes	No
Regulation for the return of space objects	Yes	Yes
Principal actor on whom the obligation expressly imposed	The Korean government	The discoverer of a space object
Situation	An emergency landing, distress, or an accident	Not specified in the provision but the title of the chapter to which the provision belongs reads "Liabilities, counterclaims and measures in the event of falling space objects"
Return to	The launching State, the State of registry, or the international organization, whichever is responsible for the launch of the artificial space object	The State of registry

the following process, once informed or returned to the Belgian government, shall be in compliance with the Rescue Agreement. Furthermore, as inferred from the context, it establishes the obligation to notify the Belgian authorities imposed upon those who have discovered the space object.

The difference in how South Korea and Belgium incorporate their international obligations into their national legislation is that the former emphasizes the Korean government's commitment to rescuing and returning astronauts and space objects, whereas the latter focuses more on the returning procedure of a space object starting from a space object discoverer to the Belgian authorities, highlighting the discoverer's duty of notification and returning to the authorities. Additionally, the territorial applicability of Belgium's clause is more limited than South Korea's as Belgium does not include the high seas in terms of applicable scope (see Table 20).

4.5.4 Concluding Remarks

As discussed in this section, the two provisions of South Korea's Space Development Promotion Act governing the rescue and return of astronauts and space objects do more than simply reaffirm the country's international obligations. Indeed, the Act broadens the scope of the Korean government's domestic obligations to a particular extent based on humanitarian considerations.

Regarding the question of which State astronauts and space objects must be returned to, the Act creates its own combined terminology of both treaties – the "launching State" from the Outer Space Treaty and "the State of registry, or the international organization, whichever is responsible for the launch of the artificial space object" not exactly the same but virtually similar to the definition of "launching authority" of the Rescue Agreement – possibly to avoid any controversy over the interpretation due to their non-identical wordings.

From a comparative law perspective, it is unusual for States to have included rescue and return obligations in their national space law. Nonetheless, Belgium and South Korea have one or two provisions in their national legal frameworks that deal with such obligations. While the inclusion of these provisions may appear unnecessary if only superficially observed, it can still provide extra clarity by stipulating a domestic procedure (such as Belgium) or can impose a supplementary duty upon the government by extending the scope of international obligations at the national level (such as South Korea). In other words, although such inclusion is neither required nor promoted by default, it should not be dismissed as a somewhat futile endeavor.[316] Moreover, as the number of space activities, notably commercial/private human space flights, is increasing and more and more space objects are launched by various emerging countries, South Korea's unique approach to conventional rescue and return obligations can help facilitate the recovery and return of astronauts and space objects in a broader sense, regardless of whether they belong to Member States of those space treaties.

316 *Cf.* Annette Froehlich and Vincent Seffinga, National Space Legislation: A Comparative and Evaluative Analysis (2018), 186.

4.6 *Safety and Security*

4.6.1 Space Accident Investigation

The Space Development Promotion Act and its Presidential Decree provide detailed measures for a space accident investigation. According to Article 16 (1) of the Act, if any of the "space accidents specified in the Presidential Decree" occur, the Minister of Science and ICT 'may' form and run a Space Accident Investigation Committee. Article 14 of the Presidential Decree defines "space accidents specified in the Presidential Decree" as any of the following accidents that the Minister of Science and ICT deems necessary to investigate for reasons such as severe damage inflicted on human life, body, or property:

i. Accidents caused by artificial space objects registered preliminarily or formally under Article 8 of the Act;[317]
ii. Accidents caused by space launch vehicles, the launch of which is authorized under Article 11 of the Act;[318]
iii. Accidents caused by artificial space objects of foreign countries, which occur in the territory of the Republic of Korea or in areas or facilities under Korean jurisdiction; and
iv. Accidents caused by artificial space objects of foreign countries to the property of the Republic of Korea or to a Korean national including a Korean juridical person.

Technically speaking, while Article 16(1) of the Act merely grants the Minister of Science and ICT the authority to establish a space accident investigation committee, Article 18(1) of the Presidential Decree further stipulates it as the Minister's duty by stating that "when a space accident under Article 14 of the Decree occurs, the Minister 'must' organize a Space Accident Investigation Committee without delay and request the Committee to conduct an investigation." The Committee is obligated to submit an investigation report to the Minister accordingly.[319] To carry out its tasks, the Committee may also investigate any of the following individuals:[320]

i. A person who has filed preliminary or formal registration of an artificial space object in accordance with Article 8;
ii. A person who has obtained permission to launch space objects in accordance with Article 11; and
iii. A person involved in the artificial space objects in question, such as manufacturers and performance testers of the artificial space objects.

---

317 *Supra* Chapter 5 §4.3.1.1.

318 *Supra* Chapter 5 §4.2.1.

319 Article 18(2) of the Presidential Decree of the Space Development Promotion Act.

320 Article 16(3) of the Space Development Promotion Act.

Individuals under investigation must comply and cooperate unless they have justifiable grounds not to. In order to facilitate investigations, the Committee's chairperson has the authority to request cooperation from the heads of relevant administrative agencies for measures such as access control of accident locations. The heads of these agencies must cooperate, unless there are compelling reasons to the contrary.[321]

The Committee's missions include discovering the causes of space accidents, collecting and analyzing accident data, drawing up investigation reports, and other tasks that the Minister of Science and ICT deems necessary for space accident investigation.[322] The Committee's operating period begins on the date it is formed and ends when the Minister considers that the Committee has completed its aforementioned duties.[323]

The Committee is composed of at least five but no more than eleven members including one chairperson. All of them are commissioned by the Minister of Science and ICT. In view of national security, however, a separate committee can be independently formed for matters prescribed by the Presidential Decree.[324] Such matters include space accidents caused by artificial space objects launched by heads of administrative agencies concerned with national security under their own space programs where the general disclosure of accident investigations would be detrimental or harmful to national security.[325] A separate investigation committee is organized under the head of the administrative agency concerned,[326] who is required to consult with the Minister of Science and ICT when necessary for the management of the separate committee.[327] This demonstrates how the Korean government takes national security into consideration in its space accident investigation.

In contrast, there are no specific provisions on space accident investigation in the UN space treaties. It is worth noting that the Korean Space Development Promotion Act and its accompanying Presidential Decree address the issue at the national level in considerable detail.

As previously discussed, Article 16(3) of the Act and Article 14 of the Presidential Decree specify the individuals who may be investigated and the space accidents possibly falling under investigation, respectively. Both

321 Article 16(4) of the Space Development Promotion Act.
322 Article 17 of the Presidential Decree of the Space Development Promotion Act.
323 Article 16(4) of the Presidential Decree of the Space Development Promotion Act.
324 Article 16(2) of the Space Development Promotion Act.
325 Article 19(1) of the Presidential Decree of the Space Development Promotion Act.
326 Article 19(2) of the Presidential Decree of the Space Development Promotion Act.
327 Article 19(4) of the Presidential Decree of the Space Development Promotion Act.

provisions identically refer to the Act's Articles 8 (space object registration) and 11 (launch permission) as being subject to investigation in cases of space accidents. This implies that a series of accident investigation procedures conducted by the Korean government can also be part of the "continuing supervision" that Article VI of the Outer Space Treaty requires. From the preliminary registration of space objects throughout launch permission and after launch, the Korean government is involved in overseeing the totality of launch activities. It should also be noted that applicants for registration and launch permission are required to submit a launch plan that includes a compensation plan in preparation for space accidents and/or a safety analysis report.[328]

In essence, the Space Development Promotion Act creates mandatory obligations in two ways: 1) a requirement of the Minister of Science and ICT (or heads of pertinent government agencies involving national security) to investigate space accidents and 2) a requirement to those involved in launch activities to cooperate with investigation procedures. The concept of space accident investigation appears to have been partially derived from the one introduced by the aviation accident investigation protocols of the Korea Aviation Accident Investigation Board (KAAIB), which is governed by the Korean Aviation and Rail Accident Investigation Act[329] under the Convention on International Civil Aviation.[330] Given the fact that South Korea's space launch industry is nascent and still in development compared to its aviation industry, operating a space-exclusive investigation committee apart from the long-lived traditional aviation system appears to be a sagacious decision. Although not explicitly stated, the fundamental aim of the investigation committee appears to be to identify the causes of space accidents, thereby preventing potential future accidents and ensuring the safety of space activities in general.[331] This is supported by the missions assigned to the investigation committee in Article 17 of the Presidential Decree of the Space Development Promotion Act as previously discussed. It is also undeniable that this Korean system for space accident investigation will further contribute to international cooperation and mutual assistance in conducting space activities in a safe and sustainable manner.

328 *Supra* Chapter 5 §4.2.1 and §4.3.1.1.

329 Act No. 7692, enacted on November 8, 2005, entered into force on July 9, 2006, as partially amended on May 18, 2021.

330 Also known as the Chicago Convention, Doc 7300 of the International Civil Aviation Organization (ICAO), signed on December 7, 1944, in Chicago, as superseded by 9th edition, 2006 (Doc 7300/9).

331 In contrast, the Aviation and Rail Accident Investigation Act explicitly stipulates these purposes and contains provisions regarding the initiation of judicial proceedings, including criminal prosecution, during aviation accident investigations. More specifically, it

4.6.2 Safety Management and Compensation Pertinent to Launch Activities

In order to ensure the safe launch of artificial space objects in Korea, the Minister of Science and ICT may request the heads of administrative agencies or the local governments to assist in controlling access to surrounding areas including territorial waters and airspace, telecommunicating, firefighting, emergency rescue and recovery.[332] Additional requests include notification of the scheduled launch time to domestic and international aircraft as well as providing weather forecasts.[333]

In instances wherein access is restricted to people, vehicles, businesses and fishing vessels resulting in economic loss as a result of launching a launch vehicle, the State and local governments are required to provide compensation.[334] A claim for compensation must be submitted to the Minister of Science and ICT within three months after the date access is restricted resulting in economic loss.[335] The Minister then provides claimants with the criteria and procedures to secure compensation including the method of payment. The Minister along with the relevant local government and the entity that launches the artificial space object negotiates the amount of compensation with claimants.[336] This process suggests that the Korean government took into consideration public safety but also compensation for the infringement of the individual interests of its people from space launch activities.

4.6.3 Security Measures and Guidelines

When implementing space development projects related to national security, the Minister of Science and ICT is required to consult with the heads of

states that the investigation must be conducted separately and independently from other judicial proceedings related to administrative, civil, and/or criminal liability (Article 30). Additionally, it ensures that any person who testifies, provides information, or otherwise participates under the Act must not face discharge, transfer, disciplinary action, or any other disadvantages (Article 32). At present, the Space Development Promotion Act does not contain explicit provisions for space accident investigations. Furthermore, there have been no space accidents under Korean jurisdiction. However, it is worth noting that aviation accident investigations have a well-established history with a dedicated law. Considering that the concept of space accident investigation is still in its early stages, one can anticipate the development of more specific principles for improved investigations in the future, drawing from the extensive example of aviation legislation.

332 Article 20(1) of the Space Development Promotion Act.

333 Article 20 of the Presidential Decree of the Space Development Promotion Act.

334 Article 20-2(1) of the Space Development Promotion Act.

335 Article 20-2(1) of the Presidential Decree of the Space Development Promotion Act.

336 Article 20-2(2) of the Presidential Decree of the Space Development Promotion Act.

relevant central administrative agencies.[337] The Minister may consult with the Minister of National Defense, the Director of the National Intelligence Service, or the Minister of Foreign Affairs.

Furthermore, the Minister of Science and ICT establishes the necessary measures and discloses the guidelines for such security-related projects, which are accessible to the public.[338] Participants in the projects are also required to implement their security measures in accordance with the Minister's guidelines.[339] The guidelines cover comprehensive matters such as security management principles, the security control system including the designation of departments and officers in charge, the classification and security control of satellite data, and the requirements and procedures for public disclosure of space development projects.[340] Given South Korea's geopolitical location and the current division between the two Koreas, the importance of national security cannot be overstated in its space development and activities.

4.7 *Promotion of Private Space Sector*

4.7.1 Private Sector-Led Space Development

In an effort to encourage private sector-led space development in light of NewSpace, the Korean National Assembly passed an amendment to the Space Development Promotion Act on June 10, 2022.[341] The amendment includes the revised Article 18 on the promotion of privately-led space development and six newly inserted Articles 18-2 to 18-7 that elaborate on the key principle enshrined in Article 18.

Article 18(1) of the Act mandates that the Minister of Science and ICT formulate and implement strategies to specifically promote space development and investment in the private sector as well as foster space enterprises in accordance with the Basic Plan for the Promotion of Space Development.[342] When formulating and implementing such strategies, the Minister may request the heads of relevant central agencies to cooperate.[343] Under this overarching principle, central and local governments may enable private space entities to access and utilize infrastructures owned by public organizations or

337 Article 21(1) of the Space Development Promotion Act.
338 Article 21(2) of the Space Development Promotion Act.
339 Article 21(3) of the Presidential Decree of the Space Development Promotion Act.
340 Article 21(2) of the Presidential Decree of the Space Development Promotion Act.
341 Act No. 18867, as amended on June 10, 2022, entered into force on December 11, 2022.
342 Article 5 of the Space Development Promotion Act, *see supra* Chapter 5 §3.3.
343 Article 18(2) of the Space Development Promotion Act.

government-funded research institutions in an attempt to promote the growth of the commercial space industry.[344]

The Korean government may carry out space development projects together with institutions or organizations by signing a contract to efficiently implement the Basic Plan.[345] The government may also enable the institutions or organizations to manufacture products of an equal quality and performance to those using technologies developed by the government through its space development projects.[346] This confirms the government's intention to transfer its space technologies to the private sector. In other words, while these new additional clauses were being drafted around 2021, the government was already preparing to provide the private sector with the launch technology which would be acquired through the Korea Space Launch Vehicle (KSLV)-II program.[347]

For space development projects, the Korean government may reimburse those who made an agreement with the government for all or a portion of the expenses associated with carrying out the projects.[348] This supports the government's willingness to promote the private space sector through its financial support given the specificity of the high-cost space development. The agreement between the government and the private sector in Korea is fundamentally governed by the Act on Contracts To Which The State Is A Party[349] which is considered as a basic law for public-private partnerships. However, the Space Development Promotion Act has an exception wherein the private sector is a party, given the 'otherwise indicated' phrase.[350] In other words, in consideration of the uniqueness of space development, the Act leaves room for not completely abiding by the contracting standards stated in the Act on Contracts To Which The State Is A Party. For instance, the Korean National Assembly is preparing a bill to lower 'liquidated damages for delay' in contracts for space development projects with the private sector: The typical rate of compensation for delays under contracts between the government and the private sector

---

344 Article 18-2(1) of the Space Development Promotion Act.

345 Article 18-3(1) of the Space Development Promotion Act.

346 Article 18-3(2) of the Space Development Promotion Act.

347 *See, supra* Chapter 2 §5.2. On June 21, 2022, South Korea successfully launched its home-built space vehicle, the KSLV-II, into orbit. Although it is not at that stage yet, once the launch technology is transferred to the private sector, it will be utilized on the commercial market.

348 Article 18-3(3) of the Space Development Promotion Act.

349 Act No. 4868, enacted on January 5, 1995, entered into force on July 6, 1995, as amended on January 5, 2021, under Act No. 17816.

350 Article 18-3(5) of the Space Development Promotion Act.

is 30%; however, for space development projects, this amount will be capped at 10%.

The Act further elaborates on the Minister of Science and ICT's duty to establish and implement policies that actively utilize the performance outcome of space development projects and promote technology transfer to the private sector. These policies specifically cover the administration and dissemination of information on the performance and technology transfer of space development projects, the promotion of organizations set up in research institutions to spread project performance and technology transfer, and the sharing and collaboration of infrastructure, technology, and human resources among those research institutions.[351] In order to facilitate the transfer of technology under space development projects, the heads of research institutions may dispatch their researchers or employees to private companies to which space technology will be transferred.[352] This provision will likely be applied for the first time when the KARI researchers or employees are deployed to space enterprises for the transfer of launch technology that the Korean government has developed.

According to Article 18-5 of the Act, the Korean government may provide the "necessary support" to foster space start-ups. Although it is unclear what would be regarded as "necessary support" which leaves room for interpretation, it can include comprehensive government assistance such as financial, technical, and educational aid as well as providing start-ups with vital infrastructure. The significance of this provision resides in the fact that the government established a 'legal' basis to support start-ups in the space industry.

Article 18-6 of the Act emphasizes the Minister of Science and ICT's additional duty to formulate and implement policies to cultivate professional human resources for space development. To that end, the Minister is required to identify the demand for space professionals, forecast mid- to long-term supply and demand for human resources, develop and support professional training programs, and assist in job creation for space professionals.

Finally, Article 18-7 of the Act establishes a concept of "New Space Technology" which is designated by the Minister of Science and ICT that is recognized to have novelty and progressiveness and is necessary to disseminate and utilize. The following technologies can be designated as "New Space Technology": 1) Technologies developed for the first time in Korea; 2) Improved technologies originally introduced from abroad; and 3) Technologies that create new added value to be applied to other fields. The Minister may request

351 Article 18-4(1) of the Space Development Promotion Act.

352 Article 18-4(4) of the Space Development Promotion Act.

central, local governments, or public institutions to preferentially purchase products manufactured using "New Space Technology." These newly added provisions demonstrate South Korea's commitment to the advancement of space technology as well as its willingness to vitalize the private sector in the domestic space industry.

Under this innovative new environment, private companies are now becoming leading actors in space activities, as opposed to only participating in government-initiated space programs. Then, what is actually required for a private company to launch a space object under the existing Korean authorization regime?

Permission for each launch activity must be obtained in order to launch a space launch vehicle.[353] Currently, there is no authorizing regulation for on-orbit operations and the launching of other space objects except for a space launch vehicle. The same applies to any instance where a private company uses/hires/leases a spaceport or other launch facilities provided by a foreign government or company; the company is required to obtain the aforementioned permission for the launching of its space launch vehicle.[354] In reality, two Korean private companies, Perigee Aerospace[355] and INNOSPACE[356] are planning on launching their launch vehicles from spaceports located in Australia (run by a private company, the Southern Launch) and Brazil (run by the Brazilian Air Force), respectively.

4.7.2 Designation of Space Industry Clusters

The "Space Industry Cluster" is a new term adopted through the amendment of June 10, 2022. It is defined as a zone that is created in conjunction with research institutions, enterprises, educational institutions, and science and technology organizations to further the convergence and development of the space industry.[357]

The cluster is designated by the Minister of Science and ICT after consultation with the heads of the relevant central administrative agencies, mayors, and governors concerned. It also requires deliberation by the National Space

353 Article 11(1) i of the Space Development Promotion Act.

354 Article 11(1) ii of the Space Development Promotion Act.

355 *Supra* Chapter 2 §4.

356 INNOSPACE, "Latest News," last accessed on October 29, 2022, available at http://www.innospc.com/shop_contents/myboard_read.htm?load_type=&page_idx=0&tag_on=&h_search_c=0&h_search_v=&me_popup=&myboard_code=sub04_02&page_limit=5&idx=188227&page=1&category_idx=.

357 Subparagraph 8 of Article 2 of the Space Development Promotion Act.

Committee.[358] The central and local governments may subsidize or lend necessary expenses to institutions, enterprises, and organizations located in the cluster.[359] As such, it is expected that South Korea's space industry will be more intensively invested and fostered by focusing on certain regions designated as the Space Industry Clusters.[360]

4.8 *Dissemination and Utilization of Satellite Data: Remote Sensing*

Article 17 of the Space Development Promotion Act titled "Dissemination and Utilization of Satellite Data" and its implementing regulations govern remote sensing activities carried out using satellites developed by the Korean government under the Basic Plan.[361] Remote sensing in South Korea commenced with the government-built and operated satellite series in the early 1990s. Although the number of private commercial operators is increasing in the remote sensing arena, there is yet no specific regulation to directly govern their activities.

According to Article 17(1) of the Act, the Minister of Science and ICT is authorized to take necessary measures to facilitate the dissemination and utilization of satellite data acquired by government-developed satellites. In such cases, the Minister is obligated to confer with the Minister of Land, Infrastructure, and Transportation about national spatial data as well as with the heads of relevant central administrative agencies when addressing national security-related data.

To better serve the purpose of Article 17(1) of the Act, the Minister of Science and ICT is empowered to create a dedicated organization. This organization is eligible for subsidies awarded by the Minister in accordance with Article 17(2) of the Act. Its missions include system construction for satellite databases; implementation of inter-agency projects for satellite data utilization; support of the satellite data industry; reproduction, processing, provision, and sale of satellite data; status inspection of satellite data utilization; and other affairs to efficiently build an integrated system for the dissemination and better utilization of satellite data.[362]

---

358 Article 22(1) of the Space Development Promotion Act.

359 Article 23 of the Space Development Promotion Act.

360 As of August 2022, the Korean government is considering the designation of three cities as Space Industry Clusters: Goheung for the launch industry, Sacheon for the satellite industry, and Daejeon for the research industry.

361 The Basic Plan for the Space Development, *supra* Chapter 5 §3.3.

362 Article 19-3(2) of the Presidential Decree of the Space Development Promotion Act.

One clear principle outlined in Article 17(3) of the Act is that the Korean government must endeavor not to invade individuals' privacy while conducting its missions utilizing satellite data. With all this framework for the management of satellite data, details for the implementation of policies under Article 17 of the Act are specified in the Orders on the Dissemination and Utilization of Satellite Data,[363] the Orders on the Security Management of Satellite Data,[364] and the Guidelines for the Organization and Operation of the Consultative Body for the Utilization of Satellite Data.[365] While these detailed regulations set forth requirements for the utilization of satellite data, strategies, and implementing procedures, they do not govern private commercial actors but are for internal purposes. Essentially, the regulations are exclusively binding on the central and local governments, government agencies, and public organizations, even if some may indirectly affect private entities.

South Korea's satellite industry and its related businesses including remote sensing are better developed than its launch vehicle industry and launch activities. Moreover, a new industrial area employing satellite data is being created in various fields. Nonetheless, it is regrettable that, aside from the satellite data regulations, there is no overarching legislation that governs satellite remote sensing activities applicable to the private sector. For the better development of commercial remote sensing, it is vital to explicitly present operational requirements and data distribution procedures for the private sector. In addition, clear standards to restrict the distribution of satellite data by private entities are required in the interest of national security. These would be a driving force to ensure business predictability while providing expanded opportunities and accelerating the development of the private sector.

4.9 *Enforcement Mechanism*

Sanctions are imposed for non-compliance with the Act's primary requirements. Depending on the significance of the violation, there are two categories of sanctions which include criminal penalties and administrative fines.

---

363 Order No. 69 by the former Ministry of Education, Science, and Technology, entered into force on July 28, 2008, as amended Order No. 195 by the Ministry of Science and ICT on February 22, 2022.

364 Amended under Order No. 132 by the former Ministry of Science, ICT and Future Planning Education on December 4, 2014.

365 Guideline No. 281 by the former Ministry of Education, Science, and Technology, entered into force on February 12, 2013, as amended Guideline No. 196 by the Ministry of Science and ICT on February 22, 2022.

First, any person who conducts launch activities without launch permission or permission for major modification faces up to five-year imprisonment or a fine of up to fifty million Korean won.[366] The fact that this criminal penalty is the Act's most severe sanction demonstrates how crucial the Korean government considers obtaining launch permissions or permissions for major modification by space actors.

Second, any of the following persons are punished with up to three-year imprisonment or a fine of up to thirty million Korean won:[367]

i. A person who takes a meteorite out of the Republic of Korea without approval by the Minister of Science and ICT for study and research purposes;[368]
ii. A person who fails to comply with the Minister's order for suspension or rectification of space activities in an emergency or in the interest of national security;[369] or
iii. A person who violates the duty of confidentiality.[370]

When a representative or an employee of a corporation or private business commits one of the aforementioned offenses while acting in the course of their employment, the corporation or private business is also fined in accordance with each penalty provision in addition to the offender. However, this joint punishment does not apply when such a corporation or private business was not negligent in paying due attention and supervision to prevent such an offense.[371]

Finally, the remaining sanctions are administrative fines imposed and collected by the Minister of Science and ICT. Any person who fails to file a preliminary or formal registration of an artificial space object as well as failure to report a minor modification for launch permission is imposed an administrative fine of up to ten million Korean won.[372] Separately, an administrative fine of up to five million Korean won is imposed on any person who has registered

366 Approximately USD 40,000 as of August 2022; Article 27(1) of the Space Development Promotion Act.

367 Approximately USD 25,000 as of August 2022; Article 27(2) of the Space Development Promotion Act.

368 *See, supra* Chapter 5 §4.3.1.3.

369 *See, supra* Chapter 5 §4.2.2.3.

370 Article 25 of the Space Development Promotion Act provides that any person who is engaging or has engaged in the Act's duties and is aware of confidential information in the course of performing the duties must not divulge or use such confidential information other than the purpose of the Act.

371 Article 28 of the Space Development Promotion Act.

372 Approximately USD 8,500 as of August 2022; Article 29(1) of the Space Development Promotion Act.

an artificial space object but fails to notify modification or give false notification or who refuses, interferes with, or evades a space accident investigation.[373]

This detailed punishment system serves as a means of not only upholding law enforcement at the national level but also of continual supervision of space activities conducted by non-governmental entities as well as exercising jurisdiction and control over activities covered by Articles VI and VIII of the Outer Space Treaty.

5 Concluding Remarks

The Space Development Promotion Act is a fundamental national space law that addresses various aspects of space and space-related activities. The Act consists of four key categories: 1) the framework for national space policies and organizations, 2) the regulations for national space activities that implement international obligations and principles of the UN space treaties and recommendations, 3) the promotion and support of private space sector, and 4) the safety, security measures and sanctions for non-compliance.

The first category features South Korea's space governance. One major characteristic is the government's periodic and detailed planning of space development along with its public announcement prior to every space program in accordance with the Act. In this proactive manner, South Korea has been able to continuously expand its space capacity starting from scratch. Meanwhile, the organizational structure in charge of space is not integrated into one single body but rather dispersed throughout the government agencies and government-funded institutes. The National Space Committee is the top decision-making body currently chaired by the Prime Minister following the amendment to the Act in 2021.

The second category sets forth the regulatory regime for authorization and supervision over space activities, registration of space objects, rescue and return of space objects and astronauts as well as liability caused by space objects. This overarching framework confirms South Korea's commitment to international obligations under the space treaties to which South Korea is a party. In addition, from the perspective of UN Resolution 68/74,[374] the Act covers almost all aspects of the suggested recommendations except for the lack of

373 Article 29(2) of the Space Development Promotion Act.

374 *Supra* Chapter 5 §4, n. 153, "Recommendations on National Legislation relevant to the Peaceful Exploration and Use of Outer Space."

a provision on the transfer of ownership and control of a space object in orbit. While the Act establishes the distinctive and thorough registration system, there is room for improvement in terms of permission or requirements for various space activities evolving in South Korea, such as remote sensing, launch site operation, and commercial human spaceflight. The rescue and return obligation and the accident investigation system are characteristics of the Act that are not commonly observed in other countries' national space laws.

The third category reflects South Korea's recent endeavor to further commercial space activities while promoting the space industry by designating Space Industry Clusters and providing financial support. With a focus on the transfer of government-developed space technologies to the private space sector, the Act adopted the concept of public-private partnerships associated with a series of space projects. As the role of the Korean government shifts from an active performer on its own toward being more of a facilitator, partnerships between the government and the private sector will likely increase, which is now supported by the Act.

Given the geopolitics affecting the Korean peninsula, national safety and security have always been a huge concern. The fourth category emphasizes the need for safety measures and security requirements. It also outlines criminal and administrative sanctions for not abiding by the requirements stated in the Act to ensure South Korea's compliance with international obligations as well as the nation's national safety and security while carrying out space activities.

As South Korea's space capacity is dramatically improving and expanding, an increasing number of private entities are engaging in space development projects accordingly. It should be noted that a more comprehensive and detailed regulatory regime can provide more certainty and predictability to the private sector which will stimulate the growth of the space industry the way South Korea expects.

CHAPTER 6

An Analysis of the Space Damage Compensation Act

1 Introduction

One of the most notable aspects of international space law is that States are liable for damage caused by space objects. According to Article VII of the Outer Space Treaty, each State Party that launches or procures the launching of a space object into outer space, as well as each State Party from whose territory or facility an object is launched, is internationally liable for damage to another State Party or to its natural or juridical persons caused by such an object or its component parts. More specifics on the liability regime are provided in the Liability Convention which was concluded around five years after the Outer Space Treaty entered into force.[1]

The key elements of the liability regime enshrined in the Liability Convention are as follows:

First and foremost, the Liability Convention defines the term "launching State" to which liability for damage is attributed. Article I(c) of the Liability Convention provides that "[a] State which launches or procures the launching of a space object" and "[a] State from whose territory or facility a space object is launched" is considered to be a "launching State."[2] Despite this definition, however, it is not unequivocal to what extent private companies' launches, their procurement of launches, or launches from private facilities would fall within the concept of a "launching State."[3]

---

1 The Outer Space Treaty was concluded on January 27, 1967, and entered into force on October 10, 1967. The Liability Convention, on the other hand, was concluded on March 29, 1972, and entered into force September 1, 1972.

2 Although Article VII of the Outer Space Treaty does not explicitly use the term "launching State," it essentially contains the concept of a launching State as described in Article I(c) of the Liability Convention.

3 *See, supra* Chapter 1 §1.3.2. For a further discussion and details, *see* Frans von der Dunk, "International Space Law," in Frans von der Dunk (ed.), Handbook of Space Law (2014), 54–56; Lesley Jane Smith & A. Kerrest de Rozavel, "The 1972 Convention on International Liability for Damage Caused by Space Objects," in Stephan Hobe, Bernhard Schmidt-Tedd and Kai-Uwe Schrogl (eds.), Cologne Commentary on Space Law, Vol. II (2013), 114; Karl-Heinz Böckstiegel, "The Term 'Appropriate State' in International Law" in Proceedings of the 37th Colloquium on the Law of Outer Space (1994), 80–82; Bin Cheng, "Convention on

 | DOI:10.1163/9789004694743_008

In addition, the term "damage" is defined in Article I(a) of the Liability Convention as "loss of life, personal injury or other impairment of health; or loss of or damage to property of States or of persons, national or juridical, or property of international intergovernmental organizations."[4] While either damage to outer space, environmental damage to the high seas, or consequential damage without direct physical contact is not included in the definition or generally recognized,[5] the compensation that the launching State is liable to pay for damage could be unlimited under international law and the principles of justice and equity.[6]

Separately, the terms "launching" and "space object" are simply defined without much elaboration: Article I(b) of the Liability Convention states that the term "launching includes attempted launching." In a similar way, Article I(d) of the Liability Convention provides that the term "space object includes component parts of a space object as well as its launch vehicle and parts thereof." Although these two terms constitute the aforementioned concept of a "launching State," the Liability Convention does not provide detailed definitions of the terms themselves other than merely stating what is included in such terms. Nevertheless, it is evident that the Liability Convention ensures the grounds for a broad interpretation in that regard by including attempted launching in the definition of "launching" and parts of a space object, its launch vehicle, and a launching vehicle's parts in the definition of "space object."

One of the notable distinctions adopted by the Liability Convention is the principle of absolute liability versus fault liability depending on where the damage occurs.[7] The principle of absolute liability applies to "damage caused

International Liability for Damage Caused by Space Objects" in Nandasiri Jasentuliyana and Roy S.K. Lee (eds.), Manual on Space Law, Vol. 1 (1979), 103.

4 For the definition of damage set forth in the Korean Space Damage Compensation Act, *see* Chapter 6 §2.

5 *Supra* Chapter 6, n. 3, Frans von der Dunk, "International Space Law," 56–58; *supra* Chapter 1, n. 54, Stephen Gorove, "Cosmos 954: Issues of Law and Policy," Journal of Space Law Vol. 6, No. 2 (1978), 141. For more discussion on the scope of damage, *see* Chapter 6 §2.

6 Article XII of the Liability Convention. Its full language is as follows: "[t]he compensation which the launching State shall be liable to pay for damage under this Convention shall be determined in accordance with international law and the principles of justice and equity, in order to provide such reparation in respect of the damage as will restore the person, natural or juridical, State or international organization on whose behalf the claim is presented to the condition which would have existed if the damage had not occurred." For more information on the term "damage" in general, Frans von der Dunk, "The 1972 Liability Convention: Enhancing Adherence and Effective Application," in Proceedings of the Forty-First Colloquium on the Law of Outer Space (1998), 369; *supra* Chapter 1, n. 54, Stephen Gorove, "Cosmos 954: Issues of Law and Policy," Journal of Space Law Vol. 6, No. 2 (1978), 140.

7 *Supra* Chapter 1 §1.3.4.

by [a] space object on the surface of the Earth or to aircraft in flight,"[8] whereas the principle of fault liability covers damages "caused elsewhere than on the surface of the Earth."[9] An exception to the principle of absolute liability is that in the cases of "gross negligence" or a willful act with "intent to cause damage" on the part of a claimant State or its representative, exoneration from absolute liability is granted.[10] The Liability Convention does not provide further explanation or reference as to what constitutes such concepts of liability, leaving room for interpretation.[11]

Another crucial distinction that the Liability Convention introduced is the differentiation between international liability and national liability. In other words, the Liability Convention does not cover damage suffered by nationals of the launching State or foreign nationals who participate in or are invited to the launch in question.[12] Consequently, only "[a] State which suffers damage, or whose natural or juridical persons suffer damage" has the right to present a claim for compensation under the Liability Convention.[13] This approach is reasonable as the main purpose of the Liability Convention is to regulate the relations between States by providing a mechanism for compensating victims through their respective States. Separately, individual victims still have the option of seeking remedies or making claims against States at the national level.[14] Furthermore, the Liability Convention does not preclude a State, or its natural or juridical persons, from pursuing a claim in the courts of a launching State, provided that such claim is not based on the same damage for which a claim is already being pursued under the Liability Convention.[15]

---

8 Article II of the Liability Convention.

9 Article III of the Liability Convention. The same principles of absolute and fault liability apply in the event of joint launch, according to Article IV of the Liability Convention.

10 Article VI(1) of the Liability Convention.

11 Frans von der Dunk, "Too-Close Encounters of the Third Party Kind: Will the Liability Convention Stand the Test of the Cosmos 2251-Iridium 33 Collision?," in the Proceedings of the International Institute of Space Law (2009), 202–205 regarding the term "fault" in particular; Ram Jakhu, "Iridium-Cosmos Collision and its Implications for Space Operations," in Kai-Uwe Schrogl (ed), Yearbook on Space Policy 2008/2009 (2010), 254–275, 2010; Tanja Masson-Zwaan, "Space Law and the Satellite Collision of 10 February 2009," in Space Research Today, COSPAR's Information Bulletin No. 174 (2009), 4–11; Martha Mejia-Kaiser, "Collision Course: 2009 Iridium-Cosmos Crash," in the Proceedings of the International Institute of Space Law (2009), 274–284.

12 Article VII of the Liability Convention.

13 Article VIII of the Liability Convention.

14 *Supra* Chapter 6, n. 3, Lesley Jane Smith & A. Kerrest de Rozavel, "The 1972 Convention on International Liability for Damage Caused by Space Objects," Cologne Commentary on Space Law, Vol. II (2013), 152.

15 Article XI(2) of the Liability Convention.

The Liability Convention also addresses procedural aspects of settling a claim. In essence, a claim to a launching State is required to be presented through diplomatic channels[16] within the time limits specified in Article X of the Liability Convention. If there is no settlement reached through diplomatic negotiations, the parties can proceed to establish a Claims Commission at their request.[17] The decision of the Claims Commission is final and binding only if the parties have thus agreed.[18]

Lastly, the Liability Convention explicitly stipulates the position of international intergovernmental organizations, which are deemed to be *de facto* parties to the Liability Convention. To obtain a comparable, albeit not fully equivalent, status under the Liability Convention, an international intergovernmental organization must declare its acceptance of the rights and obligations set forth in the Liability Convention. Furthermore, a majority of the States members of the organization must be parties to both the Liability Convention and the Outer Space Treaty.[19] These three prerequisites are necessary for an international intergovernmental organization to be granted a status similar to that of a State under the Liability Convention. Although the Liability Convention applies to such organizations, certain provisions concerning ratification, signature, accession, amendment, and withdrawal apply exclusively to States.[20]

This international liability regime specified in the Liability Convention serves as a motivator for States to take necessary precautions to reduce the likelihood of damage and prevent the hazards and risks inherent in space development. In this regard, enacting national space legislation can be the most desirable means of achieving these purposes. Although national space legislation is not allowed to modify the international liability regime, it can domestically establish the nation's own procedures and regulations to minimize the risk of damage and thus lowering the possibility of holding international liability.

The Space Damage Compensation Act is South Korea's national space law that is dedicated to addressing the principle of liability for space damage and its domestic protocols. As mentioned in the previous chapter, the enactment

16 Article IX of the Liability Convention.

17 Article XIV of the Liability Convention.

18 Article XIX(2) of the Liability Convention.

19 Article XXII(1) of the Liability Convention. For more discussions, *see supra* Chapter 6, n. 3, Frans von der Dunk, "International Space Law," Handbook of Space Law (2014), 92; Lesley Jane Smith & A. Kerrest de Rozavel, "The 1972 Convention on International Liability for Damage Caused by Space Objects," Cologne Commentary on Space Law, Vol. II (2013), 204–205.

20 Articles XXIV to XXVII of the Liability Convention.

of the Act is legally based on Article 14 of the Space Development Promotion Act: It provides that i) a person who launches an artificial space object is liable for damage caused by the artificial space object and that ii) the scope of compensation for damage, limitation of liability, and other relevant matters will be regulated by a separate law.[21] As a result, the Space Damage Compensation Act was enacted in 2007 two years after the Space Development Promotion Act entered into force.

1.1 *Legislative History*

On February 5, 2007, twelve members of the National Assembly proposed a draft bill of the Space Damage Compensation Act. After several deliberations by the National Assembly's Science, Technology, Information and Telecommunication Committee, as well as the Legislation and Judiciary Committee, the modified bill was subsequently adopted on November 22, 2007, and promulgated on December 21 of the same year.[22] In accordance with its Addenda, the Act entered into effect on June 22, 2008, six months after the promulgation date. Since the Act's enactment was already intended to conform with the Space Development Promotion Act, its legislative process from the proposal through the passing of the bill was relatively expeditious.

1.2 *The Structure and Purpose of the Act*

The Act is composed of nine Articles, which include the right to recourse, strict and fault liability, the maximum amount of compensation, insurance, and the measures taken by the government (see Table 21). The Act aims to specify the extent of compensation and the limitation of liability in the event of space accidents, thus ensuring the protection of victims and contributing to the sound advancement of space development initiatives.[23]

The Reasons for the Enactment of the Act, which were released concurrently with the Act's promulgation, go into additional detail about the legislative background and the purpose of the Act:[24]

---

21 *See, supra* Chapter 5 §4.4.

22 The National Assembly of the Republic of Korea, "Bill Information," last accessed on September 13, 2022, available at https://likms.assembly.go.kr/bill/billDetail.do?billId=PRC_P0X7P0M2M0T7D1X5V4T2C2H1W9Y4C2.

23 Article 1 of the Space Damage Compensation Act.

24 The Korean Law Information Center, "The Reasons for the Enactment of the Act," last accessed on September 13, 2022, available at https://www.law.go.kr/lsInfoP.do?lsiSeq=81874&ancYd=20071221&ancNo=08714&efYd=20080622&nwJoYnInfo=N&efGubun=Y&chrClsCd=010202&ancYnChk=0#0000.

TABLE 21 Main contents of the Space Damage Compensation Act

Articles	Contents
1	Purpose
2	Definitions
3	Relation with the Liability Convention and Other Nations
4	Extent of Liability
5	Maximum Amount of Compensation
6	Third-Party Liability Insurance
7	Measures to be Taken by the Government and Its Financial Support
8	Period for Exercising the Right to Claim
9	Regulatory Review

Countries around the globe have been actively carrying out various space development programs. The advent of private entities including commercial satellite operators has raised the need to prepare for space accidents that are increasingly likely to occur. However, since space technology is a specialized field where aerospace, electronics, telecommunications, and materials engineering are combined, it is not appropriate to apply the existing civil law liability principle to damages caused by space objects. Moreover, requiring private entities to compensate for all the massive damage makes it difficult for the private sector to aggressively participate in space development. As a result, it is necessary to establish a distinct compensation system – the Space Damage Compensation Act. The purpose of the Act is to provide specific standards and procedures for the scope of compensation and limitations of liability caused by space accidents in relation to the launch of space objects, satellite operations, and other space development activities.[25]

25 Translated by the author.

2 The Definitions of the Terms in the Act

The Act provides for the definitions of four terms: i) a space object, ii) a person who launches a space object, iii) the launching of a space object, and iv) space damage.[26]

Since the term "space object" is already defined in the Space Development Promotion Act as discussed in the previous chapter, the Act does not explicitly describe the term again. Instead, the Act cites the definition provision of the Space Development Promotion Act, which defines a space object as an object designed and manufactured for use in outer space including a space launch vehicle, a satellite, a spacecraft, and component parts thereof.[27]

The terms "a person who launches a space object" and "the launching of a space object" are also explained in relation to the particular provisions of the Space Development Promotion Act. A person who has made a preliminary registration or formal registration of a space object in accordance with Article 8 of the Space Development Promotion Act, or a person who has obtained permission for launching a space launch vehicle in accordance with Article 11 of the same Act is regarded as "a person who launches a space object."[28]

Furthermore, "the launching of a space object" is defined as launching a space object by a person who has obtained launch permission pursuant to Article 11 of the Space Development Promotion Act. The Act also highlights that "the launching of a space object" includes preparation of launch, test launch, and failed launch.[29] Similarly, Article 1(b) of the Liability Convention states that the term "launching" includes 'attempted launching.' What should then be considered to be an 'attempted launching'? According to the Oxford Dictionary, the verb 'attempt' means "to make an effort or try to do something, especially something difficult."[30] Based on this lexical meaning and the context of a space launch activity, 'attempted launching' should be understood in a broad way that includes activities from preparation through launch, even if failed. Therefore, the definition provided by the Act seems appropriate and more detailed as it elaborates on the meaning of 'attempted launching' from South Korea's perspective.

26 Article 2 of the Space Damage Compensation Act.

27 Subparagraph 3 of Article 2 of the Space Damage Compensation Act quotes Subparagraph 3 of Article 2 of the Space Development Promotion Act.

28 Subparagraph 2 of Article 2 of the Space Damage Compensation Act.

29 Subparagraph 3 of Article 2 of the Space Damage Compensation Act.

30 Oxford Learner's Dictionaries, last accessed on September 19, 2022, available at https://www.oxfordlearnersdictionaries.com/definition/american_english/attempt_2.

Lastly, the legislators of the Act introduced the concept of "space damage" for the first time in Korean domestic legislation. Under the Act, "space damage" is defined as bodily and material damage caused by the launch, operation, and suchlike of a space object. Furthermore, as for bodily damage, the Act specifies that it includes loss of life, personal injury, or other impairment of health to a third party. The Act also states that material damage includes destruction or loss of or damage to property.[31] This is similar to the definition provided by the Liability Convention, where "damage" is prescribed as 'loss of life, personal injury or other impairment of health; or loss of or damage to property of States or of persons, national or juridical, or property of international intergovernmental organizations.'[32] However, it is still unclear whether indirect damage is covered by the Act, just as there are differing opinions as to what extent constitutes "damage" according to the Liability Convention.[33] In the end, the scope of "space damage" under the Act would ultimately be consistent with the Korean compensation system, which is widely accepted by domestic jurists and allows for the consideration of consequential damages in exceptional circumstances only where there is a strong and clear causal link between the damage and its effects/consequences.

One notable wording to pay attention to regarding causality is that the Act defines space damage as 'caused by the launch, operation, and suchlike of a space object.' In other words, the Act does not identically adopt the phrase 'caused by a space object' as used in the Liability Convention.[34] Although it is arguable, damage 'caused by a space object' is generally construed as the damage arising directly from physical or kinetic contact and not the damage resulting from indirect events such as erroneous signals due to malfunctioning of a satellite system.[35] Nonetheless, since the Korean Act refers to 'the launch, operation, and suchlike of a space object,' there is room for interpretation as to whether the Act recognizes a broader range of damage rather than being restricted to immediate, direct contact or physical collision of the space object.

In this regard, contentious questions may arise pertaining to the scope of the Act: Would indirect damage such as consequences deriving from electronic or laser interference also be compensated under the Act? Would damage caused by improper satellite transmissions be included in the Act?[36] Given

---

31 Subparagraph 4 of Article 2 of the Space Damage Compensation Act.

32 Article I(a) of the Liability Convention.

33 *See, supra* Chapter 1 §3.3.3.

34 Articles II and III of the Liability Convention.

35 *Supra* Chapter 6, n. 3, Lesley Jane Smith & A. Kerrest de Rozavel, 111; *supra* Chapter 1, n. 54, Stephen Gorove, "Cosmos 954: Issues of Law and Policy," 141.

36 *Supra* Chapter 6, n. 3, Frans von der Dunk, 85.

the language, particularly the phrase 'operation and suchlike of a space object,' it may sound plausible to argue that such damage could fall within the Act's definition. Since there has been no active discussions yet among domestic jurists on this subject, examining the 'statement of reasons for passing the bill' at the time of the Act's enactment may provide insight into the legislative intent when adopting those phrases.

According to the statement, the ground for enacting the Act was to establish specific standards and procedures for the scope of compensation and limitation of liability in cases of 'space accidents' related to space development such as 'launching space objects, operating satellites, and suchlike.'[37] A noteworthy wording in the statement is a 'space accident,' which indicates in what circumstances the Act applies in conjunction with the term 'space damage' employed in the Act.

Then, what does the term 'space accident' mean? It remains undefined within the Space Damage Compensation Act, and the Liability Convention does not mention the term either; rather, it merely references 'damage caused by a space object.' Nonetheless, the Space Development Promotion Act, which was examined in the previous Chapter 5, defines 'space accident' as "a breakdown, crash, collision, explosion, and suchlike of an artificial space object occurring in the course of launching (including preparation for launch, test launch, and unsuccessful launch) and operating the space object."[38]

Considering expressions such as 'crash' and 'collision' in particular, it can be comprehended that the term 'space accident' pertains to an occurrence involving physical or kinetic events. Additionally, as the Act is a kind of 'spin-off' legislation under the mandate of the Space Development Promotion Act, the concept of 'space accident' can also be borrowed from the Space Development Promotion Act to provide a more in-depth understanding of the Act. It should be re-emphasized that Article 14 of the Space Development Promotion Act explicitly stipulates that the scope and limit of liability for damages caused by 'space accidents' are governed by a separate legislation, which is the Space Damage Compensation Act.[39]

Consequently, based on the legislative background and a comprehensive interpretation of both Acts, it can be inferred that the scope of damage under

37 The Statement of Reasons for Enacting the Space Damage Compensation Act, on December 21, 2007, last accessed on December 14, 2022, available at https://www.law.go.kr/LSW//lsInfoP.do?lsiSeq=81874&ancYd=20071221&ancNo=08714&efYd=20080622&nwJoYnInfo=N&efGubun=Y&chrClsCd=010202&ancYnChk=0#0000.

38 *Supra* Chapter 5 §2.

39 *Supra* Chapter 5 §4.4.

the Act apparently involves direct, immediate damage essentially encompassing physical events.

3 Major Provisions of the Act

3.1 *The Government's Right to Recourse and the Principle of Reciprocity*

The Korean government establishes two norms in Article 3 of the Act under the title of "Relations with the International Treaty and Other Nations." Paragraph 1 of Article 3 grants the Korean government the authority to request reimbursement or indemnification from the person who launched a space object in cases where compensation has been paid by the government for damage to a foreign government in accordance with the Liability Convention. Paragraph 2 of Article 3 enshrines the principle of reciprocity by stating that the Act may not be applied to any foreign individual, organization, or government that prohibits or restricts payment of compensation to a South Korean national, organization, or government. This means that the benefits and rights provided by the Act are fundamentally based on reciprocity between nations.

A possible scenario in relation to Paragraph 2 would be when a Korean citizen files a claim for compensation for damage in a domestic court of the launching State, and the amount of compensation the Korean citizen can obtain is limited to, for example, 100 billion Korean won pursuant to the launching State's law.[40] In this case, despite the Korean Act providing up to 200 billion Korean won for compensation, the maximum compensation for a citizen of that country who presents a claim in a Korean court can equally be limited to 100 billion Korean won. Additionally, if another State's domestic law applies fault-based liability to space damage compensation as opposed to the Korean Act's non-fault-based/strict liability that benefits victims, South Korea may not apply the principle of strict liability under the Act to a lawsuit filed by a citizen of that country in the Korean court. In this scenario, the victim of another State would be required to prove the Korean launch company's fault in court.

40 According to Article 5 of the Korean Space Damage Compensation Act, the maximum amount of compensation for damage is 200 billion Korean won. Therefore, in this scenario, the law of the launching State provides for a lower amount of compensation compared to Korean law. For a more in-depth discussion on the maximum compensation under the Act, *see infra* Chapter 6 §3.3.

TABLE 22 Liability for space damage under the Space Damage Compensation Act

Who	Situation	Liability
A person who launched a space object	When space damage by the definition of the Act occurs	Strict liability
	In the event of space damage occurring in an emergency or in outer space	Fault (intent or negligence) liability

3.2 *The Liability Regime of South Korea versus that of the Liability Convention*

According to the first sentence of Article 4(1) of the Act, in the event of "space damage," a person who has launched a space object at issue is obliged to pay compensation for the damage. However, its second sentence stipulates that in the event of "space damage caused by armed conflicts or hostilities between nations, civil disturbances or mutinies" or "space damage caused in outer space," the first sentence only applies to cases where space damage occurred by intent or negligence.

In other words, a person who launched a space object is fundamentally liable to pay compensation for space damage, but in an instance of damage occurring in an emergency or in outer space, the person is liable only if the damage is caused intentionally or negligently (see Table 22).

In comparison, the relevant provisions of the Liability Convention do not entirely correspond to the aforementioned Korean principle (see Table 23). Notably, the Liability Convention differentiates between absolute liability and fault liability based on where the damage occurred.[41] A launching State[42] is "absolutely liable to pay compensation for damage caused by its space object on the surface of the Earth or to aircraft in flight."[43] Nevertheless, "[i]n the event of damage being caused elsewhere than on the surface of the Earth to a space object of one launching State or to persons or property on board such a space object by a space object of another launching State," the latter is "liable

41 *See, supra* Chapter 1 §1.3.4.

42 For the definition of a launching State, *see supra* Chapter 1 §1.3.2.

43 Article II of the Liability Convention.

TABLE 23 Liability for damage under the Liability Convention

Who	Situation	Liability
launching State(s)	When damage is caused by a space object on the surface of the Earth or to aircraft in flight	Absolute liability (Exoneration from absolute liability to the extent of gross negligence or an act done with intent on the part of a claimant State)
	In the event of damage being caused elsewhere than on the surface of the Earth to a space object or to persons or property on board a space object	Fault liability

only if the damage is due to its fault or the fault of persons for whom it is responsible."[44] Exoneration from absolute liability is granted to the extent that a launching State establishes that the damage has resulted from gross negligence or from an act or omission with intent to cause damage on the part of a claimant State.[45] These principles of absolute and fault liability apply to cases where States are jointly and severally liable to a third State.[46]

Essentially, both the Act and the Liability Convention share the principle of fault liability when damage caused by a space object occurs in outer space. However, the Act explicitly mentions intent or negligence, whereas the Liability Convention does not specify the meaning of the term 'fault.'

The Act also provides for the right to recourse that can be exercised by a person, the launcher who paid compensation in accordance with Article 4(1). Specifically, in the event of space damage being caused due to a third party's intent or negligence, the compensator may request the third party to indemnify

44 Article III of the Liability Convention.

45 Article VI(1) of the Liability Convention.

46 Article IV(1) of the Liability Convention.

the amount of compensation.[47] This concept of recourse is essentially similar to the Korean government's right to recourse against the launcher as previously discussed. In other words, under Korean national space legislation, the launcher who paid compensation also has the right to request indemnification from a faulty third party. In this manner, a chain reaction may occur from the Korean government's compensation under the international space law to the launcher's compensation and to the third party's obligation to indemnify under the national space law (See Table 24).

One restriction on the launcher's right of recourse to the third party is that in the event of the damage being caused by the supply of materials or services (including labor services) to be provided for the launch, operation, and suchlike of a space object, a request for the indemnification of the compensation can only be made when the aforementioned supplier or his/her employees acted with intent or gross negligence.[48]

In addition, the Act succinctly states that the Product Liability Act[49] does not apply to space damage.[50] In order to comprehend the meaning of this clause, it is necessary to briefly examine the purpose of the Product Liability Act. The Product Liability Act aims to establish the liability of manufacturers and suchlike for damages caused by the defects of their products and thus thoroughly protecting injured persons and contributing to the safety of the citizens' life and the sound development of the national economy.[51] To that end, the Product Liability Act establishes a strengthened liability of manufacturers to better protect consumers. This approach is reflected in provisions such as the presumption of product defects[52] and strict exoneration from compensation,

---

47 The first sentence of Article 4(2) of the Space Damage Compensation Act.

48 The second sentence of Article 4(2) of the Space Damage Compensation Act.

49 Enacted on January 12, 2000, Act No. 6109, enforced on July 1, 2002, as partially amended on April 18, 2017, Act No. 14764.

50 Article 3 of the Space Damage Compensation Act.

51 Article 1 of the Product Liability Act.

52 Article 3 *bis* of the Product Liability Act stipulates as follows:

In cases where the injured person proves the following facts, it shall be presumed that the product had a defect at the time the product was supplied and thus the damage was caused because of the defect:

1. The fact that the damage was caused to the injured person while the product was being used normally;

2. The fact that the damage referred to in subparagraph 1 was attributable to a cause practically controllable by the manufacturer; and

3. The fact that the damage referred to in subparagraph 1 would not ordinarily be caused if it were not for the relevant defect of the product.

TABLE 24 The right to recourse and/or obligation to indemnify in the event of space damage

	The Korean government	The launcher	The third party
When / Situation	The Korean government has paid compensation in accordance with the Liability Convention	The Korean government who has paid compensation in accordance with the Liability Convention requests indemnification and/or the launcher has paid compensation under the Space Damage Compensation Act	The launcher who has paid compensation under the Space Damage Compensation Act requests indemnification
Right / Obligation	Right to recourse to the launcher	Obligation to indemnify compensation to the Korean government and/or right to recourse to the intentional or negligent third party	Obligation to indemnify compensation to the launcher

which is rarely granted to manufacturers who have provided the product in question due to rigorous requirements.[53]

53 Article 4 of the Product Liability Act provides as follows:

(1) In cases where a person who is liable for damages in accordance with the provisions of Article 3 proves any of the following facts, he/she shall be exempted from any liability for damages under this Act:

Unlike the Product Liability Act, the purpose of the Act is more focused to limit the liability of private space actors and to promote the development of South Korea's space industry. Therefore, since the principles of the Product Liability Act are not compatible or consistent with the aim of the Space Damage Compensation Act, it seems reasonable that the Space Damage Compensation Act precludes the application of the Product Liability Act.

3.3 *The Maximum Amount of Compensation and Liability Insurance*

Article 5 of the Act establishes that the maximum amount of compensation for which registrants of space objects and launch licensees are liable[54] is 200 billion Korean won.[55] This indicates that in any case, these registrants and licensees are only required to pay up to that maximum amount, the so-called 'maximum of maximum.' The Korean government's right of recourse against the person is likewise limited to that amount.

The same maximum amount is also referenced in Article 6 of the Act, which establishes the principle of compulsory third-party liability insurance to be followed by launch licensees. Under Paragraph 1 of Article 6, each person seeking permission to launch a space launch vehicle in accordance with Article 11 of the Space Development Promotion Act must obtain third-party liability insurance.[56] Further, Paragraph 2 of Article 6 specifies that the amount of

---

1. The fact that the manufacturer did not supply the product;

2. The fact that the existence of the defect could not be identified by the state of scientific or technical knowledge of the time when the manufacturer supplied the product;

3. The fact that the defect is attributable to the manufacturer who complied with the standard prescribed by any Act or subordinate statute of the time when he/she supplied the product; or

4. In the case of raw materials or components, the fact that the defect is attributable to the design or the instruction on manufacturing by the manufacturer of the product made of the relevant raw materials or components.

(2) If the person who is liable for damages under the provisions of Article 3 fails to take appropriate measures to prevent damage caused by the defect, although he/she is either aware of or would have been able to know the existence of such defect after he/she supplied the product, he/she shall not be entitled to any exemption referred to in paragraph (1) 2 through 4.

54 The national liability regime of South Korea applies to those who comply with the obligations established in Articles 8 and 11 of the Space Development Promotion Act, which respectively require the domestic registration of artificial space objects and obtaining permission to launch space launch vehicles. *See*, *Supra* Chapter 5 §4.4.

55 Approximately USD 150 to 200 million depending on currency exchange rates.

56 Therefore, registrants of artificial space objects under Article 8 of the Space Development Promotion Act are not obliged to obtain third-party liability insurance. However, in practice, it is highly recommended by the Korean government that registrants obtain such insurance during the preliminary registration process.

TABLE 25 The maximum amount of compensation and liability insurance

	Registrants of artificial space objects	Launch licensees
Maximum Amount of Compensation	200 billion Korean won (USD 150–200 million)	
Obligation of Liability Insurance	N/A	Maximum of 200 billion Korean won

insurance coverage is determined by the Minister of Science and ICT, within the maximum amount stipulated in Article 5, which is 200 billion Korean won (see Table 25). The Minister considers various factors such as the characteristics of the space object, technical complexities, launch site surroundings, and available domestic and international insurance markets.[57]

The insurance coverage determined by the Minister of Science and ICT is publicly announced after the Minister sets the limit based on the aforementioned assessment of the launch activity. In theory, the insurance coverage can thus vary case by case, depending primarily on the risks involved; however, in practice, since the Act's enactment, the Minister has been applying the same maximum of 200 billion Korean won to the launches of KSLV-I and II, which are South Korea's home-grown launch vehicles. Specifically, on April 23, 2021, the Minister announced that the insurance coverage of the KSLV-II shall be 200 billion Korean won.[58] The announcement also includes a clause of the

57 In the United States, the maximum amount of third-party liability insurance is limited to USD 500 million, and it cannot exceed the available insurance coverage on the global market at a reasonable cost.

51 U.S.C. § 50914(3) states:

For the total claims related to one launch or reentry, a licensee or transferee is not required to obtain insurance or demonstrate financial responsibility of more than—

(A) (i)$500,000,000 under paragraph (1)(A) of this subsection; or

(ii)$100,000,000 under paragraph (1)(B) of this subsection; or

(B) the maximum liability insurance available on the world market at reasonable cost if the amount is less than the applicable amount in clause (A)(i) or (ii) of this paragraph.

For further information with respect to the US third-party liability regime, *see* Matthew Schaefer, "The Need for Federal Preemption and International Negotiations Regarding Liability Caps and Waivers of Liability in the US Commercial Space Industry," Berkeley Journal of International Law, Vol. 33, Issue 1 (2015), 230–233.

58 Public Notice No. 2021-32 issued by the Ministry of Science and ICT.

Minister's obligation to reassess the said coverage every 3 years beginning on January 1, 2022.[59] By conducting this review, the Minister can take into account evolving technologies and other variables and subsequently reflect those aspects in the insurance coverage over time.

Similar clauses are found in the previous announcements for the insurance coverages of the KSLV-I. Its first and second launches were carried out in 2009 and 2010, respectively, but both attempts failed. In its third launch, the KSLV-I successfully placed a science satellite into orbit. Regarding the insurance coverage for those launches, the announcement issued on September 23, 2009, states that the insurance coverage is 200 billion Korean won for both the first and second launches of the KSLV-I. It further specified that the deadline for repealing or amending the said coverage by taking into account new statutes and other factors was September 22, 2012.[60] As a result, on June 27, 2012, another announcement for the third launch of the KSLV-I was made by the Minister following his review, even though the coverage amount was the same as the previous announcement. Unless there are significant changes in the launch environment around the Korean peninsula, South Korea will likely continue the set maximum coverage for a while.

While the Act establishes an insurance obligation imposed on a licensee of launching a launch vehicle, it is silent about satellite insurance that a satellite owner/operator may purchase. Nonetheless, in practice, the Korean government strongly advises owners/operators of satellites and other space objects to take out third-party liability insurance when registering their objects in compliance with Korean national space legislation.

3.4 *Measures and Financial Support by the Government*

Article 7(1) of the Act under the title of Government Measures states that in the event of space damage, the government must take measures necessary for the rescue of victims and the prevention of further damage. This is the declaration of the Korean government's commitment not only to preventing space damage but also to taking the proper action in case of actual occurrence.

Furthermore, Article 7(2) of the Act specifies the possibility of financial support from the Korean government in the event of space damage. Specifically, if the amount of compensation for damage to be compensated by a person who launched a space object exceeds insurance coverage, which is up to 200 billion Korean won, the government may offer necessary support to the person if it is

59 Article 3 of Public Notice No. 2021-32.

60 Public Notice No. 2009-37 issued by the Ministry of Science and ICT.

deemed necessary to achieve the purpose of the Act. This means that in some cases where compensation is beyond the insurance coverage, the government may step in and guarantee to pay the excess amount. In this instance, the assistance rendered by the government must be within the parameters set forth by the Korean National Assembly's resolution, which is a prerequisite for such assistance according to Article 7(3) of the Act.

Nevertheless, it should still be noted that the principle of maximum compensation of 200 billion Korean won only applies domestically and it does not affect South Korea's international obligation as a party to the Liability Convention. For example, if a foreign individual files a lawsuit for compensation for space damage in a Korean court against a Korean launch company which took out a thirty-party liability insurance of 100 billion Korean won, the amount of compensation by the Korean company to the foreign individual would always be limited to maximum 200 billion Korean won under the Act. If the compensation exceeds the company's insurance coverage of 100 billion Korean won, then the government may pay the excess amount to the foreign individual, but the total compensation would still be up to 200 billion Korean won. However, if the same foreign individual presents a claim through his/her State in accordance with the Liability Convention, then it is possible that South Korea as a launching State would pay more than 200 billion Korean won since the compensation under the Liability Convention is unlimited. In short, the bottom line is that the Korean domestic system of governmental support for compensation has a beneficial effect on the commercial space sector, which applies to amounts exceeding the compulsory insured ceiling level. While liability insurance is more readily available than before and taking out the insurance is compulsory under the Act, not all space-related risks are covered or affordable as insurance markets also place limits on insurance coverage. In this regard, the government support system will likely serve as an incentive for the commercial space industry by filling the gap between the insurance coverage and the amount of compensation.

3.5 *The Period for Claims*

Article 8 of the Act addresses the time limits for presenting a claim under the Act, which contains two paragraphs. Each paragraph deals with a specific scenario involving the awareness of space damage, the identification of the person responsible for compensation for the damage, and the occurrence of the damage itself with the deadlines for a claim under the Act.

Paragraph 1 specifies that the right to claim compensation for damage under the Act shall be terminated if not exercised within one year following the date on which the victim or his/her legal representative has learned of the damage and the person responsible for compensation. This establishes the time frame when the one-year limitation commences; if the identity of the person who is responsible for compensation is known at the time the damage occurs, the time limit then starts running; if the damage and the person responsible for compensation are discovered later, the time limit begins to run from the date the victim becomes aware of the requisite information.

There has not been any actual court case of space damage compensation in Korea, but the meaning of the 'date when knowing the damage and the person responsible for compensation' can be inferred from the ruling of the Korean Supreme Court. In other damage compensation cases, the Supreme Court clarifies that it means the time when the victim realistically and specifically becomes aware of the existence of an incident, the occurrence of space damage, and the significant causal link between the incident and the damage.[61]

Paragraph 2 stipulates an additional time limit for lodging a compensation claim from a different perspective. It states that if three years have passed from the date of the occurrence of space damage, the right to claim compensation under this Act shall not be exercised. In other words, this three-year period commences immediately from the day when space damage occurs, regardless of whether the victim or his/her legal representative learned of the damage and the person responsible for compensation. Thus, according to paragraph 2 together with paragraph 1 comprehensively, even if the victim is going to file a claim within one year from his/her awareness of the requisite information, the right to claim compensation shall not be exercised if three years have passed since the occurrence of space damage.

Similarly but not identically, Article X of the Liability Convention deals with the issue of time limits for presenting a claim under the Convention. Paragraph 1 of Article X specifies the general rule for a claim for damage compensation, which requires a claim must be presented to a launching State "not later than one year following the date of the occurrence of the damage or the identification of the launching State which is liable."[62] The last part of this clause acknowledges the challenges involved in determining which State is considered to be the launching State. Notably, it establishes that even if the identification of the launching State takes longer than one year after the incident, a claim for compensation for damages will still be admissible as the one-year time limit for filing a claim begins on the day the launching State is identified.

61 The Korean Supreme Court Ruling on June 30, 2022, Case No. 2022DA206384, available at https://www.law.go.kr/LSW/precInfoP.do?mode=0&precSeq=223319.

62 Paragraph 1 of Article X of the Liability Convention.

Paragraph 2 of Article X addresses an instance wherein a "State does not know of the occurrence of the damage or has not been able to identify the launching State." In this instance, the claimant State can "present a claim within one year following the date on which it learned of the aforementioned facts." However, paragraph 2 also requires the claimant State to exercise due diligence by stating that the period will "not exceed one year following the date on which the State could reasonably be expected to have learned of the facts."

The one-year period applies regardless of whether the full extent of the damage has yet to be known.[63] Nonetheless, the claimant State has the right to revise the level of damage and submit additional information until one year after the full extent of the damage is known.[64]

Essentially, the Liability Convention sets the one-year time limit as its standard; what varies is the precise moment from when the one-year period beings to apply, which relies on the prescribed situations. However, this time frame only affects claims presented under the Liability Convention, and the time limit may differ under national law when a claim is filed before national courts. In this regard, the time limit set by Korean space legislation is a good example; the period of one year or three years for a claim for space damage compensation is domestically applicable under the Space Damage Compensation Act, apart from an international claim according to the Liability Convention.

One point to note is that the time limit specified in the Space Damage Compensation Act is relatively shorter than the general timeframe for tort claims under the Korean Civil Act. More specifically, paragraphs 1 and 2 of Article 766 of the Civil Act provide a concept of time limitation similar to that of space damage compensation: i) The right to claim for damage resulting from an unlawful act shall be terminated if not exercised within three years commencing from the date on which the victim or his/her legal representative becomes aware of such damage and the identity of the person who caused it; and ii) If ten years have elapsed from the time when the tort was committed, the right for compensation shall not be exercised. As such, while both the Space Damage Compensation Act and the Civil Act have similarly structured clauses for time limits, they differ in the length of the period (see Table 26).

In essence, the Space Damage Compensation Act appears to reflect the legislator's intent to swiftly resolve legal relations concerning space damage by way of forfeiting the right to claim in a relatively short period of time. However, eleven members of the Korean National Assembly have recently

63 The first sentence of paragraph 3 of Article X of the Liability Convention.
64 The second sentence of paragraph 3 of Article X of the Liability Convention.

TABLE 26 Time limits for claims under the Space Damage Compensation Act versus the Civil Act

	Space Damage Compensation Act	Civil Act
From the date of learning the damage and the responsible person	1 year	3 years
From the date of the occurrence of the event	3 years	10 years

TABLE 27 A comparison between current Article 8 of the Space Damage Compensation Act and the proposed revision by the National Assembly members

	Current	Proposed
From the date of learning the damage and the person responsible for compensation	1 year	3 years
From the date of the occurrence of space damage	3 years	10 years 30 years, in the case of physical injury, disease, or death.

submitted a proposal to extend the time period for filing a space damage claim. The proposal contends that, given the risk of space damage growing as space development activities are steadily increasing, the existing time limits are too short to enable active and effective compensation for such damage.[65] The draft revision suggested by the National Assembly members is as follows (see Table 27):

65 A proposal for the partial revision of the Space Damage Compensation Act, submitted on June 15, 2021, Proposed Bill No. 2110790, available at the Korean National Assembly website https://likms.assembly.go.kr/bill/billDetail.do?billId=PRC_Q2M1M0C5I2I4X1E3X1W8X3D7N5H6I3.

After the submission of the proposal in June 2021, it was reviewed by the National Assembly's Committee of Science, Technology, Information and Telecommunication. In addition, the Subcommittee on the Review of the Science, Technology and Atomic Energy Bill deliberated the proposal in November 2021. However, the Ministry of Science and ICT, the major government department for this subject matter, as well as the Ministry of Government Legislation and the Ministry of Foreign Affairs did not positively receive the proposed revision.[66] As a result, it is still in the review process and has yet to be presented to the plenary session of the National Assembly.[67]

In terms of protecting victims, there may be a beneficial aspect in strengthening the time period for exercising the right to claim compensation for space damage. However, it is necessary to comprehensively analyze some points:

First, eleven members of the National Assembly proposed to revise the Space Damage Compensation Act to match the claim period under the Nuclear Damage Compensation Act, where the claim right must be exercised within three years, ten years, or thirty years.[68] However, unlike nuclear damage which can take a long time to confirm the occurrence of damage such as cancer or disease, space damage tends to be rather immediate with no significant lag between the occurrence of the incident and the damage.[69]

---

66 Report submitted by the Committee of Science, Technology, Information and Telecommunication, "The Expansion of the Right to Claim a Space Damage Compensation," November 9, 2021, at 5.

67 As of September 2022.

68 Enacted and enforced on March 17, 2010, Act No. 10089 as amended on January 20, 2015. The full language of Article 13 *bis* of the Nuclear Damage Compensation Act is as follows:

(1) The right to present a claim for compensation for nuclear damage under this Act shall lapse by prescription if it is not exercised within three years from the date upon which a victim or his/her legal representative became aware of such damage and the identity of the person liable for such damage as prescribed in Article 3.

(2) The right to present a claim for compensation for nuclear damage under this Act shall lapse by prescription if it is not exercised within ten years from the date upon which a nuclear incident occurred: Provided, that the right to claim for nuclear damage due to personal injury, disease or loss of life shall lapse by prescription if it is not exercised within thirty years commencing from the date upon which the nuclear incident occurred.

69 As revealed in the crash of the Russian satellite 'Cosmos 954,' which was equipped with a nuclear reactor to provide power for its mission, a space accident may also involve a problem of the control of nuclear energy. Nonetheless, the aforementioned proposal by eleven members of the Korean National Assembly does not indicate any discussion about or consideration for the possibility of nuclear-related damage being involved in space accidents; it merely argues that the Space Damage Compensation Act needs longer claim deadlines than currently provided by introducing an example of the Nuclear Damage Compensation Act in order to better support victims of space accidents as space activities and accompanying risks are increasing. In addition, there has not been any academic

Second, the Liability Convention basically sets a one-year time period for a damage claim. The only variable is the moment from which the period commences depending on the awareness of the occurrence of damage or the identity of the launching State. Moreover, if the claim is filed in a domestic court, there is a possibility that Korean nationals will bear heavier responsibilities for compensation than those of other States.

Third, the right to claim damage compensation under the Civil Act, which is considered relatively long as previously discussed, is only three years or ten years. Thus, from the legislative policy perspective, it is questionable whether there is a special reason for a longer 30-year period.

This will ultimately be a matter of balancing the promotion of the commercial space industry and the protection of third parties. Considering the pros and cons of extending the time limit, the current period of one or three years under the Space Damage Compensation Act does not seem that short; rather,

---

commentary on the application of the Space Damage Compensation Act versus the Nuclear Damage Compensation Act in cases of space accidents involving nuclear damage. As a result, with no actual case or clear guidelines available, questions may arise pertaining to whether space damage involving nuclear damage like the Cosmos 954 incident falls under the Nuclear Damage Compensation Act and thus victims can benefit from its longer deadlines.

According to Article 1 of the Nuclear Damage Compensation Act, its purpose is to provide for standards and procedures for compensation for nuclear 'damage caused by the operation and suchlike of nuclear reactors' so as to protect victims and to contribute to the safe and sound advancement of 'nuclear businesses.' This can be compared to Article 1 of the Space Damage Compensation Act, which states that its purposes are to prescribe the scope of compensation for space damage and limitation of liability in the event of 'damage caused by space objects' so as to protect victims and to contribute to the sound advancement of 'space development businesses.'

While both the Nuclear Damage Compensation Act and the Space Damage Compensation Act are special laws for the general damage compensation principles by the Civil Act, when it comes to space accidents and damage, the Space Damage Compensation Act would likely be applicable in priority. Comparing the two Acts' purposes, the Nuclear Damage Compensation Act addresses damage generating directly from the operation of nuclear reactors in relation to the nuclear power business, whereas the Space Damage Compensation Act focuses on damage caused by space accidents that occur in the course of space development projects. In addition, the concept of space damage can include nuclear-related damage caused by a space object in its interpretation. Meanwhile, some lawmakers' attempt to revise the existing deadline provision itself may be based on the premise that as far as space damage is concerned, the Space Damage Compensation Act takes precedence over the Nuclear Damage Compensation Act. Since the relation between the two Acts has not yet been clearly identified, further discussions are expected in the future.

it seems to be a reasonable term setting forth enough time/opportunity to present a claim in front of the domestic courts.

3.6 *Regulatory Review of the Period for Claims*

Article 9 of the Space Damage Compensation Act is a rather uncommon provision, which was introduced to the Act in 2015. While the Act itself was originally proposed and enacted by the members of the National Assembly in 2007, the addition of Article 9 to the then-existing Act was initiated by the government in 2014.[70]

Article 9 of the Act stipulates that the Minister of Science and ICT has the obligation to review whether Article 8 requires revision – namely, whether the period of exercising the right to compensation claim requires abolishment, relaxation, or maintenance – every two years commencing from January 1, 2016.[71]

Back in 2014, the idea of adding Article 9 to the Act was simply for administrative purposes and had nothing to do with the Act's uniqueness concerning space damage. More specifically, when the Framework Act on Administrative Regulations was amended in 2013,[72] a new clause was inserted in the Framework Act, which requires the heads of government departments to set a review period for existing regulations in the relevant laws.[73] As a result, the Ministry of Science and ICT, the government department in charge of the Space Damage Compensation Act, created Article 9 of the Act to establish a timeline for regulatory review in accordance with the Framework Act.

Intriguingly, the Liability Convention has a comparable review-provision; the difference is that the provision addresses the whole question of reviewing the Liability Convention, as opposed to the Space Damage Compensation Act, which solely deals with the time limits for the compensation claim. The

---

70 The Korean National Assembly, Bill Information, available at https://likms.assembly.go.kr/bill/billDetail.do?billId=ARC_C1T4F1Y2B2K6V1B4O1A7G0E5M4Q9F5.

71 Act No. 13516, newly inserted on December 1, 2016.

72 Enacted on August 22, 1997, Act No. 5368, entered into force on March 1, 1998. The Framework Act on Administrative Regulations prescribes basic matters concerning administrative regulations. It aims at facilitating creative initiative in social and economic activities and enhancing national competitiveness, through the repeal or revision of unnecessary, inefficient administrative regulations.

73 Article 19 *bis* (1) of the Framework Act on Administrative Regulations provides that the head of a central administrative agency shall stipulate the effective period or review period of regulations in the relevant statutes or regulations after an examination on the existing regulations.

provision also specifies the procedure of convening a conference to review the Liability Convention:

> Ten years after the entry into force of this Convention, the question of the review of this Convention shall be included in the provisional agenda of the United Nations General Assembly in order to consider, in the light of the past application of the Convention, whether it requires revision. However, at any time after the Convention has been in force for five years, and at the request of one-third of the States Parties to the Convention, and with the concurrence of the majority of the States Parties, a conference of the States Parties shall be convened to review this Convention.[74]

Apparently, the purpose of Article 9 of the Act to periodically assess the appropriateness of the time limit seems reasonable. However, it is debatable whether it makes sense to mandatorily conduct a review every two years. So far, not a single claim for space damage compensation has been filed since the enactment of the Act in 2007. Additionally, the one or three-year exercise period under the Act does not seem unusual compared to the one-year standard under the Liability Convention.

As discussed in the previous section, the revision proposal for extending the time limits was submitted by members of the National Assembly, and it is irrelevant to Article 9 of the Act, which stipulates the Minister's obligation to review. According to the report issued by the National Assembly's Committee of Science, Technology, Information and Telecommunication, the Ministry of Science and ICT currently believes that there is no need to revise the time limits set forth in Article 8 of the Act.[75]

4 Concluding Remarks

The Space Damage Compensation Act effectively implements the principles of the Liability Convention by establishing a clear framework for compensating victims of space damage. The Act's provisions for strict and absolute liability, as well as its domestic allocation and distribution of risks and liabilities between private actors and the Korean government, serve to efficiently and timely compensate those affected by space-related incidents.

---

74 Article XXVI of the Liability Convention.

75 Submitted on November 9, 2021, available at https://likms.assembly.go.kr/bill/billDetail.do?billId=PRC_Q2M1M0C5I2I4X1E3X1W8X3D7N5H6I3.

In the context of a private actor's risk and liability, a person who preliminarily or formally registered a space object or who obtained permission for launch is obliged to pay compensation for space damage up to 200 billion Korean won. The person who paid compensation has the right to request indemnification from a faulty party who caused the damage with intention or negligence.

From the Korean government's perspective, if the amount of compensation the private actor has to pay exceeds the insured amount, the Korean government may render financial assistance within the scope of the National Assembly's resolution. Separately, if the Korean government paid compensation to a foreign State under the Liability Convention, it has the right to request indemnification from the private actor.

Notably, regardless of whether it is for damage compensation, insurance, or indemnification, the total amount the private actor is liable to pay is limited to a maximum of 200 billion Korean won, or approximately 150 to 200 million US dollars. This system ensures that the Korean private sector will not face unlimited liability and thus provides legal certainty for the commercial space industry.

However, whether the maximum amount of 200 billion Korean won is appropriate is another matter to be revisited. Since the Act was enacted in 2007, the maximum amount has remained the same until the present. The space industry and the environment of space activities, as well as the currency value, have continually changed during the last fifteen years. The year 2007 was prior to South Korea acquiring its own launch capabilities however the current circumstances are different; South Korea is transferring the most recent space technologies developed by the government to the private sector. Furthermore, the private sector has its own launch capabilities and continues to expand. Therefore, it is anticipated that the space launch market in Korea will become increasingly active.

Although there is a possibility that the Korean government *may* provide financial assistance for damage compensation that exceeds the insured amount, it is not entirely guaranteed by the Act, as is clear from its wording. Moreover, in light of the current scale of the space insurance market, even if the compensation limit is raised, various insurance providers and their policies will be able to cover the increased cap. The maximum amount of liability should be more flexible and adaptable to keep up with the space market trend and the current space capabilities in Korea. This may also benefit the Korean private space sector to enhance its international competitiveness.

Conclusion

1 Introduction

The previous chapters have analyzed the Korean domestic space laws on the premise that national space legislation is the most desirable method of establishing the rights and obligations of private space entities. Prior to an in-depth analysis of each law, Chapters 1 and 2 have explored South Korea's participation in international space law and relevant activities as well as the nation's space governance including its space programs. Since space law and policy are inextricably linked or closely intertwined with one another, it is critical to identify the status of South Korea's space activities and the government strategies in relation to the regulatory framework.

South Korea has made significant progress since announcing its first plan for national space development in the mid-1990s. Since it had already initiated satellite development and secured its own technologies, the Korean government has focused more on developing a space launch vehicle that employs independent and domestic technologies through its national space programs. Finally, on June 21, 2022, South Korea became the world's seventh country capable of placing a satellite weighing more than one ton into orbit aboard a homegrown launch vehicle from its soil.

South Korea's space development programs have been accompanied by space policymaking in conjunction with space legislation and the revision of relevant laws. In this regard, it should be reiterated that examining the past, current, and future of Korea's space development and policy is as crucial as assessing the existing space legislation.

As mentioned in the introductory part of this book, the main objective of this study is to comprehend the framework of Korean space legislation, to identify the extent of its implementation of and conformity to international space law, and to provide recommendations for the advancement of national space law in light of future space development and policy in South Korea. To that end, Chapters 3 through 6 have analyzed provisions of each Korean space law and presented how South Korea implements international obligations and governs the nation's space-related activities.

The following sections of this concluding part will, first, summarize the features of Korean space legislation and identify the key findings of each Korean space law. This will provide a basis for assessing whether South Korea's regulatory framework for the space sector is properly specified in accordance with international space law. Second, based on this, proposed suggestions will arise

 | DOI:10.1163/9789004694743_009

for amendments to the existing laws or recommendations for a better space regulatory regime that is suitable for South Korea's status of space development and policy. Finally, in view of the global trend of space activities as well as in the context of the NewSpace era, this book will be concluded by presenting perspectives regarding the future of Korean space legislation and the way forward for South Korea's space development.

2 The Findings of the Analysis of Korean Space Legislation

2.1 *The Aerospace Industry Development Promotion Act of 1987*

The Aerospace Industry Development Promotion Act is unquestionably the first law of its kind in South Korea that was enacted with the express purpose of advancing the space industry. Although the Radio Waves Act was legislated much earlier than the Act, it did not govern space-related activities from the beginning; regulations regarding satellites, space stations, and frequency bands were later added to the Radio Waves Act. In contrast, the Aerospace Industry Development Promotion Act was proposed by repealing the then-existing Aviation Industry Promotion Act and explicitly introducing the concept of space development for the first time. This is the core value of the Act in Korean space legislative history.

As the title of the Act indicates, the Act uses the term "aerospace" to address both the aviation and the space industries. However, space missions or activities are not specifically governed by the Act. The Act aims to contribute to the national economy and people's lives via effective research and development of aerospace science and technology and rational support and promotion of the aerospace industry. To that end, the Act provides a framework for policymaking and technical standards in the aerospace sector, which includes the establishment of a development plan for the aerospace industry, the designation of the specialized complex for the aerospace industry, the government's financial support, and the procedures for the inspection of the performance and quality of aerospace craft, and suchlike.

Ten articles of the Act have been repealed since its enactment, as circumstances in the aerospace industry changed or initial goals were achieved. In particular, under the influence of the military dictatorship post-Korean War, various industries in the early stages were developed by government initiatives, and the aerospace sector was no exception. In this regard, the original Act featured a number of government support programs for certain aerospace businesses. However, since the industry has been developed to a certain level, the provisions pertaining to government-led promotion and support were ultimately abolished to enable fair competition in the sector.

Then, what is the fundamental significance of this Act? Does the Act still have a valid, intrinsic value of its own?

The Act indeed served as the foundation for the initial assistance given to the aerospace sector and a legal basis for the establishment of the Korea Aerospace Research Institute (KARI). However, as discussed, it should be reiterated that those original objectives were achieved. Moreover, KARI is now regulated by a separate law along with other government-funded research institutions. The majority of the Act's remaining provisions include the formulation of a master plan for aerospace industry development, the basic level of general government support that is still in place, and technical standards for evaluating the performance and quality of aerospace craft and other equipment.

As far as the space sector is concerned, it should also be noted that most of the parts of the master plan mentioned above may potentially overlap with the plans established under the Space Development Promotion Act of 2005. Furthermore, the Space Development Promotion Act contains government support provisions specifically for the space sector, which can also be incorporated into the plans formulated under the Space Development Promotion Act.

Additionally, given the fact that the Space Development Promotion Act provides a significant number of clauses in detail for the development of the commercial space industry, it can be debatable whether the Act retains its peculiar value for the space sector, apart from the aviation industry. It is time to consider if the Act is worth upholding except for its technical standard regulations and the aviation section and to entirely review and reorganize its provisions as the situations have changed since its enactment.

2.2 *The Radio Waves Act of 1961 as Amended in 2000*

When the Radio Waves Act was first enacted in 1961, the Act primarily dealt with radio broadcasting including the management of radio waves. With the rising need for satellite-based services and the rapid expansion of the telecommunications sector, the Act underwent extensive amendments in 2000 by adding chapters to the Act regarding spectrum management and space communications. The Act seeks to effectively execute the ITU principles and requirements.

Like other space-related laws in Korea, the Act requires the Minister of Science and ICT to formulate master plans, including a plan to encourage efficient usage of frequency bands. The Act also stipulates South Korea's regime of spectrum use and the management of spectrum frequencies. In addition, domestic procedures to secure satellite frequencies and to record satellite networks internationally are prescribed in detail following the ITU Radio Regulations.

A wide range of satellite-related matters is comprehensively covered by the Act, which includes the regulations for the establishment of a space station, the transfer of space station facilities, and the submission of a satellite operation plan by a private entity. Of particular importance is that the international registration of satellites with the United Nations under Article VIII of the Outer Space Treaty and Articles III and IV of the Registration Convention is governed by the Act rather than the Space Development Promotion Act.

It should also be noted that the Act expressly recognizes the value of finite frequency resources and firmly establishes the government's commitment to international cooperation for the sustainable use of frequencies as well as monitoring spectrum interference and the space weather.

The majority of the Act's provisions are clearly defined and more detailed than the ITU principles. Separately, some provisions addressing matters that may potentially change under the ITU Radio Regulations succinctly stipulate that they must comply with the relevant ITU provisions. This demonstrates how flexible the Act's approach is to follow up on new situations or possible scenarios. Moreover, the ITU regime and other international space law requirements have swiftly been embraced by the Act's amendments, which is a good illustration of how well South Korea has implemented and abided by its international obligations concerning the telecommunications sector.

Nonetheless, regulations on the operation of satellites other than those for communication purposes are insufficient. Furthermore, the Act lacks regulations for remote sensing in particular. South Korea's geopolitical situation and its dynamic terrain require systematic monitoring and analysis. In addition, from the humanitarian perspective, satellite data from Earth observations can contribute to a better understanding and protection of our planet.

As South Korea goes beyond the era of utilizing satellites primarily for communications, it is now vital to consider creating legislation pertaining to remote sensing and satellite data security. This will provide legal certainty for private satellite operators as well as maximize the efficient use of satellite data and the development of innovative remote sensing technologies.

2.3 *The Space Development Promotion Act of 2005*

The Space Development Promotion Act is undoubtedly a foundational piece of Korean space legislation, which encompasses diverse facets of space activities as well as international principles and obligations in compliance with the four UN space treaties to which South Korea is a party. Since its enactment, the framework of the Act has been adjusting to the ever-changing and developing environment of the space sector. The history of the Act's amendments demonstrates how the Act has been responding to emerging situations and issues that, at first, were focused on the government-initiated space programs but are now turning attention to the increasing private activities in progress. In this regard, organizing the major amendments made to the Act so far would be useful in identifying areas in which the Act could be improved. The most significant amendments were made between 2014 and 2022, as summarized in the following section.

2.3.1 The Findings in the Amendments to the Act

2.3.1.1 *The 2014 Amendment*

The 2014 Amendment introduced novel systems regarding i) space situational awareness and ii) satellite data utilization. The 2014 Amendment added new terms and definitions that form the framework for the newly introduced systems: The term "space hazards" is defined as risks of the crash, collision, and suchlike of space objects in outer space, and the term "satellite data" means information such as images, voice, sound, and data acquired by using satellites or processed information combined.

The system of space situational awareness provides thorough knowledge and comprehension of space hazards, which includes monitoring of near-Earth objects (NEOs) as well as tracking of artificial space objects and space weather forecasting. In order to do this, the 2014 Amendment mandates that the government periodically establish a long-term plan for preparedness against space hazards every ten years and a detailed action plan every year. In addition, the government designated a space surveillance institute in accordance with the 2014 Amendment.

Furthermore, the 2014 Amendment requires the government to formulate a five-year basic plan and an annual action plan to promote the dissemination and utilization of satellite data.[1] The Working Committee for the Utilization of Satellite Date was subsequently created, with the Presidential Decree setting forth specifics.[2]

Overall, the 2014 Amendment focused on policy aspects such as monitoring the space environment and utilizing satellite data collected through remote sensing. This is a step forward from South Korea's early space technology development to ensure the safety of citizens and various applications of space activities that will enhance the quality of life for long-term sustainability.

1 *See, supra* Chapter 5 §3.7.

2 *See, supra* Chapter 5 §3.8 and §4.8.

Since the 2014 Amendment, there have been a significant number of private remote sensing companies founded, with startups operating in a variety of industries such as agriculture, disaster relief, and environmental protection. Nonetheless, the aforementioned provisions and governmental guidelines apply exclusively to state-developed satellites. As a result, there is currently no regulation that governs private companies' remote sensing activities using privately owned satellites for commercial purposes. Thus, it is suggested that remote sensing legislation be enacted for legal certainty and predictability, which can encourage private sector involvement in the remote sensing business and contribute to the advancement of commercial use of satellite data.

2.3.1.2 *The 2015 Amendment*

The 2015 Amendment introduced a unique and intriguing system for meteorite registration. Specifically, the Act inserted new procedural provisions for meteorite registration in between national and international registration of an artificial space object and it also amended the Act's existing definitional provision to include a definition of a meteorite.[3] In other words, it established a distinction between a natural space object that is subject to registration according to the 2015 Amendment and an artificial space object that is required to be registered under international space law.

The idea of registering a meteorite is certainly effective for research purposes and its scientific value. Additionally, the inclusion of two registration systems of both artificial and natural space objects in the Act is remarkable in the broad context of outer space. However, it is still questionable whether it is desirable to incorporate meteorite management in the Act's registration system merely because the concept is similar. It should be reminded that the Act's primary purpose is to implement South Korea's international obligations set forth in the space treaties, with a special focus on governing private space activities. Therefore, it is suggested that provisions pertaining to meteorite registration for scientific research purposes be preferably transferred to one of the scientific laws or, if legislation on space resources is formulated in the future, included into such resources law.

2.3.1.3 *The 2021 Amendment*

In 2021, significant organizational changes occurred to the National Space Committee, South Korea's top deliberation body in the space sector.

---

3 *See, supra* Chapter 5 §2.

Prior to the 2021 Amendment, the National Space Committee had been chaired by the Minister of Science and ICT and consisted of fifteen vice ministers of the central government as well as civilian space experts. This composition raised concerns because the Committee's *de facto* status was less than ideal despite its critical roles and tasks. In response to this criticism, the 2021 Amendment restructured the National Space Committee such that, as of November 11, 2021, it is chaired by the Prime Minister and composed of ministers, rather than vice ministers, of the central government.[4]

Another remarkable change to the National Space Committee was the establishment of the Working Committee for Space Security under the National Space Committee. This reflects South Korea's growing recognition of outer space as a crucial domain for national defense and security.[5]

The 2021 Amendment is noteworthy since it reorganized and strengthened the status of the National Space Committee and broadened the nation's perspective on outer space toward national security, not merely focusing on the development of space technology itself. However, there is still room for improvement regarding the Committee's current standing. In order for the National Space Committee to make resolute and definitive decisions that are inherently interrelated throughout administrations, it would be preferable for the President, the head of the Korean government administration, to consider chairing the Committee, which is the supreme space decision-making body of South Korea.

2.3.1.4 *The 2022 Amendment*

Most recently, the Act included terms and definitions for "launch vehicle," "space business person," and "space industry cluster" to the existing Article 2, in relation to promoting the private space sector in Korea.[6] In this regard, it also introduced new provisions to reinforce the commercial space industry, such as i) opening up space development infrastructures to space business operators, ii) fostering public-private partnerships in space development projects, iii) promoting the transfer of space technology to the private sector, iv) designating space industry clusters, and v) providing government funding for organizations/institutes that reside in space industry clusters.[7]

4 *See supra* Chapter 5 §3.4.

5 *See supra* Chapter 5 §3.9.

6 *See supra* Chapter 5 §2; According to Subparagraph 3 *bis* of Article 2 of the Act, the definition of a launch vehicle explicitly excludes a weapon. For more details on the term of space industry cluster, *see supra* Chapter 5 §4.7.2.

7 *See supra* Chapter 5 §4.7.

TABLE 28 National space policy plans

Promotion of space development		Utilization of satellite data		Preparation of space hazards	
Basic Plan	Action Plan	Master Plan	Action Plan	Basic Plan	Action Plan
5 years	1 year	5 years	1 year	10 years	1 year

In order to implement the amendments, the government has established detailed guidelines and procedures, which became effective on December 11, 2022.[8] It will be crucial in this regard to pay close attention to the implications of the 2022 Amendment on the private space sector in the coming years.

2.3.2 The Findings on the Subject Matter

2.3.2.1 *The Framework for National Space Policies and Organizational Structure*

As South Korea's primary space legislation, the Space Development Promotion Act embodies the nation's overall approach to space governance. One distinctive feature is that, in accordance with the Act's detailed clauses, the government periodically formulates and makes public announcements of national space policy plans. They include the Basic and Action Plan for the Promotion of Space Development, the Master and Action Plan for the Utilization of Satellite Data, and the Basic and Action Plan for the Preparation of Space Hazards. These Plans are established on a one-, five-, or ten-year basis (see Table 28) and are deliberated and finalized by the National Space Committee.

The most significant of these is the Basic Plan for the Promotion of Space Development, a blueprint for South Korea's space programs for a five-year period. Under this Basic Plan, the Action Plan, which contains specific strategies and procedures to implement those programs, is created annually. Before the National Space Committee deliberates these plans, public hearings are held to review drafts and gather feedback from the public that will be taken into account when finalizing drafts. This engagement provides the public with the

8 Act No. 18867, partially amended on June 10, 2022, entered into force on December 11, 2022. Additionally, on November 29, 2022, the Cabinet meeting passed the amendments to the Presidential Decree of the Space Development Promotion Act, which also entered into force on December 11, 2022.

opportunity to participate in space policymaking, which may have an impact on the interests of stakeholders, private companies, and individuals' daily life.

The governmental bodies that address space-related activities from a regulatory and policy perspective are dispersed throughout the central administrations and government-funded research institutes (see Table 29). As discussed, the National Space Committee is the top committee that deliberates almost every aspect of space activities including the drafts of aforementioned space plans. The Committee is chaired by the Prime Minister and has three working committees under its authority: the Working Committee for the Promotion of Space Development, the Working Committee for the Utilization of Satellite Data, and the Working Committee for National Space Security.

The Ministry of Science and ICT is the overarching governmental administration for South Korea's space development and activities, and its Minister is essentially in charge of authorization and supervision of private space activities. Furthermore, space activities concerning national defense and security are governed by the Ministry of Defense, and various administrative bodies are involved in satellite development and international cooperation such as the Ministry of Foreign Affairs, the Ministry of Land, Infrastructure and Transport, the Ministry of Environment, and the Korea Meteorological Administration.

In addition to the government administrations and ministries above, numerous government-funded research institutions contribute to South Korea's space research and development. The Korea Aerospace and Research Institute (KARI) is unquestionably the core institute that leads and executes national space programs. Under the Act, KARI is the one and only institution designated as specializing in space development. It is currently transferring its satellite and launch technologies to the private sector through public-private partnerships.

The Korea Astronomy and Space Science Institute (KASI) is a scientific research institute that operates the National Space Situational Awareness Organization (NSSAO) under the Act. NSSAO monitors space hazards such as collisions of near-Earth objects (NEOs) and forecasts space weather that may affect citizens' lives on Earth.

The Satellite Technology Research Center (SaTRec) is an academic institution affiliated with the Korea Advanced Institute of Science and Technology (KAIST). SaTRec focuses on developing satellites and remote sensing technologies while nurturing space professionals.

The most recent government-funded establishment in 2021 is the Space Policy Research Center (SPREC) which develops space policies and provides analyses to government agencies. SPREC is affiliated with the Science and

Technology Policy Institute (STEPI) and is considered a Korean space policy think tank.

Separately, the Agency for Defense Development (ADD) conducts research and development of defense space technologies and reconnaissance satellite systems.

As demonstrated above, however, concerns have been raised that South Korea's governance structure for space development lacks a central, integrated government body responsible for coordinating space-related activities. While the National Space Committee has some authority in terms of deliberating national space policy and launch permission, it is not a permanent entity and therefore has limitations in its ongoing role. Additionally, the lack of a dedicated agency for space development and activities has led to various governmental agencies executing their own space projects, resulting in redundancy and inefficiency.

Furthermore, while KARI plays a key role in conducting space research and development as well as leading South Korea's space programs, it does not have the authority to make decisions on behalf of the Korean government or to represent the nation in the international space community. Despite being designated as a specialized space development institution under the Act, this designation does not provide any additional legal significance or specify KARI's authority or responsibility. It is, therefore, possible that South Korea's space development governance could be improved by establishing an independent and centralized government body with greater authority and decision-making power, as well as more distinct roles and duties enshrined in law.

Opportunely on November 28, 2022, South Korean President Sukyeol Yoon pledged to launch a national aerospace agency by the end of 2023. The proposed agency, tentatively named the Korea AeroSpace Administration (KASA),[9] will be positioned within the Ministry of Science and ICT. Its intended role is to provide an integrated management framework for national space programs which are presently dispersed across various ministries and institutions. This endeavor is a commendable step towards strengthening Korea's technological capabilities and promoting scientific innovation in the space sector.

9 우주항공청 in Korean. During their visit to NASA's Goddard Space Flight Center on April 25, 2023, President Sukyeol Yoon and US Vice President Kamala Harris agreed to strengthen the space alliance between South Korea and the United States. The two nations signed a joint statement to enhance partnerships in space communications, navigation, and research on the Moon. Notably, President Yoon mentioned the English acronym KASA for the first time, emphasizing that cooperation between KASA and NASA will play a pivotal role in forging a robust space alliance between the two nations.

TABLE 29 Major space governance structure in South Korea

National Space Committee			
– Chaired by Prime Minister – Deliberation of overall space policy and programs including launch permission			
Central Ministries			
Ministry of Land, Infrastructure and Transport, Ministry of Environment, and Korea Meteorological Administration	*Ministry of Science and ICT*	*Ministry of Foreign Affairs*	*Ministry of Defense*
– Satellite utilization	– Oversight of space activities – Issuance of launch permission	– International cooperation	– Space defense and security
Government-Funded Institutes			
Korea Aerospace and Research Institute (KARI)	*Korea Astronomy and Space Science Institute (KASI)*	*Korea Advanced Institute of Science and Technology (KAIST)*	*Agency for Defense Development (ADD)*
– Civilian space technology development – Conducting national space programs	– National Space Situational Awareness Organization (NSSAO)	– Satellite Technology Research Center (SaTRec)	– National defense and security space development

Nonetheless, some concerns are still raised regarding the envisioned agency's position under the Ministry of Science and ICT, rather than being directly under the President or an independent agency. Apart from the issue that the envisioned agency encompasses both the aviation and space sectors rather than being solely dedicated to space, it would be preferable for it to be independent status or a similar degree of autonomy. If KASA is established under the Ministry of Science and ICT as announced by the President, it may face limitations in managing and controlling all relevant ministries and agencies. To address these concerns, a special law for the establishment of the agency should clearly specify KASA's authority and position, empowering it to make decisions and represent the Korean government both domestically and internationally. Furthermore, in order for KASA to fully optimize its function as South Korea's national aerospace agency, the government should reconsider its decision to position KASA under the Ministry of Science and ICT. In short, KASA should ideally operate as an independent agency rather than belonging to any specific ministry.

2.3.2.2 *The Implementation of International Obligations*

The Space Development Promotion Act addresses almost all significant elements of international obligations enshrined in the four UN space treaties to which South Korea is a party. These include i) authorization and supervision over space activities by non-governmental entities, ii) national and international registration of space objects, iii) rescue and return of astronauts and space objects, and iv) liability for damage caused by space objects.

First, the Act stipulates that any person who intends to launch a space launch vehicle must obtain launch permission from the Minister of Science and ICT in cases where it is launched from Korean territory or areas/facilities under Korean jurisdiction or where it is launched outside of Korea on board a launch vehicle owned by the Korean government or citizen.[10] This authorization regime, one of the most crucial aspects of the Act, demonstrates how South Korea implements the international principle of authorization and continuing supervision over national space activities set forth in Article VI of the Outer Space Treaty. However, this does not appear to be sufficient to fully regulate potential space activities taking place within South Korea's jurisdictional purview.[11] For better governance, space activities that could need authorization should not be limited only to launching a space launch vehicle.

10 *See supra* Chapter 5 §4.2.1.

11 *See supra* Chapter 5 §4.2.2.

Given South Korea's responsibility for national space activities and its liability for damage as a launching State under the Outer Space Treaty and the Liability Convention, space activities falling under South Korea's jurisdiction or control should be incorporated into the Act's authorization regime. The appropriate scope should preferably cover more diverse space activities conducted from the Korean territory, by Korean nationals from or outside of Korea, and activities involved in space objects registered by Korea. Therefore, it is suggested that South Korea should consider expressly incorporating its nationals in the Act's personal scope of launch permission like the Act's (quasi-) territorial scope in order to have legal control over activities conducted by Koreans in general. Additionally, space activities that may possibly be recognized as South Korea's national activities should ideally fall under the Act's authorization regime. These would include the operation of a launch site, the control over space objects in orbit, and the launch of space objects broadly. In the foreseeable future, the operation of a re-entry site or the return of a space object may also need to be included in the Act's scope as the Korean government is currently developing its re-entry capabilities while a Korean private launch company built a reusable rocket and is test-launching.

Second, the Act provides detailed procedures and requirements for the national and international registration of space objects. It demonstrates how South Korea implements the principle of registration under Article VIII of the Outer Space Treaty and the Registration Convention. South Korea's national registration system consists of two steps: One, preliminary registration 180 days before the scheduled launch date; and two, formal registration 90 days after launch. The Act mandates that any Korean person who intends to launch a space object – but excluding a launch vehicle – must register the space object. For a non-Korean person, on the other hand, national registration is required only if it is launched from Korean territory or areas/facilities under Korean jurisdiction or if it is launched outside of Korea on board a launch vehicle owned by the Korean government or citizen. Space objects that have completed formal domestic registration are eligible for international registration with the United Nations. The Act explicitly requires the Minister of Science and ICT to proceed to the UN registration in accordance with the Registration Convention.

While South Korea's registration regime appears comprehensive and thorough, it could be excessive or insufficient in some instances. In terms of personal jurisdiction, applying the registration obligation to non-Koreans outside of Korea might only give South Korea the burden to maintain registration records and track any changes to them.[12] With regard to material scope, it should be reconsidered whether excluding a launch vehicle from the subject to the registration is appropriate.[13] In governing private space activities, South Korea's approach is to regulate the launch of a launch vehicle through launch permission and other activities through the registration of payloads. However, it should be noted that registration is not enough to replace permission and such a dichotomy may result in a legal loophole in controlling the hazards and risks inherent in space activities.

Third, the Act embodies the principles of rescue and return of astronauts and space objects enshrined in Articles V and VIII of the Outer Space Treaty as well as the Rescue Agreement. It is not common for national space law to stipulate the rescue and return obligations in separate provisions. This is especially true given that the Act contains a general provision that explicitly states the Korean government's obligation to comply with the UN space treaties that it signed.

Nevertheless, the Act has its own significance since it requires the government to fulfill the rescue and return obligation regardless of whether the nations involved in the emergency are treaty parties. This expands South Korea's obligation to non-signatory nations from a humanitarian perspective. Furthermore, the Act pragmatically combines both terminologies – the launching State and the launching authority – from the Outer Space Treaty and the Rescue Agreement, respectively. This allows for avoiding any potential argument over interpretation regarding the question of which nation the rescued astronauts and space objects should be returned to.[14]

Fourth, the Act concisely outlines the principle of liability for damage caused by a space object set forth in Article VII of the Outer Space Treaty and the Liability Convention. Since South Korea has a separate law dedicated to liability issues, the Act only provides a foundation for compensation for space damage in terms of who is domestically liable in what circumstances. The Act expressly states that details such as the scope of compensation and limitation of liability will be regulated by another law, which is the Space Damage Compensation Act enacted two years after the Act's enforcement.

Overall, it is concluded that the Space Development Promotion Act adequately reflects the key principles of the UN space treaties and implements South Korea's obligations, notwithstanding the potential for improvement to better regulate varied commercial space activities.

---

12 For more details, *see supra* Chapter 5 §4.3.2.1.

13 For further discussion, *see supra* Chapter 5 §4.3.2.2.

14 For further discussion, *see supra* Chapter 5 §4.5.2.3.

2.3.2.3 *The Promotion of the Private Space Sector*

Another notable finding in the Act is that it contains a number of provisions for the promotion of the private space sector. The Act allows private space entities to access and utilize infrastructure owned by public organizations or government-funded research institutions. The Act also provides the procedures for how the government carries out space development projects with private entities as well as the reimbursement of expenses incurred in relation to those projects. Further, the Act stipulates the transfer of space technology developed by the government to the private sector.

To that end, the Act specifies the Minister of Science and ICT's duty to formulate and execute strategies for facilitating the transfer of space technology and promoting the performance outcomes of space projects. This demonstrates the Korean government's dedication to advancing its commercial space industry. In other words, the Act reflects the government's intention to incentivize the private sector to participate in space development through public-private partnerships.[15]

2.3.2.4 *Space Accident Investigation*

In order to prepare for space mishaps, the Act and its implementing Presidential Decree established a framework for conducting a space accident investigation, which is not commonly addressed in other nations' national space legislation. The Act essentially creates two domestic obligations: One is for the Minister of Science and ICT to form and operate the Space Accident Investigation Committee in the event of an accident. The other is for those involved in the space activities at issue to cooperate with the investigation. The accident investigation system is anticipated to contribute to the prevention of potential mishaps and ensure the safety of space activities in general.[16]

2.3.2.5 *Satellite Data Utilization and Distribution*

The Act and its implementing regulations address issues pertaining to the utilization and distribution of satellite data acquired through government-developed satellites. The Act requires the Minister of Science and ICT to facilitate and maximize the use of satellite data, and the Minister established a dedicated governmental body for this purpose. While these regulations do not regulate the activities of commercial operators, they set forth requirements and procedures for government agencies and public organizations.

---

15 For further discussion, *see supra* Chapter 5 §4.7.

16 For more details on space accident investigation, *see supra* Chapter 5 §4.6.

Given the prosperous satellite and accompanying data processing industry in South Korea, it is suggested that a comprehensive law including operational requirements and data distribution procedures should be established for the private sector of the remote sensing and Earth observation industry. This would contribute to satellite data security and promote business predictability through regulatory certainty.[17]

2.3.2.6 *Sanctions for Non-compliance*

The Act imposes penalties for non-compliance with the Act's requirements, which include criminal penalties and administrative fines depending on the gravity of the infraction. The most severe criminal penalty is for conducting launch activities without permission, whereas administrative fines are imposed for failing to file a preliminary or formal registration of a space object, as well as interfering with or evading a space accident investigation.[18] These sanctions serve to uphold the Act's regime and ensure the supervision and control of space activities.

2.4 *The Space Damage Compensation Act of 2007*

As its title indicates, the Space Damage Compensation Act is committed to providing South Korea's liability regime for space damage, compensation, and insurance.

Essentially, a person who registered a space object or obtained launch permission is liable to compensate for space damage up to 200 billion Korean won, approximately 150 to 200 million US dollars. Furthermore, any person who seeks to obtain launch permission is required to take out third-party liability insurance within the maximum of 200 billion Korean won. The Korean government can render financial assistance if the compensation exceeds the insured amount. The government has the right of recourse if it paid compensation as a launching State under the Liability Convention.

However, the analysis of the Act reveals two aspects for possible improvements. First, it is suggested that South Korea should consider raising the existing limit of 200 billion Korean won given the increasing number of space activities and the current space industry and insurance market trend. Second, the insurance obligation under the Act should preferably be extended to other private entities such as the registrant of a space object or satellite operator.

17 For further discussion, *see supra* Chapter 5 §4.8.

18 For specifics of penalties, *see supra* Chapter 5 §4.9.

The existing obligation only applied to those who intend to obtain launch permission, which is not sufficient to ensure the protection of third-party victims.

3 Recommendations and Suggestions for Better Space Governance in Korea

3.1 *The Need to Reform the Existing Space Legislation and Enact New Regulations for Emerging Space Activities*

As inferred from the analysis of each space law of South Korea in the prior chapters, Korean national space legislation is composed of a series of laws and regulations that govern certain aspects of space activities as well as a number of general norms that affect the space industry. This is a reflection of South Korea's progressive engagement in space development and its approach to addressing legal challenges as they arise. As a result of this reactive approach, South Korea lacks an overarching, all-inclusive piece of legislation that would regulate all of its national space activities. Nonetheless, Korean space legislation is overall thorough and encompasses each possible aspect of the exploration and use of outer space under international space law.

South Korea's legal regime in the space sector has been executed by various administrative agencies and government-funded institutions involved in the governance of space activities and national space programs. The fabric of Korean space governance is a patchwork of processes centered on South Korea's early viable space activities. This framework, however, has become ill-suited for the present climate of the space industry and emerging space technologies. After three decades of South Korea's involvement in space development, it is now time to revisit the existing national space legislation and reform its system.

3.2 *The Aerospace Industry Development Promotion Act*

Notwithstanding its significance in the Korean space development history, it is questionable whether the Aerospace Industry Development Promotion Act still retains its own value and effectiveness. The Act was created to support the nation's initial aerospace industry. A number of provisions of the Act have been repealed over time as the aerospace industry has evolved or early goals have been achieved. The Act served as the foundation for governmental assistance in the primary stage of the aerospace industry as well as the legal basis for the establishment of the Korea Aerospace Research Institute (KARI).

However, these objectives have been accomplished or are now governed by other laws. For instance, KARI is regulated by a separate law together with other government-funded institutions. National space programs and specialized space industry clusters are now created and governed by the Space Development Promotion Act. Therefore, it is recommended that South Korea should reconsider whether the Aerospace Industry Development Promotion Act is still imperative. The Act should be entirely reviewed, and its remaining minor provisions for technical standards need to be rearranged into a technical law in light of the changes and advancements since its enactment in 1987.

3.3 *The Radio Waves Act*

Based on the analysis of the Radio Waves Act, it is suggested that the current spectrum utilization system of South Korea be restructured into a more streamlined and unified licensing regime to better manage frequency resources. Under the current system, it is complicated and difficult to understand the dispersed concepts and requirements of frequency assignment, the approval of frequency usage, and the frequency designation, which were added one by one to the Act each time as needed. A single and encompassing license regime would be desirable that integrates each concept of spectrum use.

Additionally, with regard to the registration of space objects, the only aspect the Radio Waves Act addresses is the 'international' registration of 'satellites' with the United Nations. However, the 'national' registration of 'satellites' as well as national and international registration of other space objects are governed by the Space Development Promotion Act. In this regard, it is worth reconsidering whether it is still effective to segregate international registration of satellites from all other registrations.

Overall, the provisions of the Radio Waves Act are clearly defined and more detailed than the ITU principles, but they do not regulate non-communication satellite operations or remote sensing. Given South Korea's unique geopolitical situation and the potential of satellite data in understanding and protecting the Earth, it is recommended to consider the creation of legislation to address these issues and provide legal clarity for private satellite operators. This would also enable the most effective utilization of satellite data and the advancement of remote sensing technology.

3.4 *The Space Development Promotion Act*

There are several areas in which the Space Development Promotion Act could be improved in order to comprehensively regulate non-governmental space activities.

Above all, the scope of application of the Act's key regime should be stipulated in a more inclusive and intuitive manner to thoroughly encompass all possible scenarios. For example, with regard to obtaining launch permission or registering space objects, the Act may plainly set both territorial and personal jurisdiction as determining the Act's standard applicable scope rather than the current complicated provision structure. Alongside this standard scope, the Act may still keep the existing launch vehicle ownership-based jurisdiction as an additional part of the scope (see Table 30). Through this approach, a case that does not currently fall under the Act – such as a Korean citizen using a non-Korean-owned launch vehicle outside Korea – can be governed by the Korean authorization system.

It is also recommended that South Korea should consider expanding the scope of application of the Space Development Promotion Act to more various space activities. For example, with regard to authorization, the Act currently requires permission only for launching a space launch vehicle, which leaves a legal loophole in coverage for other diverse space operations that may be considered as South Korean national space activities under international space law. To address this, it is suggested to broaden the Act's authorization scope to include other activities such as the operation of a launch site and the control over space objects in orbit. The operation of a re-entry site, the return of a space object, or human spaceflight can also be included as a number of private companies in South Korea are already involved in these areas and improving their capabilities. In this regard, South Korea may further consider introducing a license system for private entities such as the launch service provider or launch site operator in addition to issuing a single launch permission for a series of launch activities.

Additionally, in some areas of space activities, there is no regulation to apply for the private sector. For example, the regulations for dissemination and utilization of satellite data acquired through remote sensing apply only to government agencies or institutions on behalf of the government using government-developed satellites. It is suggested that South Korea should consider establishing regulations for non-government entities to operate private remote sensing space systems under the jurisdiction or control of South Korea as well as a necessary license system and data security regulations.

In light of South Korea's ongoing space program, it is proposed that South Korea should prepare to create regulations governing the operation of the Korea Positioning System (KPS). Furthermore, given the growing interest of the Korean private sector in space mining and South Korea's participation in the Artemis Accords, regulations on space resources may also be required in the near future. This trend is driven by the increasing value of space resources, as well as the development of new technologies that enable cost-effective extraction of these resources.

TABLE 30 An example of amending the current Article 11(1) of the Act

Structure of the current Article 11(1) of the Act	Recommendation
A person who intends to launch a launch vehicle must apply for launch permission in the following cases: i. where a launch vehicle lifts off from South Korean territory or areas/facilities under South Korean jurisdiction; or ii. where a launch vehicle is owned by the Korean government or a Korean national despite being intended to launch outside of Korea.	A launch permission is required for: i. a person to launch a launch vehicle inside South Korea or under South Korean jurisdiction; ii. a Korean citizen to launch a launch vehicle outside South Korea; or iii. a person to use the Korean government- or citizen-owned launch vehicle.

Meanwhile, regarding space debris, there is the Korean government's Recommendations for Space Debris Mitigation applicable to satellite operators. Although the Recommendations are guidelines and not legally binding, the Korean government, in practice, strongly advises satellite operators to include space debris mitigation strategies including post mission disposal when applying for their registration of satellite networks. As South Korea is earnestly developing technology including active debris removal that will be employed soon, it would be worthwhile to take into account to transform the Recommendations into legally obligatory regulations. Eventually, space debris mitigation requirements should be incorporated in national licensing processes.[19]

Lastly, the organizational structure under the Space Development Promotion Act would need to be reformed with the discussion on the novel concept of a Korean space agency. In South Korea, a number of central ministries and government-funded institutes are all involved in space-related activities from decision-making to execution. At the top of the hierarchy is the National Space

19 This approach is employed by certain space-faring nations, such as the United States, the United Kingdom, and France. *See, supra* Chapter 1 §3.2 and Chapter 1, n. 194.

Committee chaired by the Prime Minister. However, the current authority and role of the National Space Committee need to be reevaluated and adjusted in light of the ongoing discussion regarding the establishment of the Korea space agency, tentatively named the Korea AeroSpace Administration (KASA). A draft bill to establish KASA should clarify its legal status and representativeness as well as allow it to have independent authority to better address interagency tasks.

3.5 *The Space Damage Compensation Act*

By reflecting the contemporary space industry and market trend, the Space Damage Compensation Act can be improved in two key areas.

The first suggestion is to increase the existing maximum compensation limit set forth in 2007. Despite the exponential growth of space activities and the change of currency value, the current maximum has remained until today, which does not reflect inflation since 2007 and is not sufficient to protect victims.

The second suggestion is to expand the insurance obligation under the Act to other private actors than launch permission holders including registrants of space objects or satellite operators. These improvements would benefit the Korean private sector for its international competitiveness as well as better protect third-party victims in the event of damages caused by space objects.

4 Perspectives and Prospects for the Future of the Korean Space Sector

The Korean space sector has been making significant strides in recent years, and the future looks promising for this burgeoning industry. As more players enter the field and the global space economy continues to grow, there are several key perspectives and prospects worth considering that are likely to shape the industry in the years ahead.

One major perspective on the future of the Korean space sector is the increasing commercialization of space activities. This trend is being driven by the rapid growth of the global space economy, which is projected to more than triple in size by 2030, reaching one trillion US dollars by 2040.[20] A significant

---

20 Michael Sheetz, "Bank of America expects the space industry to triple to a $1.4 trillion market within a decade," Oct 4, 2020, last accessed January 11, 2023, available at https://www.cnbc.com/2020/10/02/why-the-space-industry-may-triple-to-1point4-trillion-by-2030.html; Michael Sheetz, "The space industry is on its way to reach $1 trillion in revenue by

portion of this growth is expected to come from the commercial sector, as more and more companies seek to leverage space-based technologies and services to improve their operations and create new revenue streams. In South Korea, a number of private companies are already active in the space sector, including satellite manufacturers and operators, launch vehicle developers, and providers of space-based services such as remote sensing and Earth observation. Furthermore, companies such as Samsung, Korea Telecommunication Corporation (KT), Hanwha, and recently Boryung[21] have made substantial investments in the space industry, and more companies are expected to follow suit in the coming years.

Another crucial perspective to consider is the role of government policy and regulations in shaping the future of the commercial space sector in Korea. The Korean government has been enthusiastically promoting the growth of the domestic space industry, through measures such as funding for research and development, tax incentives, and the establishment of a regulatory framework for non-governmental space activities. Beyond that, the government should concentrate on creating a more favorable and conducive regulatory environment for the industry to function and compete efficiently while ensuring safety, security, and other public interest concerns. As the Korean space sector continues to grow and evolve, government policy and regulations will play an increasingly important role in determining its future.

An additional point of view is the emphasis on increasing international cooperation and collaboration. As commercial space activities become more globalized, it is essential for countries to work together in order to attain common goals and share expertise and resources. To ensure the long-term sustainability of space activities, cooperation and collaboration among States is crucial in the areas of space security, space debris mitigation and remediation, and space traffic management. In South Korea, there has been a significant increase in international cooperation in recent years, with the country working closely with other space-faring powers such as the United States and the European Union. This trend towards international collaboration will be

---

2040, Citi says," May 21, 2022, last accessed January 11, 2023, available at https://www.cnbc.com/2022/05/21/space-industry-is-on-its-way-to-1-trillion-in-revenue-by-2040-citi.html.

21 At a board of directors meeting on December 21, 2022, Boryung, a South Korean pharmaceutical company, voted to make a strategic investment of USD 50 million in Axiom Space, the world's first commercial space station leader. The company is dedicated to exploring space-based healthcare solutions and stated that its investment in Axiom Space is significant in terms of securing a business ecosystem and laying the foundation for seeking new business opportunities in the private space industry.

particularly important for commercial, non-governmental space activities, as private companies will be more likely to engage in international partnerships, joint ventures, and other forms of collaboration.

South Korea has made remarkable progress in its space sector over the past decades. From establishing the Korea Aerospace Research Institute (KARI) in 1989 and launching its first-developed satellite in 1992, to sending its first astronaut to the International Space Station in 2008, to successfully launching its home-grown launch vehicles, KSLV-I in 2013 and II in 2022, and to exploring the Moon by sending the Korean Pathfinder Lunar Orbiter (KPLO) in 2022, South Korea has continuously demonstrated its ambition and capability in the space field.

The Korean government has also made several policy efforts to support the growth of the space industry, most recently through President Sukyeol Yoon's keynote speech at the Korea Space Forum in November 2022 and the National Space Committee's announcement in December 2022 of the Fourth Basic Plan for the Promotion of Space Development for the years from 2023 until 2027. These endeavors seek to not only enhance South Korea's self-reliance in space technology, but also to foster the growth of the domestic space industry, aiming to increase the value of the industry 8 trillion Korean won, or approximately 7 billion US dollars by 2030. Further, the objectives include uncrewed landing on the Moon in 2032 and on Mars in 2045 by focusing on the development of South Korea's own technology for space exploration and thus launching a crewed spacecraft in 2045. To attain these goals, President Yoon pledged to double the government's budget for space development over the next five years from 2023 and invest a minimum of 100 trillion Korean won, or approximately 85 billion US dollars in the space sector by 2045.[22]

The achievement of South Korea's ambitious plans for space exploration is contingent upon its capacity to proactively address both current and future legal challenges. The existing legal framework is not sufficient to adequately regulate and safeguard the rights and interests of all stakeholders involved in space activities. Consequently, there is a pressing need for the Korean government to improve and update its space legislation to keep up with the fast-evolving space sector.

The contemporary space industry is witnessing a new paradigm shift. The growing participation of private and non-governmental entities in the industry is adding a layer of complexity to the governance of space activities. It is thus

22 In 2022, 734 billion Korean won, or approximately 600 million US dollars was earmarked for South Korea's space budget.

more crucial to have a clear and consistent regulatory regime in place. A robust legal framework will help provide predictability and clarity for investors and industry players. This will enable South Korea to harness the full potential of its space activities, positioning the Korean space industry to compete more effectively in the global market.

In conclusion, the Korean space sector has come a long way in a relatively short period of time, with the aim to become one of the global leaders in the commercial satellite market, space exploration, and technology development. To achieve this, South Korea must address the legal challenges associated with these endeavors. The government should update the legal framework and revamp the existing space legislation, which has become a patchwork of elements over time.

Despite the challenges, the future of South Korean space activity appears bright, with a range of opportunities waiting to be explored. The role of the Korean government, notably in terms of policy and regulations, is a key that will determine the success of space industry in the years to come. With a firm commitment to regulatory reform from the government, the Korean space sector is expected to generate substantial benefits for the nation and the world, while also emerging as a major player in shaping the future of space activities.

Bibliography

ABS, "Asia Broadcast Satellite Acquires Koreasat-2," accessed on February 13, 2021, available at https://absatellite.com/asia-broadcast-satellite-to-acquire-koreasat-2/.

ABS, "Asia Broadcast Satellite Acquires Koreasat-3," accessed on February 13, 2021, available at https://absatellite.com/asia-broadcast-satellite-acquires-koreasat-3/.

Adnan Al Rais *et al.*, "DubaiSat-1: Mission Overview, Development Status and Future Applications," in 2009 IEEE International Geoscience and Remote Sensing Symposium (2009).

Airbus, "New Space: Europe should shape the future of space," accessed November 14, 2019, http://www.airbus.com/public-affairs/brussels/our-topics/space/new-space.html.

Annette Froehlich and Vincent Seffinga, "National Space Legislation: A Comparative and Evaluative Analysis," (2018).

Armel Kerrest, "Remarks on the Responsibility and Liability for Damage Caused by Private Activity in Outer Space" in Proceedings of the 42nd Colloquium on the Law of Outer Space (1997).

Atomic Heritage Foundation, "Limited or Partial Test Ban Treaty (LTBT/PTBT)," June 10, 2016, available at https://www.atomicheritage.org/history/limited-or-partial-test-ban-treaty-ltbtptbt.

Bernhard Schmidt-Tedd and Kai-Uwe Schrogl (eds.), Cologne Commentary on Space Law, Vol. I (2013).

Bernhard Schmidt-Tedd, Nataliia Malysheva and Olga Stelmakh, "The 1975 Convention on Registration of Objects Launched into Outer Space" in Stephan Hobe, Bernhard Schmidt-Tedd and Kai-Uwe Schrogl (eds.), Cologne Commentary on Space Law, Vol. II (2013).

Bert W. Rein and Carl R. Frank, "The Legal Commitment of the United States to the INTELSAT System," 14 N.C. J. Int'l L. and Com. Reg. 219 (1989).

Bin Cheng, "Article VI of the 1967 Space Treaty Revisited: 'International Responsibility,' 'National Activities' and 'The Appropriate State'," Journal of Space Law 26 (1998).

Bin Cheng, "Convention on International Liability for Damage Caused by Space Objects" in Nandasiri Jasentuliyana and Roy S.K. Lee (eds.), Manual on Space Law, Vol. 1 (1979).

Bin Cheng, "International Responsibility and Liability for Launch Activities," Air and Space Law 20, no. 6 (1995).

Bin Cheng, "Studies in International Space Law," Clarendon Press Oxford (1997).

Brian Kim, "US lifts missile restrictions on South Korea, ending range and warhead limits," Defense News, May 25, 2021, available at https://www.defensenews.com/global/asia-pacific/2021/05/25/us-lifts-missile-restrictions-on-south-korea-ending-range-and-warhead-limits/.

Caleb Henry, "Backed by Samsung, South Korean startup Perigee aims for 2020 maiden launch," SpaceNews, October 23, 2019, https://spacenews.com/backed-by-samsung-south-korean-startup-perigee-aims-for-2020-maiden-launch/.

Carl Q. Christol, "International Liability for Damage Caused by Space Objects," American Journal of International Law 74 (1980).

Carl Q. Christol, "The Modern International Law of Outer Space," (1982).

China Daily, "Launch propels ROK into space age," January 31, 2013, accessed on July 23, 2020, http://usa.chinadaily.com.cn/epaper/2013-01/31/content_16190866.htm.

Christopher J. LeMon, "International Law and North Korean Nuclear Testing," American Society of International Law Insights, October 19, 2006, https://www.asil.org/insights/volume/10/issue/27/international-law-and-north-korean-nuclear-testing#_edn6.

Committee on the Peaceful Uses of Outer Space: Membership Evolution, accessed on March 3, 2020, https://www.unoosa.org/oosa/en/ourwork/copuos/members/evolution.html.

CONTEC, http://contec.kr/index.

Daniel Rietiker, "The (Il)legality of Nuclear Weapons Tests Under International Law: Filling the Possible Legal Gap by Ensuring the Comprehensive Test Ban Treaty's Entry into Force," American Society of International Law Insights, March 16, 2017, https://www.asil.org/insights/volume/21/issue/4/illegality-nuclear-weapons-tests-under-international-law%E2%80%94filling-possible.

Dasol Kim, "S. Korea joins elite space club as 7th member," The Korea Herald, last accessed on January 21, 2023, available at https://www.koreaherald.com/view.php?ud=20220621000810.

David S. Jonas, "The Comprehensive Nuclear Test Ban Treaty: Current Legal Status in the United States and the Implications of a Nuclear Test Explosion," New York University Journal of International Law and Politics 39, no. 4 (2007).

David Kelley and Eugene Milone, "Exploring Ancient Skies: A Survey of Ancient and Cultural Astronomy," Springer Science & Business Media (2011).

David A. Koplow, "Nuclear Arms Control by a Pen: Effectuating the Comprehensive Test Ban Treaty without Ratification," Georgetown Journal of International Law 46, no. 2 (2015).

Donald R. Rothwell, *et al.*, "International Law: Cases and Materials with Australian Perspectives (3rd ed.)," Cambridge University Press (2018).

Felix Kim, "South Korea accelerates space defense program," Indo-Pacific Defense Forum, November 14, 2021, https://ipdefenseforum.com/2021/11/south-korea-accelerates-space-defense-program/.

Francis Lyall, "On the Privatization of INTELSAT," Journal of Space Law 28, no. 2 (2000).

Francis Lyall, "Protection of the Public Interest in the Light of the Commercialization and Privatization of the Providers of International Satellite Telecommunications," Proceedings on the Law of Outer Space 47 (2004).

Francis Lyall, "Who is an astronaut? The inadequacy of current international law," Acta Astronautica 66 (2010).

Francis Lyall and Paul B. Larsen, "Space law: A Treatise," Ashgate Publishing (2009).

Frans von der Dunk, "Advanced Introduction to Space Law" (2020).

Frans von der Dunk, "A Sleeping Beauty Awakens: The 1968 Rescue Agreement after Forty Years," Journal of Space Law 34, no. 2 (2008).

Frans von der Dunk, "Fundamental Provisions for National Space Laws," Space, Cyber, and Telecommunications Law Program Faculty Publications 11 (2006).

Frans von der Dunk, "International Organizations in Space Law," in Frans von der Dunk (ed.), Handbook of Space Law, Edward Elgar Publishing (2014).

Frans von der Dunk, "International Space Law," in Frans von der Dunk (ed.), Handbook of Space Law, Edward Elgar Publishing (2014).

Frans von der Dunk, "International Trade Aspects of Space services," in Frans von der Dunk (ed.), Handbook of Space Law, Edward Elgar Publishing (2015).

Frans von der Dunk, "Legal Aspects of Satellite Communications," in Frans von der Dunk (ed.), Handbook of Space Law, Edward Elgar Publishing (2015).

Frans von der Dunk, "Private Enterprise and Public Interest in the European 'Spacescape': towards harmonized national space legislation for private space activities in Europe," Leiden, International Institute of Air and Space Law (1998).

Frans von der Dunk, "Registration Convention: Background and Historical Context," Proceedings on the Law of Outer Space 46 (2003).

Frans von der Dunk, "Scoping National Space Law: The True Meaning of 'National Activities in Outer Space' of Article VI of the Outer Space Treaty," in Proceedings of the International Institute of Space Law 2019, Eleven International Publishing (2020).

Frans von der Dunk, "The Origins of Authorization: Article VI of the Outer Space Treaty and International Space Law," in Frans von der Dunk (ed.), National Space Legislation in Europe (2011).

Frans von der Dunk, "The 1972 Liability Convention: Enhancing Adherence and Effective Application," in Proceedings of the Forty-First Colloquium on the Law of Outer Space (1998).

Frans von der Dunk, "Too-Close Encounters of the Third Party Kind: Will the Liability Convention Stand the Test of the Cosmos 2251-Iridium 33 Collision?" in The Proceedings of the International Institute of Space Law (2009).

Gary Martin, "NewSpace: The Emerging Commercial Space Industry," accessed November 14, 2019, https://ntrs.nasa.gov/archive/nasa/casi.ntrs.nasa.gov/20160001188.pdf.

George Bunn, "The Status of Norms against Nuclear Testing," The Nonproliferation Review (1999).

Geunhong Park, "The Advance of a Korean Institute: A Brief History of KAIST," KAIST Herald, April 21, 2011, available at https://www.herald.kaist.ac.kr.

Government of Dubai, "Mohammed Bin Rashid Space Centre," November 15, 2017, last accessed December 23, 2021, available at https://herald.kaist.ac.kr/news/articleView.html?idxno=158.

Gunter's Space Page, "Korea Pathfinder Lunar Orbiter," accessed on May 9, 2020, https://space.skyrocket.de/doc_sdat/kplo.htm.

Hamid Kazemi, S. Hadi Mahmoudi and Ali Akbar Golroo, "The Need to Regulate New Space Activities on Exploration of Space Resources and Off-Earth Mining," in Proceedings of the International Institute of Space Law 2017 (2018).

Hanneke L. van Traa-Engelman, "Problems of State Responsibility in International Space Law" in Proceedings of the 26th Colloquium on the Law of Outer Space (1983).

Helaine Selin, "Encyclopedia of the History of Science, Technology, and Medicine in Non-Western Cultures," Springer Science & Business Media (2013).

Henri A. Wassenbergh, "The Law Governing International Private Commercial Activities of Space Transportation," Journal of Space Law 21, no. 2 (1993).

Hiroko Yotsumoto *et al.*, "The Space Law Review: Japan," last accessed February 25, 2022, available at https://thelawreviews.co.uk/title/the-space-law-review/japan.

Hyungjin Kim, "South Korea to have solid-fuel rockets in major deal with US," Defense News, July 28, 2020, available at https://www.defensenews.com/global/asia-pacific/2020/07/28/south-korea-to-have-solid-fuel-rockets-in-major-deal-with-us/.

IADC, "An overview of the IADC annual activities," in 53rd Session of the Scientific and Technical Subcommittee United Nations Committee on the Peaceful Uses of Outer Space, February 22, 2016, available at https://iaaweb.org/iaa/Scientific%20Activity/debrisminutes09164.pdf.

IADC, "What's IADC," accessed on January 26, 2020, https://www.iadc-home.org/what_iadc.

INNOSPACE, "Latest News," last accessed on October 29, 2022, available at http://www.innospc.com/shop_contents/myboard_read.htm?load_type=&page_idx=0&tag_on=&h_search_c=0&h_search_v=&me_popup=&myboard_code=sub04_02&page_limit=5&idx=188227&page=1&category_idx=.

InSpace, https://www.inspace.co.kr/.

International Maritime Organization, "IMO Convention on the International Maritime Satellite Organization," https://www.imo.org/en/About/Conventions/Pages/Convention-on-the-International-Maritime-Satellite-Organization.aspx.

Irmgard Marboe, "Agreement on the Rescue and Return of Astronauts and Objects Launched into Outer Space," The Oxford Research Encyclopedias, 7, available at https://oxfordre.com/planetaryscience/view/10.1093/acrefore/9780190647926.001.0001/acrefore-9780190647926-e-65.

Irmgard Marboe, Julia Neumann, and Kai-Uwe Schrogl, "Preamble ARRA," in Stephan Hobe, Bernhard Schmidt-Tedd and Kai-Uwe Schrogl (eds.), Cologne Commentary on Space Law, Vol. II (2013).

ISO, accessed on November 19, 2020, https://www.iso.org/about-us.html.

Istvan Herczeg, "Problems of Interpretation of the Space Treaty of 27 January 1967" in Proceedings of the 10th Colloquium on the Law of Outer Space (1967).

ITSO "About us," available at https://itso.int/about-us/.

ITSO, "Milestones," accessed on November 10, 2020, available at https://itso.int/about-us/milestones/.

ITSO, accessed on November 11, 2020, available at https://itso.int/about-us/more/.

ITU, "About ITU," last accessed on October 27, 2020, https://www.itu.int/en/about/Pages/default.aspx.

ITU, "Cost Recovery for Satellite Network Filings," accessed on February 1, 2021, available at https://www.itu.int/ITU-R/go/space-cost-recovery/en.

ITU, "E-Submission of Satellite Network Filings," accessed on February 1, 2021, available at https://www.itu.int/en/ITU-R/space/e-submission/Pages/default.aspx.

ITU, "International monitoring," accessed on February 24, 2021, https://www.itu.int/en/ITU-R/terrestrial/monitoring/Pages/default.aspx.

ITU, "List of member states," accessed on January 27, 2020, https://www.itu.int/online/mm/scripts/gensel.

ITU Media Center, "5G – Fifth generation of mobile technologies," accessed on January 27, 2020, https://www.itu.int/en/mediacentre/backgrounders/Pages/5G-fifth-generation-of-mobile-technologies.aspx.

ITU, "Monitoring Program band 406–406.1 MHz," accessed on February 24, 2021, https://www.itu.int/en/ITU-R/terrestrial/monitoring/Pages/Res205.aspx.

ITU, "Regular Monitoring Program in frequency bands between 2 850 kHz and 28 000 kHz," https://www.itu.int/en/ITU-R/terrestrial/monitoring/Pages/Regular.aspx.

Jack M. Beard, "The Nuclear Nonproliferation Regime and Nuclear Realities: Repair or Reassessment," American Society of International Law Proceedings 101 (2007).

JAXA, "About JAXA," last accessed December 15, 2021, https://global.jaxa.jp/about/.

Jerzy Rajaki, "Convention on International Liability for Damage caused by Space Objects – An Important Step in the Development of the International Space Law," Proceedings on the Law of Outer Space 17 (1974).

Jerzy W. Vonau, "Restructured Inmarsat and Public Service Obligations," Annals of Air and Space Law 26 (2001).

Jill M. Sheldon, "Nuclear Weapons and the Laws of War: Does Customary International Law Prohibit the Use of Nuclear Weapons in All Circumstances," Fordham International Law Journal 20, no. 1 (1996).

Jitae Jang, "방아 찧는 토끼 (A rabbit pounding rice cakes [English title added])," Busanilbo, October 31, 2012, https://news.naver.com/main/read.nhn?oid=082&aid=0000362799.

Joanne Wheeler, "Space Debris: Legal Framework, Issues Arising and New ISO Guidelines," in 2010/2011, in Peter Hulsroj, Spyros Pagkratis and Blandina Baranes (eds.), Yearbook on Space Policy 2010/2011: The Forward Look (2013).

Joseph A. Burke, "Convention on International Liability for Damage Caused by Space Objects: Definition and Determination of Damages After the Cosmos 954 Incident," Fordham International Law Journal 8 (1984).

Joseph N. Pelton, "Space Debris and Other Threats from Outer Space," (2013).

Julian Hermida, "Legal Basis for a National Space Legislation," McGill University (2003).

KAI, "Compact Advanced Satellite," accessed on August 2, 2020, https://www.koreaaero.com/EN/Business/CAS500_01.aspx.

KAI, "Korea Space Launch Vehicle," accessed on August 2, 2020, https://www.koreaaero.com/EN/Business/KoreaSpaceLaunchVehicle.aspx.

KAIST history, https://www.kaist.ac.kr/_prog/history/?site_dvs_cd=en&menu_dvs_cd=010202&site_dvs_cd=en&menu_dvs_cd=010202, accessed on November 19, 2019.

KAIST SaTRec, "History," accessed on July 1, 2020, http://satrec.kaist.ac.kr/e_01_02.php.

KARI, "Cooperative Convergence Research on Lunar Exploration," accessed on May 6, 2020, https://www.kari.re.kr/eng/sub03_04_02.do#link.

KARI, "Future Vision 2050," accessed on April 30, 2020, https://www.kari.re.kr/eng/sub01_06.do.

KARI, "Introduction to Korea Lunar Exploration Program and KPLO Mission," August 2016.

KARI, "Korea Space Launch Vehicle (Nuri)," accessed on March 17, 2020, https://www.kari.re.kr/eng/sub03_03_01.do.

KARI, "Lunar Exploration," accessed on May 7, 2020, https://www.kari.re.kr/eng/sub03_04.do.

KARI, "Naro Space Center," accessed on July 23, 2020, https://www.kari.re.kr/eng/sub03_03_04.do.

KARI, "30th Anniversary Statement, " accessed on November 19, 2019, available at https://www.kari.re.kr/kor/sub01_10.do.

KARI, "2017 Korea Aerospace Research Institute Promising Technologies for Commercialization".

KARI, "Welcome to KARI," accessed on July 29, 2020, https://www.kari.re.kr/eng/sub01_01.do.

KARI and Korea Association for Space Technology Promotion (KASP), "우주산업실태조사 2017 (Survey on the Korea's Space Industry 2017 [English title added])".

Karl-Heinz Böckstiegel, "The Term 'Appropriate State' in International Space Law," in International Institute of Space Law, Proceedings of the 37th Colloquium (1994).

Kenneth Katkin, "Communication Breakdown: The Future of Global Connectivity after the Privatization of INTELSAT," Vanderbilt Journal of Transnational Law 38, no. 5 (2005).

Kenneth Katkin, "The Global Broadband Satellite Infrastructure Initiative," University of Louisville Law Review 48, no. 4 (2010).

Khrunichev State Research and Production Space Center, "Korea Space Launch Vehicle-KSLV (South Korea)," accessed on April 15, 2020, http://www.khrunichev.ru/main.php?id=73&lang=en.

Korea Communications Agency (KCA), accessed on March 3, 2021, https://www.kca.kr/eng/.

Korea Communications Commission (KCC), accessed on March 1, 2021, https://kcc.go.kr/user/ehpMain.do.

Korea ITU Committee, "History," accessed on July 20, 2020, https://www.koreaitu.or.kr/introduce_ITU/menu4/intro_history.do?menu_gubun=mid&menu_no=0&menu_no2=3&menu_no3=&params=.

Korea ITU Committee, "Annual Report of Korea ITU Committee 2017".

Korea Radio Promotion Association (RAPA), "Business," accessed on March 4, 2021, available at https://www.rapa.or.kr/en/un/un01/list.do.

KSR-I, http://www.astronautix.com/k/ksr-i.html.

KSR-II, "Part of KSR," accessed on May 10, 2020, http://www.astronautix.com/k/ksr-ii.html.

KSR-III, "Part of KSR," accessed on May 10, 2020, http://www.astronautix.com/k/ksr-iii.html.

KT Sat, "Facilities," accessed on April 1, 2020, https://www.ktsat.net/kr/content/view.do?cttNm=facilities&cttNo=011.

Lesley Jane Smith and A. Kerrest de Rozavel, "Article I (Definitions) LIAB," in Stephan Hobe, Bernhard Schmidt-Tedd and Kai-Uwe Schrogl (3ds.), Cologne Commentary on Space Law, Vol. II (2013).

Lesley Jane Smith and A. Kerrest de Rozavel, "The 1972 Convention on International Liability for Damage Caused by Space Objects," in Stephan Hobe, Bernhard Schmidt-Tedd and Kai-Uwe Schrogl (eds.), Cologne Commentary on Space Law, Vol. II (2013).

Lotta Viikari, "Environmental Aspects of Space Activities," in Frans von der Dunk (ed.), Handbook of Space Law (2014).

Lotta Viikari, "The Environmental Element in Space Law: Assessing the Present and Charting the Future," (2008).

Luxembourg Space Agency, "Expertise," last accessed December 15, 2021, https://space-agency.public.lu/en/expertise/space-directory/contec.html.

Luxembourg Space Agency, "International Collaboration," last accessed December 22, 2021, https://space-agency.public.lu/en/agency/international-collaboration.html.

Luxembourg Space Agency, "Our Team," last accessed December 22, 2021, https://space-agency.public.lu/en/agency/lsa/team.html.

Luxembourg Space Agency, "Space Resources," last accessed December 16, 2021, https://space-agency.public.lu/en/space-resources/the-initiative.html.

Luxembourg Space Agency, "The Agency," last accessed December 15, 2021, https://space-agency.public.lu/en/agency/lsa.html.

Malcolm Shaw, "International Law," last accessed February 3, 2022, available at https://www.britannica.com/topic/international-law/Jurisdiction.

Manfred Lachs, "The Law of Outer Space: An Experience in Contemporary Law-Making," (1972), 30.

Mark J. Sundahl, "Regulating Non-Traditional Space Activities in the United States in the Wake of the Commercial Space Launch Competitiveness Act," Air and Space Law 42, no. 1 (February 2017).

Mark J. Sundahl, "Rescuing Space Tourists: A Humanitarian Duty and Business Need," in Proceedings of the Fiftieth Colloquium on the Law of Outer Space (2008).

Mark J. Sundahl, "The Duty to Rescue Space Tourists and Return Private Spacecraft," Journal of Space Law 35, no. 1 (Spring 2009).

Martha Mejia-Kaiser, "Collision Course: 2009 Iridium-Cosmos Crash," in The Proceedings of the International Institute of Space Law (2009).

Matthew Schaefer, "The Contours of Permissionless Innovation in the Outer Space Domain," University of Pennsylvania Journal of International Law 39, Fall (2017).

Matthew Schaefer, "The Need for Federal Preemption and International Negotiations Regarding Liability Caps and Waivers of Liability in the US Commercial Space Industry," Berkeley Journal of International Law 33, no. 1 (2015).

Matthew Schaefer, "What Level of Detail in National Commercial Space Legislation Is Ideal for the Harmonization and Enforcement of Such Legislation and Outer Space Treaty?" Proceedings of the International Institute of Space Law 62 (2019).

Max Blenkin, "Southern Launch signs rocket launch deal with Korean space company," October 2, 2019, https://www.spaceconnectonline.com.au/launch/3783-southern-launch-signs-rocket-launch-deal-with-korean-space-agency.

Michael Gerhard, "Article VI," in Stephan Hobe, Bernhard Schmidt-Tedd and Kai-Uwe Schrogl (eds.), Cologne Commentary on Space Law, Vol. I (2013).

Michael Sheetz, "Bank of America expects the space industry to triple to a $1.4 trillion market within a decade," October 4, 2020, last accessed January 11, 2023, available at https://www.cnbc.com/2020/10/02/why-the-space-industry-may-triple-to-1point4-trillion-by-2030.html.

Michael Sheetz, "The space industry is on its way to reach $1 trillion in revenue by 2040, Citi says," May 21, 2022, last accessed January 11, 2023, available at https://www.cnbc.com/2022/05/21/space-industry-is-on-its-way-to-1-trillion-in-revenue-by-2040-citi.html.

Michel Bourely, "Is it Necessary to Renegotiate the Convention on Registration," Proceedings on the Law of Outer Space 31 (1988).

Michel Bourely, "Rules of International Law Governing the Commercialization of Space Activities," in Proceedings of the 29th Colloquium on the Law of Outer Space (1986).

Mikyung Kim, "DMB Market and Audience Attitude," in Encyclopedia of Multimedia Technology and Networking, Second Edition (2009).

Ministry of Foreign Affairs, "Multilateral Treaties, Multilateral Treaties," accessed on January 15, 2020, http://www.mofa.go.kr/www/wpge/m_3835/contents.do.

Ministry of Foreign Affairs, "우주활동의 자유와 국가주권관련 국제법적 문제에 대한 연구 (A Study on the International Legal Issues Regarding Space Activities and National Sovereignty [English title added])" conducted by Wonwha Park, September 25, 2009.

Ministry of Science and ICT, Press release on July 24, 2020, "우주 쓰레기 경감을 위한 우주비행체 개발 및 운용 권고 (Recommendations for Space Debris Mitigation in the Course of Developing and Operating Spacecraft) [English title added by the author]".

Ministry of Science and ICT, "2019 우주산업실태조사 (Space Industry Survey 2019 [English title added])".

Ministry of Science and ICT, Press release, on January 15, 2023, "South Korea-UAE's MOU for Space Cooperation," last accessed on January 17, 2023, available at https://www.msit.go.kr/bbs/view.do?sCode=user&mId=113&mPid=238&pageIndex=&bbsSeqNo=94&nttSeqNo=3182635&searchOpt=ALL&searchTxt=.

Ministry of Science and ICT, "International Space Cooperation," October 16, 2014, accessed on January 30, 2020, https://doc.msit.go.kr/SynapDocViewServer/viewer/doc.html?key=fa1aa5adfe3d4186bf924848e5dd49ea&convType=img&convLocale=ko_KR&contextPath=/SynapDocViewServer.

Ministry of Science and ICT on February 5, 2018, "우주를 향한 대한민국의 새로운 도전 (South Korea's New Challenge for Space [English title added])," available at https://www.msit.go.kr/web/msipContents/contentsView.do?cateId=_policycom2&artId=1374583.

Ministry of Science and ICT on January 10, 2019, "정부, 민간주도 우주개발 생태계조성으로 미래 혁신성장동력을 창출한다 (The government, creating innovative space environment led by private sector [English title added])," available at http://www.korea.kr/news/pressReleaseView.do?newsId=156312526.

Ministry of Science and ICT on February 28, 2019, "The Second Master Plan for Promotion of Utilization of Satellite Data [English title added]," available at http://www.korea.kr/archive/expDocView.do?docId=38652.

Ministry of Science and ICT, "The Establishment of the Five-Year Master Plan for Radio Waves Promotion (2019–2023) [English title added]," accessed on January 20,

2021, available at https://www.msit.go.kr/publicinfo/view.do?sCode=user&mPid=62&mId=63&publictSeqNo=19&publictListSeqNo=2&formMode=R&referKey=19,2.

Ministry of Science and ICT, "The Establishment of the Five-Year Master Plan for Radio Waves Promotion (2019–2023) [English title added]," accessed on January 20, 2021, available at https://www.msit.go.kr/publicinfo/view.do?sCode=user&mPid=62&mId=63&publictSeqNo=19&publictListSeqNo=2&formMode=R&referKey=19,2.

Ministry of Science and ICT, Press release on June 18, 2018, the Results of the 5G Spectrum Auction, accessed on February 7, 2021, available at https://www.msit.go.kr/bbs/view.do?sCode=user&mId=113&mPid=112&bbsSeqNo=94&nttSeqNo=1386500.

Ministry of Science and ICT, Press release on May 30, 2019, "Launch of the Radio-Frequency Policy Advisory Meeting [English title added]," available at https://www.msit.go.kr/bbs/view.do?sCode=user&mId=113&mPid=112&bbsSeqNo=94&nttSeqNo=1994901.

Ministry of Science and ICT, Press release on June 10, 2021, "한미 정상회담을 통한 우주개발 성과의 실현을 위한 '제19회 국가우주위원회 개최' (The Nineteenth National Space Committee Held to Fulfill the Achievements of Space Development Following the Korea-US Summit) [English title added by the author]."

Ministry of Science and ICT, Press release, "글로벌 우주 이슈, 범 부처 공동 대응 강화 – 국가우주위원회 우주개발국제협력소위원회 출범 (Reinforcing Cross-Ministerial Responses to Global Space Issues – the Launch of the Subcommittee on International Space Cooperation [English title added by the author])," January 25, 2019, available at https://www.msit.go.kr/bbs/view.do?sCode=user&mId=113&mPid=112&bbsSeqNo=94&nttSeqNo=1502086.

Ministry of Science and ICT, Press release on May 30, 2014, "The First Master Plan for Promotion of Utilization of Satellite Data [English title added]" available at https://www.korea.kr/archive/expDocView.do?docId=35262.

Ministry of Science and ICT, Press release on September 30, 2014, "The 2014 Action Plan for Promotion of Utilization of Satellite Date [English title added]," available at https://www.korea.kr/archive/expDocView.do?docId=35723.

Ministry of Science and ICT, Press release on January 29, 2021, "The 2021 Action Plan for Promotion of Utilization of Satellite Date [English title added]," available at https://www.korea.kr/archive/expDocView.do?docId=39358.

Ministry of Science and ICT, Press release on February 13, 2023, "한-태국 우주 발사장 구축 타당성 조사 협력 이행약정 체결 (Implementation Agreement on Feasibility Study on the Establishment of Spaceport in Thailand)," available at https://www.msit.go.kr/bbs/view.do?mId=113&bbsSeqNo=94&nttSeqNo=3182721.

Ministry of Science and Technology (current Ministry of Science and ICT), "2005 과학기술연감, Science and Technology Annual" (2006).

Ministry of the Office for Government Policy Coordination, Press release on August 24, 2016, "the Deliberation and Resolution of the Fourth Frequency Deliberation Committee," accessed on March 3, 2021, available at https://www.korea.kr/news/pressReleaseView.do?newsId=156151354.

Mohammed bin Rashid Space Centre (MBRSC), "DubaiSat-1," available at https://www.mbrsc.ae/satellite-programme/dubai-sat-1, and "DubaiSat-2," available at https://www.mbrsc.ae/satellite-programme/dubai-sat-2, last accessed December 23, 2021.

NARA Space Technology, https://www.naraspace.com/.

NASA, "Republic of Korea Joins List of Nations to Sign Artemis Accords," last accessed on October 3, 2022, available at https://www.nasa.gov/feature/republic-of-korea-joins-list-of-nations-to-sign-artemis-accords.

National Archives, "Dwight D. Eisenhower, Presidential Library, Museum and Boyhood Home," last accessed on December 13, 2021, available at https://www.eisenhowerlibrary.gov/research/online-documents/early-history-and-development-national-aeronautics-and-space.

National Archives of the Republic of Korea, accessed on December 18, 2019, http://theme.archives.go.kr/viewer/common/archWebViewer.do?bsid=200300839869&dsid=000000000019&gubun=search#1.

National Archives of the Republic of Korea, "The Minutes of the National Assembly on December 12, 1948," accessed on January 20, 2020, https://dl.nanet.go.kr/SearchDetailView.do.

National Assembly of Republic of Korea, "Bill Information," accessed on January 15, 2020, http://likms.assembly.go.kr/bill/billDetail.do?billId=008797&ageFrom=20&ageTo=20.

National Radio Research Agency, "Introduction," accessed on March 3, 2021, https://www.rra.go.kr/en/intro/object.do.

Oktokki Space Center, accessed on November 17, 2019, http://www.oktokki.com/.

Oxford Learner's Dictionaries, last accessed on September 19, 2022, available at https://www.oxfordlearnersdictionaries.com/definition/american_english/attempt_2.

Oxford University Press, "Oxford Learner's Dictionaries," last accessed on April 29, 2022, available at https://www.oxfordlearnersdictionaries.com/definition/english/distress_1.

Peter Cramton, "Spectrum Auctions," in Martin Cave, Sumit Majumdar and Ingo Vogelsang (eds.), Handbook of Telecommunications Economics (2002).

Peter Malanczuk, "Akehurst's Modern Introduction to International Law," Seventh Edition (1997), 109–117; Malcolm Shaw, "International Law," Ninth Edition (2021).

Ram Jakhu, "Emerging Legal Issues of Satellite Telecommunications and Broadcasting," Proceedings on the Law of Outer Space 43 (2000).

Ram Jakhu, "Iridium-Cosmos Collision and its Implications for Space Operations," in Kai-Uwe Schrogl (ed.), Yearbook on Space Policy 2008/2009 (2010).

Ram Jakhu, "Legal Issues Relating to the Global Public Interest in Outer Space," Journal of Space Law 32, no.1 Summer (2006).

Renata Knittel Kommel *et al.*, "Exploring Insights from Emerging Space Agencies," The George Washington University Elliott School of International Affairs, October 2020, at 1 and 8. NASA, "The Birth of NASA," March 28, 2008, last accessed on December 13,2021, available at https://www.nasa.gov/exploration/whyweexplore/Why_We_29.html.

Ricky J. Lee, "Liability Arising from Article VI of the Outer Space Treaty: States, Domestic Law, and Private Operators," in Proceedings of the 48th Colloquium on the Law of Outer Space (2005).

Sacheon, "Support for the specialized aerospace complex," accessed on September 28, 2020, https://www.sacheon.go.kr/aerospace/02811/02813.web.

Sakif Alam, "Do North Korea's nuclear tests violate international law?," The Daily Star Opinion, October 03, 2017, https://www.thedailystar.net/opinion/global-affairs/do-north-koreas-nuclear-tests-violate-international-law-1470622.

SaTRec, "Research and Development: KITSAT-1," accessed on November 19, 2019, http://satrec.kaist.ac.kr/e_02_01.php.

Seokmin Oh, "Lifting of US missile restrictions signifies Seoul's missile sovereignty, Washington's China strategy: experts," Yonhap News Agency, May 22, 2021, last accessed January 22, 2022, available at https://en.yna.co.kr/view/AEN20210522003900325.

Setusko Aoki, "In Search of the Current Legal Status of the Registration of Space objects," Proceedings of the International Institute of Space Law 53 (2010).

Setsuko Aoki, "Space Legislation in Japan," last accessed February 25, 2022, available at https://www.unoosa.org/documents/pdf/copuos/lsc/2019/tech-05E.pdf.

S. G. Sreejith, "When Sputnik orbits Geneva: Legal Reflections on WTO Governance in Respect of Commercial Space Activities," Proceedings on the Law of Outer Space 47 (2004).

SIIS, https://www.satreci.com/sub0301.

SI's products, "World-leading solution provider for Earth observation missions," accessed on July 31, 2020, https://www.satreci.com/sub0301.

Sisoo Park, "South Korea to develop reusable rocket with 100-ton thrust engines," last accessed February 12, available at https://spacenews.com/south-korea-to-develop-reusable-rocket-with-100-ton-thrust-engines/.

"South Korea and the ITU Plenipotentiary Conference, 우리나라와 ITU 전권회의 [English title added]," October 19, 2014, available at https://www.etnews.com/20141017000139.

"South Korean rocket startup to launch from South Australia," accessed on August 3, 2020, https://studyadelaide.com/whats-happening/south-korean-rocket-startup-launch-south-australia.

South Korean Scientist and Astronaut, accessed on April 24, 2020, https://www.britannica.com/biography/Yi-Soyeon.

Space Debris Mitigation Guidelines of the Committee on the Peaceful Uses of Outer Space, accessed on November 19, 2020, available at https://www.unoosa.org/pdf/publications/st_space_49E.pdf.

SpaceNews, "South Korea signs Artemis Accords; Brazil, New Zealand likely next," last accessed on October 3, 2022, available at https://spacenews.com/south-korea-signs-artemis-accords/.

SPACE SOLUTIONS, http://www.spacesolutions.co.kr/.

Space Weather, "Members," accessed on February 23, 2021, available at http://www.spaceweather.org/ISES/rwc/rwc.html.

"Statement of Republic of Korea," accessed on January 30, 2020, https://www.unoosa.org/documents/pdf/copuos/2018/hls/04_02E.pdf.

Stephen Clark, "South Korea's all-domestic satellite launcher reaches orbit for first time," Spaceflight Now, last accessed January 21, 2023, available at https://spaceflightnow.com/2022/06/21/south-koreas-all-domestic-satellite-launcher-reaches-orbit-on-test-flight/.

Stephen Gorove, "Cosmos 954: Issues of Law and Policy," Journal of Space Law 6 (1978).

Stephen Gorove, "Liability in Space Law: An Overview," Annals of Air and Space Law 8 (1983).

Stephan Hobe, "Space Law," Bloomsbury Publishing PLC, Oxford, United Kingdom (2019).

Steve Colantuoni, the Central American Group, "The Costa Rican Space Agency has been created," June 3, 2021, last accessed January 13, 2022, available at https://www.thecentralamericangroup.com/costa-rican-space-agency-has-been-created/.

Sylvia Ospina, "International Satellite Organizations: Their Evolution from ISOS to GSCS and the Further Privatization/Commercialization of Space Activities," Proceedings of the International Institute of Space Law 53 (2010).

Table of Frequency Allocations of the Republic of Korea is Notification No. 2020-11 issued on January 6, 2021. Available in Korean at https://www.law.go.kr/ LSW/conAdmrulByLsPop.do?&lsiSeq=218931&joNo=0009&joBrNo=00&datClsCd=010102&dguBun=DEG&lnkText=%25EA%25B3%25A0%25EC%258B%259C%25ED%2595%2598%25EC%2597%25AC%25 EC%2595%25BC%2520%25ED%2595%259C%25EB%258B%25A4&admRulPttninfSeq=6256 #AJAX, accessed on February 4, 2021.

Tanja Masson-Zwaan, "Space Law and the Satellite Collision of 10 February 2009," Space Research Today, COSPAR's Information Bulletin 174 (2009).

Tanja Masson-Zwaan and Mahulena Hofmann, "Introduction to Space Law," 4th edition, Wolters Kluwer (2019).

The bill of ratification of the Liability Convention, "The minutes of the Foreign Affairs Subcommittee of the 103rd National Assembly," available at http://likms.assembly.go.kr/bill/billDetail.do?billId=008797&ageFrom=20&ageTo=20.

The Central Radio Management Service, "Organization," accessed on February 24, 2021, https://www.crms.go.kr/en/lay1/S192T196C199/contents.do.

The Committee of Science, Technology, Information and Telecommunication, "The Expansion of the Right to Claim a Space Damage Compensation," November 9, 2021.

The Fédération Aéronautique Internationale (FAI), "100km Altitude Boundary for Astronautics," last accessed on October 24, available at https://www.fai.org/page/icare-boundary.

The IADC Space Debris Mitigation Guidelines; A/AC.105/C.1/L.260, available at https://www.unoosa.org/oosa/oosadoc/data/documents/2003/aac.105c.1l/aac.105c.1l.260_0.html.

The International Charter Space and Major Disasters, "Charter Members," last accessed January 19, 2021, available at https://disasterscharter.org/web/guest/home;jsessionid=B5E7A1D8FB97850C79683D1D84615350.APP1#portlet-wrapper-56_INSTANCE_NqTgFexnyH9p.

The International Charter Space and Major Disasters, last accessed January 28, 2023, https://disasterscharter.org/web/guest/home;jsessionid=B5E7A1D8FB97850C79683D1D84615350.APP1#portlet-wrapper-56_INSTANCE_NqTgFexnyH9p.

The International Space Environment Service, "Organization," accessed on February 23, 2021, https://spaceweather.rra.go.kr/eng/Hello.do.

The Korea Communications Commission, Press release on October 26, 2010, available at https://www.korea.kr/news/pressReleaseView.do?newsId=155695908.

The Korea Herald, "S. Korea signs US-led Moon exploration accord," last accessed on October 3, 2022, available at https://www.koreaherald.com/view.php?ud=20210527000099.

The Korean Law Information Center, "The Reasons for the Enactment of the Act," last accessed on September 13, 2022, available at https://www.law.go.kr/lsInfoP.do?lsiSeq=81874&ancYd=20071221&ancNo=08714&efYd=20080622&nwJoYnInfo=N&efGubun=Y&chrClsCd=010202&ancYnChk=0#0000.

The Korean National Assembly, a proposal for the partial revision of the Space Damage Compensation Act, submitted on June 15, 2021, Proposed Bill No. 2110790, available at website https://likms.assembly.go.kr/bill/billDetail.do?billId=PRC_Q2M1M0C5I2I4X1E3X1W8X3D7N5H6I3.

The Korean National Assembly, "Bill Information," available at https://likms.assembly.go.kr/bill/billDetail.do?billId=ARC_C1T4F1Y2B2K6V1B4O1A7G0E5M4Q9F5.

The Korean Space Weather Center, "Introduction," accessed on February 23, 2021, https://spaceweather.rra.go.kr/eng/Survey.do.

The Korean Space Weather Center, "Space Weather Data," accessed on February 23, 2021, https://spaceweather.rra.go.kr/eng/spaceenvtoday.do.

The Korean Supreme Court Ruling on June 30, 2022, Case No. 2022DA206384, available at https://www.law.go.kr/LSW/precInfoP.do?mode=0&precSeq=223319.

"The minutes of the 103rd National Assembly plenary session," No. 10, December 3, 1979.

The Moon rabbit, image sources available at http://news20.busan.com/content/image/2012/10/31/20121031000079_0.jpg and http://img.kbs.co.kr/cms/1tv/sisa/science/vod/__icsFiles/artimage/2011/01/11/c_1tc_dvin2/EMB00000d0c2e71.jpg respectively, accessed November 17, 2019.

The National Archives of Korea, "우주개발중장기기본계획 (the Mid-to Long-Term Basic Plan for the Promotion of Space Development [English Title added])," by the Minister of Science and Technology, available at, https://www.archives.go.kr/next/search/showDetailPopup.do?rc_code=1310377&rc_rfile_no=200802067513&rc_ritem_no=000000000009.

The National Assembly Bill Information, "The Draft of the Aerospace Industry Development Promotion Act (October 16, 1987) [English title added]," available at http://likms.assembly.go.kr/bill/billDetail.do?billId=010578&ageFrom=21&ageTo=2.

The National Assembly of the Republic of Korea, "Bill Information," last accessed on September 13, 2022, available at https://likms.assembly.go.kr/bill/billDetail.do?billId=PRC_P0X7P0M2M0T7D1X5V4T2C2H1W9Y4C2.

The National Law Information Center, "Reasons for the Partial Revision," accessed on January 25, 2021, https://www.law.go.kr/LSW/lsInfoP.do?lsiSeq=177652&ancYd=20151222&ancNo=13588&efYd=20160623&nwJoYnInfo=N&efGubun=Y&chrClsCd=010202&ancYnChk=0#0000.

The NEXTSat project, SaTRec, "Research and Development," accessed on May 1, 2020, http://satrec.kaist.ac.kr/e_02_08.php.

The Reason for the Amendments to the Space Development Promotion Act, Act No. 13009, last accessed on March 22, 2022, available at https://www.law.go.kr/LSW/lsInfoP.do?efYd=20150721&lsiSeq=167384&ancYd=20150120&nwJoYnInfo=N&ancNo=13009&chrClsCd=010202&efGubun=Y#0000.

"The Reason for the Amendment to the Telecommunications Business Act, 전기통신 사업법 개정이유 [English title added]" released in 1997, available at http://www.law.go.kr/lsInfoP.do?lsiSeq=6303&ancYd=19970828&ancNo=05385&efYd=19980101&nwJoYnInfo=N&efGubun=Y&chrClsCd=010202&ancYnChk=0.

The Space Policy Research Center, available at https://stepi.re.kr/site/sprec/main.do.

The Statement of Reasons for Enacting the Space Damage Compensation Act on December 21, 2007, last accessed on December 14, 2022, available at https://www.law.go.kr/LSW//lsInfoP.do?lsiSeq=81874&ancYd=20071221&ancNo=08714&efYd=20080622&nwJoYnInfo=N&efGubun=Y&chrClsCd=010202&ancYnChk=0#0000.

The Subcommittee on Disaster Reduction of the US National Science and Technology Council, accessed on February 23, 2021, https://www.sdr.gov/docs/185820_Space_FINAL.pdf.

The UK Department for Business, "Energy & Industrial Strategy and Ministry of Defense," National Space Strategy 40, September 27, 2021, available at https://www.gov.uk/government/publications/national-space-strategy.

The UK Government, "List of Cabinet Committees," accessed on October 14, 2021, https://www.gov.uk/government/publications/the-cabinet-committees-system-and-list-of-cabinet-committees.

The White House, "Presidential Executive Order on Reviving the National Space Council," June 30, 2017, available at https://trumpwhitehouse.archives.gov/articles/president-trump-issues-executive-order-reviving-national-space-council/.

The World Trade Organization, "WTO Memberships," Republic of Korea, https://www.wto.org/english/thewto_e/countries_e/korea_republic_e.htm.

UAE Space Agency, "About UAE Space Agency," last accessed January 7, 2022, available at https://space.gov.ae/Page/20120/20230/About-UAE-Space-Agency.

UAE Space Agency, "Advisory Committee," last accessed January 7, 2022, available at https://space.gov.ae/AdvisoryCommittee.

UAE Space Agency, "Agency Achievements," last accessed January 7, 2022, available at https://space.gov.ae/Page/20120/20161/Achievements.

UAE Space Agency, "Chairperson of Board of Directors," last accessed January 7, 2022, available at https://space.gov.ae/Page/20120/20126/CHAIRPERSON.

UEL, https://www.facebook.com/unmannedexplorationlab.

UN Archives, available at https://treaties.un.org/Pages/showDetails.aspx?objid=08000002800361b4&clang=_en.

UN Doc. ST/SG/SER.E/297, January 16, 1995, "Note verbale dated 4 January 1995 from the Permanent Mission of the Republic of Korea to the United Nations (Vienna) addressed to the Secretary-General," last accessed on April 11, 2022, available at https://www.unoosa.org/oosa/en/spaceobjectregister/national-registries/index.html.

UN Doc. ST/SG/SER.E/304/Add.1, January 13, 2014, "Note verbale dated 13 December 2013 from the Permanent Mission of the Republic of Korea to the United Nations (Vienna) addressed to the Secretary-General," last accessed on April 11, 2022, available at https://www.unoosa.org/oosa/en/spaceobjectregister/national-registries/index.html.

UN Doc. ST/SG/SER.E/580, May 21, 2021, "Note verbale dated 4 May 2021 from the Permanent Mission of the Republic of Korea to the United Nations (Vienna) addressed to the Secretary-General," last accessed on April 11, 2022, available at https://www.unoosa.org/oosa/en/spaceobjectregister/national-registries/index.html.

UN Doc. ST/SG/SER.E/990, October 7, 2009, "Note verbale dated 24 September 2009 from the Permanent Mission of the Republic of Korea to the United Nations (Vienna) addressed to the Secretary-General," last accessed on April 11, 2022, available at https://www.unoosa.org/oosa/en/spaceobjectregister/national-registries/index.html.

UN Doc. ST/SG/SER.E/INF.23, April 16, 2009, "Note verbale dated 15 January 2009 from the Permanent Mission of the Republic of Korea to the United Nations (Vienna) addressed to the Secretary-General," last accessed on April 8, 2022, available at https://www.unoosa.org/oosa/en/spaceobjectregister/national-registries/index.html.

UN Treaty Series, accessed on January 20, 2020, https://treaties.un.org/doc/Publication/UNTS/Volume%20510/volume-510-A-6964-English_French.pdf.

UN Treaty Series, volume 533, at 366, accessed on January 20, 2020, https://treaties.un.org/doc/Publication/UNTS/Volume%20533/v533.pdf.

UNA STELLA, https://www.unastella.co/.

United Nations, Proceedings of the United Nations/International Institute of Air and Space Law Workshop on Capacity Building in Space Law (2004).

United Nations General Assembly, "The Problem of the Independence of Korea," Yearbook of the United Nations, 1947–48, New York: Department of Public Information, United Nations (1949).

United Nations Treaty Collection, accessed on December 18, 2019, https://treaties.un.org/Pages/showDetails.aspx?objid=080000028012504f.

United Nations Treaty Collection, "Status of Treaties," accessed on November 15, 2020, available at https://treaties.un.org/pages/ViewDetails.aspx?src=TREATY&mtdsg_no=XXVI-4&chapter=26.

UNOOSA, "Committee on the Peaceful Uses of Outer Space: Membership Evolution," accessed on January 21, 2020, https://www.unoosa.org/oosa/en/ourwork/copuos/members/evolution.html.

UNOOSA, "Our Work: Worldwide Space Agencies," last accessed January 15, 2022, available at https://www.unoosa.org/oosa/en/ourwork/space-agencies.html.

UZURO Tech (우주로테크), accessed on August 2, 2020, available at https://m.post.naver.com/viewer/postView.nhn?volumeNo=27197207&memberNo=6307839&vType=VERTICAL.

Valérie Kayser, "Commercial Exploitation of Space: Developing Domestic Regulation," Annals of Air and Space Law 17 (1992).

Vladimir Kopal, "The 1975 Convention on Registration of Objects Launched into Outer Space in View of the Growth of Commercial Space Activities," in Benko, Marietta and Kroll, Walter (eds.), Air and Space Law in the 21st Century (2001).

WTO, "The Schedule of Specific Commitments: Republic of Korea," accessed on April 1, 2020, http://i-tip.wto.org/services/ComparativeReports.aspx.

Xiaodan Wu, "NewSpace in China in Needs of New Laws," in Proceedings of the International Institute of Space Law 2017 (2018).

YonhapNews, January 9, 2019, "우주개발 민간주도 전환, 2021년 우주산업 3조7천억으로 확대 (Shift to private sector-led space development, economic expansion of space industry to 3.7 trillion Korean won by 2021 [English title added])," https://www.yna.co.kr/view/AKR20190109070300017?input=1195m.

Youngshin Ahn, "Recent Developments in the Republic of Korea's Space Policy: An Overview of Space Activities and National Laws," Air and Space Law 44, no. 2 (2019).

Yvon Henri *et al.*, "Regulation of telecommunications by satellites," in Ram Jakhu and Paul Stephen Dempsey (eds.), Routledge Handbook of Space Law, Routledge (2019).

Index

www.ingramcontent.com/pod-product-compliance
Lightning Source LLC
Chambersburg PA
CBHW071230230926
51849CB00001B/64
* 9 7 8 9 0 0 4 6 9 4 7 3 6 *